The Senses: Classical and Contemporary Philosophical Perspectives

PHILOSOPHY OF MIND

Series Editor
David J. Chalmers, Australian National University

What Are We?
A Study in Personal Ontology
Eric T. Olson

Thinking without Words
José Luis Bermúdez

The Conscious Brain
Jesse Prinz

Simulating Minds
The Philosophy, Psychology, and Neuroscience of Mindreading
Alvin I. Goldman

Supersizing the Mind
Embodiment, Action, and Cognitive Extension
Andy Clark

Perception, Hallucination, and Illusion
William Fish

Phenomenal Concepts and Phenomenal Knowledge
New Essays on Consciousness and Physicalism
Torin Alter and Sven Walter

Phenomenal Intentionality
George Graham, John Tienson, and Terry Horgan

The Character of Consciousness
David J. Chalmers

The Senses
Fiona Macpherson

The Senses: Classical and Contemporary Philosophical Perspectives

EDITED BY
Fiona Macpherson

OXFORD
UNIVERSITY PRESS

OXFORD

UNIVERSITY PRESS

Oxford University Press, Inc., publishes works that further
Oxford University's objective of excellence
in research, scholarship, and education.

Oxford   New York
Auckland   Cape Town   Dar es Salaam   Hong Kong   Karachi
Kuala Lumpur   Madrid   Melbourne   Mexico City   Nairobi
New Delhi   Shanghai   Taipei   Toronto

With offices in
Argentina   Austria   Brazil   Chile   Czech Republic   France   Greece
Guatemala   Hungary   Italy   Japan   Poland   Portugal   Singapore
South Korea   Switzerland   Thailand   Turkey   Ukraine   Vietnam

Published by Oxford University Press, Inc.
198 Madison Avenue, New York, New York 10016

www.oup.com

Oxford is a registered trademark of Oxford University Press

Library of Congress Cataloging-in-Publication Data
The senses : classic and contemporary philosophical perspectives /
    edited by Fiona Macpherson.
p. cm. — (Philosophy of mind)
Includes bibliographical references and index.
ISBN 978-0-19-538596-0 (pbk. : alk. paper)
ISBN 978-0-19-538597-7 (hard cover : alk. paper)
1. Senses and sensation. I. Macpherson, Fiona.
BD214.S46 2010
128'.3—dc22

9 8 7 6 5 4 3 2 1

Printed in the United States of America
on acid-free paper

For my mother, Margaret, who imparted her love, support and common sense, but also her sense of wonder.

Preface and Acknowledgements

The nature of the nonvisual senses and the relationship between the senses has been unjustifiably neglected in philosophy. Philosophers of perception heretofore focused almost exclusively on providing an account of visual perception. One can understand why. Sight is very important to humans. People often single it out as being the sense that they would least like to lose. Arguably, one would be more hampered by losing one's vision than by losing any of the other senses. (However, somewhat surprisingly, recent evidence has shown that the loss of the sense of smell can be rather devastating long-term as it can lead to severe depression.) In addition, more is known about the physiology of the visual system—the nature of the sensory organ (the eye) and the nature of the visual processing that takes place in the brain—in comparison with the other senses. Furthermore, there are many interesting and well-documented ways that vision can break down, from which we can learn a lot. (One example is blindsight, in which subjects claim to be blind but who guess well above chance in forced-choice paradigms about what is in front of them. Other examples come in the form of the various visual agnosias, in which subjects fail to recognize objects or some features of objects by sight while retaining other visual discriminatory capacities.) Philosophers of perception often simply assume that theories of visual perception can be easily or unproblematically extended to cover perception in the other sensory modalities.

Investigating this assumption involves investigating the nature of the nonvisual senses—their relation and interaction. When one does so, one finds that the other senses differ from vision and from each other in many respects. When one examines these differences, an obvious question arises: What makes a sense a sense of vision rather than a sense or hearing or touch and so on? Answering this question will involve identifying, comparing and contrasting the senses and determining the nature of each.

This is the topic of this volume: What makes the senses different from each other, and on principles should we use to determine the number and types of senses? There is a small literature on this topic within the philosophical canon. However, I predict that, as more physiological and psychological evidence about the nonvisual senses accumulates and as philosophers begin to directly address the question of the nature of perception in the nonvisual sensory modalities (as, for example, Matthew Nudds and Casey O'Callaghan have begun doing for audition), this question will become an important locus of study in the philosophy of perception.

This volume presents key works that have been written on the topic of the individuation of the senses in the last fifty years (with the exception of the piece Aristotle wrote more than two thousand years ago). In addition, it showcases a series of new essays on that topic and which also examine the similarities and differences between the senses and the interactions between them. I hope that this volume will serve as a starting point for those wishing to investigate this topic and that it will inspire and promote further work in this area.

Most of the new contributions to this volume began their life as papers presented to an interdisciplinary conference on "Individuating the Senses" in December 2004 at the University of Glasgow, which I organized with Matthew Nudds (of the University of Edinburgh). I would like to thank the British Academy, the Mind Association, the Scots Philosophical Club, the Analysis Trust, and the Faculty of Arts and the Department of Philosophy at the University of Glasgow for supporting the conference. I would also like to thank the speakers: Austen Clark, Naomi Eilan, Richard Gray, John Harrison, John Heil, Robert Hopkins, M. G. F. Martin, A. D. Smith, and Charles Spence.

The conference was held under the auspices of the Centre for the Study of Perceptual Experience (CSPE), which is based in the Department of Philosophy at the University of Glasgow. The primary aim of the CSPE is to conduct and facilitate analytical, philosophical research into the nature of perceptual experience. A secondary aim is to facilitate communication and collaboration between researchers in philosophy and other disciplines whose research remit includes perceptual experience. At the time of writing, in its five-year history, the CSPE has organized many international conferences, including: "The Individuation of the Senses"; "Disjunctivism: Perception, Action, Knowledge"; "Graduate Interdisciplinary Conference on Perception"; "The Admissible Contents of Experience"; "Hallucination on Crete"; and "Varieties of Experience Graduate Conference". This is in addition to numerous smaller workshops and events. Further information about these events and the CSPE is available on the internet: http://www.gla.ac.uk/philosophy/cspe/.

I would like to thank all of the contributors to this volume for their contributions and for their patience. I am, of course, also very grateful to them for producing excellent, thought-provoking essays.

Finally, I would like to thank Jon Bird, Michael Brady, Stuart Crutchfield, John Heil, Brian Keeley, Richard King, Matthew Nudds, Susanna Siegel, Barry Smith, and two anonymous referees from Oxford University Press for their comments and advice in preparing the volume and the introduction. And, of course, I owe much to Peter Ohlin and his staff at Oxford University Press for publishing the book and helping me to bring it to press.

FM
Glasgow, May 2010

Contents

SECTION II: NEW WORKS

Notes on Contributors

Aristotle (384 bc–322 bc) was a Greek philosopher. He was a student of Plato and teacher of Alexander the Great. He wrote on many subjects, including natural science, metaphysics, logic, and the arts.

Tim Bayne is university lecturer in the philosophy of mind at the University of Oxford and a fellow of St. Catherine's College. He has research interests in the philosophy of psychology, with a particular focus on consciousness. He is the editor (with Jordi Fernández) of *Delusion and Self-Deception: Affective and Motivational Influences on Belief Formation* (Psychology Press, 2008) and (with Axel Cleeremans and Patrick Wilken) *The Oxford Companion to Consciousness* (Oxford University Press, 2009). He is completing a monograph on the unity of consciousness.

Austen Clark is professor of philosophy at the University of Connecticut. In addition to numerous articles he is author of three books: *Psychological Model and Neural Mechanisms: An Examination of Reductionism in Psychology* (Oxford University Press, 1980), *Sensory Qualities* (Oxford University Press, 1993), and *A Theory of Sentience* (Oxford University Press, 2000).

C. A. J. Coady is professor at the University of Melbourne and is a professorial fellow in applied philosophy at the Centre for Applied Philosophy and Public Ethics (CAPPE). Best known for his work on the epistemology of testimony, he has also written on political and applied philosophy. His publications include *Testimony* (Oxford University Press, 1994) and *Messy Morality* (Oxford University Press, 2008).

Richard Gray is senior lecturer in the School of English, Communication, and Philosophy at the University of Cardiff. He has published articles on synesthesia, representationalism, and the senses.

H. P. Grice (1913–1988) studied and taught at the University of

Oxford before moving for the last two decades of his life to the University of California–Berkeley. He wrote extensively on the philosophy of language and is famous for his discussion of speaker meaning, linguistic meaning, and their interactions, as well as of conversational maxims. He also wrote on the philosophy of perception, mind, and logic. Many of his essays are reprinted in his book *Studies in the Way of Words* (Harvard University Press, 1989).

John Heil is an honorary research associate at Monash University, professor of philosophy at Washington University in St. Louis, and author of *Perception and Cognition* (University of California Press, 1983) and, more recently, *From an Ontological Point of View* (Oxford University Press, 2003). His work currently focuses on issues in metaphysics and the philosophy of mind.

Robert Hopkins is professor in the department of philosophy at the University of Sheffield. His interests lie in the philosophy of mind, epistemology, and aesthetics. He is the author of a book on pictorial representation and picture perception, *Picture, Image, and Experience* (Cambridge University Press, 1998) and has published papers on many topics, including Molyneux's question, the senses and sensory imaginings, and the relation between empirical and

philosophical work in areas of inquiry where phenomenology looms large. In 2001 he received a Philip Leverhulme Prize for his research.

Brian L. Keeley is associate professor of philosophy at Pitzer College, Claremont, California. He has written many papers on the philosophy of mind and neuroscience, as well as neuroethology and animal behavior.

Mark Leon is professor in the department of philosophy at the University of the Witwatersrand, Johannesburg. He has written numerous papers on epistemology, metaphysics, and the philosophy of mind.

Fiona Macpherson is senior lecturer in philosophy at the University of Glasgow and director of the Centre for the Study of Perceptual Experience. She is also a research fellow at the Centre for Consciousness at the Australian National University. She has published many articles on the philosophy of mind, psychology, and perception. She is editor (with Adrian Haddock) of *Disjunctivism: Perception, Action, Knowledge,* (Oxford University Press, 2008).

M. G. F. Martin is professor of philosophy at University College London and Mills Visiting Professor at the department of philosophy, University of California–Berkeley. He has written at length on the nature of perception and, in particular, on disjunctivism and naïve realism. His current research includes work on the emotions, desires, pain, the work of David Hume, and the psychology of visual cognition.

Norton Nelkin (1941–1995) spent his career at the University of New Orleans, where he became a professor. He wrote on the nature of pain, sensation, consciousness, subjectivity, intentionality, and representation. His theory of consciousness appears most fully in his book, *Consciousness and the Origins of Thought* (Cambridge University Press, 1996).

Matthew Nudds is a senior lecturer in philosophy at the University of Edinburgh. His research interests are in the philosophy of mind and perception, especially auditory perception.

John O'Dea is lecturer in the College of Arts and Sciences at the University of Tokyo and a member of the University of Tokyo's Center for Philosophy. His research interests include the philosophical problems of consciousness and perception.

J. W. Roxbee Cox was a faculty member at Queen's University of Belfast and the University of Lancaster. He wrote several articles on the philosophy of mind and perception.

A. D. Smith is professor of philosophy at the University of Warwick. He is the author of *The Problem of Perception* (Harvard University Press, 2002) and *Husserl and the Cartesian Meditations* (Routledge, 2003).

Richard Sorabji is Cyprus Global Distinguished Professor of Classics at New York University; emeritus professor of philosophy, King's College London; honorary fellow, Wolfson College, University of Oxford; and adjunct professor at the University of Texas–Austin. He is founder and director of the international "Ancient Commentators on Aristotle" project, devoted to the publication of translations of philosophical texts of the period 200–600 ad, texts that formed the necessary bridge between ancient philosophy and later thought both in medieval Islam and in the Latin-speaking West. To date more than sixty volumes have been completed. In addition, he has written ten monographs, most recently *Self: Ancient and Modern Insights about Individuality, Life, and Death* (Chicago University Press and Oxford University Press, 2006), published a large number papers, and edited six additional volumes.

The Senses: Classical and Contemporary Philosophical Perspectives

1

Introduction: Individuating the Senses

Fiona Macpherson

The senses, or sensory modalities, constitute the different ways we have of perceiving the world, such as seeing, hearing, touching, tasting, and smelling. But what makes the senses different? How many senses are there? How many could there be? What interaction takes place between the senses? This introduction is a guide to thinking about these questions.

One reason that these questions are important is that we are receiving a huge influx of new information from the sciences that challenges some traditional philosophical views about the senses. This information needs to be incorporated into our view of the senses and perception. Can we do this while retaining our preexisting concepts of the senses and of perception, or do we need to revise our concepts? If they need to be revised, then in what way should that be done? Research in diverse areas such as the nature of human perception, varieties of nonhuman animal perception, the interaction between different sensory modalities, perceptual disorders, and possible treatments for them calls into question the platitude that there are five senses, as well as the presupposition that we know what we are counting when we count them as five (or more). In the following sections I provide an overview of the main issues. In addition to explicating existing views of how to individuate the senses, I advance my own view about how one should do so by providing a framework within which we can situate our existing notions of the senses and other actual and possible ones. Finally, I provide an overview of the classic works and the new work commissioned for this volume.

It is an exciting time to be interested in the senses. One reason, mentioned earlier, is that scientists are now uncovering lots of interesting facts about the way in which nonhuman animals sense the world. The apparently wide and varied nature of senses in the animal kingdom provides lots of new empirical data to consider. For example, scientists claim that some animals can perceive the world by means of magnetic fields (e.g., pigeons), electric fields (e.g., many fish), infrared (e.g., pit vipers and some beetles), and echolocation (e.g., bats and dolphins).

Another reason is that scientists are discovering a great deal about the human senses on three fronts. First, they are discovering ways in which our senses and ways of perceiving the world can break down—ways that previously might not have been thought possible. For example, in blindsight, people claim to have either no visual experience or none in one portion of their visual field, typically half of their visual field. With respect to that portion, they claim to be blind and, for the most part, interact with the world the way blind people do.[1] The brain damage that they have suffered to their visual cortex backs up their claim that their vision is damaged. Yet, with respect to the blind portion of their visual field, these people can make accurate guesses (up to 99 percent accurate) about what is before them in the world in a forced-choice paradigm (that is, when asked to select between certain options presented to them). For example, if a vertical line were presented in the blind portion of a subject's visual field, the subject would not spontaneously be able to say what was there. However, if the subject were asked to guess whether a line that was there was vertical or horizontal, the subject would be able to guess correctly. Weiskrantz reports that subjects with blindsight:

> are able, in their blindfield hemifields, to detect the presence of stimuli, to locate them in space, to discriminate direction of movement, to discriminate orientation of lines, to be able to judge whether stimuli in the blindfield match or mismatch those in the intact hemifield, and to discriminate between different wavelengths of light, that is, to tell colours apart. (1997, 23)

This illustrates that information about the world is still being processed by the subjects' visual systems and can, to a limited degree, affect the subjects' behavior.

Another example comes from people suffering from a form of visual agnosia. Due to their condition they cannot identify common objects by sight—objects that we know they are familiar with and can identify using their other senses—despite the fact that they can draw the objects on the basis of their current visual experience of them.[2] A third example is that some people with damage to the visual cortex appear to be able to detect certain properties that we can detect with our eyes, but not all. For example, they may be able to detect movement but not shape or color. Thus, their visual experiences must be very degraded compared to those of normal subjects.

These types of cases are interesting as they demonstrate the existence of forms of experience or perception that are very different from our own and which theories of the sensory modalities ought to be able to account for. For example, some people think that the blindsight case provides a

---

[1] Total blindsight is rare. Blindsight has been studied and discussed by Weiskrantz (1986, 1997).
[2] See Farah (2004).

challenge to traditional accounts of perception that analyze perception in terms of having appropriate kinds of perceptual experiences because it is an example of perception in the absence of perceptual experience. The other cases provide examples of apparently degraded experience which challenges traditional accounts of the differences between the senses that appeal to characteristic kinds of experience associated with each sense. Can such accounts be preserved? Can we provide better ones? Or should such cases make us think that there can be amodal perception?

The second front on which science is making progress concerning human perception is in creating forms of prosthetic vision. There are now devices that allow the output from a camera placed on a subject's forehead to directly stimulate the subject's retina or visual cortex, apparently creating some crude form of visual experience that subjects can use to navigate obstacles. There are also sensory substitution devices that take output from a camera mounted on the subject's head and convert it to aural or haptic (tactile) signals that are then given to a subject. For example, a camera might drive a series of vibrating pins on a subject's back corresponding to the levels of light and dark that the camera detects. These devices allow the subject to detect three-dimensional objects at a distance from the subject's body and on the basis of this information navigate through space.[3] Again, a theory of the sensory modalities should be able to account for such novel means of apparently perceiving the world and be able to classify them. These cases of prosthetic perception will create particular difficulties for theories that try to categorize the senses by virtue of the sensory mechanisms or physical processes that partly constitute them.

The third front on which scientists are discovering facts about human perception concerns the mechanisms underlying ordinary human perception. For example, more is being learned about the mechanisms underlying our sense of touch. It turns out that there are very different and fairly discrete mechanisms for detecting properties associated with the sense of touch such as pressure, temperature, and pain. In addition, scientists are studying other types of receptors in the body that detect and process information: the semicircular canals, which deliver information about position with respect to gravity; the stretch receptors in the muscles, which deliver information about the position and movement of parts of the body; receptors for detecting pheromones in the Jacobson's organ in the nose. These facts have suggested to some that humans may have more ways of perceiving the world than has been traditionally thought.[4]

All these scientific advances provide a rich seam of empirical facts for philosophers of the senses to troll and mine in developing theories of the nature and individuation of the senses.

---

[3] See Bach-y-Rita (1972) and section 2.2.9 below.
[4] See section 2.1 below.

1. HOW MANY SENSES: THE *TOKEN* QUESTION

Of any creature we can ask:

(1) How many token senses does it have?

(2) What types are those senses?

Types are general kinds of thing, and tokens are instances of types. For example, in the word "proclivities," there are ten types of letter but twelve letter tokens. This is because there are three tokens of the same type: "i."

Questions 1 and 2 are very different questions, and it is important to keep them separate. This is not always as easy as it may seem, however, and failure to do so can lead to confused thinking.

To illustrate what we would be asking if we asked question 1, imagine that we came across a creature very much like a human but for the fact that it had four eyes—one pair above another. Call the creature "Four-Eyes." Four-Eyes might have one sense of vision, as we do, with all four eyes contributing to it, as our two eyes contribute to ours. Or Four-Eyes might have two distinct senses of vision, with each set of eyes contributing to its two different visual senses. If the latter were the case, and if Four-Eyes had no other senses, then it would have only one *type* of sensory modality, but it would have two *tokens* of that type. (Of course, for all I have said, Four-Eyes might indeed have three or four tokens of the visual sensory modality type, corresponding to its many eyes, and, if it is in other respects like a normal human, it will have other types of sensory modality such as hearing and touch. Moreover, for all I have said, depending on how we further specify the case, there may even be some reason to think that not all of the senses associated with Four-Eyes' eyes are senses of vision.[5])

To answer question 1, one might begin by thinking about the following questions:

(3) Which processes are perceptual processes?

and

(4) Which processes constitute the totality of processes associated with a modality, and which constitute just parts of the processes associated with a modality?

---

[5] Grice (1962/this volume chapter 4) considers a creature like Four-Eyes. However, he puts his imagined creature to very different philosophical use than I do. Grice assumes that his creature has two token senses—one associated with each pair of eyes—and then asks what conditions would have to be in place for us to think that these senses were both senses of vision and what conditions would have to be in place for us to think that one of these senses was a new nonvisual sense that we had not yet encountered. In contrast to this, I am not considering what types of senses Four-Eyes has but how we might decide how many token senses it has, irrespective of their type.

Not all bodily processes are perceptual ones. Digestion, for example, is a process that few would take to constitute a perceptual process.[6] How does one tell which bodily processes are the perceptual ones or part of perceptual ones? One might think that perceptual processes are those that allow a subject to gain information about the world. So perhaps all and only these are perceptual ones.

However, this definition requires further elucidation if it is to be helpful. To make progress, let us consider some familiar facts. In a typical case of perception, say vision, light—which consists of electromagnetic waves—is reflected off objects and enters our eyes. Light-sensitive cells in our retinas detect this light, and then an incredibly complex chain of brain processing begins. The cells in the retina send signals to other cells in the eye, and these send signals to cells that make up the optic nerve—a chain of neurons leading from the eye into the brain. Although signals from the eyes get sent to many areas of the brain, we know that there is an important pathway along which information from the eyes gets sent. This pathway leads to the visual cortex, an area of the brain at the back of the head in which most of the visual processing goes on. This area seems to be crucial for vision. If it is destroyed, for example by a stroke, then blindness ensues even if the eyes are not damaged.[7]

In a typical case of perception, in addition to mere brain activation, we also have a visual experience. That is to say, we go into a conscious state in which we are aware of the world around us. We know that states of one's visual cortex and states of visual consciousness are closely related. There appear to be correlations between the two. The evidence suggests that having one's visual cortex in a certain state is necessary in order to have a certain visual experience (and damage to one's visual cortex can impair one's visual experience). However, the relationship between visual experiences and states of the brain is highly disputed among both scientists and philosophers. Philosophers identify many different relationships that could obtain between the brain and conscious perceptual experiences that would be consistent with the facts that we know. For example, identity theorists think that particular brain states are to be identified with perceptual experiences. Many functionalists think that perceptual experiences are to be identified with any state of the brain that fulfils a certain causal role or with a higher-order state, such as the state of being in a state in which some physical state plays the causal role in question. Some dualists think that brain states may cause mental

---

[6] Some people have suggested that we do have a sense that detects the emptiness and fullness of our stomachs. However, even if that were true, it would not mean that digestion itself was a perceptual process, merely that there was some perceptual process associated with it, perhaps monitoring it.

[7] However, as was briefly mentioned earlier, the condition called "blindsight" may be present.

states to come into existence, but mental states are not physical states of the brain; indeed, they think that they are not physical states at all.[8]

Visual experiences are states that have phenomenal character—which is to say that there is "something that it is like" for one to be in such a state.[9] Most philosophers also think that visual experiences represent the world to be a certain way.[10] When one perceives the world, the world seems a certain way to one, and the way it seems is the way that the experience represents the world as being. When one specifies what one's experience represents, one specifies the content of the experience. One's experience may be veridical (that is, represent accurately), or it may be inaccurate (either partially or completely). An example of partial inaccuracy would occur when one suffers from some illusion: One sees the world but misperceives it in a certain way. For example, when one looks at the Müller-Lyer illusion, one perceives the two lines but misperceives the lines to have unequal length. One's experience represents one line as longer than the other when they are in fact the same length. An example of complete inaccuracy would be if one suffered a hallucination in which what one seemed to see bore no relation to what was really in front of one. (However, hallucinations need not, by their very nature, be inaccurate; one might have a veridical hallucination, for example, a hallucination of a dagger, and by chance there might be a dagger of the sort that one seems to see in the position in which one seems to see it.)

Ascribing content to a subject's visual experiences is a good way to make sense of the subject's behavior. For example, why a subject did something may be explained by how the subject's experience represented the world to be to the subject, and that way may be accurate or inaccurate. Providing a good explanation of behavior and explaining the accuracies and inaccuracies that we think experiences can have are two reasons to think experiences have content.

(Beliefs and desires are the paradigms of states that have content. These form part of the class of propositional attitudes distinguished by being states in which a subject forms an attitude toward some proposition. For example, when believing, one forms the attitude of holding some proposition to be true, say, that there are seashells on the beach. When desiring, one desires some proposition to be true, say, that there are seashells on the beach. The proposition in question specifies the content of the belief or desire. The content specifies a way the world could be, and the world may or may not be that way.)

---

[8] The question of what it is for something to be physical is a complex one. Some would say that being spatiotemporally located is a necessary and sufficient feature. Others would say that being a posit of our best fundamental science, physics, is essential.

[9] See Nagel (1974).

[10] A few philosophers deny that we should think of perceptual experiences as being representational states. Furthermore, there is enormous debate within philosophy about the nature of perceptual content. These debates lie well beyond the scope of this introduction. An overview can be found in Siegel (2008) and Macpherson (2011).

Figure 1.1 The Müller-Lyer Illusion.

When one perceives an object or a property, what one perceives is called the *distal stimulus*. If one sees a seashell, then the seashell would be the distal stimulus. We can also identify what is called the *proximal stimulus*, that is, whatever it is that directly stimulates the sensory organ. In the example of seeing the seashell, the proximal stimulus would be the light hitting our eyes. In the case of touch, the proximal stimulus might be pressure; in the case of hearing, pressure waves in some medium like air or water, and so on.

So now that we have gone over the simple facts about what happens in a typical case of perception, can we be more specific about what a perceptual process is, as opposed to some nonperceptual process, beyond saying that perceptual process are the ones that allow a subject to gather information about the world?

First, a number of further questions would have to be settled to determine the conditions that are *necessary* for perception. For example, what is it for a subject to obtain information? Must the subject come to form relevant beliefs? Or is that not necessary, as some people have thought, because animals and young children can perceive without believing since they are not cognitively sophisticated enough creatures? Moreover, if the formation of relevant beliefs is not required, then what, exactly, is? Must the subject use that information or be in a position to use it to guide action? Or is that not required because it seems reasonable to think that a completely paralyzed person could perceive while having no possibility of acting? Must the subject have a conscious experience with relevant content in order to perceive? Or is unconscious perception possible? (On the one hand, cases like blindsight, discussed earlier, might make one think unconscious perception is possible, but, on the other hand, it is not obvious that the very limited abilities that blindsight subjects possess, such as guessing from among options presented to them, really amounts to the ability to perceive the world.)

Second, it will not be easy to determine the *sufficient* conditions for a process to be perceptual. For example, one can imagine a subject coming to consciously believe things about the world—perhaps even true, justified things—in a way that seems to involve nonperceptual processes. For instance, verrucas are caused by the human papilloma virus. If one had a verruca, one might thereby come to believe, truly and justifiably, that one was infected with the human papilloma virus. However, plausibly, having a verruca is not a perceptual process or even a part of one. The seeing of the verruca is surely the perceptual process involved in the belief acquisition, but the having of the verruca is not. We need to think of some way to distinguish processes that are (or are part of) perceptual processes and those that are not.

Question 4 (which processes constitute the totality of processes associated with a modality, and which constitute just parts of the processes associated with a modality?) is a difficult question, too. Recall the creature, Four-Eyes, described earlier. How would one determine whether Four-Eyes had one sense of vision or two, three, or four?

One might think that the creature's physiology would settle the matter. For example, one might think that each sense consists in discrete and completely independent ways of processing information about the world. One might think that the processing of signals from the eyes is completely separate from the processing of signals from the ears. In short, one might think that there are physically isolable systems in the brain corresponding to each sense. Thus, one might think that the number of physiologically discrete perceptual mechanisms Four-Eyes has inside it relating to its eyes will determine how many senses it has. However, when you look at human physiological mechanisms pertaining to our different senses, we find that they are not completely discrete. Two examples illustrate different kinds of lack of discreteness.

One is the McGurk effect.[11] This phenomenon illustrates that there is interaction between what are almost always taken to be two separate sensory modalities in humans: vision and audition. When subjects listen to the sound of a spoken speech phoneme, such as a /ba/, in normal conditions with no visual input, or when looking at the lips of someone who is making a /ba/ sound, they will report that sound. However, if they listen to that sound in normal conditions except for the fact that they are looking at a video in which a person is making the lip movements suitable for producing a /ga/ sound, subjects report that they hear a different sound, in this case a /da/. Such interaction shows that the mechanisms in humans associated with different modalities are not completely distinct. There must be connections between the mechanisms that explain these, and other, cross-modal interactions.[12]

The second example arises from the fact that the deliverances of our senses feed into our one cognitive system (the system comprising and governing beliefs, desires, thoughts, and other propositional attitudes).

---

[11] See McGurk and MacDonald (1976). Other striking cross-modal effects continue to be discovered. For example, the auditory motion aftereffect is affected by perceived visual motion. See Vroomen and de Gelder (2003). An excellent reference work on cross-modal interaction is Calvert, Spence, and Stein (2004).

[12] There is increasing evidence of such interaction between sensory systems in the early stages of perceptual processing. For example, it is well documented between taste and smell. See Auvray and Spence (2008).

So, for example, if I hear a scream and I see a dagger, then I can come to have one belief about what I have seen and heard—I can come to have the one belief that there are both a scream *and* a dagger in my environment. This suggests that, although the sensory mechanisms may initially be rather distinct at the point of information reception, there is a convergence of these mechanisms in the cognitive system, which explains how we can have thoughts and beliefs as a result of the deliverances of multiple senses. Thus, one might think that many sensory mechanisms are linked at least at some high level, and therefore it will not be easy to determine just how separate physiological mechanisms must be in order for two or more sensory modalities to be present as opposed to one.

One might resist this thought by holding, as many people do, that sensory mechanisms end as they interface with the cognitive system, so that even if the deliverances of the senses feed into the one cognitive system, this does not undermine the distinctness of the senses. However, plausible as this idea seems, it can be resisted. One might think that perception and hence the sensory modalities are "cognitively penetrable"—that is to say that one's perceptual experiences, specifically the content of one's perceptual experiences, can be influenced by the content of one's beliefs, thoughts, and desires and other states of the cognitive system, not just in the sense that the cognitive states influence what we choose to perceive via moving our heads and eyes and perhaps focusing attention, but that once those factors are fixed, the cognitive states can influence the nature of that perceptual processing and yield experiences that are different from what would otherwise have been produced in the absence of those cognitive states. Whether the senses are cognitively penetrable or not is a highly disputed matter in contemporary philosophy and psychology.[13] However, if one believed it to be true, one would think that one cannot neatly carve up physiological mechanisms into two sets of isolated mechanisms: all and only those involved in perception (the precognitive) and all and only those involved in cognition (postperception). Therefore, one might think that the sensory mechanisms are not discrete since they each have the cognitive system as a common part.

In summary, the last two examples show that to determine how distinct physiological perceptual processes must be in order for there to be distinctive sensory modalities is a tricky business. It is made even more difficult by some awkward physiological facts surrounding some of our senses. For example, we normally think of touch as one sensory modality, but scientists have revealed that there are in fact at least four different, somewhat discrete physiological mechanisms corresponding to the detection of pressure, pain, warmth, and cold. Here we face a decision: Does this evidence show that one sensory modality can have distinctive

---

[13] The debate about whether perception is cognitively penetrable or not is reported and discussed in, among others, Churchland (1979), Fodor (1983), Pylyshin (1999), and Macpherson (forthcoming).

physiological sensory mechanisms associated with it, or does it show that what we typically think of as one sense is really four separate ones? The difficulty in making progress on this question shows that determining the physiological facts may not always be of great help in determining how many senses there are.

Another possible answer to the question of how one determines how many sensory modalities a creature has makes reference to the number of experiences a creature has. For example, consider Four-Eyes again. One might think that whether its eyes yielded one visual experience—as our two eyes do—or whether they yielded two, three, or four separate visual experiences will determine the number of token visual modalities it has. However, it is not obvious that there are good criteria for what makes "one" experience or multiple ones. There are a number of competing views on this issue.

One view is that there are separate experiences just to the extent that there are separate sensory modalities. Such an answer would not be helpful in determining what was a sensory modality on pain of circularity.

A second view is that at any one time we do not have multiple experiences—be they visual, auditory, tactile, or smaller units. Rather, we just have one "large" or "total" experience at any one time. On this view, this experience should not be thought of as having parts that could be enjoyed by themselves and that would constitute experiences. Whatever the merits or demerits of this view, like the previous one, it would not be helpful in determining the number of token visual senses that Four-Eyes had since, in every case, it would claim that Four-Eyes had only one experience.[14]

A third view is a counterfactual one. To see this view, consider the individuation of experiences (not modalities). Call the totality of one's experiences at a time one's "total" experience. One might think that one's total experience comprises states that are themselves experiences. The parts of one's total experiences that are themselves experiences would be those parts that could be had, counterfactually, without any other experiences. For example, it seems plausible that I could have my auditory experience of music right now without my visual experience or my tactile one or one in any other modality. It also seems fairly plausible that I could have the visual experince of the left-hand side of my visual field without that of the right-hand side. But, it does not seem plausible that I could have the experience as of the shape of the square that I am now having without an experience as of its size or position that I am now having. Given these facts, according to a counterfactual view, my auditory experience would comprise an experience, and the visual experience of each half of my visual field would constitute experiences, but my visual experience as of the shape of the square would not for it is not

---

[14] This view is advocated by Tye (2003).

a separate experience from that as of its size or position. (Of course the experience of the square together with all its visible properties might constitute an experience.)

One could use such a counterfactual view to try to settle the question of how many token senses Four-Eyes has. Here is one suggestion for how one might do so. Suppose there is some way of dividing up Four-Eyes' total visual experience into parts, each of which could be had alone and each of which corresponds to the contribution of a whole number of eyes, and no eye contributes to more than one such part of the experience. Then one could reasonably claim that number of parts is the number of token visual senses that the creature has. For example, if Four-Eyes' experience was such that there were only two parts, each of which could be had alone, and one part was had when Four-Eyes closed its top pair of eyes and the other part was had when Four-Eyes closed its bottom pair of eyes—then according to this view Four-Eyes would have two token senses of vision. The sense organ of one of these senses would be the top pair of eyes; the organ of the other would be the bottom pair.

However, one might object to the counterfactual view. Recall that the McGurk effect seems to show that some auditory and visual experiences had simultaneously by the one subject cannot be divided into parts, each of which is attributable to different sense organs. Thus, the counterfactual view would count them on this occasion as one sense. Nonetheless, vision and hearing seem to be different modalities, and one would have to be radically revisionary to think otherwise. Thus, one might think that the proposed counterfactual methodology may lead one to count too few senses.

One might solve this by insisting that the division of the senses using this technique take place when there is no illusion involved. Then one could hope that cross-modal effects of the McGurk kind all involve illusion—although whether this is true is a matter for further investigation. Alternatively, one might insist that the division of the senses depends on whether the test would be *typically* passed by Four-Eyes' visual experiences and parts of experience. Thus, one might allow that cross-modal effects can take place on some occasions as long as they are not the norm. Thus, one might hope that cross-modal effects rarely occur.[15] If these hopes do not transpire, then one could do one of two things. One could just conclude that what were thought to be two senses really are one. Or one could hold that sometimes a creature has two senses, say vision and audition, but sometimes the mechanisms underlying these senses combine to produce a different third sense, an audiovisual sense. (At that time, the original senses [vision and audition] could still be operative, producing other "pure" visual and auditory experiences, but they need

---

[15] However, this seems unlikely in the face of recent research. Cross-modal effects may be more the rule than the exception. See, for example, Auvray and Spence (2008).

not be. Audition and vision could cease to be activated, and only the new, special, audiovisual experience might exist.)

In fact, it might be rather plausible to hold a view like this concerning taste and smell. It is widely noted that what are commonly taken to be experiences of taste are really experiences created by both taste and smell. For example, when one has a bad cold and loses one's sense of smell, one's food tastes bland. Of course, we can have pure taste experiences and pure smell experiences. However, what we usually take to be experiences of taste (and are often in modern parlance dubbed experiences of "flavor" to distinguish them from pure experiences of taste) are produced by mechanisms required for both pure taste and smell. When these mechanisms work together to produce experiences of flavor, one could reasonably say that the modality in operation was the flavor modality.

In short, one's theory of how to individuate experiences will significantly alter the position one might take here as to what is to count as one experience. In turn, this will affect whether this criterion for identifying whole modalities will be useful, and, if it is helpful, it will affect the results that such a criterion might yield.

We have seen then, in this section, that there are a large number of complex issues to think about when considering the question of how to count the number of token senses that humans and other creatures have. The physiology of the creature may be an important consideration as may be the nature of its experiences.

2. HOW MANY SENSES: THE *TYPE* QUESTION

So far I have been discussing issues involved in answering question 1 (how many token senses does a creature have?) and the closely associated questions 3 and 4. But how should one go about answering question 2 (what types of senses does a creature have?)? One would need to know the following:

(1) How many token senses does it have?
(5) What types of senses are there?
(6) What makes a token sense an instance of one type rather than another?

I have dealt with question 1 in the preceding section. In the next section I look at question 5, and then in the following section I examine question 6 at length.

2.1. What Types of Senses Are There?

Many people have thought that there are only five types of senses. For example, Aristotle, in *De Anima*, famously said that there are five and only five senses: sight, hearing, touch, taste, and smell.[16] (He is talking here both about the number and kind of senses that humans have and the number and kind that animals have.) This view has echoed down the centuries, advocated by a number of scholars, most recently perhaps by Matthew Nudds. Nudds says that it is "obvious" that humans have five senses and that their having this number is a truth of folk psychology. Moreover, he thinks that it is not the case that "common-sense embodies the kind of proto-scientific understanding of the senses which is *liable* to revision or replacement."[17] Therefore, he holds that no amount of extra data from science, of the kind referred to at the beginning of this introduction, could change our minds on the question of how many types of senses there are.

The commitment to the existence of only a relatively small, specifiable number of types of senses—typically, but not necessarily, five—forms part of what I call the "sparse view" of the counting question. The sparse view maintains the following:

• The number of possible sensory modalities is relatively limited.
• The sensory modalities are discrete.[18]

To say that the modalities are discrete is to say that all of the possible modalities are rather different and distinct from each other (not that the modalities cannot interact).

Should one believe the sparse view? I think not, for two reasons. First, there is evidence that many more than five sensory modalities *actually* exist. From these cases we can go on and extrapolate and thus come to believe that the number of *possible* sensory modalities is large.

One candidate sense in humans in addition to the Aristotelian five is proprioception, which consists of awareness of the position of the parts of the body. It also encompasses awareness of movement of the body and of how much force is required to move the body.[19] Scientists commonly distinguish between *exteroceptive* senses (such as sight and hearing),

---

[16] See book III, chapter 1. It is reasonably clear that Aristotle was claiming that as a matter of fact there are only five senses, and, given the nature of the world as he took it to be (composed of elements, each of which had different properties), there could be only five senses. Thus, he was claiming that it is nomologically necessary that we have only five senses. He was not claiming that it is metaphysically necessary.

[17] Nudds (2004, 35). On the same page, not only does he say that he has "not come across a good argument" for the idea that the folk notion of the senses is liable for revision, but he also says, "There have been authors who attempt to give a 'scientific' account of the senses, but they do nothing to show that they haven't simply changed the subject. Whatever they are giving an account of, it's not the senses as we commonly understand them" (fn11).

[18] It may be that no one has ever held the sparse view that I outline here, but parts of it have certainly been avowed, and the position serves as a useful stalking horse.

[19] The term "kinesthesia" is sometimes used interchangeably with "proprioception" thus defined. However, sometimes "kinesthesia" is used exclusively as a term for our sense of awareness of the movement of the body, while "proprioception" is reserved for the sense of the body's position.

which detect objects and properties in the world external to the body, and *interoceptive* senses, which detect changes to the body. They classify proprioception as one of the interoceptive senses. Furthermore, there appears to be good reason to classify it as a sense.

First, proprioception involves a detection of information via dedicated receptors in the muscles, tendons, and joints, and these receptors can be regarded as constituting the sensory organ of this sense. Many people have claimed that there cannot be a sense unless there is a dedicated sense organ. It is not obvious, in fact, whether this criterion *has* to be met in order for a sense to exist; however, for those who think it is crucial, proprioception passes this test.

Second, subjects frequently have experiences with phenomenal character corresponding to the information picked up by the stretch receptors, and they can come to know the position of their body by virtue of having these experiences. (Interestingly, proprioceptive experiences often quickly disappear—as experiences of smell do—upon prolonged exposure to a stimulus, due to habituation.) Of course, the proprioceptive process can go wrong, and one can have illusions of bodily position. Proprioceptive illusions of size, position, and movement of limbs, fingers, and other body parts, as well as illusions of the force exerted by one's muscles, can occur after brain damage or can be induced in a variety of ways.[20] For example, illusions of movement can be induced by applying vibrations to muscle groups. Illusions of bodily position can be induced by anesthetizing a limb and asking a subject to move it. When such subjects cannot see the results of their efforts, they estimate on the basis of the illusory experience that they have that the limb is not in its original position (which it is) but is where they intended to move it. There can also be proprioceptive hallucinations, for example, when subjects who have lost a limb nonetheless feel that it is present and in a particular position.[21]

These features of proprioception and proprioceptive experiences—the existence of dedicated receptors that carry information, the existence of distinctive experiences that allow subjects to come to know this information, and the existence of cases of accurate perception, illusion, and hallucination—are shared by perceptual experiences in the traditional five Aristotelian modalities and together make a strong case that proprioception is a sensory modality.

Another candidate sense in humans is the vestibular sense, or sense of balance. Equilibrioception, as it is also known, provides us with awareness of the head's orientation with respect to gravity and informs us of the movement, particularly acceleration, of the head: up and down, side to side, and rotationally. As opposed to proprioception, equilibrioception

---

[20] See, for example, Head and Holmes (1911), Jones (1988), Paqueron et al. (2003), and Gandevia et al. (2006).
[21] See Ramachandran and Hirstein (1998).

is typically classified as an exteroceptive sense because it detects some-thing outside the body—the gravitational field—although it also detects the relationship of the head to that field. Like proprioception, the sense of balance has a dedicated sense organ: the fluid-filled, semicircular canals (which respond to rotation), and the otolithic organs (which respond to linear accelerations) in the ears. Also like proprioception, subjects typically have distinctive conscious experiences corresponding to the information detected by equilibrioception. For example, if one's vestibular sense is stimulated when one's eyes are closed, one has an experience of self-movement. A more specific example is that when one is in an elevator, one can come to know by one's experience whether the elevator is moving up or down even when one has no visual experience to drawn on. Another example is that, if one is sitting in a swivel chair in the dark, one can come to know whether one has been spun clock-wise or counterclockwise via the experiences of rotational movement. Via their equilibrioceptive experiences, subjects can come to know the position of their head with respect to gravity and whether their head is moving and accelerating. Again, as was the case in proprioception, one can also have illusions and hallucinations of equilibrioception. For example, after getting off a roundabout or merry-go-round, one may still feel as if one is rotating. Illusions and hallucinations from the vestibu-lar sense, particularly when the information from vision conflicts with it, often makes people unstable, vertiginous, and nauseous. Sufferers of Ménière's disease experience such strong illusions of vertigo, or feelings of being pushed or pulled, that they may fall. Permanent or temporary damage to the vestibular sense from inner ear infections, brain tumors, and brain damage can cause persistent, unpleasant equilibrioceptive hallucinations.[22]

Despite these reasons to think that proprioception and equilibriocep-tion are senses, counterarguments could be mounted from several direc-tions. One might argue that proprioception is not a sense as information about the world external to the body is not detected—and one might think that this is crucial for something's being a sense. Such an argu-ment could not be mounted against equilibrioception, however, as it is an exteroceptive sense. In any case, it is not clear why one should accept this restriction on what is to count as a sense.

Another reason one might proffer in order to deny that propriocep-tion and equilibrioception are sensory modalities is that proprioception and equilibrioception are really parts of other senses. For example, one might think that proprioception is really a part of touch. When we per-ceive the shape of something—say the roundness of the rim of a glass on which all and only the fingertips of one hand rest, the detection of the location of our fingertips relative to each other is crucial for detecting

---

[22] See Baloh and Honrubia (2001).

the shape of the rim. Similar but lesser-known interactions between touch and proprioception exist. How hot or cold an object feels partly determines how heavy it feels. Objects that feel cold feel heavier than ones that feel hot. Perceived temperature can also affect tactile acuity.[23] Thus, touch and proprioception often influence each other and work in unison, and so one might think this warrants thinking of proprioception as just a part of the sense of touch.

It is more difficult to assimilate equilibrioception within another sense. On the one hand, one might think that it forms part of the sensory modality that comprises touch and proprioception because it provides another a way of determining information about the position, location, and movement of one's body. On the other hand, there are also close links between equilibrioception and vision. The vestibulo-ocular reflex refers to the involuntary mechanism whereby information from the vestibular system about head movement feeds into the system that controls eye movement to allow fixation on an object despite head movements, both large and small. This reflex is essential for having clear, nonblurry vision because we cannot but help small movements of our head.[24] Thus, it is not even clear which sensory modality equilbrioception should be assimilated to, if indeed it should be assimilated to any.

These points do not decisively show that proprioception or equilibrioception are not separate modalities. We know that there can be substantial intermodal links between the traditional Aristotelian senses, such as the interaction between hearing and vision, which occurs in the McGurk effect, described earlier, which suggests that the existence of links between senses should not automatically lead to the assimilation of the two. It seems then that we must weigh various factors in determining whether proprioception and equilibrioception are distinctive senses. Certainly many scientists think that they are. Investigations into each of these sensory systems form significant research areas, which are as independent as the study of the Aristotelian senses. I am inclined to think that on balance we should count these as distinctive senses.

A third candidate for a sense in humans in addition to the Aristotelian five is the vomeronasal system, which detects pheromones using the Jacobson's organ in the nose. This system is distinct from the olfactory system. The existence of this system in some nonhuman animals is uncontroversial, and detection of pheromones clearly affects these creatures' behavior—particularly sexual behavior. The existence of a working vomeral system in humans, however, is highly disputed, but there is some evidence that it exists and that the detection of pheromones may have an effect on human behavior.[25] If this system does exist in humans, then it has some claim to be a sensory system, but not as much claim as

---

[23] See Stephens (1982) and Stephens and Hooper (1982).
[24] See Cohen and Raphan (2004).
[25] See Hughes (1999) and Meredith (2001).

the proprioceptive or vestibular systems. One reason is that it does not seem to produce conscious experiences. Thus, whether it is a sense will depend on whether a sensory modality might operate in an unconscious fashion—a question on which people could hold rather disparate views.

Candidates for yet more human senses include, as briefly mentioned earlier, distinctive pain, temperature and pressure senses instead of one more general sense of touch. Scientists have found that there are distinctive receptors that detect temperature, pressure, and painful stimuli and that there are separate spots in the skin receptive to pressure, warmth, cold, and painful stimuli. This has been the main reason that has persuaded some people that there are several senses here. However, in addition to this, some people have thought that the experiences of pressure, temperature, and pain are fairly distinctive; that is, they have rather different phenomenal characters. For example, it is sometimes claimed that Plato thought that temperature perception was a sense separate from that of touch and also that he thought pain was distinctive, being a sensation or "passion of the soul."[26] Moreover, he did this not because he knew of the differences in physiology that we know of today, for they were not known at the time, but did so at least in part on phenomenological grounds. He was not alone in doing so prior to the new physiological knowledge coming to light. A number of other scholars, including Aristotle's commentator Themistius, Avicenna, Averroes and Galen, thought that more than one sense was associated with touch.[27] So, based on considerations of phenomenal character and physiology, a good number of people have claimed that there are in fact multiple distinctive senses here, whereas the mainstream view is that we have one unified sense of touch.

Whether these are good enough reasons to postulate many senses in this case is highly disputed. One might doubt that pain, temperature, and pressure are particularly phenomenologically distinct. There seems, for example, to be a phenomenological continuity between experiences of excesses of pressure and temperature and experiences of pain. We also have evidence that a physiological overlap exists between the sensors that detect pressure, temperature, and painful stimuli—in both normal and pathological conditions. For example, pain seems to be elicited by extreme pressure or temperature (both hot and cold), suggesting that the mechanisms underlying experiences of each are not separate. However, this result might be explained away because it is hard to stop intense pressure and temperature stimuli from stimulating adjacent pain receptors in the skin. Nonetheless, there is more persuasive evidence in favor of continuity. Experiences of cold or vibration can inhibit the feeling of pain, and tactile acuity is diminished by painful heat experiences. Indeed, there is evidence of "multireceptive" neurons that are responsive

---

[26] See Classen (1993, 2).
[27] The history of the early debate over whether touch is one sense or not is explicated in great detail in Dallenbach (1939).

to two or even three of these allegedly separate modalities, which some commentators claim indicate that the allegedly separate modalities are integrated centrally in the brain.[28]

Critics of the aforementioned evidence may think that these interactive phenomena are merely similar to the McGurk effect—and thus think of them simply as intermodal interactions between different senses. So, unfortunately, such evidence does not clearly settle the matter. Moreover, appeal to phenomenology to settle these issues is not straightforward since phenomenal facts are notoriously subject to dispute. Thus, there seems to be a large open question about whether there is one sense of touch or multiple, distinctive tactile senses.

Other candidates that have been considered as being additional human senses include senses of hunger, thirst, wet and dry, the weight of objects, fullness of the bladder, suffocation and respiration, sexual appetite, and lactiferousness.[29] Indeed, in their survey of the human senses, Rivelin and Gravelle have concluded that "Five is obviously just not enough to account for the huge range of sensory possibilities of which the human species is capable; seventeen senses is probably a more accurate count."[30] Some other estimates are even higher and may be well beyond the number one should endorse, but their survey gives an indication of the number of candidates that one may have to consider.

Outside the human sphere, there are even more candidates in the animal kingdom for being senses in addition to the Aristotelian five. For example, pigeons and other birds seem sensitive to the magnetic field of the Earth, which gives them a fantastic sense of direction.[31] It has also been shown that trout can be trained to strike at targets distinguished only by their position in a magnetic field. Moreover, a distinctive sensory organ and sensory system have been identified in trout that detect magnetic fields. This evidence has led people to think that all of the conditions required for positing a magnetoreceptive sense in trout have been established.[32]

Many fish and sharks seem to have an electric sense. Sometimes this sense takes a passive form, meaning that the creatures can detect electric fields that exist independently of them in the environment. However, there is another active form of the sense where the creatures produce an electric field and then sense changes to it. Some fish use this active electric sense for navigation and to detect other living creatures.[33]

---

[28] The evidence adduced here about touch is summarized in Craig (1996). Craig claims that temperature and pain processing are closely coupled structurally in the brain and that brain lesions rarely affect one without the other. The brain's processing of pressure is structurally more distinct.

[29] See Dallenbach (1939). The last three were proposed, among others, by Erasmus Darwin. Of course, one might dispute whether these are particularly good candidates, but that is beside the point.

[30] Rivelin and Gravelle (1984, 17)

[31] See Hughes (1999).

[32] See Walker et al. (1997), reported in Hughes (1999).

[33] See Hughes (1999).

A further apparently distinctive animal sense is infrared (IR) detection. All pit vipers and some boid snakes have pits on their heads that contain cells that are sensitive to infrared light. The pits are organs distinct from the snakes' eyes and nostrils and can be used to accurately detect prey when the eyes are covered.[34]

From this evidence, one can see that many good candidates exist for being a sense, distinct from the Aristotelian five.[35] Even if we required further information about these cases before we confidently asserted that they constituted senses, these examples suggest that there at least *could* be senses of many different kinds other than the Aristotelian five. The only way to resist this thought would be to claim, as we saw Nudds do earlier, that the folk psychological notion of the senses is such that, according to it, there are only the five Aristotelian senses and that this concept of the senses is such that it is not liable to revision or replacement by scientific discovery. Do we have good reason to believe that the folk conception of the senses is as Nudds claims? I think the answer is no.

One reason to think that the folk notion of a sense is not restricted to the Aristotelian five is that scientists are some of "the folk" and the number of senses that they recognize has frequently been altered. As we have already seen, the debate about how many senses there are is a present concern to scientists. Moreover, as Rivelin and Gravelle (1984) claim, although the recent debate about the number of the senses, provoked by the vast increase in knowledge about human and animal physiology and behavior since the 1950s, has been the most notable and revisionary, the debate is not a modern phenomenon. The number of senses has been disputed throughout history by both philosophers and scientists. The historical debate is outlined in Dallenbach (1939).

Another reason is that it is very plausible to think that if ordinary people heard the facts about other creatures' sensitivity to things such as magnetic fields, and they found out how creatures can act because of such sensitivity, or if they heard the facts about human proprioception and equilibrioception, they would, I believe, unhesitatingly think of these as senses. I am happy to do so, and, in my experience, the average person shows no resistance to doing so.

An even more telling fact in favor of the view that the folk concept of the senses is not restricted to the Aristotelian five is that, in popular culture, the idea of senses other than the Aristotelian five abounds. How could this be unless the folk concept of a sense was such that it countenanced the possibility of additional senses? For example, in fiction there are accounts of possible senses such as these:

- X-ray vision
- mind-reading sense

---

[34] See ibid.
[35] There are other examples that I have not discussed here. See, for example, ibid. and the essays in this volume.

- sixth sense—the ability to perceive the future, ghosts, and so on
- the Predator's infrared perception
- the Terminator's perception, which can analyze the composition of objects
- spider sense—the ability to perceive danger via a special tingling in the extremities

Thus, I see no good reason to think that the folk conception of the senses is committed to there being five and only five senses. Thus, I see no need to revise the folk conception in light of scientific evidence. I believe that the folk concept is simply silent with regard to the question of how many number of senses there are.[36] The number of senses seems to be left open by the concept of the senses that we have. The folk already embrace the idea that the number of *actual* senses is a matter to be determined by empirical findings, and they embrace the idea that the number of *possible* senses is greater than this. Thus, I believe, the folk concept is such that when new empirical evidence of the right kind is brought to light, that which is taken to fall under the concept of the senses can easily be enlarged without changing or revising the concept. This, together with the facts mentioned earlier, gives us good reason to think that there are, and could be, many more sensory modalities than the Aristotelian five. How many actually exist is a question that only progress in science, together with philosophical investigation into the conditions required for the existence of sensory modalities, will be able to shed light on.

Can we say anything further about the question: How many senses could there be? The answer depends in part on the question that forms the main topic of the next section. Therefore, I return to this question after considering how to individuate the senses.

2.2. What Makes a Token Sense an Instance of One Type Rather Than Another?

Consider the final question that one would need to answer in order to determine what types of senses a creature has:

(6) What makes a token sense an instance of one type rather than another?

To answer this question one would need to know what determines that a sensory modality is of one particular modality rather than another. In other words, one would need to have a principle for *individuating the*

---

[36] Matthew Nudds (personal correspondence) is concerned that my account does not explain why people do say that there are five senses when asked and why this has not changed. I think that it is changing. Some people do not reply that there are five. Others who do, quickly rescind the view when other candidate senses are mentioned to them. No doubt most people have given the question little thought and reply automatically with the answer they learned from their preschool books.

senses. That is, you would need to be able to say what establishes that a sense is visual, say, rather than auditory, tactile, gustatory, or olfactory.

This individuation question has been the focus of much of the work in philosophy concerning the senses. As noted at the end of the last section, there is an obvious relationship between this question and that of how many senses there are. I believe that an explicit or a tacit acceptance of the sparse view about how many senses there are has influenced what people have often said about the individuation question—in a detrimental fashion. After elucidating the standard answers to the individuation question, I suggest another answer that rejects the sparse view and suggests that the number of actual and nomologically possible senses is rather larger than many have thought.

There are four main philosophical approaches to individuating the senses.[37] Important versions of the first two are broadly experiential approaches, holding that which sense is being used is determined by which features the perceptual experiences produced by the sense have. The other two are broadly physical approaches that hold that which physical factors are at play in the use of a sense determine which sense is being used. I discuss them in turn.

2.2.1. The Representational Criterion

One predominantly experiential approach is that a sense is individuated by which objects and properties the experiences in that modality represent. The classic Aristotelian view is one variety of this approach. According to Aristotle, there are "common sensibles"—objects or properties that can be detected by more than one sense. For example, shape is a common sensible as it can be detected by both sight and touch. Others include motion, rest, magnitude number, and unity. There are also "proper sensibles"—objects or properties that can be detected by only one sense. With one exception, each sense has its own proper sensible, and representation of it is what makes the sense the sense that it is. For example, the proper sensibles of hearing, tasting, smelling, and seeing are sound, flavor, odor, and color, respectively. Touch is the odd man out as it has multiple proper sensibles, which Aristotle thinks are reducible to four basic ones: dry, fluid, hot, and cold.

There are many variants of the representation view. For example, one might think that there are a number of features, representation of which is necessary or sufficient or both for a sense to be the sense that it is. For example, one might think that vision essentially involves representation of the shape and size of objects in three-dimensional space at a distance from one's body, as well as color and shades of light and dark. One might think that touch essentially involves the representation of the shape and

---

[37] See Grice (1962/this volume chapter 4).

size of objects that are in contact with one's body and must involve the representation of temperature, pressure, and texture. What exactly one specifies for each of these senses will depend on thinking through a large number of examples of instances of sight and touch.

Another variant of the representation view would insist that the representation that we should consider when individuating a sense should not be, or should not *just* be, what is represented in experience at the conscious, personal level but what is represented by unconscious, subpersonal brain states or mechanisms. In other words, they would invoke an information-processing notion of representation wherein one attributes content to (perhaps) unconscious brain states involved in perceptual processing. In the same way that words are symbols that carry meaning, information-processing states of the brain are thought of as vehicles or symbols that carry information that is determined by the cause (and perhaps effect) of those brain states and perhaps the evolutionary history, or function, of such states.

Some people will think that what is crucial in individuating a sense is the behavior that the sense allows a creature to engage in. For example, a sense might allow a creature to negotiate through its environment, avoiding obstacles at a distance from its body, or it might allow the creature to determine its position with respect to gravity or to magnetic fields. It is not unreasonable to include positions that make essential reference to behavior under the representational criterion. This is because when we ask how a creature can behave, the answer will very likely depend on what it knows or believes about the environment—in short, how it represents the environment to be. Some people might resist this because they hold a view of perception that denies that, in perception, representations are created in one's mind or one's brain. Rather, when perceiving, a creature directly responds either to the world or to the pattern of light in space and time that directly stimulates it.[38] However, although these views deny that representations are involved, one can argue that there is always at least a minimal sense in which perceptual states are representational. This is because, at the very least, experiences or other perceptual states of the creature can be assessed for accuracy, and the conditions in which the experience or state would be accurate can be taken to specify what representation is involved.[39] Alternatively, one could claim that the accurate description of the actions involved can be used to generate a set of objects and properties taken to specify a relevant representational content. For example, if a creature can "avoid the obstacle to its left" or "bat the ball," then these descriptions of actions in part specify ways the world is or could be and thus could

---

[38] Some disjunctivists, followers of J. J. Gibson's ecological approach, as well as sensorimotor theorists, hold such a position.

[39] This has been argued for by Susanna Siegel (2010), where accuracy is elucidated as the conditions in which there is freedom from error.

be taken as descriptions of representations relevant to determining the sense involved.

No doubt some philosophers would prefer to keep separate a representational criterion and a behavior or action criterion. However, nothing of import turns on this for my purposes. As long as one is clear about what form of representation, behaviour, or action one is using to individuate the senses, it does not matter whether one calls this type of criterion a representational one, a behavioural one, or an action one.

2.2.2. The Phenomenal Character Criterion

A second experiential approach is to think that what makes a sense the type of sense it is will be the nature of the phenomenal character of the experiences that the sense produces or involves. Immediately, however, one is faced with the question of how one might specify the sort of phenomenal character that all of the experiences of one sensory modality must have. It seems that when we specify the phenomenal character of an experience, we almost always say what it was an experience as of—that is, what the experience represented, whether or not that representation was accurate. So one might specify a class of experiences with a certain phenomenal character by specifying a class that represents certain things. In this respect, the phenomenal character criterion could turn out to look very much like the representational criterion. (Indeed, whether the nature of the phenomenal character of an experience can be fully specified *just* in terms of what the experience represents is a point much disputed in the philosophy of mind.[40]) For those philosophers that think the phenomenal character of experience can be identified with the representational content of experience, the representational criterion and the phenomenal character criterion will be the same, but for those philosophers who deny this, they will be distinct.

Another way one might specify the sort of phenomenal character that all the experiences of one sense must have is to specify one type of experience and then cite a group of experiences related to it. An important and influential way of doing this is to define classes of experiences using the notion of indiscriminability. If two experiences are discriminable, then they have different phenomenal characters. If two experiences have the same phenomenal character, then they will be indiscriminable. However, it is not true that if two experiences are indiscriminable, then they have the same phenomenal character, for A might be indiscriminable from B and B from C, yet A and C might be discriminable.[41]

---

[40] Tye (1995) and Dretske (1995), among others, argue that it is. I (2003, 2005, 2006), among others, argue that it is not.

[41] Plausibly this situation would arise, and one would have such experiences when one looked at color samples in the world where one sample was indiscriminable from a second, the second from a third, yet the first and third were discriminable. See Clark (1993).

Furthermore, B cannot have the same phenomenal character as either A or C as they can each be discriminated from something that B cannot. One can define sameness of phenomenal character, however, by appealing to global indiscriminability: Two experiences would have the same phenomenal character if they were indiscriminable and if there were no other experience that could be discriminated from either A and not B or B and not A. One can form a similarity class of experiences by identifying groups of indiscriminable experiences that are related by sharing one or more members. For example, if A and B were indiscriminable and B and C were indiscriminable, then A, B, and C would be members of the similarity class.[42] One might hope that if one took an arbitrary but clear case of an experience in a particular modality, one would be able to define a similarity class using the methodology described earlier and that the experiences in this similarity class would correspond to all and only those experiences that we intuitively would think of as experiences in that modality. One might then define that sensory modality as being the one that produces the experiences in that similarity class.

For example, one might take an experience as of a shade of color, say a mid-red, and then identify all indiscriminable experiences to it. Each of these experiences might belong to different groups of indiscriminable experiences, some as of slightly darker shades of red and some as of slightly lighter shades of red. One could imagine that the similarity class comprising all of the members of all of these groups of experiences might be identical to the class of all color experiences. In fact, one might imagine that it is possible to construct a similarity class that encompassed all visual experiences. One might be able to form a similarity class of experiences of all sounds in this way, too, providing a similarity class for audition, and so on, for each of the sensory modalities. Advocates of this view would hold that one could never form a group that encompassed both color and sound experiences if they thought vision and hearing were different senses.

2.2.3. The Proximal Stimulus Criterion

A physical approach, and one quite unlike the two typically experiential approaches so far considered, is to individuate the senses by the nature of the proximal physical stimuli that affect the sense organ. The proximal stimulus is that which directly impinges on the sensory organ of the sense. For example, one might think that electromagnetic waves of between 380 and 750 nanometers are the proximal stimuli of vision, for those are what directly stimulate the cells in the eye. On this view, one is seeing if and only if one's method of perceiving the world involves the direct stimulation of one's sensory organ by such electromagnetic

---

[42] For more information on this methodology see ibid.

waves. One might think that pressure waves in a medium are the proximal stimuli associated with hearing. Thus, one would be hearing if and only if the proximal stimuli that affect the organ that one is using to perceive are pressure waves in some medium such as air or water. One might think the proximal stimuli of smell are the members of a class of airborne chemicals. One could identify similar proximal stimuli for each sense.

2.2.4. The Sense-Organ Criterion

The second physical approach is to individuate the senses by the nature of the sense organ that one is using when perceiving. One might think that if eyes are used, then one is seeing; if ears, then one is hearing, and so on. However, it would seem incumbent on one to then give an account of what made something an eye, an ear, and so on.

One tempting way to do this would be to specify the nature of the sensory organs by specifying the nature of the proximal stimulus that affected them. For example, perhaps one might define an eye as being an organ that detects light waves and ears as organs that detect pressure waves, and so on. If one proceeded in this way, then the difference between this approach and the previous one would essentially collapse.

One could also define the sensory organs in physical ways. Thus, the physical makeup of the organ would be important. Indeed, one might not only want to mention the physical makeup of just the sensory organ but also include as part of the criterion the physiology of the whole sensory system, such as the nature of the nerves leading to the brain and even the relevant parts of the brain itself, in particular the cortical regions to which each sensory system projects. When I speak of sense-organ approaches, I include approaches such as these that include the whole sensory system.

2.2.5. The Standard Views and the Aristotelian Senses

Much of the philosophical literature on individuating the senses involves presenting reasons to favor one of these views over another. For the most part, the five Aristotelian senses differ fairly markedly on all four approaches from each other when they are operating normally and in optimal conditions. Those who support the sparse view of the senses would claim that this is evidence for their view that the senses are very different and discrete. To illustrate this, see the following table, which displays how one might think the Aristotelian senses the criteria different theories may use to individuate the senses.[43]

---

[43] Of course, there are some reasons to question this neat dichotomy, even for the Aristotelian senses, as we will see in due course. In particular, it turns out that distinguishing taste and smell is particularly difficult.

The criteria different theories may use to individuate the senses*

	Vision	Touch	Hearing	Taste	Smell
Representation	Colour, shape and movement at a distance from our body in front of our eyes	Temperature, pressure, shape and movement at the surface of our body	Sounds, volume, pitch, objects being struck or vibrated at locations in and at distance from and all around our body	Flavours (sweet, salty, bitter, sour, umami) in the mouth or on the tongue or in the food touching the tongue	Odours located either in the nose or in the air around the nose, perhaps coming from a certain direction
Phenomenal Character	Visual experiences	Tactile experiences	Auditory experiences	Taste experiences	Olfactory experiences
Proximal Stimulus	Electromagnetic waves	Mechanical pressure and temperature	Pressure waves in a medium such as air or water	Chemicals that affect receptors on the tongue	Volatile molecules that affect the epithelium
Sense Organ	Eyes, particularly the retina	Skin or receptors in the skin	Ears, particularly the cochlea	Tongue, particularly the taste-buds on the tongue	Nose, particularly the nasal epithelium

* Of course, there are some reasons to question this neat dichotomy, even for the Aristotelian senses as we will see in due course. In particular, it turns out that distinguishing taste and smell is very difficult.

However, the following create havoc with this neat taxonomy:

(1) non-Aristotelian senses
(2) tampering with the Aristotelian senses
(3) malfunction of the Aristotelian senses
(4) the Aristotelian senses operating in odd environments

These cases show (as will shortly be illustrated) that none of the four criteria allow us to neatly categorize each of the senses as being one of the Aristotelian senses or as being one of a small number of discrete senses. Furthermore, the four criteria pull us in different directions when we try to determine which type of sense a given sense is. This is one reason that people have thought that one has to choose between the four criteria for individuating the senses—they have thought that one has to pick the best out of the *competing* theories for individuating the senses. However, after outlining four examples that bring to light the most important problems these theories face, I suggest an alternative approach to individuating the senses. I claim that, in light of these examples, we have reason not to be sparse theorists and that, once we give up that commitment, we can come to see the four criteria in a new light. They are criteria that can be used together to allow us to accurately, nonarbitrarily, and in a fine-grained manner taxonomize the actual and possible senses.

2.2.6. The Standard Views and Bat Echolocation

Bats send out a high frequency "chirrup" and listen for the returning echo. Both the time it takes for the sound to bounce off objects and return to the bat and the direction from which the sound is returned (determined by the different times at which each ear is stimulated by the returning echo) are used to determine the size, shape, and position of objects at a distance in front of the bat. This means of perception allows bats to negotiate through their environment skillfully and quickly, dodging obstacles and catching moths and other prey in the dark.[44]

What do your intuitions say about this sense?

(1) Bats have an incredible form of hearing.
(2) Bats can see in the dark using this mechanism.
(3) Bats have a sense that we do not: echolocation.

The proximal stimulus and sense-organ criteria tend to suggest that the bat has a form of hearing because the proximal stimulus is pressure waves and the sensory organ is an ear, or at least something more like our ears than any other organ. However, the frequencies that bats can hear are different from those that we can hear. So, to judge that

---

[44] Further details of the bat's echolocation, together with excellent informed speculation on the representational and phenomenal nature of the bat's experience, is given in Akins (1993).

the bat is hearing is to think that hearing involves the detection of any frequency of pressure wave, as opposed to just those that humans can detect. Similarly, the bat's ears are not physically exactly like ours. In addition, if within the sense-organ criterion we wish to include the brain mechanisms that process the signals coming from the ear, then because a bat's brain receives or calculates so much more information from its auditory signal compared to humans, there are numerous differences between the bat's brain and ours. So the bat's sensory organs are somewhat like ours, but somewhat not. In short, while the proximal stimulus and sense-organ criterion most naturally suggest that the bat is hearing, one could hold that the proximal stimulus and the sense organ are different enough from ours that the bat should be counted, on application of these criteria, as having a sense that we do not.

The representational criterion yields unclear results. One might think that it will yield the result that the bat is seeing because, using this sense, the bat can detect three-dimensional objects at a distance from its body, which humans can do with their sense of sight. However, the bat does not detect color, and some people have thought that perception of color is required for seeing. So alternatively, one might think that the bat really has a sense of hearing, for surely the bat's experiences will represent the sound that bounces back in the form of the echo. And indeed, one might question whether the bat's experiences represent where objects are at a distance from its body. One might think that instead, postperception, the bat judges where these objects are on the basis of things that it hears.[45] Alternatively again, one might be inclined to think that the bat's experiences represent both sound *and* objects at a distance from its body. If this is right, then perhaps the bat both sees and hears with the one sensory organ. Or perhaps it would be best to say that it has a different sense altogether from any of the ones that we have.

The phenomenal character criterion is unhelpful in this case. To the extent that we can imagine what it is like to be a bat one might think that the experiences share some auditory and visual characteristics and perhaps some unlike either of these.[46]

So what should we decide? In part we are ignorant of some facts, knowledge of which might help us determine which sense the bat has. However, I believe that even if we knew all of the relevant facts, our intuitions and criteria would tell us that the bat's sense is like our vision in some respects and like our hearing in others and like neither in some respects. Before exploring what we should do in the face of this, consider the other cases.

---

[45] Whether we can draw a sharp line between perceptual content and judgment is a highly debatable matter.
[46] Famously, philosophers have thought that one cannot know what it is like to be a bat. (See Nagel [1974].) However, Akins (1993) persuasively claims that we can know quite a lot about what it is like, even if not everything.

2.2.7. The Standard Views and Bee "Vision"

Bees are sensitive both to what we call visible light and also to ultraviolet (UV). If we look at many flowers in visible light, they often look like the flower on the left of figure 1.2—they have a small dark center and then a uniform color on the petals. However, if we photograph them using a camera sensitive to ultraviolet light, then the flowers often look like the flower on the right of the figure. The extra markings that can be detected using ultraviolet are called the "nectar guide" pattern, and they guide the bees to the source of the nectar.

It is natural to say that bees have vision—a form of vision in which both the human visible spectrum and ultraviolet light are detected by the bees' eyes. But should we? Recall the nature of the electromagnetic spectrum, of which visible light and ultraviolet are parts. It simply consists of all of the wavelengths of electromagnetic waves. The shortest wavelengths are gamma rays, at around 0.0005 nanometers (nm). Next are X-rays (around 0.5 nm), then ultraviolet wavelengths (around 250 nm). Slightly longer still, the visible spectrum consists of wavelengths between 380 nm and 760 nm. Above that are infrared wavelengths, centered around 10,000 nm. Microwaves have longer wavelengths still, up to about 1 meter, and wavelengths longer than that are classified as radio waves.

The proximal stimulus criterion is the reason for mentioning these facts. If we think that bee "vision" really is vision, and we think we should individuate the senses by the proximal stimulus criterion, then one must think that the proximal stimulus of vision is wider than the visible spectrum and also includes ultraviolet electromagnetic waves. However, if one is willing to extend the proximal stimulus beyond visible light, then should one extend it to the whole electromagnetic spectrum? One might

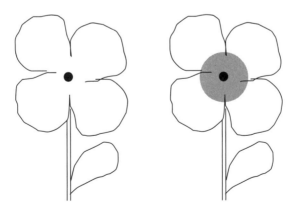

Figure 1.2 Diagram of typical markings on flowers: in visible light on the left, and in ultraviolet light on the right.

think that one ought to. After all, one might think that all the wave-lengths form a natural kind. What makes them different is merely their wavelength. However, if one does that, then one would be committed to thinking that a creature that detected only radio waves was seeing and that one that detected only gamma rays was seeing. Nevertheless, it is far from obvious that creatures with such detecting mechanisms, even if we were confident that they constituted senses, would really be ones that we would want to count as vision. I certainly would want to know a lot more about the sense in question, such as the nature of the sense organ, what the subject's experiences represented, and what their phenomenal character was before I would feel confident that the sense was vision.

Alternatively, perhaps we should limit the proximal stimulus of vision to encompass just visible light. In that case, the bee would either have vision plus some other sense, an ultraviolet sense, or just some sense other than vision—one that detected both ultraviolet and visible light. (A further case for the thought that we should limit the proximal stimulus of vision is outlined when we come to discuss snake infrared perception later.)

The sense-organ criterion yields unclear results. We do classify the bees' organs that detect visible light and ultraviolet light as eyes. Nonetheless, bee eyes are very different from human eyes. Bees have two large, compound eyes and three small, simple eyes (called "ocelli") arranged in a triangle on their forehead. When we learn just how different the organ of the bees' "vision" is to ours, it is not completely obvious that we should think of bees as having eyes.

The representational criterion perhaps delivers the clearest verdict that bees have vision. They would seem to represent what we represent—three-dimensional objects at a distance from our bodies. Perhaps they represent all of the qualities that we represent the world as having, plus some others visible only to those who can detect ultraviolet. Still, if that is right, then perhaps we should think that they have their own special vision-plus-ultraviolet sense. This is made all the more plausible when we consider that it is not clear that bees simply represent more than us—some extra ultraviolet facts. Humans have three types of cells in their eyes that are responsive to long, medium, and short wavelengths of visible light. The nature of these cells, plus subsequent processing, determines the kind of color vision that we have. Bees have three kinds of receptor, too, but their receptivity spans both the visible and the ultraviolet ranges. Thus, the kind of "color vision" that bees have is rather different from ours. Bees do not see the colors that we see plus some other colors. They do not see, for example, how the flower looks to us under visible light *and* how it appears to us in a picture taken by a camera sensitive to ultraviolet light. Rather, they see the flower in just one way, determined by both the reflectance of visible light and ultraviolet light and by the nature of their light-sensitive cells. Because of this, it is tempting to describe the case as one in which bees do not see colors—or at the very least do not see the colors we do. And then if, with Aristotle, we thought that what made a sense vision was the representation of the colors—or at least the ones we see—it would be right to conclude that the bees do not see, although they do something similar.

Finally, think about the phenomenal character criterion. Of course, it is hard to know what the phenomenology of bee experience is like, but our best guess would be that to some extent it is the same and to some extent different from human vision.[47] The facts that make us think that what the bees' experience represents partially overlaps with human visual experience and partly does not motivates this thought. Here, a mixture of our ignorance and our best guess leaves us unsure as to how to classify bee "vision." It is somewhat like our vision and somewhat not.

Thus, although a few criteria suggest that bees have vision, the sense they have is sufficiently different from our vision that one might think it a different sense, even if it is most like our vision. This case shows that for each proposed criterion for individuating the senses, it will be difficult to decide upon the necessary and sufficient conditions that it takes to have a particular sense. We will see this problem manifest itself further in the next example.

2.2.8. The Standard Views and Snake Infrared Perception

It is interesting to contrast and compare the case of bee vision with that of snake infrared perception. Some snakes, such as pit vipers and boid snakes, have organs separate from their eyes that detect infrared. These organs are situated on the front of the snakes' faces, below the eyes and close to the snakes' nostrils. They consist of pits lined with infrared detecting cells.[48] Using this sense alone, snakes can detect prey in front of them and discriminate the shape of the prey enough to allow them to make precise strikes on vulnerable parts of the prey's body. (This ability has been documented in a congenitally blind rattlesnake.[49]) Snakes can also detect the heat trails of prey that have passed by their location some time previously and then follow that trail to the creature's burrow and thus find their meal. Is this a form of vision or not? Let us run through the list of criteria again.

The proximal stimulus criterion is unclear. As with bee "vision" we face a decision as to whether we should extend the proximal stimulus of vision beyond that of human visible light, this time to include not ultraviolet but infrared radiation. If one thinks that one should do it for ultraviolet, then it will be hard to find principled grounds on which to

---

[47] Some people might even wonder whether bees (and other animals) are the subjects of any states with phenomenal character.
[48] See Hughes (1999). The relevance of this case to individuating the senses is also discussed by Gray (2005).
[49] See Kardong and Mackessy (1991).

exclude an extension to infrared. Then again, the question comes up, Should it be extended to include detection of any part of the electromagnetic spectrum, including gamma or radio waves even if, intuitively, the detection of these waves would not yield a sense like vision?

The sense-organ criterion does not yield perspicuous results, either. The snakes' pits are like our eyes in some respects but not very many. The obvious question facing this criterion on consideration of this example is, What is it for something to be an eye? Right away we can see that any criteria for being an eye will be very malleable. For example, is an eye any electromagnetic detector or just a detector of all and only visible light or something else?

Another interesting question that the snake infrared sense raises, in addition to that of which sense it is, is whether it is a separate sense from what is commonly taken to be the snake's visual sense. Certainly the eyes and the infrared pits are different sensory systems to the extent that we think of them as formed by just the physiological structures near the surface of the snake's head. However, if we think of the sense organs as composing the whole physiological structure leading from the cells that light and infrared impinge upon to the central parts of the brain, which process the information gathered by those cells, the issue is far from clear. It has been found that the maplike visual and infrared representations of the world in the snake's brain are partly overlaid in the optic tectum. Some neurons in the tectum respond only to visual stimulation or only to infrared stimulation; others respond to either visual or infrared stimulation; still others respond only to a combination of visual and infrared stimulation. There may be enough overlap that one is tempted to think that both sets of organs (the snakes' eyes and infrared pits) are really organs of the one sense in the way our two eyes are organs of the one sense.

The question of whether the snake has one visible-light-plus-infrared sense or two token senses—either vision and an infrared sense or two token senses of vision—muddies the water in considering the nature of the snake's senses. For the rest of this section, I assume that there are two token senses and address the question of whether the sense that detects infrared is a sense of vision or not.

What does the representational criterion tell us? It is a reasonable assumption that three-dimensional objects at a distance from the snake's body are represented on account of the precise targeting of prey by snakes using only this sense. The infrared sense then shares a representational aspect with human vision. Nonetheless, the snake's infrared sense detects heat and does not detect the color properties that we detect, so there are considerable differences with regard to representation, too. These representational similarities and differences suggest that the phenomenal character of the snake's infrared sense may be somewhat like our vision but somewhat different. It is hard to say very much more than this.

In summary, the snake infrared sense is somewhat like our vision and somewhat not. Unlike the case of bee "vision," which involves detection of the part of the electromagnetic spectrum humans can detect plus an additional part, snake infrared perception does not involve detection of a part of the electromagnetic spectrum that humans can detect, merely detection of shorter wavelengths.

2.2.9. The Standard Views and Tactile-Visual Sensory Substitution

Tactile-visual sensory substitution (TVSS) devices try to replace the sense of sight by exploiting the sense of touch. A camera image drives a grid of vibrating pins that press against the back or other suitable expanse of skin. Areas of the camera image correspond to isomorphic areas of the grid of pins, and pressure and vibration against the skin correspond to the light levels the camera detects. With practice, subjects can use the system to skillfully navigate their way through the world and identify three-dimensional objects at a distance from their body.[50]

At first, subjects report that they are aware of the sensations on their skin, but as they continue to use the system they stop paying attention to or noticing the tactile stimulation, at least *as such*, and instead attend to or notice what seems to them to be the objects in the world in front of them. Reports about such subjects suggest that their experiences have much in common with visual experiences, particularly with regard to their spatial nature. For example, Nicholas Humphrey reports the following:

> By making use of information in the image about perspective and motion parallax, the blind subjects came to perceive external objects as being located in a stable three-dimensional world. They did not locate objects as lying up against their skin—any more than we with normal vision locate objects as lying up against the retina of our eyes—but immediately perceived them as being out there in space. (1993, 59)

Are people who use TVSS devices seeing, feeling, or perceiving in some different way? That is, are we replacing their vision, or are we extending their existing sense of touch to allow the detection of objects and properties it usually cannot detect, or are we creating a brand new sense? The sensory-organ criterion would yield different answers depending on what we say the sense organ here is. If it is the camera, then perhaps we should think that the sense at play is vision. If it is the skin, then we should think it touch. If it is the camera plus the skin, then perhaps the sense is neither vision nor touch but a new sensory modality. The proximal stimulus criterion is open to just the same sort of speculation. Is the stimulus the pressure on the skin, light on the camera, or both? Which one decides upon will determine whether the sense is touch, vision, or neither.

---

[50] See Bach-y-Rita (1972).

What does the representational criterion tell us? Certainly at first, when using the TVSS system, there is a representation of the pins touching the body. This surely remains over time as the subject gets used to the TVSS system, even if it is not the main focus of subject's attention. The subject also seems to acquire a representation of objects in three-dimensional space in front of them. To this extent their experiences seem to represent in part what visual experiences do (minus color). Then again, if the subject has experiences with both vision-like and touch-like representational characteristics, then perhaps the subject has a sense that ordinary humans do not. The phenomenal character criterion yields much the same result here: one imagines the experiences, phenomenally speaking, to be partly like touch, partly like vision, and partly distinctive.

Thus, people who use a TVSS system, at least once they have adapted to it, are using a sense partly like vision, partly like touch, and partly unique.

2.2.10. Rejection of the Sparse View and How to Individuate the Senses

The criteria and our intuitions tell us that in each of the following cases:

- echolocation
- UV vision
- IR vision
- tactile vision

the sense involved is in some respects like our vision and in some respects different—sometimes like another one of our senses and sometimes different altogether. I suggest that these examples and others show that the actual and the possible senses cannot be clearly divided into a limited number of discrete kinds. The differences between the senses amounts more to a difference of degree rather than a difference of kind.

Rather than try to pigeonhole all of the senses into a small number of discrete categories we should simply note what each sense is like with regard to each of the four criteria proposed by philosophers:

- proximal stimulus
- representation
- phenomenal character
- sense organ

(and perhaps others if they are required to fully capture all of the important aspects of the senses). For each criterion we can note how different or similar each sense is to one of the five Aristotelian senses if we like, but that is relatively unimportant. We should stop trying to artificially determine or stipulate which Aristotelian sense any sense is—or to shoehorn each sense into one of a small number of discrete kinds. It is because people have tried to do this and because the four criteria pull in different directions in problem cases that people have thought that they have to choose among the four criteria—rather than embrace them all.

For example, Matthew Nudds has suggested that our choice of which of the standard criteria we use to individuate the senses should be determined by their significance. This seems like a good methodology. We should ask, Why does distinguishing the senses matter to us? Nudds's own answer is that, "In distinguishing different senses we are distinguishing different ways of perceiving" (2004, 45). He goes on to explain that different ways of perceiving will involve perceiving different ranges of properties. Telling you which sense I am using to perceive something lets you know the type of properties that I (normally) know about.

However, I think that distinguishing the senses matters to us because we care about all of the following:

- representation
- proximal stimulus
- phenomenal character
- sense organ

Philosophers have argued over which is important, but why not think they all are? All can matter practically, and all can matter for determining both philosophical and scientific issues.

I hold that the four criteria are relatively independent dimensions along which different possible kinds of senses could take different values. We can think of these four criteria as defining a multidimensional space within which we can locate each of the Aristotelian senses, the four examples of unusual senses discussed earlier, and any other sense. Thus, human vision, bee "vision," snake infrared perception, and TVSS perception would each be located at a different place in the multidimensional space. Indeed, this multidimensional space is a way of delineating the space of all possible senses. All possible senses will occupy a place in the space.[51] (The actual senses will occupy a small number of these places.[52])

---

[51] In the actual world there will of course be contingent connections between the criteria. For example, the proximal stimulus and the sense organ/physiology of the sense probably partly determine the representational properties and the phenomenal character of perceptual experience. The extent to which any necessary connections exist among the criteria is a difficult question and one's answer to it will depend on one's views on (at least) the following: the nature of phenomenal character, what types of metaphysically possible worlds there are, and whether a sense must generate conscious experiences. Thus, one might hold that while each possible sense will occupy some place in the multidimensional space, not every position in the space is a place that a possible sense could occupy.

[52] Of course, when faced with certain senses we may be ignorant of the nature of those senses with regard to the facts pertaining to one or more of the criteria, but that is merely our unfortunate epistemic situation. When we embrace all four criteria and resist shoehorning all of the senses into a few discrete kinds, we can simply note, for each criterion, all of the facts we know. For example, in assessing the nature of the sensory organ in TVSS we should mention both the camera and the skin of the subject and the connection between them.

Plotting the actual senses in this space will allow one to see the similarities and connections between them yet, at the same time, to individuate the types of sense in a nonsparse, fine-grained manner. When we do such a plotting for the actual senses, we could do it for each token instance of a sense, or we could do it for idealized versions of the senses in each species. If we did the former, then my sense of vision might turn out to be a different sense from yours, for I may be much more nearsighted than you. If we did the latter, then we would have the same sense, for we each have tokens of the idealized sense of vision in humans. Also, if we did the latter, we might find that the actual senses are to be found in clusters in this space. For we will find, for example, that human vision and bee "vision" are closer together in this space than human vision and bat echolocation. Perhaps these clusters would correspond to the Aristotelian senses or the Aristotelian senses plus a few others. I suspect this might be the case. This would show us that the folk were trying to reflect complex facts about the types of senses that we find in the world using an oversimplistic model, but one whose origin is explicable given the facts. However, if two senses are close together in this space, we should not concern ourselves with the question of whether they are the same sense. Once we have plotted their location in the space and noted their similarities and differences, we have said everything we need to say about the senses. That is when we should cease to ask how to individuate the senses.

3. THE CLASSIC WORKS

The issues that I have outlined in this introduction are explored at length by the essays in this volume.

In the classic works section, Aristotle's famous contribution outlining his version of the representational criterion, in which the senses are individuated in terms of the objects and properties that can be discerned by means of them, is followed by a detailed and erudite commentary by Richard Sorabji. Sorabji explores not only what Aristotle's view was but also whether any version of Aristotle's view can plausibly be held. He concludes that the sense that is the most difficult to individuate in the way Aristotle recommends is touch.

Grice's essay opens by considering when it would be appropriate to claim that a creature has a sense that is not one of the senses that humans possess. After a short discussion of how to distinguish perceptual processes from nonperceptual ones he lists the four main criteria, outlined in this introduction, that one might use to individuate the senses. He discusses their relations and plausibility. He then argues that there is an ineliminable role for the phenomenal character of experiences in individuating the senses.

In addition to considering how one might individuate the senses, Roxbee Cox discusses how a subject can know from the inside which sense is being employed to perceive. He claims that a representational view is the best approach to answering both questions. He develops in detail his version of this view, which he calls the "key feature" view.

Coady discusses Grice's work at length and the idea that the phenomenal character of experience is essential to individuating the senses. He rejects the idea and discusses the extent to which one could practically determine or know about this criterion. He concludes that the other criteria, particularly the representational criterion, are important.

The proximal-stimulus criterion for individuating the senses is explored and developed in Heil's essay. Heil comments that the senses may not be sharply distinguished from one another, but to the extent that they can, he believes this criterion is the best. He acknowledges the work of J. J. Gibson in developing his approach.

Like Grice, defending the ineliminability of the phenomenal criterion is Leon's purpose. He also discusses the representational nature of experience at length and in doing so tries to distinguish perception from other belief-forming mechanisms. He raises problems for the representational criterion for individuating the senses.

Nelkin defends the idea that the senses are to be individuated by a combination of the types of belief that are formed using the sense and the nature of the sensory organ in which the belief-forming process originated.

Martin's essay examines to the extent to which one can use the phenomenal criterion to individuate the senses. He shows that an account of the phenomenal differences between the experiences in different modalities can be given by reference to the various structural properties of those experiences. He argues that sight can be differentiated from touch because, in sight, a perceptual field contributes to seeing in a way that any field associated with touch does not contribute to touch.

Finally, Keeley draws our attention to the criteria used in science and to neuroethology in particular, which is regularly faced with the task of classifying the senses in unusual animals. He argues that four criteria are required to individuate the senses: the proximal stimulus; the nature of the sensory organ and the relevant, associated brain mechanisms; the creature's ability to discriminate between stimuli associated with one type of proximal stimulus; and the evolutionary or developmental importance of the sense to the creature.

4. THE NEW WORKS

Gray contrasts a scientific picture of the senses as natural kinds, which would be individuated in the manner that Keeley suggests in his work, with what he takes to be the antirealist position of Nudds (2004). He claims that Nudds holds that the way we individuate the senses is, largely, a conventional matter. Thus, Nudds merely seeks to elucidate the folk criteria by which we do individuate the senses. Gray defends the scientific approach over the antirealist approach.

Perceiving is often thought to have something in common with sensory imagining. For example, it is often said that such imagining is phenomenally similar to perceiving, simply less vivid or lively (as Hume famously suggested). Might one make progress with individuating the senses by thinking about how to individuate sensory imaginings? Hopkins argues in favor of this idea. Taking sight and touch as examples, he claims that different forms of perspective are involved in each. He explores this idea and, like Martin earlier, thinks that the structural features of experiences play some part in individuating the senses.

In Heil's new contribution to this volume he further defends the view he set out in his earlier work. He claims that we should distinguish the senses on the basis of the kinds of information-bearing stimulation to which they are sensitive.

O'Dea defends a representational theory of phenomenal character from Grice's contention that some phenomenal aspects of experiences are not representational. O'Dea argues that our perceptual experiences represent not only things in the world but also which organ of sense we are using to perceive. Thus, he claims that perceptual experiences have an interoceptive, as well as an exteroceptive, aspect, which can allow subjects of experience to know which sense or senses are employed when they perceive.

The questions of individuating the senses and what constitutes a sensory modality occupy Nudds in his contribution to this volume. Unlike O'Dea, he claims that it is doubtful that the operations of the different sensory mechanisms are available to us in introspection. He thus claims that we should not give an experiential (representational or phenomenal) account of the individuation of the senses. Rather, we distinguish the senses in light of our understanding of the different mechanisms that allow us to perceive and their connection to the experiences that we have. So the senses, according to Nudds, are different forms of sensory mechanism. However, he goes on to argue that, although our concept of the senses is that there are five, we do not find five sorts of sensory mechanism in humans. In light of this, he claims that either we are mistaken about how many senses there are or our concepts of the senses are not concepts of natural kinds. Nudds provides reasons to think that the latter position is correct and suggests that our concepts of the senses may be social ones.

Smith's essay focuses on the question of what makes an experience a perceptual one or at least a perceptual experience of something other than our own body. Focusing on the case of experiences of pain, he investigates the reason we do not locate painful qualities in the objects that produce experiences of pain and finds an answer in a detailed investigation of the nature of the phenomenal character of pain experiences.

As we have seen in this introduction, there are many candidate sensory modalities in humans and animals besides the Aristotelian five. One candidate is the sense of agency—the sense of acting. Taking this as a case study, Bayne considers whether it is right to think that there is a sense of agency and concludes that there are some good reasons to think that agentive experiences are produced by a dedicated perceptual system that represents one's own agency and makes these representations available to the cognitive system in experiential form.

Finally, Clark looks at intriguing new evidence concerning cross-modal effects involving spatial attention. Reflection on these results, he claims, gives us new reasons to think that spatial properties are common sensibles of all sensory modalities.

5. CONCLUSION

The topic of individuating the senses is a fascinating field, one that not only is of interest in its own right but also promises to provoke further investigation into the nature of perception and perceptual experience in modalities other than vision—an area of philosophical inquiry long overdue for attention. It promises to provoke an investigation of perception in all of the modalities that must reflect the ever-growing number of fascinating empirical results on the nature of perception—in each modality and across and between modalities—and to find a role for those findings. As we have seen, the responses to those findings can be many and varied. Finally, it promises to uncover interesting avenues of investigation for thinking about the nature of perception itself in all its myriad forms.

References

Akins, K. 1993. What Is It Like to Be Boring and Myopic? In *Dennett and His Critics*, ed. B. Dahlbom, pp. 124–160. Cambridge, Mass.: Blackwell.

Auvray, M., and C. Spence. 2008. The Multisensory Perception of Flavour. *Consciousness and Cognition* 17: 1016–31.

Bach-y-Rita, P. 1972. *Brain Mechanisms in Sensory Substitution*. New York: Academic Press.

Baloh, R. W., and V. Honrubia. 2001. *Clinical Neurophysiology of the Vestibular System*, 3rd ed. New York: Oxford University Press.

Calvert, G. A., C. Spence, and B. E. Stein, eds. 2004. *The Handbook of Multisensory Processes*. Cambridge, Mass.: MIT Press.

Churchland, P. M. 1979. *Scientific Realism and the Plasticity of Mind*. New York: Cambridge University Press.

Clark, A. 1993. *Sensory Qualities*. New York: Oxford University Press.

Classen, C. 1993. *Worlds of Sense: Explaining the Senses in History and across Cultures*. London: Routledge.

Cohen, B., and T. Raphan. 2004. The Physiology of the Vestibuloocular Reflex (VOR). In *The Vestibular System*, ed. S. M. Highstein, R. R. Fay, and A. N. Popper, pp. 235–285. New York: Springer.

Craig, A. D. 1996. Pain, Temperature, and the Sense of the Body. In *Somesthesis and the Neurobiology of the Somatosensory Cortex*, ed. O. Franzén, R. J. Lars, and Y. Terenius, pp. 27–39 Basel: Birkhäuser.

Dallenbach, K. M. 1939. Pain: History and Present Status. *American Journal of Psychology* 52(3): 331–47.

Dretske, F. I. 1995. *Naturalizing the Mind*. Cambridge, Mass.: MIT Press.

Farah, M. J. 2004. *Visual Agnosia*, 2nd ed. Cambridge, Mass.: MIT Press.

Fodor, J. A. 1983. *The Modularity of Mind*. Cambridge, Mass.: MIT Press.

Gandevia, S. C., J. L. Smith, M. Crawford, U. Proske, and J. L. Taylor. 2006. Motor Commands Contribute to Human Position Sense. *Journal of Physiology* 571(3): 703–10.

Gray, R. 2005. On the Concept of a Sense. *Synthese* 147(3): 461–75.

Grice, H. P. 1962. Some Remarks about the Senses. In *Analytical Philosophy*, first series, ed. R. J. Butler, 133–53. Oxford: Blackwell. Reprinted in this volume, chapter 4.

Head, H., and G. Holmes. 1911. Sensory Disturbances from Cerebral Lesions. *Brain* 34: 102–254.

Hughes, H. C. 1999. *Sensory Exotica*. Cambridge, Mass.: MIT Press.

Jones, L. A. 1988. Motor Illusions: What Do They Reveal about Proprioception? *Psychological Bulletin* 103(1): 72–86.

Kardong, K. V., and S. P. Mackessy. 1991. The Strike Behaviour of a Congenitally Blind Rattlesnake. *Journal of Herpetology* 25(2): 208–11.

Macpherson, F. 2003. Novel Colours and the Content of Experience. *Pacific Philosophical Quarterly* 84(1): 43–66.

———. 2005. Color Inversion Problems for Representationalism. *Philosophy and Phenomenological Research* 70(1): 127–52.

———. 2006. Ambiguous Figures and the Content of Experience. *Noûs* 40(1): 82–117.

———. 2011. The Admissible Contents of Experience. In *The Admissible Contents of Experience*, ed. Katherine Hawley and Fiona Macpherson, 1–15. Wiley-Blackwell.

———. Forthcoming. Cognitive Penetration of Color Experience: Rethinking the Issue in Light of an Indirect Mechanism. *Philosophy and Phenomenological Research*.

McGurk, H., and J. MacDonald. 1976. Hearing Lips and Seeing Voices. *Nature* 264(5588): 746–48.

Meredith, M. 2001. Human Vomeronasal Organ Function: A Critical Review of Best and Worst Cases. *Chemical Senses* 26: 433–45.

Nagel, T. 1974. What Is It Like to Be a Bat? *Philosophical Review* 83: 435–50.

Nudds, M. 2004. The Significance of the Senses. *Proceedings of the Aristotelian Society* 104(1): 31–51.

Paquerson, X., M. Leguen, D. Rosenthal, P. Coriat, J. C. Willwe, and N. Danaziger. 2003. The Phenomenology of Body Image Distortions Induced by Regional Anaesthesia. *Brain* 126: 702–12.

Pylyshyn, Z. W. 1999. Is Vision Continuous with Cognition? The Case for Cognitive Impenetrability of Visual Perception. *Behavioral and Brain Sciences* 22: 341–423.

Ramachandran, V. S., and W. Hirstein. 1998. The Perception of Phantom Limbs: The D. O. Hebb Lecture. *Brain* 121: 1603–30.

Rivelin, R., and K. Gravelle. 1984. *Deciphering the Senses: The Expanding World of Human Perception*. New York: Simon and Schuster.

Siegel, S. 2008. The Contents of Perception. In *The Stanford Encyclopedia of Philosophy*, ed. E. N. Zalta (Winter edition). http://plato.stanford.edu/archives/win2008/entries/perception-contents/.

———. 2010. Do Visual Experiences Have Contents? In *Perceiving the World*, ed. B. Nanay. New York: Oxford University Press.

Stephens, J. C. 1982. Temperature Can Sharpen Tactile Acuity. *Perception and Psychophysics* 31: 57–80.

———, and J. E. Hooper. 1982. How Skin and Object Temperature Influence Touch Sensation. *Perception and Psychophysics* 32: 282–85.

Tye, M. 1995. Ten Problems of Consciousness: A Representational Theory of the Phenomenal Mind. Cambridge, Mass.: MIT Press.

———. 2003. *Consciousness and Persons: Unity and Identity.* Cambridge, Mass.: MIT Press.

Vroomen, J., and B. de Gelder. 2003. Visual Motion Influences the Contingent Auditory Motion Aftereffect. *Psychological Science* 14(4): 357–61.

Walker, M., C. Diebel, C. Haugh, P. Pankhurst, J. Montgomery, and C. Green. 1997. Structure and Function of the Vertebrate Magnetic Sense. *Nature* 390: 371–76.

Weiskrantz, L. 1986. *Blindsight: A Case Study and Implications.* New York: Oxford University Press.

———. 1997. *Consciousness Lost and Found.* New York: Oxford University Press.

Section: I

CLASSIC WORKS

2

Excerpt from *On the Soul (De Anima)*

Aristotle

BOOK II

· ·

6 · In dealing with each of the senses we shall have first to speak of the objects which are perceptible by each. The term 'object of sense' covers three kinds of objects, two kinds of which we call perceptible in themselves, while the remaining one is only incidentally perceptible. Of the first two kinds one consists of what is special to a single sense, the other of what is common to any and all of the senses. I call by the name of special object of this or that sense that which cannot be perceived by any other sense than that one and in respect of which no error is possible; in this sense colour is the special object of sight, sound of hearing, flavour of taste. Touch, indeed, discriminates more than one set of different qualities. Each sense has one kind of object which it discerns, and never errs in reporting that what is before it is colour or sound (though it may err as to what it is that is coloured or where that is, or what it is that is sounding or where that is). Such objects are what we call the special objects of this or that sense.

Common sensibles are movement, rest, number, figure, magnitude; these are not special to any one sense, but are common to all. There are at any rate certain kinds of movement which are perceptible both by touch and by sight.

We speak of an incidental object of sense where e.g. the white object which we see is the son of Diares; here because being the son of Diares is incidental to the white which is perceived, we speak of the son of Diares as being incidentally perceived. That is why it in no way as such affects the senses. Of the things perceptible in themselves, the special objects are properly called perceptible and it is to them that in the nature of things the structure of each several sense is adapted.

Aristotle, (350 BC) *On the Soul*, Book II, Chapters 6–12 and Book III, Chapters 1 & 2, from Jonathan Barnes (ed.) *The Complete Works of Aristotle: The Revised Oxford Translation*, 1984. (Copyright, 1986, Princeton University Press. Reprinted by permission of Princeton University Press.)

7 · The object of sight is the visible, and what is visible is colour and a certain kind of object which can be described in words but which has no single name; what we mean by the second will be abundantly clear as we proceed. Whatever is visible is colour and colour is what lies upon what is in itself visible; 'in itself' here means not that visibility is involved in the definition of what thus underlies colour, but that that substratum contains in itself the cause of visibility. Every colour has in it the power to set in movement what is actually transparent; that power constitutes its very nature. That is why it is not visible except with the help of light; it is only in light that the colour of a thing is seen. Hence our first task is to explain what light is.

Now there clearly is something which is transparent, and by 'transparent' I mean what is visible, and yet not visible in itself, but rather owing its visibility to the colour *of something else*; of this character are air, water, and many solid bodies. Neither air nor water is transparent because it is air or water; they are transparent because each of them has contained in it a certain substance which is the same in both and is also found in the eternal upper body. Of this substance light is the activity—the activity of what is transparent *qua* transparent; where this power is present, there is also the potentiality of the contrary, viz. darkness. Light is as it were the proper colour of what is transparent, and exists whenever the potentially transparent is excited to actuality by the influence of fire or something resembling 'the uppermost body'; for fire too contains something which is one and the same with the substance in question.

We have now explained what the transparent is and what light is; light is neither fire nor any kind whatsoever of body nor an efflux from any kind of body (if it were, it would again itself be a kind of body)—it is the presence of fire or something resembling fire in what is transparent. It is certainly not a body, for two bodies cannot be present in the same place. The opposite of light is darkness; darkness is the absence from what is transparent of the corresponding positive state above characterized; clearly therefore, light is just the presence of that.

Empedocles (and with him all others who used the same forms of expression) was wrong in speaking of light as 'travelling' or being at a given moment between the earth and its envelope, its movement being unobservable by us; that view is contrary both to the clear evidence of argument and to the observed facts; if the distance traversed were short, the movement might have been unobservable, but where the distance is from extreme East to extreme West, the strain upon our powers of belief is too great.

What is capable of taking on colour is what in itself is colourless, as what can take on sound is what is soundless; what is colourless includes what is transparent and what is invisible or scarcely visible, i.e. what is dark. The latter is the same as what is transparent, when it is potentially, not of course when it is actually transparent; it is the same substance which is now darkness, now light.

Not everything that is visible depends upon light for its visibility. This 419ᵃ1
is only true of the 'proper' colour of things. Some objects of sight which
in light are invisible, in darkness stimulate the sense; that is, things that
appear fiery or shining. This class of objects has no simple common
name, but instances of it are fungi, horns, heads, scales, and eyes of fish.   5
In none of these is what is seen their own proper colour. Why we see
these at all is another question. At present what is obvious is that what
is seen in light is always colour. That is why without the help of light
colour remains invisible. Its being colour at all means precisely its having
in it the power to set in movement what is actually transparent, and the   10
actuality of what is transparent is just light.

The following makes the necessity of a medium clear. If what has
colour is placed in immediate contact with the eye, it cannot be seen.
Colour sets in movement what is transparent, e.g. the air, and that,
extending continuously from the object of the organ, sets the latter in
movement. Democritus misrepresents the facts when he expresses the   15
opinion that if the interspace were empty one could distinctly see an
ant on the vault of the sky; that is an impossibility. Seeing is due to an
affection or change of what has the perceptive faculty, and it cannot be
affected by the seen colour itself; it remains that it must be affected by
what comes between. Hence it is indispensable that there be *something*
in between—if there were nothing, so far from seeing with greater dis-   20
tinctness, we should see nothing at all.

We have now explained the cause why colour cannot be seen otherwise than in light. Fire on the other hand is seen both in darkness
and in light; this double possibility follows necessarily from our theory, for it is just fire that makes what is potentially transparent actually
transparent.

The same account holds also of sound and smell; if the object of either   25
of these senses is in immediate contact with the organ no sensation is
produced. In both cases the object sets in movement only what lies
between, and this in turn sets the organ in movement: if what sounds or
smells is brought into immediate contact with the organ, no sensation
will be produced. The same, in spite of all appearances, applies also to
touch and taste; why there is this apparent difference will be clear later.   30
What comes between in the case of sounds is air; the corresponding
medium in the case of smell has no name. But, corresponding to what
is transparent in the case of colour, there is a quality found both in air
and water, which serves as a medium for what has smell; for animals that
live in water seem to possess the sense of smell. Men and all other land
animals that breathe, perceive smells only when they breathe air in. The 419ᵇ1
explanation of this too will be given later.

8 · Now let us, to begin with, make certain distinctions about sound
and hearing.

5   Sound may mean either of two things—actual and potential sound. There are certain things which, as we say, have no sound, e.g. sponges or wool, others which have, e.g. bronze and in general all things which are smooth and solid—the latter are said to have a sound because they can make a sound, i.e. can generate actual sound between themselves and the organ of hearing.

Actual sound is always of something in relation to something and in
10   something; for it is generated by an impact. Hence it is impossible for one body only to generate a sound—there must be a body impinging and a body impinged upon; what sounds does so by striking against something else, and this is impossible without a movement from place to place.

As we have said, not all bodies can by impact on one another produce sound; impact on wool makes no sound, while the impact on bronze or
15   any body which is smooth and hollow does. Bronze gives out a sound when struck because it is smooth; bodies which are hollow owing to reflection repeat the original impact over and over again, the body originally set in movement being unable to escape from the concavity.

Further, sound is heard both in air and in water, though less distinctly in the latter. Yet neither air nor water is the principal cause of sound.
20   What is required for the production of sound is an impact of two solids against one another and against the air. The latter condition is satisfied when the air impinged upon does not retreat before the blow, i.e. is not dissipated by it.

That is why it must be struck with a sudden sharp blow, if it is to sound—the movement of the whip must outrun the dispersion of the air, just as one[16] might get in a stroke at a heap or whirl of sand as it was travelling rapidly past.

25   An echo occurs, when, a mass of air having been unified, bounded, and prevented from dissipation by the containing walls of a vessel, the air rebounds from this mass of air like a ball from a wall. It is probable that in all generation of sound echo takes place, though it is frequently only indistinctly heard. What happens here must be analogous to what happens in the case of light; light is always reflected—otherwise it would not be dif-
30   fused and outside what was directly illuminated by the sun there would be blank darkness; but this reflected light is not always strong enough, as it is when it is reflected from water, bronze, and other smooth bodies, to cast a shadow, which is the distinguishing mark by which we recognize light.

It is rightly said that an empty space plays the chief part in the production of hearing, for people think that the air is empty, and the air is what causes hearing, when it is set in movement as one continuous mass; but
420ª1   owing to its friability it emits no sound, unless what is impinged upon is smooth. But then it becomes a single mass at the same time because of the surface; for the surface of the smooth object is single.

---

[16] Retaining τις.

What has the power of producing sound is what has the power of setting in movement a single mass of air which is continuous up to the organ of hearing. The organ of hearing is physically united with air, and because it is in air, the air inside is moved concurrently with the air   5
outside. Hence animals do not hear with all parts of their bodies, nor do all parts admit of the entrance of air; for even the part which can be moved and can sound has not air everywhere in it. Air in itself is, owing to its friability, quite soundless; only when its dissipation is prevented is its movement sound. The air in the ear is built into a chamber just to prevent this dissipating movement, in order that the animal may accu-   10
rately apprehend all varieties of the movements of the air outside. That is why we hear also in water, viz. because the water cannot get into the air chamber or even, owing to the spirals, into the outer ear. If this does happen, hearing ceases, as it also does if the tympanic membrane is damaged, just as sight ceases if the membrane covering the pupil is damaged. It is also a sign of whether we hear or not that the ear does or does not   15
reverberate like a horn; the air inside the ear has always a movement of its own, but the sound we hear is always the sounding of something else, not of the organ itself. That is why we say that we hear with what is empty and echoes, viz. because what we hear with is a chamber which contains a bounded mass of air.

Which is it that sounds, the striking body or the struck? Is not the   20
answer that it is both, but each in a different way? Sound is a movement of what can rebound from a smooth surface when struck against it. As we have explained not everything sounds when it strikes or is struck, e.g. if one needle is struck against another, neither emits any sound. In order, therefore, that sound may be generated, what is struck must be smooth, to enable the air to rebound and be shaken off from it in one piece.   25

The distinctions between different sounding bodies show themselves only in actual sound; as without the help of light colours remain invisible, so without the help of actual sound the distinctions between sharp and flat sounds remain inaudible. Sharp and flat are here metaphors, transferred from their proper sphere, viz. that of touch, where they mean respectively what moves the sense much in a short time, and what   30
moves the sense little in a long time. Not that what is sharp really moves fast, and what is flat, slowly, but that the difference in the qualities of the one and the other movement is due to their respective speeds. There seems to be a sort of parallelism between what is sharp or flat to hearing and what is sharp or blunt to touch; what is sharp as it were stabs, while $420^b 1$
what is blunt pushes, the one producing its effect in a short, the other in a long time, so that the one is quick, the other slow.

Let the foregoing suffice as an analysis of sound. Voice is a kind of   5
sound characteristic of what has soul in it; nothing that is without soul utters voice, it being only by a metaphor that we speak of the voice of the flute or the lyre or generally of what (being without soul) possesses the power of producing a succession of notes which differ in length

and pitch and timbre. The metaphor is based on the fact that all these differences are found also in voice. Many animals are voiceless, e.g. all
10 non-sanguineous animals and among sanguineous animals fish. This is just what we should expect, since voice is a certain movement of air. The fish, like those in the Achelous, which are said to have voice, really make the sounds with their gills or some similar organ. Voice is the sound made by an animal, and that with a special organ. As we saw, everything that makes a sound does so by the impact of something against some-
15 thing else, across a space filled with air; hence it is only to be expected that no animals utter voice except those which take in air. Once air is inbreathed, Nature uses it for two different purposes, as the tongue is used both for tasting and for articulating; in that case of the two functions tasting is necessary for the animal's existence (hence it is found more widely distributed), while articulate speech serves its possessor's well-being; similarly in the former case Nature employs the breath both
20 as an indispensable means to the regulation of the inner temperature of the living body and also as the matter of articulate voice, in the interests of its possessor's well-being. Why its former use is indispensable must be discussed elsewhere.

The organ of respiration is the windpipe, and the organ to which this is related as means to end is the lungs. The latter is the part of the body
25 by which the temperature of land animals is raised above that of all others. But what primarily requires the air drawn in by respiration is not only this but the region surrounding the heart. That is why when animals breathe the air must penetrate inwards.

Voice then is the impact of the inbreathed air against the windpipe, and the agent that produces the impact is the soul resident in these parts
30 of the body. Not every sound, as we said, made by an animal is voice (even with the tongue we may merely make a sound which is not voice, or without the tongue as in coughing); what produces the impact must have soul in it[17] and must be accompanied by an act of imagination, for voice is a sound with a meaning, and is not the result of any impact of the breath as
421ª1 in coughing; in voice the breath in the windpipe is used as an instrument to knock with against the walls of the windpipe. This is confirmed by our inability to speak when we are breathing either out or in—we can only do so by holding our breath; we make the movements with the breath so checked. It is clear also why fish are voiceless; they have no windpipe.
5 And they have no windpipe because they do not breathe or take in air. Why they do not is a question belonging to another inquiry.

9 · Smell and its object are much less easy to determine than what we have hitherto discussed; the distinguishing characteristic of smell is less obvious than those of sound or colour. The ground of this is that

---

[17] Retaining ἔμψυχον.

our power of smell is less discriminating and in general inferior to that   10
of many species of animals; men have a poor sense of smell and our
apprehension of its objects is bound up with pleasure and pain, which
shows that in us the organ is inaccurate. It is probable that there is a parallel failure in the perception of colour by animals that have hard eyes:
probably they discriminate differences of colour only by the presence or   15
absence of what excites fear, and that it is thus that human beings distinguish smells. It seems that there is an analogy between smell and taste,
and that the species of tastes run parallel to those of smells—the only
difference being that our sense of taste is more discriminating because it
is a sort of touch, which reaches in man the maximum of discriminative
accuracy. While in respect of all the other senses we fall below many   20
species of animals, in respect of touch we far excel all other species in
exactness of discrimination. That is why man is the most intelligent of
all animals. This is confirmed by the fact that it is to differences in the
organ of touch and to nothing else that the differences between man and
man in respect of natural endowment are due; men whose flesh is hard   25
are ill-endowed with intellect, men whose flesh is soft, well-endowed.

As flavours may be divided into sweet and bitter, so with smells. In
some things the flavour and the smell have the same quality, e.g. both
are sweet, in others they diverge. Similarly a smell may be pungent,   30
astringent, acid, or succulent. But, as we said, because smells are much
less easy to discriminate than flavours, the names of these varieties are   421ᵇ1
applied to smells in virtue of similarity; for example sweet belongs to
saffron or honey, pungent to thyme, and so on.

In the same sense in which hearing has for its object both the audible
and the inaudible, sight both the visible and the invisible, smell has for
its object both the odorous and the inodorous. Inodorous may be either   5
what has no smell at all, or what has a small or feeble smell. The same
holds of the tasteless.

Smelling too takes place through a medium, i.e. through air or water—
for water-animals too (both sanguineous and non-sanguineous) seem
to smell just as much as land-animals; at any rate some of them make   10
directly for their food from a distance if it has any scent. That is why
the following facts constitute a problem for us. All animals smell in the
same way, but man smells only when he inhales; if he exhales or holds his
breath, he ceases to smell, no difference being made whether the odorous object is distant or near, or even placed inside the nostril; it is com-   15
mon to all not to perceive what is in immediate contact with the organ of
sense, but our failure to apprehend what is odorous without the help of
inhalation is peculiar to man (the fact is obvious on making the experiment). Now since bloodless animals do not breathe, they should have
some other sense apart from those mentioned. But this is impossible,   20
since it is scent that is perceived; a sense that apprehends what is odorous
and what has a good or bad odour cannot be anything but smell. Further,

25 they are observed to be deleteriously effected by the same strong odours
as man is, e.g. bitumen, sulphur, and the like. These animals must be
able to smell without breathing. The probable explanation is that in man
the organ of smell has a certain superiority over that in all other animals
just as his eyes have over those of hard-eyed animals. Man's eyes have in
the eyelids a kind of shelter or envelope, which must be shifted or drawn
30 back in order that we may see, while hard-eyed animals have nothing
of the kind, but at once see whatever presents itself in the transparent
medium. Similarly in certain species of animals the organ of smell is like
the eye of hard-eyed animals, uncurtained, while in others which take
422ª1 in air it probably has a curtain over it, which is drawn back in inhalation, owing to the dilating of the veins or pores. That explains also why
5 animals that breathe cannot smell under water; to smell they must first
inhale, and that they cannot do under water.

Smells are of what is dry as flavours of what is moist. Consequently
the organ of smell is potentially dry.

10 · What can be tasted is always something that can be touched, and
just for that reason it cannot be perceived through an interposed foreign
body, for no more is it so with touch. Further, the flavoured and taste-
10 able body is suspended in a liquid matter, and this is tangible. Hence,
if we lived in water, we should perceive a sweet object introduced into
the water, but the water would not be the medium through which we
perceived; our perception would be due to the solution of the sweet substance in the water, just as if it were mixed with some drink. There is
no parallel here to the perception of colour, which is due neither to any
15 blending nor to any efflux. In the case of taste, there is no medium; but as
the object of sight is colour, so the object of taste is flavour. But nothing
excites a perception of flavour without the help of liquid; what acts upon
the sense of taste must be either actually or potentially liquid like what
is saline; it must be both itself easily dissolved, and capable of dissolving
20 along with itself the tongue. Just as sight apprehends both what is visible
and what is invisible (for darkness is invisible and yet is discriminated
by sight; so is, in a different way, what is over-brilliant), and as hearing
apprehends both sound and silence, of which the one is audible and the
25 other inaudible, and also over loud sound as sight does what is bright (for
as a faint sound is inaudible, so in a sense is a loud or violent sound; and as
one thing is called invisible absolutely (as in other cases of impossibility),
another if it is adapted by nature to have the property but has not it or
has it only in a very low degree, as when we say that something is footless
or stoneless—so too taste has as its object both what can be tasted and
30 the tasteless—the latter in the sense of what has little flavour or a bad
flavour or one destructive of taste. The primary difference seems to be
that between what is drinkable and what is undrinkable—both are tasteable, but the latter is bad and tends to destroy taste, while the former is
natural. What is drinkable is a common object of both touch and taste.

Since what can be tasted is liquid, the organ for its perception can- 422ᵇ1
not be either actually liquid or incapable of becoming liquid. Tasting is
being affected by what can be tasted as such; hence the organ of taste
must be liquefied, and so to start with must be non-liquid but capable of
liquefaction without loss of its distinctive nature. This is confirmed by 5
the fact that the tongue cannot taste either when it is too dry or when
it is too moist; in the latter case there is contact with the pre-existent
moisture, as when after a foretaste of some strong flavour we try to taste
another flavour; it is in this way that sick persons find everything they
taste bitter, viz. because, when they taste, their tongues are overflowing
with bitter moisture.

The species of flavour are, as in the case of colour, simple, i.e. the two 10
contraries, the sweet and the bitter, secondary, viz. the succulent and
the saline; between these come the pungent, the harsh, the astringent,
and the acid; these pretty well exhaust the varieties of flavour. It follows
that what has the power of tasting is what is potentially of that kind, and
that what is tasteable is what has the power of making it actually what 15
it itself already is.

11 · Whatever can be said of what is tangible, can be said of touch,
and vice versa; if touch is not a single sense but a group of senses, there
must be several kinds of what is tangible. It is a problem whether touch
is a single sense or a group of senses. It is also a problem, what is the 20
organ of touch; is it or is it not the flesh (including what in certain animals is analogous to flesh)? On the second view, flesh is the medium of
touch, the real organ being situated farther inward. Every sense seems to
be concerned with a single pair of contraries, white and black for sight,
sharp and flat for hearing, bitter and sweet for taste; but in the field of 25
what is tangible we find several such pairs, hot cold, dry moist, hard
soft, &c. This problem finds a solution, when it is recalled that in the
case of the other senses more than one pair of contraries are to be met
with, e.g. in sound not only sharp and flat but loud and soft, smooth and 30
rough, &c.; there are similar contrasts in the field of colour. Nevertheless
we are unable clearly to detect in the case of touch what the single subject is which corresponds to sound in the case of hearing.

To the question whether the organ of touch lies inward or not (i.e.
whether we need look any farther than the flesh), no indication can be
drawn from the fact that if the object comes into contact with the flesh it 423ᵃ1
is at once perceived. For even under present conditions if the experiment
is made of making a sort of membrane and stretching it tight over the
flesh, as soon as this web is touched the sensation is reported in the same
manner as before, yet it is clear that the organ is not in this membrane.
If the membrane could be *grown* on to the flesh, the report would travel 5
still quicker. That is why the flesh plays in touch very much the same
part as would be played by an air-envelope growing round our body; had

we such an envelope we should have supposed that it was by a single organ that we perceived sounds, colours, and smells, and we should have taken sight, hearing, and smell to be a single sense. But as it is, because

10 that through which the different movements are transmitted is not naturally attached to our bodies, the difference of the various sense-organs is evident. But in the case of touch the obscurity remains.

For no living body could be constructed of air or water; it must be something solid. Consequently it must be composed of earth along with these,

15 which is just what flesh and its analogue tend to be. Hence the body must be the medium for the faculty of touch, naturally attached to us, through which the several perceptions are transmitted. That they are several is clear when we consider touching with the tongue; we apprehend at the tongue all tangible qualities as well as flavour. Suppose all the rest of our flesh was sensitive to flavour, we should have identified the sense of taste and the

20 sense of touch; but in fact they are two, for they do not correspond.

The following problem might be raised. Let us assume that every body has depth, i.e. has three dimensions, and that if two bodies have a third body between them they cannot be in contact with one another; let us remember that what is liquid is not independent of body and must be or contain water, and that if two bodies touch one another under water,

25 their touching surfaces cannot be dry, but must have water between, viz. the water which wets their bounding surfaces; from all this it follows that in water two bodies cannot be in contact with one another. The same holds of two bodies in air—air being to bodies in air precisely what

30 water is to bodies in water—but the facts are not so evident to our observation, because we live in air, just as animals that live in water would not notice that the things which touch one another in water have wet surfaces. The problem, then, is: does the perception of all objects of sense

423^{b}1 take place in the same way, or does it not, e.g. taste and touch requiring contact (as they are commonly thought to do), while all other senses perceive over a distance? The distinction is unsound; we perceive what is hard or soft, as well as the objects of hearing, sight, and smell, through a medium, only that the latter are perceived over a greater distance than

5 the former; that is why the facts escape our notice. For we do perceive everything through a medium; but in these cases the fact escapes us. Yet, to repeat what we said before, if the medium for touch were a membrane separating us from the object without our observing its existence, we

10 should be relatively to it in the same condition as we are now to air or water in which we are immersed; in their case we fancy we can touch objects, nothing coming in between us and them. But there remains this difference between what can be touched and what can be seen or can sound; in the latter two cases we perceive because the medium produces a certain effect upon us, whereas in the perception of objects of touch we are affected not *by* but *along with* the medium; it is as if a man were

15 struck through his shield, where the shock is not first given to the shield and passed on to the man, but the concussion of both is simultaneous.

In general, flesh and the tongue are related to the organs of touch
and taste, as air and water are to those of sight, hearing, and smell.
Hence in neither the one case nor the other can there be any percep-   20
tion of an object if it is placed immediately upon the organ, e.g. if a
white object is placed on the surface of the eye. This again shows that
what has the power of perceiving the tangible is seated inside. Only so
would there be a complete analogy with all the other senses. In their
case if you place the object on the organ it is not perceived, here if you
place it on the flesh it is perceived; therefore flesh is the medium of   25
touch.

What can be touched are distinctive qualities of body *as* body; by
such differences I mean those which characterize the elements, viz. hot
cold, dry moist, of which we have spoken earlier in our treatise on the
elements.[18] The organ for the perception of these is that of touch—that   30
part of the body in which primarily the sense of touch resides. This is
that part which is potentially such as its object is actually: for all sense-   424ª1
perception is a process of being so affected; so that that which makes
something such as it itself actually is makes the other such because the
other is already potentially such. That is why we do not perceive what is
equally hot and cold or hard and soft, but only excesses, the sense itself
being a sort of mean between the opposites that characterize the objects
of perception. It is to this that it owes its power of discerning the objects   5
in that field. What is in the middle is fitted to discern; relatively to either
extreme it can put itself in the place of the other. As what is to perceive
white and black must, to begin with, be actually neither but potentially
either (and so with all the other sense-organs), so the organ of touch
must be neither hot nor cold.   10

Further, as in a sense sight had for its object both what was visible
and what was invisible (and there was a parallel truth about all the other
senses discussed), so touch has for its object both what is tangible and
what is intangible. Here by intangible is meant what like air possesses
some quality of tangible things in a very slight degree and also what possesses it in an excessive degree, as destructive things do.

We have now given an outline account of each of the several senses.   15

12 · Generally, about all perception, we can say that a sense is what
has the power of receiving into itself the sensible forms of things without
the matter, in the way in which a piece of wax takes on the impress of   20
a signet-ring without the iron or gold; what produces the impression is
a signet of bronze or gold, but not *qua* bronze or gold: in a similar way
the sense is affected by what is coloured or flavoured or sounding not
insofar as each is what it is, but insofar as it is of such and such a sort and
according to its form.

---

[18] See *Gen Corr* II 2–3.

A primary sense-organ is that in which such a power is seated. The sense and its organ are the same in fact, but their essence is not the same. What perceives is, of course, a spatial magnitude, but we must not admit that either the having the power to perceive or the sense itself is a magnitude; what they are is a certain form or power in a magnitude. This enables us to explain why excesses in objects of sense destroy the organs of sense; if the movement set up by an object is too strong for the organ, the form which is its sensory power is disturbed; it is precisely as concord and tone are destroyed by too violently twanging the strings of a lyre. This explains also why plants cannot perceive, in spite of their having a portion of soul in them and being affected by tangible objects themselves; for their temperature can be lowered or raised. The explanation is that they have no mean, and so no principle in them capable of taking on the forms of sensible objects but are affected together with their matter. The problem might be raised: Can what cannot smell be said to be affected by smells or what cannot see by colours, and so on? Now a smell is just what can be smelt, and if it produces any effect it can only be so as to make something smell it, and it might be argued that what cannot smell cannot be affected by smells and further that what can smell can be affected by it only in so far as it has in it the power to smell (similarly with the proper objects of all the other senses). Indeed that this is so seems clear as follows. Light or darkness, sounds and smells leave bodies quite unaffected; what does affect bodies is not these but the bodies which are their vehicles, e.g. what splits the trunk of a tree is the air which accompanies thunder. But bodies are affected by what is tangible and by flavours. If not, by what are things that are without soul affected, i.e. altered in quality? Must we not, then, admit that the objects of the other senses also may affect them? Is not the true account this, that all bodies are capable of being affected by smells and sounds, but that some on being acted upon, having no boundaries of their own, disintegrate, as in the instance of air, which does become odorous, showing that some effect is produced on it by what is odorous? What is smelling more than such an affection by what is odorous? Is it that air, when affected quickly, becomes perceptible, but that smelling is actually perceiving?

BOOK III

1 · That there is no sense in addition to the five—sight, hearing, smell, taste, touch—may be established by the following considerations:—

We in fact have sensation of everything of which touch can give us sensation (for all the qualities of the tangible qua tangible are perceived by us through touch); and absence of a sense necessarily involves absence of a sense-organ; and all objects that we perceive by immediate contact with them are perceptible by touch, which sense we actually possess, while all objects that we perceive through media, i.e. without immediate contact, are perceptible by or through the simple elements, e.g. air and water. Now this is so arranged that if more than one kind of sensible object is perceivable through a single medium, the possessor of a sense-organ homogeneous with that medium has the power of perceiving both kinds of objects (for example, if the sense-organ is made of air, and air is a medium both for sound and for colour); and if more than one medium can transmit the same kind of sensible objects, as e.g. water as well as air can transmit colour, both being transparent, then the possessor of either alone will be able to perceive the kind of objects transmissible through both. And of the simple elements two only, air and water, go to form sense-organs (for the pupil is made of water, the organ of hearing is made of air, and the organ of smell of one or other of these two, while fire is found either in none or in all—warmth being an essential condition of all sensibility—and earth either in none or, if anywhere, specially mingled with the components of the organ of touch; hence it would remain that there can be no sense-organ formed of anything except water and air); and these sense-organs are actually found in certain animals. Thus all the possible senses are possessed by those animals that are not imperfect or mutilated (for even the mole is observed to have eyes beneath its skin); so that, if there is no fifth element and no property other than those which belong to the four elements of our world, no sense can be wanting to such animals.

Further, there cannot be a special sense-organ for the common sensibles either, i.e. the objects which we perceive incidentally through this or that special sense, e.g. movement, rest, figure, magnitude, number, unity; for all these we perceive by movement, e.g. magnitude by movement, and therefore also figure (for figure is a species of magnitude), what is at rest by the absence of movement: number is perceived by the negation of continuity, and by the special sensibles; for each sense perceives one class of sensible objects. So that it is clearly impossible that there should be a special sense for any one of the common sensibles, e.g. movement; for, if that were so, our perception of it would be exactly parallel to our present perception of what is sweet by vision. That is so because we have a sense for each of the two qualities, in virtue of which when they happen to meet in one sensible object we are aware of both contemporaneously. If it were not like this our perception of the common qualities would always be incidental, i.e. as is the perception of Cleon's son, where we perceive him not as Cleon's son but as white, and the white thing happens to be Cleon's son.

But in the case of the common sensibles there is already in us a common sensibility which enables us to perceive them non-incidentally; there is therefore no special sense required for their perception: if there were, our perception of them would have been exactly like what has been above described.

30   The senses perceive each other's special objects incidentally; not
because the percipient sense is this or that special sense, but because all
425ᵇ1 form a unity: this incidental perception takes place whenever sense is
directed at one and the same moment to two disparate qualities in one
and the same object, e.g. to the bitterness and the yellowness of bile;
the assertion of the identity of both cannot be the act of either of the
senses; hence the illusion of sense, e.g. the belief that if a thing is yellow
it is bile.

5   It might be asked why we have more senses than one. Is it to prevent a
failure to apprehend the common sensibles, e.g. movement, magnitude,
and number, which go along with the special sensibles? Had we no sense
but sight, and that sense no object but white, they would have tended
to escape our notice and everything would have merged for us into an
indistinguishable identity because of the concomitance of colour and
magnitude. As it is, the fact that the common sensibles are given in the
10   objects of more than one sense reveals their distinction from each and
all of the special sensibles.

        2 · Since it is through sense that we are aware that we are seeing or
hearing, it must be either by sight that we are aware of seeing, or by some
sense other than sight. But the sense that gives us this new sensation
must perceive both sight and its object, viz. colour: so that either there
will be two senses both percipient of the same sensible object, or the
15   sense must be percipient of itself. Further, even if the sense which perceives sight were different from sight, we must either fall into an infinite
regress, or we must somewhere assume a sense which is aware of itself.
If so, we ought to do this in the first case.

        This presents a difficulty: if to perceive by sight is just to see, and
what is seen is colour (or the coloured), then if we are to see that which
sees,[19] that which sees[20] originally must be coloured. It is clear therefore
20   that 'to perceive by sight' has more than one meaning; for even when we
are not seeing, it is by sight that we discriminate darkness from light,
though not in the same way as we distinguish one colour from another.
Further, in a sense even that which sees is coloured; for in each case the
sense-organ is capable of receiving the sensible object without its matter.
25   That is why even when the sensible objects are gone the sensings and
imaginings continue to exist in the sense-organs.
        The activity of the sensible object and that of the sense is one and
the same activity, and yet the distinction between their being remains.
Take as illustration actual sound and actual hearing: a man may have
hearing and yet not be hearing, and that which has a sound is not always

---

[19] Retaining τὸ δρῶν.
[20] Retaining τὸ δρῶν.

sounding. But when that which can hear is actively hearing and that which can sound is sounding, then the actual hearing and the actual sound come about at the same time (these one might call respectively hearkening and sounding).

426ª1

If it is true that the movement, i.e. the acting, and the being acted upon,[21] is to be found in that which is acted upon, both the sound and the hearing so far as it is actual must be found in that which has the faculty of hearing; for it is in the passive factor that the actuality of the active or motive factor is realized; that is why that which causes movement may be at rest. Now the actuality of that which can sound is just sound or sounding, and the actuality of that which can hear is hearing or hearkening; 'sound' and 'hearing' are both ambiguous. The same account applies to the other senses and their objects. For as the acting-and-being-acted-upon is to be found in the passive, not in the active factor, so also the actuality of the sensible object and that of the sensitive subject are both realized in the latter. But while in some cases each has a distinct name, e.g. sounding and hearkening, in some one or other is nameless, e.g. the actuality of sight is called seeing, but the actuality of colour has no name: the actuality of the faculty of taste is called tasting, but the actuality of flavour has no name. Since the actualities of the sensible object and of the sensitive faculty are one actuality in spite of the difference between their modes of being, actual hearing and actual sounding appear and disappear from existence at one and the same moment, and so actual savour and actual tasting, &c., while as potentialities one of them may exist without the other. The earlier students of nature were mistaken in their view that without sight there was no white or black, without taste no savour. This statement of theirs is partly true, partly false: 'sense' and 'the sensible object' are ambiguous terms, i.e. may denote either potentialities or actualities: the statement is true of the latter, false of the former. This ambiguity they wholly failed to notice.

5

10

15

20

25

If voice is a concord, and if the voice and the hearing of it are in one sense one and the same, and if concord is a ratio, hearing as well as what is heard must be a ratio. That is why the excess of either the sharp or the flat destroys the hearing. (So also in the case of savours excess destroys the sense of taste, and in the case of colours excessive brightness or darkness destroys the sight, and in the case of smell excess of strength whether in the direction of sweetness or bitterness is destructive.) This shows that the sense is a ratio.

30

426ᵇ1

That is also why the objects of sense are pleasant when e.g. acid or sweet or salt, being pure and unmixed, are brought into the proper ratio; then they are pleasant: and in general what is blended—a concord—is more pleasant than the sharp or the flat alone; or, to touch, that which is

5

---

[21] Ross excises 'and the being acted upon'.

capable of being either warmed or chilled:[22] the sense and the ratio are identical; while excess is painful or destructive.

10 Each sense then is relative to its particular group of sensible qualities: it is found in a sense-organ as such and discriminates the differences which exist within that group; e.g. sight discriminates white and black, taste sweet and bitter, and so in all cases. Since we also discriminate white from sweet, and indeed each sensible quality from every other, with what[23] do we perceive that they are different? It must be by sense; for what is before us is sensible objects. (Hence it is also obvious that

15 the flesh cannot be the ultimate sense-organ: if it were, the discriminating power could not do its work without immediate contact with the object.)

Therefore discrimination between white and sweet cannot be effected by two agencies which remain separate; both the qualities discriminated must be present to something that is one and single. On any other supposition even if I perceived sweet and you perceived white, the differ-

20 ence between them would be apparent. What says that two things are different must be one; for sweet is different from white. Therefore what asserts this difference must be self-identical, and as what asserts, so also what thinks or perceives. That it is not possible by means of two agencies which remain separate to discriminate two objects which are separate, is therefore obvious; and that it is not possible to do this in separate

25 moments of time may be seen if we look at it as follows. For as what asserts the difference between the good and the bad is one and the same, so also the time at which it asserts the one to be different and the other to be different is not accidental to the assertion (as it is for instance when I now assert a difference but do not assert that there is now a difference); it asserts thus—both now and that the objects are different now; the objects therefore must be present at one and the same moment. Both the discriminating power and the time of its exercise must be one and undivided.

30 But, it may be objected, it is impossible that what is self-identical should be moved at one and the same time with contrary movements in so far as it is undivided, and in an undivided moment of time. For if what is sweet be the quality perceived, it moves the sense or thought

427ª1 in this determinate way, while what is bitter moves it in a contrary way, and what is white in a different way. Is it the case then that what discriminates, though both numerically one and indivisible, is at the same time divided in its being? In one sense, it is what is divided that perceives two separate objects at once, but in another sense it does so

5 qua undivided; for it is divisible in its being, but spatially and numerically undivided.

---

[22] Ross, following Dittenberger, excises the sentence 'or, to touch,…chilled'.
[23] Reading τίνι for τινί.

But is not this impossible? For while it is true that what is self-identical and undivided may be both contraries at once *potentially*, it cannot be self-identical in its being—it must lose its unity by being put into activity. It is not possible to be at once white and black, and therefore it must also be impossible for a thing to be affected at one and the same moment by the forms of both, assuming it to be the case that sensation and thinking are properly so described.

Just as what is called a point is, as being at once one and two, properly   10
said to be divisible,[24] so here, that which discriminates is *qua* undivided one, and active in a single moment of time, while *qua* divisible it twice over uses the same dot at one and the same time. So far then as it takes the limit as two, it discriminates two separate objects[25] with what in a sense is separated; while so far as it takes it as one, it does so with what is one[26] and occupies in its activity a single moment of time.

About the principle in virtue of which we say that animals are per-   15
cipient, let this discussion suffice.

---

[24] Ross adds: 'and indivisible'.

[25] Ross excises 'two separate objects'.

[26] Reading ἐνί, ἐνί.

3

Aristotle on Demarcating the Five Senses

Richard Sorabji

I. SENSES AND THEIR OBJECTS

IN THE *De Anima*, Book II, Chapter 6, Aristotle tells us that sensible qualities are related to the senses as *kath hauta*. In other words, one is defined by reference to the other.[1] I believe that Aristotle has no special interest in defining sense objects by reference to senses.[2] If he has not,

Richard Sorabji, "Aristotle on Demarcating the Five Senses", *Philosophical Review*, Volume 80, No. 1, pp. 55–79. (Copyright, 1971, Sage School, of Philosophy at Cornell University. All rights reserved. Used by permission of the Publisher, Duke University Press.)

---

[1] *D. A.* 418a8–25. For this sense of *Kath Hauta*, see *An. Post.* 73a34-b24. There are admittedly other senses. The following abbreviations are used in this paper:

An. Post.	*Posterior Analytics*
Phys.	*Physics*
G. & C.	*De Generatione et Corruptione*
D.A.	*De Anima*
D.S.	*De Sensu*
Som.	*De Somno*
Insom.	*De Insomniis*
Resp.	*De Respiratione*
H.A.	*Historia Animalium*
P.A.	*De Partibus Animalium*
Metaph.	*Metaphysics*

[2] If one looks at his definitions of color, light, sound, odor, flavor, hot, cold, fluid, dry, one will find that they very seldom mention the senses. (*D.A.* 418b9–10; 418b16–17, b20, 419a9–11, 420a8–9, a21–23, b11; *D.S.* 439a19–20, b11–12, 441b19–21, 443a7; G. & C. 329b26–32; *P.A.* 648a20–650a3.) Much less do the so-called common objects, properties perceptible by more than one sense, get defined by reference to the senses (e.g., unity: *Metaph.* 1015b16–1017a3, 1052a15–1053b8; change: *Phys.* 201a9–15). This is the more surprising, in view of the theory of actually functioning color at *D.A.* 425b26–426a26, which links color closely to sight.

Admittedly, the definitions of color and light bring in the notion of transparency. But the connection between transparency and sight is stressed only in the definition of light (not strictly a sense object at all) at 418b9–10. Here light is defined by reference to the idea that when the air or water around us is dark, it is only potentially seeable-through whereas when it is light, we can actually see through it.

Allowance should be made, of course, for Aristotle's purposes, which vary considerably in these different passages and which can influence the content of his definitions. But, nonetheless, it should not be supposed that he thinks the best or most scientific definition then his point must be rather that the senses should be defined by reference to their objects. But the interpretation of *kath hauta* here may be controversial.[3] And we have no need to rest our case upon it, if we want to establish Aristotle's interest in defining senses by reference to sense objects.

That he wants to define (and in general to get clear about) the senses by reference to their objects is evident, if we consider the structure of the *De Anima*. Here Aristotle sets out to give an account of the soul. It emerges by Book II, Chapter 3,[4] that if one wants to give an account of the soul suitable for a specialized treatise, and not merely an account in very general terms, one should describe one by one the powers of which the soul consists; the power to think, the power to perceive, the power to absorb nutrition, and so on. And in the next chapter,[5] it turns out that in order to say what one of these powers is—for example, the power to perceive—one should first say what the corresponding activity is—the act of perceiving. That in turn requires that one should first study the object of the activity—for example, the objects of the senses. This point is made in Chapter 4, and in Chapter 6 of Book II.[6] It is this latter chapter which contains the statement that sensible qualities are related to the senses as *kath hauta*. And though this statement, taken on its own, may be ambiguous, the closing sentence of the chapter is not. It says that qualities like color, which are perceived by only one sense, the so-called *proper* objects of the senses, are the things to which the very being of each sense is naturally related.[7] It is already clear that Aristotle means to analyze the senses by reference to their objects, and the next five chapters (II, 7–11) carryout the analysis, each chapter being devoted to one of the five senses. The analysis gives prominence to the sense objects throughout. The account of vision, for example, begins with an investigation of its object.[8] And when the account of the five senses is complete, and we move on to Book III, we there get our first, and on some views our only, conception of what the so-called *common* sense is, from hearing about its objects, motion, rest, shape, magnitude, number, unity.[9]

---

of sense objects, or the one that gives their essence, will mention the senses. The essence of color is stated at *D.A.* 419a9–11, without any very direct reference to sight.

[3] In a valuable series of publications, Professor Hamlyn has argued that the point is that sense objects must be defined by reference to senses, either instead of, or as well as, the other way round. ("Aristotle's account of Aesthesis in the *De Anima*," *Classical Quarterly* [1959], *passim*; "Koine Aesthesis," *Monist* [1968], esp. p. 205; "Seeing Things as They Are," Inaugural Lecture, Birkbeck College, 1965, esp. p. 12; *Aristotle's De Anima, Books II and III*, Clarendon Aristotle Series (Oxford, 1968), esp. pp. 105, 108, 117.

[4] 415a12–13.

[5] II.4, 415a14–20.

[6] 415a20–22; 418a7–8. It had already been mentioned as a possibility in I.1, 402b14–16.

[7] 418a24–25. Compare the statement at *Metaph.* 1021a29-b3, that sight is a relative term, related to color or to something like color.

[8] 418a26.

[9] 425a14–30.

We should expect this pattern to be continued in the other psychological treatises. For whatever the date at which they were first drafted, the treatises included in the so-called *Parva Naturalia* are, in their final form, so presented that they will read as a continuation of the *De Anima*. Sure enough, we do find there the same tendency to define, distinguish, and identify sensory powers by reference to their objects. Thus, for example, in the *De Sensu* and *De Somno* Aristotle speaks of a central sense faculty which is responsible for various functions that a single sense could not perform on its own. This central sense faculty has a certain unity because it is dependent on a single bodily organ, the heart. But it differs in its being and in its definition, says Aristotle, according to the different *objects* that it perceives.[10]

Another example of the importance of sense objects for identifying senses is to be found in Aristotle's insistence that since fish and other animals perceive odor, we must allow that they exercise smell.[11] Evidently, the perception of odor is to be counted as smell, in spite of considerable differences in the mechanism involved. For the medium through which water animals perceive odor is not air, as it is for us, but water.[12] Correspondingly, the organ they use for perceiving odor contains water, in Aristotle's view, not air.[13] Nor is the organ used at all like our nostrils in structure. Fish use their gills, dolphins their blowhole, and insects the middle part of their body, according to Aristotle.[14] And neither fish nor insects, he says, inhale when perceiving odor.[15] In spite of these differences, their perception of odor is to be counted as smelling.[16] Similarly, the perception of sound is to be counted as hearing, and the perception of flavor as tasting, in spite of large differences in the mechanism involved.[17]

We have been arguing that Aristotle puts considerable stress on the sense objects in defining, distinguishing, and identifying the senses. In this, he shows himself faithful to a claim that Plato makes in the *Republic*.[18] For before asserting that knowledge and opinion have different

---

[10] D.S. 449a16–20; *Som.* 455a21–22.
[11] D.S. 444b10, b15, b16; D.A. 421b21.
[12] D.S. 442b29–443a3; D.A. 421b9–13.
[13] D.A. 425a5.
[14] P.A. 659b14–19.
[15] D.S. 443a4–6, 444b15–28; D.A. 421b13–422a6.
[16] The differences of mechanism must not be exaggerated. For gills and the middle part of insects' bodies, though different in structure from nostrils, are analogous in function, according to Aristotle, who thinks they serve to cool the body. Again, the fact that we need to inhale in order to smell is due merely to the need to open a certain lid, which in some animals is not present. Inhalation is clearly then only an incidental feature of our smelling. Nor will every difference of mechanism be permissible. For all smelling must involve an organ becoming smelly. And all smelling must be done at a distance from the object smelled.
[17] H.A. IV, 8- And for differences of mechanism: P.A. 656a35–37, 657a17–24, 658b27–659b19, 660a14–661a30, 678b6–13; H.A. 492a23–29, 503a2–6, 504a20–23, 505a33–35, 532a5–14; G.A. 781b23–24; *Resp.* 473a25–27.
[18] 477c-478b.

objects, Plato maintains that in general different capacities have different objects, and different objects imply different capacities. Sight and hearing are adduced as examples of capacities.

We must not, however, exaggerate the unity of the passages cited from Aristotle. We should distinguish several different things he wants to do. (*i*) Firstly, he wants to get clear about what sight is, what hearing is, and so on, by means of a protracted discussion. For this purpose, the sense objects are important. And one needs to consider them in detail, not merely to mention them. However, it is not only the sense objects that one needs to investigate. One should also know, for example, how the sense objects interact with the environment, so as to affect the sense organs, and what the process in the sense organs is (*D.A.* II, 7–12).

(*ii*) Different from a protracted discussion is a definition. Assuming Aristotle had not abandoned the scientific method described in the *Posterior Analytics*, he would have hoped eventually to obtain a definition of sight, of hearing, and so on. The definition would mention only some of the facts about sight and hearing, but it could be used in deducing and explaining other facts about them. Evidently, his definition of sight and hearing would mention their objects, color and sound. But we know it would not be confined to this. For in the *De Anima*,[19] he says that one should refer to the physiological process involved, when one defines any mental *pathos*. Thus in the definition of sight, he would mention not only the sense objects, but also the coloration of the eye-jelly, which is, in his opinion, the physiological process involved.[20] His reason for including mention of the physiological process is probably not so much to help in distinguishing sight from other things, as to produce a definition fitted for scientific purposes, one which can be used in generating deductions and explanations.

(*iii*) Different again from giving a scientific definition of sight is the process of simply distinguishing sight from other things, and of showing what cases are to be counted as cases of sight. For this purpose, Aristotle puts a very heavy stress on the sense objects and attaches much less importance to other criteria. We should, however, make a disclaimer on his behalf. For he is not particularly interested in giving us logically necessary and sufficient conditions for something's counting as a case of sight. And so he is not suggesting that reference to the sense objects

---

[19] 403*a*25-*b*9.

[20] Notice that reference to the physiological process will reimport reference to the sense objects. For according to Aristotle, the physiological process involved in sense perception is one in which the sense organ takes on the sense object. For example, the eye-jelly takes on color.

His theory is not the silly one, commonly attributed to him, that the whole eye, or the pupil, goes colored. What goes colored is merely the *Korê* (*D.A.* 431*a*17–18; *H.A.* 491*b*21; *P.A.* 653*b*25), which is the eye-jelly (*D.S.*438*a*16, *b*5–16; *H.A.* 491*b*21; *D.A.* 425*a*4; *G.A.* 780*b*23).

would supply such conditions. He is interested in demarcating the sensory powers that a zoologist can expect to find in this world, rather than ones which could exist in logically possible worlds. So in assessing the criteria by which he demarcates the senses, we ought to consider whether they are adequate for this zoological purpose.

Enough of exegesis, for the present. I want now to raise a philosophical question, which may appear to take us away from Aristotle. Is it good advice, that we should stress the sense objects in defining the senses? The question may appear to take us away from Aristotle, because obviously our concept of definition is not his. But I should want of a definition some of the things that he wants. A definition of sight should include and exclude the right cases. And it should also bring out what, if anything, unites the various cases of sight. To answer the question, I propose to see how far one could get toward defining the senses, if one took things to an extreme and sought to define the senses solely by reference to their objects. Let us try defining hearing simply as the perception of sound, taste simply as the perception of flavor, smell simply as the perception of odor, and sight simply as the perception of color and other properties.[21] We need not expect that these definitions will prove adequate. But in seeing where they do and where they do not fail, we may learn what value there is in stressing the sense objects. And this in turn may help us to see whether Aristotle is well advised to emphasize the sense objects, as he does.

Concentrating on the case of sight, I shall consider three objections to this kind of definition. The first objection is that there is such a large variety of objects that can be perceived by sight. Consequently, it would be laborious to define sight by reference to its objects. Moreover, it would conceal what unity there is in the concept, and make it a mystery that the single name "sight" should be used to cover such a heterogeneous list. Certainly, sight has many more objects than the two which Aristotle lists as its proper objects—namely, color and the brightness of things that can be seen in the dark.[22] (By calling these proper objects he means that they can be perceived by no other sense.) In addition to these two properties, one can also see other kinds of brightness. One can see size and shape, motion or rest, texture, depth, or the location of things. One might be said to see darkness or light,[23] the warmth of a fire or, somewhat less

---

[21] This is a more promising kind of formula, I think, than the kind studied by Grice in "Some Remarks about the Senses" (*Analytical Philosophy*, ed. by R. J. Butler, Series 1 [Oxford, 1962] [and this volume, chapter 4]). The latter kind is couched in terms of perceiving a material object to have such and such properties.

[22] *D.A.* 418a26–29, 419a1–9.

[23] I am here following Aristotle's distinction between brightness and light. By light he means that state of the air or water around us in which we can actually see through to colors at a distance from us. His idea is that when it's dark, we cannot actually see colors through the air or water. So the air and water are only potentially transparent. Light is the state in which they are actually transparent. This is all he means by the

naturally, the sweetness of a ripe fruit.[24] How could an Aristotelian reply to this objection, that the objects of sight are too many and various?

One line of reply would be to say that the objects of sight just listed fall into two, possibly overlapping, groups. Firstly, there is a group that includes such properties as color, brightness, and darkness. This group is small, and its members are somewhat akin to each other, both phenomenologically and, as is now known, in their physical basis, since they are all effects of the behavior of light. Secondly, there are objects of sight like size and shape, some of which are not at all like color, but which are perceived *by* perceiving color or what is like it. If this is so, then sight, as it operates in the everyday world, will be firstly the perception of color and of things like color,[25] and secondly the perception of other things by means of perceiving these.[26]

The expression "by" or "by means of" here covers a variety of different relations.[27] If anyone objects that the words are being stretched too far, we can drop them from our account of sight altogether. And we can simply say that one sees, if and only if one perceives color, brightness, or darkness. The idea that one cannot see shape and so forth without perceiving color, brightness, or darkness is put forward as applying at least to any cases that Aristotle was likely to encounter in his zoological enquiries. Whether it is a logically necessary truth is something that the reader may decide for himself.

This account of sight, if correct, will meet the present objection. For the list of objects of sight will be a short one. One probably need not mention more than color, brightness, and darkness. Moreover, the account reveals what unity there is in the concept of sight. For color and brightness or darkness have a certain kinship with each other.

---

formidable-sounding definition of light as the actualized state of the transparent (*D.A.* 418*b*9–10, 419*a*11). It should be clear from this that light, a state of the surrounding medium, is quite different from brightness.

[24] Somewhat less naturally. These cases are not very like each other. For warmth consists of such powers as the power to melt things or make them red hot. And the fact that something is melting or red hot is something I can be said to see. Sweetness does not in the same way consist of powers whose exercise can be seen.

[25] Under "color" I include the three aspects of color: hue, saturation, and brightness. Under "hue" I include black and white along with the other hues. Under "things like color" I include brightness and darkness.

[26] When I say that one sees shape (etc.) by *perceiving* color (etc.), I do not mean that one has to *notice what colors are present*, in order to see the shape.

[27] Thus, in the case of three-dimensional shape, often colors, highlights, and shadows serve merely as clues to the shape of something. But in the case of two-dimensional shape, the relation between color and shape is often closer than this. For example, if there is a sharp boundary between an area of one color (hue, saturation, or brilliance) and an area of another, and if we see where the boundary runs, this *is* to see (part of) the shape of the areas.

Seeing sweetness is more like the first case, in that color and shine serve merely as clues to sweetness. Seeing warmth is, in some instances, more like the second case. For the relation between red (hot) and warmth is a much closer relation than that between a clue and what the clue points to.

The materials for such a reply can be found in Aristotle himself. Brightness he mentions as being like color (*D.S.* 439*b*2). By light, as distinct from brightness, he means that state of the air or water around us which permits us actually to see through it (*D.A.* 418*b*9–10, 419*a*11), and this could be treated in either of the two ways proposed. For on the one hand, he insists that light is very like color (*D.A.* 418*b*11; *D.S.* 439*a*18); indeed, like white color; darkness, like black (*D.S.* 439*b*14–18). But on the other hand, he would prefer to deal with the present question by saying that we perceive light by perceiving that we are successfully perceiving color through the air or water around us. And we perceive darkness by perceiving that we are unsuccessful (*D.A.* 422*a*20–21, 425*b*20–22). He might wish to add that it is better not to talk of *seeing* light and darkness, but more noncommittally of perceiving them by means of sight (*D.A.* 425*b*20–22). As for the use of sight to perceive size and shape, he explicitly says that size and shape are perceived through the perception of other properties such as color. And in general the common objects are perceived by perceiving the proper objects (*D.S.* 437*a*5–9, perhaps *D.A.* 425*a*19). The same point is made about the use of sight to perceive sweetness (*D.A.* 425*a*22–24, *a*30–*b*4). In these cases, we see a color and know from past experience that sweetness is associated with it. All this suggests the view that to see is to perceive color or properties akin to color, and other things only through the perception of these.

I have said that the *materials* for this view are present in Aristotle. But I must add it is not clear that it is quite the view he states. For he seems to think he can get clear about what sight is without referring to sense objects other than color (which is seen in the light) and the brightness of phosphorescent things (which is seen in the dark). Why does he not mention other kinds of brightness? Surely he would have to do so if he took the view just outlined. One possible (though far from certain) answer is that he includes the brightness of things that shine in the light under the heading of color and therefore does not need to mention it separately. This would not be a normal way to use the English word "color." But Greek color words often did double duty, and were used as much to denote degrees of darkness and brightness as to denote hues.[28] So it is just possible that under the heading of color Aristotle means to include cetain kinds of brightness.

Before we leave the present objection, we should notice one further point. The suggested solution claimed to be able to exhibit the concept of sight as having a certain unity. It did so by insisting on the kinship between color and brightness or darkness. But part of this kinship was a phenomenological one. And to appeal to phenomenology is to appeal to the kind of experience to which these sense objects give rise. It becomes a question, then, whether the suggested definition of sight in terms of

---

[28] See Platnauer, "Greek Colour Perception," *Classical Quarterly* (1921). Also Cornford, *Plato's Cosmology*, p. 277.

color, brightness, or darkness appeals only to sense objects. Is it not also appealing to something other than sense objects—namely, to the kind of experience to which these sense objects give rise?

I now turn to a second objection that may be raised to the idea of relying on sense objects in defining the senses. For may not senses other than sight sometimes perceive color? If so, we cannot define sight simply as the power to perceive color and so forth, for other senses will fall under the description. An unfanciful example is provided by the ability of some people to tell the colors of flowers by smell. In the typical case, however, what happens here is most naturally described by saying that an odor is smelled and is known to be correlated with a certain color, not that a color is smelled.[29] Aristotle discusses such cases in the *De Anima* at 425*a*22–24 and *a*30-*b*4. He calls such perception a merely incidental perception of color. And with a view to meeting the present objection he could rule that such incidental perception of color does not count as seeing.

But what if we turn to the more unusual kind of case reported by psychologists, or resort to imaginary examples? Cannot we then expect to find cases in which there is non-incidental perception of color without there being an exercise of sight? A case that excited some interest recently was that of Rosa Kuleshova, reported in *Time* (January 25, 1963, p. 58). She allegedly distinguished colors and read ordinary print with her fingertips, without relying on the texture of the paper. Later the case was declared by T.A.S.S. to be a fraud. She peeped. But meanwhile other psychologists had reported that similar capacities were known in man and in other animals. May not cases such as this supply counterexamples to the claim that the non-incidental perception of color is always an exercise of sight?

It is by no means so easy to find counterexamples as one might at first suppose. Had the case of Rosa Kuleshova been genuine, we should have needed a lot of information about her before we could decide whether to say she was feeling color, or seeing color with an unusual part of the body, or feeling some such property as warmth and inferring to color.

---

[29] No doubt, this description would be preferred in fact. But is there good reason for preferring it? A partial answer can be gained by comparing the relation between odor and color with that between, say, being red (hot) and warmth, or between the shape things look and the shape they feel. Different as these latter two cases are from each other, they both involve a relationship such that we do not feel obliged to say merely that one property is seen and the other is known to be correlated with it. The first case has been mentioned in notes 24 and 27. Excellent discussions bearing on the second case can be found in H.P. Grice, *loc. cit.*, and in Jonathan Bennett, "Substance, Reality and Primary Qualities," *American Philosophical Quarterly* (1965). The point is that we do not have to talk of seeing visual shape and knowing that tactual shape is correlated with it. We can talk more boldly of seeing shape. For the shape things look and the shape they feel do not vary independently of each other. Nor is this a mere accident that could easily have been otherwise. If we try to imagine it otherwise, we will find we can no longer speak of there being physical objects and of these objects having a definite location in the imagined situation. For details, see the two articles mentioned.

Only if she was feeling color would she supply a counterexample. To establish that she was feeling color, we should have to show (*a*) that hers was a case of feeling, not of seeing with an unusual part of the body. (It would help to show this, if she could distinguish colors with any part of her body surface.) But we should also have to show (*b*) that her perception of color was nonetheless non-incidental, in other words that she was not simply inferring to color. And the trouble is that the performance of one of these tasks is liable to impede the performance of the other.[30]

We may add that if a case of feeling color can be described at all, it will very likely not be a case that a scientist can expect to meet in the real world. And if not, it will not be a case of a kind that Aristotle is particularly concerned to classify.

Finally, we should raise a third objection against the appeal to sense objects. May not people be said to see when they are subject to total hallucination, or when they have afterimages, or when their eyes are closed and there is some stimulation of the optic nerve, or in other cases where there is no real color, brightness, or darkness in the objective world which they are perceiving? If so, it is not true that all seeing involves the perception of color, brightness, or darkness. Aristotle's own response would be to allow that in these cases no objective color is perceived, but to deny that they are cases of seeing. Rather, they are exercises of *phantasia*, the faculty of imagination. At least, this is the usual trend in Aristotle, though there are faint traces of a different trend.[31]

The Aristotelian answer is not satisfactory, for surely the examples in question are cases of seeing in the ordinary sense. Is there any other way of meeting the present objection, so as to preserve the idea that all seeing involves the perception of color, brightness, or darkness? It may

---

[30] Particularly important would be the question of what kind of experience she had. If the experience were too like that involved in seeing, we should be inclined to say she was seeing. If the experience were too like that involved in, say, feeling warmth, we might be inclined to say she was feeling, but that the perception of color was merely incidental. The solution might seem to be to look for a case in which the experience involved was neutral—i.e., neither too like that involved in recognized cases of seeing, nor too like that involved in recognized cases of feeling. But it is not clear that even this would enable us to classify the case as one of feeling color. For could we say her perception of color was non-incidental if the color did not give rise to the kind of experience normally associated with color? The answer to this will no doubt depend in part on one's conception of color, and on how closely one supposes the notion of color to be linked to a certain kind of experience. One might argue that the notion of color is connected not only with a certain kind of experience, but also with the behavior of light. So if we can show she is reacting to the behavior of light, and not to some by-product of light, such as temperature, we shall have reason to say her perception of color is non-incidental. (For experiments ruling out reaction to temperature, see *Nature*, August 29, 1964, p. 993.) But this suggestion in its turn creates a difficulty. For if she perceives by means of light receptors, this will make her unable to perceive by direct contact, and so cast doubt again on the idea that she is feeling. This is perhaps enough to indicate some of the difficulties.

[31] For the predominant trend see, e.g., *D.A.* 428a16 and *Insom.* 458b7–9, 459a1–21. For traces of a different trend see *D.A.* 425b22–25, which is tempted by the idea that when one has an afterimage, one does perceive real, objective color—namely, the color taken on by one's eye-jelly, as a result of looking at the bright object.

be urged that when one sees with closed eyes, one is at least perceiving subjective color, even if there is no objective color in the external world that one is seeing. But one who thus appeals to subjective color should notice what he is doing. He is in effect appealing to something which initially we might have been inclined to distinguish from color itself— namely, the kind of experience to which color gives rise. He is saying that the experience is like that of perceiving objective color. He is not wrong, for the character of the experience is part of the reason why seeing with one's eyes closed is counted as a kind of seeing. But on the other hand, it is not clear whether the definition can still be said to confine itself to the mention of sense objects only.

What conclusions can we now draw from our attempt to define sight as the perception of color, brightness, or darkness? The definition goes a long way toward picking out the right cases, though, as the third objection shows, it does not, without special interpretation, cover quite all the standard cases of sight.

A more interesting point that has emerged en route is the importance of the kind of experience that is involved in sight. We found ourselves appealing to the character of this experience, firstly when we talked of the phenomenological kinship between color and brightness or darkness, secondly when (in note 30) we argued against the possibility of feeling color, and thirdly when we spoke of subjective color. It looks as if the character of the experience is an important element in the concept of sight. And part of the reason why it is helpful to mention the sense objects in a definition of sight is that reference to the sense objects implies in turn a reference to the kind of experience to which the sense objects give rise.[32]

A further conclusion is that we should be cautious in claiming that the attempted definition confines itself to the sense objects. For not only does the mention of color, brightness, and darkness import a reference to the kind of experience involved, but also there was an appeal to the notion of perception. Sight was treated as one species of the genus, perception. Now, if we were to analyze the generic notion of perception in its turn, we might well have to refer to the kind of physical mechanisms that distinguish sense perception from other forms of cognition. And if so, the attempted definition of sight in its turn involves an implicit appeal to these mechanisms.

Finally, we have been laying stress on two criteria, the sense objects and the kind of experience involved. But we should remember that it may be necessary to appeal to other criteria as well, at least when we leave the standard cases of sense perception and consider how to classify imaginary and logically possible cases. Here we may need to take into

---

[32] Grice arrives at a similar conclusion, traveling by a somewhat different route, in his valuable paper, *loc. cit.*

account the behavior involved, the mechanisms within the perceiver's body, and the mechanisms in the surrounding environment.[33]

Where does this discussion leave Aristotle? It suggests that his stress on the sense objects is helpful. For reference to these does pick out most of the standard cases of sight and does bring out the unity of the concept. But reference to the objects alone, we have seen, will not suffice. And so we may be glad that in his protracted discussion of the senses, the emphasis on sense objects does not lead to the exclusion of other aspects of each sense. With some qualifications, then, the verdict so far is in favor of Aristotle. But I have hitherto excluded from discussion a certain one of the five senses—namely, the sense of touch. To this I shall now have to turn.

II. THE SENSE OF TOUCH

There is an exception to what we have been saying about the importance of sense objects. This exception is the sense of touch. I have in mind the layman's conception of touch, rather than the refined concept of psychologists, which has been influenced by neurophysiological discoveries. The layman's concept includes, roughly speaking, those perceptual powers which are called powers of *feeling* sensible properties, but only sensible properties of a kind that can belong to non-sentient bodies and not, for example, such properties as hunger or pain. In speaking of touch, I am using the noun "touch," not the verb. The verb that goes with it is not the verb "to touch," but the verb "to feel."

It would be unsatisfactory to rely heavily on the objects of touch in defining the sense. For one thing, the objects of touch are extremely varied.[34] Not only would it be laborious to define touch by reference to its many objects, but also knowledge of what these objects are would give no indication of what unites the varieties of touch, nor of why some kinds of sense perception are excluded. Again, given the diversity that already exists, one would meet less difficulty than in corresponding cases with other senses, in classifying under touch new perceptual powers which

---

[33] These possibilities are discussed in detail by Grice, *loc. cit.*

[34] Aristotle might be able to shorten the list of objects somewhat, thanks to his view that coarse and fine, viscous and brittle, hard and soft, come from dry and fluid (G. & C. 329*b*32–34). In fact, he says all the other objects of touch are reducible to the basic four, dry and fluid, hot and cold (G. & C. 329*b*34, 330*a*24–26). If this is so, might he not be able to specify the objects of touch as dry and fluid, hot and cold, and other properties reducible to these? Such a specification runs two opposite risks. It would let in the objects of other senses, if any of these are reducible to dry, fluid, hot, or cold. At the same time, it is not clear how it would accommodate heavy and light, rough and smooth. For he does not show how these are reducible to dry and fluid, hot and cold, though he does bring out some causal connections between them. In any event, he can at best shorten the list of objects of touch. He cannot eliminate the irreducible difference between the pair, hot and cold, and the pair, dry and fluid.

have quite different objects from any of those currently recognized as objects of touch. So one does not want a definition that restricts too much the list of objects. A further inconvenience (though a surmountable one) for someone who lays stress on the objects of touch is that so many of the objects apprehended by touch are apprehended by other senses too, as, for example, are size and shape, rough and smooth, sharp and blunt, and perhaps hot and cold.

In view of these difficulties, it is not surprising to find people defining touch by reference to something other than its objects. We shall encounter two criteria that were canvassed in ancient times.

(a) *The contact criterion.* The criterion that impresses Aristotle is that touch, in his view, operates by direct contact with the body.[35] In saying this, he may be influenced by the etymology of the word for touch—namely, *haphê*, a word which was still often used with its original meaning of contact. At any rate, he says in the *De Anima* (435a17–18) that the sense of touch gets its name from the fact that it operates through direct contact.

Aristotle's appeals to the contact criterion are fairly numerous. Thus when perception occurs through direct contact, we quite often find him treating this as reason enough for classifying a perceptual power as a form of touch. In the *De Sensu*, for example (442a29-b3), he accuses Democritus of reducing all the senses to touch, apparently on the grounds that Democritus makes all the senses operate through direct contact between the body and the atoms that stream off the object perceived. Again, in the *De Anima*, at least on one interpretation of lines 434b11–18, he argues from the fact that an animal needs to perceive a thing when in direct contact with it, to the conclusion that it needs the sense of touch. In the immediately following lines, 434b18–19, again on one interpretation, he argues from the fact that taste apprehends something with which we are in direct contact—namely food—to the conclusion that taste is a variety of touch. Elsewhere in the *De Anima*, at 424b27–28, we find the statement "And all things that we perceive when in contact with them are perceived by touch."

An argument in the opposite direction is offered at *De Anima* 422a8–16. Not only does perception by direct contact indicate the sense of touch, but all exercises of taste (a form of touch, in Aristotle's view) are through contact. This is in spite of appearances to the contrary, which might suggest that fish taste food thrown into the water at a distance from them, or that we taste through the intervening liquid the sugar at the bottom of our drink. Aristotle's argument travels in the

---

[35] This is not to say that touch operates through direct contact with the sense organ. For the organ of touch is within, according to Aristotle, in the region of the heart (*D.S.* 439a1).

same direction when he says, "What is perceived by touch is directly contacted" (*D.A.* 434*b*12–13).

In these remarks, Aristotle has not abandoned the idea of distinguishing the other four senses by reference to their objects. On the contrary, he is presupposing it. And he thinks this way of distinguishing them fits in with the definition of touch by reference to direct contact. His idea is that sight, hearing, and smell (where these are defined as the power to perceive color [and so forth], sound and odor) are *never* exercised through direct contact (*D.A.* 419*a*11–21, 419*a*25–30, 421*b*16–18, 422*a*14–15, 423*b*20–25). Taste, however (where this is defined as the power to perceive flavor and is regarded as a form of touch), is *always* so exercised (*D.A.* 422*a*8–16). It is given these facts that we can, in his opinion, safely distinguish touch (including taste) as operating through direct contact with the body. He does not say how things would need to be classified, if some acts of perceiving flavor were performed at a distance or some acts of perceiving color were through direct contact.

Though Aristotle is wise to lay stress on something other than the *objects* of touch, his choice of the direct contact mechanism is difficult to work with. And this applies whether with him we take touch as including taste, or not. To bring this out, let us first notice which perceptual powers he lists under touch. He includes the power to perceive hot and cold, fluid and dry, hard and soft, heavy and light, viscous and brittle, rough and smooth, coarse and fine, as well as the power to perceive flavor. These lists are taken from the *De Anima*[36] and from the *De Generatione et Corruptione*.[37] Elsewhere, rough and smooth are distinguished from the others, as being objects of sight as well as of touch—in other words, as being common objects.[38] Other common objects are size, shape, sharp and blunt, motion and rest, number and unity.[39] It is only when these common objects are perceived by direct contact that Aristotle thinks of them as being perceived by touch.

There are several difficulties to be mentioned in applying the contact criterion. Firstly, one can by the sense of touch feel the heat of a stove while at a distance from it. Again, though one sometimes tastes by direct contact, one can sometimes also taste the olive at the bottom of the martini without being in direct contact with it. Aristotle might wish to reply to the first example that one is really feeling the heat of the air that intervenes between the stove and oneself. Certainly, he says that fire warms a distant body by warming the intervening air.[40] As for the second example, he discusses a case of this kind and protests that the flavored object which is at a distance from one dissolves and gets mixed

---

[36] 422*b*25–27.
[37] 329*b*18–20.
[38] *D.S.* 422*b*5–7.
[39] *D.S.* 442*b*5–7; *D.A.* 425*a*16.
[40] *G. & C.* 327*a*3.

with the intervening fluid. So one really is in direct contact with the flavored object after all.[41] But if these are legitimate ways of showing that
touch and taste always operate by direct contact, could they not have
been used with equal plausibility to show that smell operates by direct
contact? What makes Aristotle so sure that one does not smell the air
intervening between oneself and the rose, or that one does not smell as a
result of bits of rose dissolving and becoming mixed with the air?

This difficulty may suggest an alternative way of applying the contact
criterion. Why did not Aristotle seek to distinguish touch (including
taste) from the other senses by saying that touch is that group of perceptual powers that *can* operate by direct contact? Not every exercise of
touch will involve direct contact, but those exercises which do not will
be similar to those which do, in ways which justify our counting them
as exercises of the same sense, touch. Unfortunately, this way of applying the contact criterion runs into an immediate difficulty. For hearing
and smell would seem to be powers which *can* operate through direct
contact,[42] even if they seldom do so in fact.

Finally, there is a difficulty of another sort in relying on a contact
criterion. It is that taste will have to be counted as a form of touch.
Aristotle is quite happy so to count it. But our own concept of touch
does not include taste. Nor did the concept that Aristotle inherited. At
any rate, when we discuss the main rival to the contact criterion, we
shall notice that a number of Aristotle's predecessors did not group taste
along with the tactual powers.[43] So the contact criterion does not pick
out existing concepts of touch. It seems more that Aristotle is making a
recommendation—namely, that we should follow the contact criterion
to its logical conclusion and include taste under touch. But the recommendation does not seem a very good one, given the way in which, as
we have seen, this criterion cuts across other criteria for distinguishing
senses.

Apart from the above difficulties involved in using the contact criterion, there was another reason why it could not be employed by certain
of Aristotle's predecessors. For Empedocles, Democritus, and, according
to Aristotle,[44] most of the other early philosophers of nature had made
all sense perception operate by direct contact. The contact, in the case of
some forms of sense perception, was with particles that streamed off the
thing perceived and into the sense organs. Contact could not therefore
be used as a criterion for distinguishing one sense from others. It characterized all forms of sense perception alike. Aristotle avoided this obsta-

---

[41] D.A. 422a8–16.
[42] One can smell the snuff lodged in one's nostrils, and hear the bath water trapped in
one's ears, though Aristotle seeks to deny this in the passage mentioned on p. 70.
[43] See pp. 74–75.
[44] D.S. 442a29–30.

cle to using the contact criterion.[45] For on his theory, the sense organs did not receive particles of matter from the thing perceived. Rather, they received form without matter.[46] The eye-jelly, for example, took on the colors of the thing perceived but did not come into contact with material particles from it.[47] It may be urged that the early philosophers of nature still could have used a contact criterion for drawing distinctions between senses. For there is a difference between being in contact with the main mass of the thing perceived, and being in contact with particles that have streamed from it. So why should not touch be distinguished as involving contact with the main mass? This new criterion no longer turns on the question of whether contact is employed, but rather on the question of what it is that is contacted. Assuming that it still deserves to be called a contact criterion, it does meet the latest objection to contact criteria. But it is not the contact criterion that Aristotle himself uses for touch, since he does not require contact with the main mass.[48] Nor, of course, would it escape the objections raised earlier against contact criteria.

(b) *The non-localization criterion.* There is evidence that some of Aristotle's predecessors had used another criterion instead of the contact criterion. The clearest example of this comes in Plato's *Timaeus*, 61D-65B. Here Plato groups together various properties that we should count as objects of touch—namely, hot, cold, hard, soft, heavy, light, smooth, and rough. But he does not use a contact criterion for grouping them, nor does he use one of the names for the sense of touch that is etymologically connected with contact—namely, *haphê* or *psausis*. Rather, he groups these properties together because, in his words, they are affections "common to the body as a whole" (64A, 65B). What he means is that they are perceived without the use of a localized organ, such as eyes, nose, ears, or tongue. Rather they can be perceived through any part of the body.[49]

Plato does not always avoid the names that are connected with contact. Thus in the *Republic* (523E) we find him using for the sense of touch the name *haphê*. This time he is talking of the perception of thick and thin, hard and soft. He uses a related word for the sense of touch at *Phaedo* 75A, and perhaps at *Theaetetus* 186B, 189A, 195 D-E.

---

[45] On this subject, see the useful article by Solmsen, "αἴσθησις in Aristotelian and Epicurean Thought," in *Mededelingen der Koninklijke Nederlandse Akademie van Wetenschappen Afd. Letterkunde* (1961).

[46] *D.A.* 424a18, 424b2, 425b22, 427a8, 429a15, 434a29, 435a22.

[47] In another sense, Aristotle did accept that all sense perception involved contact. The object seen must be in contact with the air, and the air in turn with the eye (*Phys.* 245a2–9).

[48] Thus, he allows that fish exercise taste, a form of touch, when in contact not with the main mass of their food, but with that part of their food that has dissolved in the water.

[49] Aristotle would not agree that touch lacks a localized organ. The organ is in the region of the heart (*D.S.* 439a1). He could still have distinguished the recognized tactual powers, if he had chosen, however, by saying that the other senses have either a localized organ at the surface of the body (ears, eyes, nose) or at least a localized channel at the surface (tongue).

There is another author who combines the non-localization criterion with the use of terminology that is connected with contact. In
Regimen I. 23, a treatise which was written perhaps around 400 B.C.,
and which belongs to the Hippocratic collection of medical writings,
there is reference to a sense called *psausis*, a name which is connected
with contact. But the author goes on to add a reference to the non-localization criterion, saying that the whole body is its organ.

For a use of the non-localization criterion without terminology suggesting contact, we may refer to Theophrastus' report (*De Sensibus* 38)
on Cleidemus, a pre-Socratic who was perhaps contemporary with
Democritus. According to this report, Cleidemus distinguished between
perception through the tongue and perception through the rest of the
body.

This last example is important for an additional reason. Not only does
it use the non-localization criterion for distinguishing a sense. But also
by its treatment of what we should call taste, it implies a rejection of the
contact criterion. For both perception through the tongue and perception through the rest of the body operate by direct contact. Yet for all
that, they are not grouped together as forming a single sense.

The same is true in the passage cited from the Hippocratic treatise,
Regimen. Even though this passage uses the name *psausis*, which is connected with contact, it does not include taste as falling under *psausis*. On
the contrary, it distinguishes between perception through the tongue
and perception through the whole body. And it is the latter that is called
psausis. In spite, then, of using a name connected with contact, the
author does not treat contact as a sufficient ground for including a form
of perception under the heading of *psausis*. He seems to have preferred
the non-localization criterion to the contact one.

The same seems to be true of other authors. At any rate, on the most natural interpretation, Democritus lists five senses in fragment II—namely,
sight, hearing, smell, taste, and touch. Though he uses a contact word,
psausis, for touch, he agrees with Cleidemus and with the author of
Regimen I, in refusing to subsume taste under the heading of touch. And
he thereby implies rejection of the contact criterion. Admittedly, an
alternative interpretation has been suggested for the passage. Solmsen[50]
remarks that the word *psausis* might be being used not to refer to the
sense of touch, but to emphasize that the other four senses named operate, in Democritus' opinion, by contact. This interpretation is very much
less natural. But even if it be correct, we still get a result of some interest. For if contact characterizes the other four senses, then Democritus
is not free to distinguish a fifth sense, touch, as the sense which employs
contact. So, as was remarked before, if he wished to use the contact criterion, he would have to use a version of it different from Aristotle's.

---

[50] *Loc. cit.*

Aristotle himself seems to have been influenced by the tradition which treats taste as distinct from touch, in so far as he devotes separate discussions in the *De Anima* to sight, hearing, smell, taste, and touch. He does not treat taste and touch together, in spite of his recommendation that we should subsume taste under touch.

Let us summarize these findings. On the one hand, we do encounter among Aristotle's predecessors the names *psausis* and *haphê*, which are connected with contact. On the other hand, a good many authors, including ones who used these names, seem to have rejected the contact criterion as a way of distinguishing the sense of touch. This rejection comes out in their insistence on treating taste as distinct from touch. (Moreover, their view that all the senses operate by direct contact commits them to rejecting Aristotle's own version of the contact criterion.) In place of the contact criterion for distinguishing touch, a number of them used the non-localization criterion. It looks as if, in spite of their choice of nomenclature, the non-localization criterion answered more faithfully to the conception which they actually had.

Certainly, the non-localization criterion is the one that corresponds most closely to the present-day concept of touch, at least if we take the layman's conception, which I referred to before. The powers that the layman groups under touch (and here the power of taste is not included) are distinguished by the fact that they operate without any obvious localized organ. If modern research has discovered localized organs, these were not apparent at the time the concept was being formed. The absence of an obvious localized organ is the only feature that is common and peculiar to the very diverse powers that are grouped under the heading of touch. This is not to say that the feature is logically necessary or logically sufficient for making a perceptual power count as a variety of touch. But at least it has served as a principle of collection for the familiar varieties. And newly encountered or imaginary perceptual powers will be classified on the basis of their similarity to these familiar ones (even though the similarity will not necessarily be in respect of non-localization).

We get a strong indication of the influence that the non-localization criterion has had, if we ask ourselves the following question. What else has led to taste being excluded, and to the perception of temperature being included, under the heading of touch? It looks, then, as if the non-localization criterion, to be found in Plato and others, has retained its influence to the present day.

Two related points of clarification need to be introduced, however. The non-localization criterion does not on its own enable us to classify individual acts of perception. For one can, for example, feel the texture of something with one's tongue or ear. So we must not suggest that each individual exercise of touch will be carried out without the aid of a localized organ. Rather, the point is that the same quality, texture, can be apprehended by the same kind of mechanism and the same kind of experience, through a quite different part of the body, at least in the case of a healthy human being. And these considerations warrant our saying that, even if a given exercise of the power is confined to a localized organ, the power itself is not so confined.

The point could be put like this. The non-localization criterion is used to classify not individual acts of perception, but perceptual powers. And in deciding which individual acts fall under a given power, we may have to appeal to criteria other than the non-localization one.

This brings us to the second point of clarification. We have been saying that under touch we include at present those perceptual powers which operate without any obvious localized organ. But the truth of this statement depends on what counts as a distinct perceptual power. Is the power to perceive shape, for example, whether visually or tactually, to be counted as a single power? If so, we will get an unfortunate result. For when we ask whether or not this single power is confined to a localized organ, either answer will be unsatisfactory. Suppose, for example, it is said that the power to perceive shape is not confined to a localized organ, on the grounds that tactual exercises of the power are not so confined. Then the entire power of perceiving shape, even the power to perceive it visually, will have to be classified under touch, which is not the result we want. The moral is that the non-localization criterion can only be used to classify powers under the heading of touch, if we have adopted the right kind of procedure for individuating powers in the first place.

Now that we have introduced the non-localization criterion, we are in a better position to evaluate two arguments of Aristotle's. In *De Anima*, Book II, Chapter 11, he introduces several imaginary situations. One of these situations involves people being able to perceive flavor with any part of the body.[51] In this situation, he says, people would identify taste with touch. Taken in one sense, Aristotle's claim is perfectly correct, as our discussion of the non-localization criterion will show. For in the envisaged situation, the perception of flavor would not be through a localized organ. Taste in that case would have at least as good a claim as the perception of temperature to be classified under touch. Admittedly, this is not the kind of point that Aristotle himself is intending to make in the passage.[52] So all we should say is that our discussion of the non-localization criterion reveals one sense in which his remark is correct.

---

[51] 423a17–21.

[52] Aristotle's own point is that in the imaginary situation described, we would fail to notice that taste is a distinct kind of perception in its own right, distinct from, say, the power of perceiving fluid and dry. For there would be no difference of organ or medium to attract our attention to its distinctness. Aristotle does think, however, that taste is a distinct kind of perception, and that it would remain so in the imaginary situation. This is not to retract his view that taste is a kind of touch, and would remain so in the imaginary situation. It is to insist that taste is, and would be, only one kind of touch. Aristotle suggests that just as in the imaginary situation we would fail to notice the distinctness of taste, so now perhaps we fail to distinguish different kinds of perception that are lumped together under the heading of touch.

The second Aristotelian argument which we can now profitably recall is his objection to Democritus, that Democritus reduces all the senses to touch.[53] The ground of this charge is apparently that Democritus makes all the senses operate through contact. Aristotle is right about one thing. The name *haphê* originally meant, and still often meant, contact. Consequently, if all the senses operate through contact, the name *haphê* is not a very appropriate one to reserve for one of them. Rather, it should be applied to all. This point is only one about nomenclature, however. There is a much more important point on which Aristotle cannot fault Democritus. He cannot say that Democritus is debarred from distinguishing between the sense that is called touch and the other four senses. For Democritus is free to draw this distinction by reference to the non-localization criterion.

RETROSPECT

We have argued that Aristotle emphasizes the sense objects in his account of four of the senses. And we found some good reasons for following such a policy. But we argued that the policy would not be a good one in connection with the sense of touch, and that Aristotle wisely stresses a different criterion in speaking of this sense. He goes wrong, however, in choosing the contact criterion for touch, rather than the non-localization criterion that had been used by several of his predecessors. Although the name *haphê*, like our word "touch," was often used to mean contact, it is in fact the non-localization criterion that corresponds most closely to the conception of touch that people have actually had.[54]

---

[53] *D.S.* 442*a*29-*b*3.

[54] Earlier drafts were read at Cornell, Princeton, and London Universities, and at a weekend meeting of Birkbeck College. I benefited from many helpful comments at these meetings. But I should like to acknowledge in particular Hidé Ishiguro, Alan Lacey, and David Hamlyn, who prepared for me on these occasions valuable comments which have led to many improvements. Some of the work for this paper was done on leave, while I held a Howard Foundation Fellowship from Brown University, and a project grant, No. H68-0-95, from the National Endowment for the Humanities. I acknowledge these sources gratefully.

4

Some Remarks About the Senses*

H. P. Grice

A claim to the effect that certain creatures possess a faculty which should be counted as a sense, different from any of those with which we are familiar, might be met in more than one way, without actual repudiation of the alleged facts on which the claim is based. It might be said that this faculty, though possibly in some way informative about the world, was not a faculty of perceiving, or it might be admitted that the exercise of the faculty constituted perception, and maintained that no new sense was involved, but only one of the familiar ones operating, perhaps, in some unfamiliar way.

About the first alternative I shall not say a great deal. It embraces a number of sub-alternatives:

(1) The faculty might be assimilated to such things as a moral sense, or a sense of humour. These are dubiously informative; and even if treated as informative, could not be regarded as telling (in the first instance) only about conditions of the world spatially and temporally present to the creature who is exercising them.

(2) The faculty might be held to be some kind of power of divination. This line might be adopted if the creature seemed to have direct (non-inferential) knowledge of certain contemporary states or events in the material world, though this knowledge was not connected with the operation of any sense-organ. We should, of course, be very reluctant to accept this sub-alternative. We should so far as possible cling to the idea that such knowledge must be connected with the operation of a sense-organ, even if we could not identify it.

(3) The exercise of the faculty—let us call it x-ing—might be denied the title of perception because of its analogy with the having of

H. P. Grice "Some Remarks About the Senses", in R. J. Bulter (ed.) *Analytical Philosophy*, First Series, Oxford: Basil Blackwell, 1962. (Reproduced with permission of Blackwell Publishing Ltd.)

* I am indebted to Rogers Albritton for a number of extremely helpful criticisms and suggestions.

sensations. It might be held that x-ing consisted in having some
sort of experience generated by material things or events in the
x-er's environment by way of some effect on his nervous system, though it did not qualify as perceiving the things or events
in question. The kind of situation in which this view might
be taken may perhaps be indicated if we consider the assaults
made by physiologists and psychologists on the so-called 'sense
of touch'. They wish, I think on neurological grounds, to distinguish three senses: a pressure-sense, a warm-and-cold sense,
and a pain-sense. Would we be happy to accept their pain-sense
as a sense in the way in which sight or smell is a sense? I think
not; for to do so would involve regarding the fact that we do not
'externalize' pains as a mere linguistic accident. That is to say,
it would involve considering as unimportant the following facts:
(*a*) that we are ready to regard 'malodorous', as distinct from
'painful' or 'sharply painful', as the name of a relatively abiding
characteristic which material things in general either possess or
do not possess; we are as a general rule prepared to regard questions of the form 'Is M (a material thing) malodorous?' as being
at least in principle answerable either affirmatively or negatively,
whereas we should very often wish to reject questions of the
form 'Is M painful?' or 'Is M sharply painful?'; and (*b*) that we
speak of smells but not of pains as being in the kitchen.

Very briefly, the salient points here seem to me as follows:

(*a*) Pains are not greatly variegated, except in intensity and location.
     Smells are.
(*b*) There is no one standard procedure for getting a pain: one can
     be cut, bumped, burnt; scraped, and so on. There is a standard
     procedure for smelling, namely, inhaling.
(*c*) Almost any type of object can inflict pain upon us, often in more
     than one way.

In consequence of these facts, our pains are on the whole very poor
guides to the character of the things that hurt us. Particular kinds of
smells, on the other hand, are in general characteristic of this or that
type of object. These considerations I hope constitute a partial explanation of the fact that we do not, in general, attribute pain-qualities to
things: we may in a special case speak of a thumb-screw, for example, as
being a painful instrument, but this is because there is a standard way of
applying thumb-screws to people.

We do not speak of pains as being in (say) the kitchen; and the reason
for this is, I think, that if a source of pain moves away from a given place,
persons arriving in this place after the removal do not get hurt. Smells,
on the other hand, do linger in places, and so are 'detachable' from the
material objects which are their source. Though pains do not linger in

places, they do linger with individuals after the source of pain has been removed. In this again they are unlike smells.

I shall now turn to discussion of the second possible way of meeting the claim of x-ing to be the exercise of a new sense. This, you will remember, took the form of arguing that x-ing, though perceiving, is merely perceiving by one of the familiar senses, perhaps through an unfamiliar kind of sense-organ. At this point we need to ask by what criteria senses are to be distinguished from one another. The answer to this question, if obtainable, would tell us how x-ing must differ from the exercise of familiar senses in order to count as the operation of a distinct sense. Four seemingly independent ideas might be involved:

I. It might be suggested that the senses are to be distinguished by the differing features that we become aware of by means of them: that is to say, seeing might be characterized as perceiving (or seeming to perceive) things as having certain colours, shapes and sizes; hearing as perceiving things (or better, in this case, events) as having certain degrees of loudness, certain determinates of pitch, certain tone-qualities; and so on for the other senses.

II. It might be suggested that two senses, for example, seeing and smelling, are to be distinguished by the special introspectible character of the experiences of seeing and smelling; that is, disregarding the differences between the characteristics we learn about by sight and smell, we are entitled to say that seeing is itself different in character from smelling.

III. Our attention might be drawn to the differing general features of the external physical conditions on which the various modes of perceiving depend, to differences in the 'stimuli' connected with different senses: the sense of touch is activated by contact, sight by light rays, hearing by sound waves, and so on.

IV. Reference might be made to the internal mechanisms associated with the various senses—the character of the sense-organs, and their mode of connection with the brain. (These suggestions need not of course be regarded as mutually exclusive. It is possible—perhaps indeed likely—that there is no one essential criterion for distinguishing the senses; that there is, rather, a multiplicity of criteria.)

One procedure at this point (perhaps the most desirable one) would be to consider, in relation to difficult cases, the applicability of the suggested criteria and their relative weights. But a combination of ignorance of zoology with poverty of invention diverts me to perhaps not uninteresting questions concerning the independence of these criteria, and in particular to the relation between the first and the second. The first suggestion (that differing senses are to be distinguished by the differing features which we perceive by means of them) may seem at first sight attractive and unmystifying; but difficulties seem to arise if we attempt to make it the sole basis of distinction between the senses.[1] It looks as if, when we try to work out suggestion (I) in detail we are brought round to some version of the second suggestion (that the senses are to be distinguished by the special introspectible characters of their exercise).

There is a danger that suggestion (I) may incorporate from the start, in a concealed way, suggestion (II): for instance, to adopt it might amount to saying 'Seeing is the sort of experience that we have when we perceive things as having certain colours, shapes, etc. If we are to eliminate this danger, I think we must treat suggestion (I) as advancing the idea that, starting with such sense-neutral verbs as 'perceive', 'seem', we can elucidate the notion of seeing in terms of the notion of perceiving things to have such-and-such features, smelling in terms of perceiving things to have such-and-such other features, and so on. In general, special perceptual verbs are to be explained in terms of general perceptual verbs together with names of special generic features which material things or events may be perceived to have. At this point an obvious difficulty arises: among the features which would presumably figure in the list of tactual qualities (which are to be used to distinguish feeling from other modes of perceiving) is that of warmth; but to say that someone perceives something to have a certain degree of warmth does not entail that he is *feeling* anything at all, for we can *see* that things are warm, and things can *look* warm.

To extricate the suggestion from this objection, it looks as if it would be necessary to introduce some such term as 'directly perceive' (and perhaps also the term 'directly seem', the two terms being no doubt definitionally linked). How precisely these terms would have to be defined I do not propose to enquire, but the definition would have to be such as to ensure that someone who saw that something was blue might be directly perceiving that it was blue, while someone who saw that something was warm could not be directly perceiving that it was warm. We then might try to define 'see' and its congeners (and primary uses of 'look' and its congeners) in terms of these specially introduced verbs. We might put up the following as samples of rough equivalences, without troubling ourselves too much about details, since all we require for present purposes is to see the general lines on which the initial suggestion will have to be developed:

(1) X sees M (material object) = X directly perceives M to have some colour and some spatial property.
(2) X feels M = X directly perceives M to have some spatial property and degrees of one or more of such properties as warmth (coldness), hardness (softness), etc.
(3) M looks (primary sense) ϕ to X = M directly seems to X to have certain spatial and colour properties, one of which is ϕ.
(4) M looks (secondary sense) ϕ to X = M directly seems to X to have certain spatial and colour properties, one or more of which indicate to X that M is or may be ϕ.

---

[1] I shall consider later the possibility of combining it with suggestions III and IV.

Analogous definitions could be provided for primary and secondary uses of 'feel' (with a non-personal subject).

This manoeuvre fails, I think, to put suggestion (I) in the clear. Some might object to the definitions of verbs like 'see' (used with a direct object) in terms of 'perceive that'; and there would remain the question of defining the special terms 'directly perceive' and 'directly seem.' But a more immediately serious difficulty seems to me to be one connected with the seemingly unquestionable acceptability of the proposition that spatial properties may be directly perceived to belong to things both by sight and by touch. Suppose a man to be resting a half-crown on the palm of one hand and a penny on the palm of the other: he might (perhaps truthfully) say, 'The half-crown looks to me larger than the penny, though they feel the same size'. If we apply the rough translations indicated above, this statement comes out thus: 'The half-crown and the penny directly seem to me to have certain spatial and colour proper-ties, including (in the case of the half-crown) that of being larger than the penny; but they also directly seem to me to have certain properties, such as certain degrees of roughness, warmth, etc., and spatial proper-ties which include that of being equal in size.'

The facts stated by this rigmarole seem to be (differently ordered) as follows:

(1) The coins directly seem to have certain spatial and colour properties.
(2) The coins directly seem to have certain properties drawn from the 'tactual' list.
(3) The half-crown directly seems larger than the penny.
(4) The coins directly seem to be of the same size.

But there is nothing in this statement of the facts to tell us whether the coins *look* different in size but *feel* the same size, or alternatively *feel* different in size but *look* the same size.

At this point two somewhat heroic courses suggest themselves. The first is to proclaim an ambiguity in the expression 'size', distinguishing between visual size and tactual size, thus denying that spatial properties are really accessible to more than one sense. This more or less Berkeleian position is perhaps unattractive independently of the current argument; in any case the introduction of the qualifications 'visual' and 'tactual', in the course of an attempt to distinguish the senses from one another without invoking the special character of the various modes of perceiv-ing, is open to the gravest suspicion. The second course is to amend the accounts of looking and feeling in such a way that, for example, 'A looks larger than B' is re-expressible more or less as follows: 'A directly seems larger than B in the kind of way which entails that A and B directly seem to have certain colour-properties'. But this seems to introduce a refer-ence to special kinds or varieties of 'direct seeming', and this brings in what seems to be only a variant version of suggestion (II).

But there is a rather more subtle course to be considered.[1] In addition to the link (whatever that may be) which may join certain *generic* properties (*e.g.*, colour, shape, size) so as to constitute them as members of a group of properties associated with a particular sense (*e.g.*, as visual properties), another kind of link may be indicated which holds between specific properties (*e.g.*, specific colours and shapes, &c.), and which might be of use in dealing with the difficulty raised by this current example. Suppose that A_1 is a specific form of some generic property which occurs only in the visual list (*e.g.*, a particular colour), that B_1 is a specific form of some generic property occurring only in the tactual list (*e.g.*, a particular degree of warmth), and that X_1 and X_2 are specific forms of a generic property occurring in both the visual and the tactual lists (*e.g.*, are particular shapes). Suppose further that someone simultaneously detects or seems to detect the presence of all these properties (A_1, B_1, X_1, X_2) in a given object. Now the percipient might find that he could continue to detect or seem to detect A_1 and X_1 while no longer detecting or seeming to detect B_1 and X_2; and equally that he could detect or seem to detect B_1 and X_2 while no longer detecting or seeming to detect A_1 and X_1; but on the other hand that he could not retain A_1 and X_2 while eliminating B_1 and X_1, or retain B_1 and X_1 while eliminating A_1 and X_2. There would thus be what might be called a 'detection-link' between A_1 and X_1, and another such link between B_1 and X_2. On the basis of this link between X_1 and a purely visual property it might be decided that X_1 was here being visually detected, and analogously it might be decided that X_2 was being tactually detected. Similarly in the example of the half-crowns one might say that there is a detection-link between inequality of size and certain purely visual properties the coins have or seem to have (*e.g.*, their real or apparent colours) and a detection-link between equality of size and certain purely tactual properties the coins have or seem to have (*e.g.*, their coldness): and thus the difficulty may be resolved.

There are three considerations which prevent me from being satisfied with this attempt to make suggestion (I) serviceable. I put them in what I regard as the order of increasing importance:

(1) Consider the possible case of a percipient to whom the two half-crowns *look* equal in size when only seen, *feel* equal in size when only felt, but look unequal and feel equal when *both* seen *and* felt. This case is no doubt fantastic, but nevertheless it *seems* just an empirical matter whether or not the way things appear to one sense is affected in this sort of way by the operation or inoperation of another sense. If such a case were to occur, then the method adumbrated in my previous paragraph would be quite inadequate to deal with it: for equality of size would be co-detectable *both* with visual properties alone *and* with tactual properties

---

[1] The idea of this was suggested to me by Mr. O. P. Wood.

alone, whereas inequality in size would be co-detectable neither with visual properties alone nor with tactual properties alone. So the percipient would, so far as this test goes, be at a loss to decide by which sense he detected (or seemed to detect) inequality. But I doubt whether this conclusion is acceptable.

(2) If it were possible for a creature to have two different senses by each of which he detected just the same generic properties, then the test suggested could not be applied in the case of those senses; for it depends on these being properties accessible to one but not both of two senses with regard to which it is invoked. It is far from clear to me that it is inconceivable that just the same set of generic properties should be detectable by either one of two different senses. (I touch again on this question later.)

(3) Whether or not the suggested test, if applied, would always rightly answer the question whether a given spatial property is on a given occasion being detected by sight or touch, it seems quite certain that we never do employ this method of deciding such a question. Indeed there seems something peculiar about the idea of using *any* method, for the answer to such a question, asked about ourselves, never seems in the slightest doubt. And it seems rather strange to make the difference between detecting (or seeming to detect) a given property by sight and detecting (or seeming to detect) it by touch turn on what would be the result of an experiment which we should never in any circumstances perform.

Suggestion (I) has a further unattractive feature. According to it certain properties are listed as visual properties, certain others as tactual properties, and so forth; and to say that colour is a visual property would seem to amount to no more than saying that colour is a member of a group of properties the others of which are.... This leaves membership of the group as an apparently arbitrary matter. I now wish to see if some general account of the notion of a visual (tactual etc.) property could be given if (as suggestion (II) would allow) we make unhampered use of special perceptual verbs like 'see' and 'look'. I shall go into this question perhaps rather more fully than the immediate purposes of the discussion demand, since it seems to me to be of some intrinsic interest. I doubt if such expressions as 'visual property', 'tactual property', etc., have any clear-cut accepted use, so what follows should be regarded as a preliminary to deciding upon a use, rather than as the analysis of an existing one. I shall confine myself to the notion of a visual property, hoping that the discussion of this could be adapted to deal with the other senses (not of course necessarily in the same way in each case).

First I suggest that we take it to be a necessary (though not a sufficient) condition of a property P being a visual property that it should be linguistically correct to speak of someone as *seeing* that some material thing M is P, and also (with one qualification to be mentioned later) of some thing M as *looking* P to someone. Within the class of properties which satisfy this condition I want to make some distinctions which belong to two non-independent dimensions, one of which I shall call 'determinability', the other 'complexity':

(1)   There are certain properties (for example that of being blue) such that if P is one of them there is no better way (though there may be an equally good way) for me to make sure that a thing M is P than to satisfy myself that, observational conditions being optimal, M looks P to me. Such properties I shall label 'directly visually determinable'.

(2)   It seems to me that there might be a case for labelling some properties as visually determinable, though indirectly so. I have in mind two possible kinds of indirectness. First, it might be the case that a primary (non-inferior) test for determining whether M is P would be not just to ensure that M looked P in the most favourable conditions for observation, but to ensure, by scrutiny, that certain parts (in a wide sense) or elements of M had certain characteristics and were interrelated in certain ways; it being understood that the characteristics and relations in question are to be themselves *directly* visually determinable. For me, though no doubt not for a Chinese, the property of being inscribed with a certain Chinese character might be of this kind; and for every one no doubt the property of having a chiliagonal surface would be of this kind. Second, a characteristic might be such that its primary test involved comparison of M (or its elements) with some standard specimen. Under this head I mean to take in both such properties as being apple-green, for which the primary test involves comparison with a colour chart, and such a property as that of being two feet seven inches long, the primary test for which is measurement by a ruler. It is to be understood that the results of such comparison or measurement are to be describable in terms of properties which are directly visually determinable.

It seems to me possible that 'visual characteristic' might be used in such a way that P would qualify as a visual characteristic only if it were directly visually determinable, or in such a way that it would so qualify if it were visually determinable either directly or indirectly. But there also seems to be a different though I think linked basis of classification, which might also be employed to fix the sense of the expression 'visual characteristic'. There will be some values of P, such an object M may be said to look P, with regard to which the question, 'What is it about the way that M looks that makes it look P?' has no answer. More generally, it will be impossible to specify anything about the way things look, when they look P, which will account for or determine their looking P. One cannot, for example, specify anything about the way things look when they look blue, which makes them look blue. Characteristics for which this rough condition is satisfied I will call 'visually simple'. But with regard to those values of P which are such that a thing may look P, but which are not visually simple, there are various possibilities:

(1) The specification of what it is about the way a thing looks which makes it look P, or determines it to look P, may consist in specifying certain characteristics (of the visually determinable kind) which M has or looks to have, the presence of which indicates more or less reliably that M is P. Warmth is such a characteristic. In this kind of case P will not be visually determinable, and I should like to say that P is not a visual characteristic, and is neither visually simple nor visually complex. P will be merely 'visually indicable'.

(2) The specification of what it is about the way a thing M looks which makes it look P or determines it to look P might take the form of specifying certain properties (of a visually determinable or visually simple kind or both) the possession of which constitutes a logically sufficient condition for being P. The property of being lopsided might be of this kind. A man's face could perhaps be said to be made to look lopsided by his looking as if he had (and perhaps indeed his actually having) one ear set lower than the other; and his actually having one ear set lower than the other would perhaps be a logically sufficient condition of his face's being lopsided. Characteristics belonging to this class I will label 'visually tightly complex'.

(3) Consider such examples as 'X's face looks friendly' or 'X looks tough'. Certainly friendliness and toughness are not themselves visually determinable: and certainly the questions 'What is there about the way his face looks that makes it look friendly?' and 'What is there about the way he looks that makes him look tough?' are in order. Nevertheless there may be considerable difficulty in answering such questions; and when the answer or partial answer comes it may not amount to saying what it is about the look of X's face (or of X) which indicates more or less reliably that X is friendly (or tough). In such cases one might be inclined to say that though toughness is not a visual characteristic, being tough-looking is.[1] The following remarks seem in point:

(1) Being tough-looking is in some way dependent on the possession of visually determinable characteristics: there would be a logical absurdity in saying that two people were identical in

---

[1] It might be thought necessary, for this type of characteristic, to relax the initial condition which visual characteristics were required to satisfy, on the grounds that one cannot speak of someone as 'looking tough-looking'. But as Albritton has pointed out to me, it does not seem linguistically improper to say of someone that (for example) he looked tough-looking when he stood in the dim light of the passage, but as soon as he moved into the room it could be seen that really he looked quite gentle.

respect of all visually determinable characteristics, and yet that one person was tough-looking and the other was not.

(2) Even if one has specified to one's full satisfaction what it is about the way X looks that makes him look tough, one has not given a logically sufficient condition for being tough-looking. If I just produced a list of X's visually determinable characteristics, the possession of which does *in fact* make him look tough, no one could strictly *deduce* from the information given that X looks tough; to make quite sure he would have to look at X himself.

(3) Though the primary test for determining whether X is tough-looking is to see how he looks in the most favourable observational conditions, this test may not (perhaps cannot) be absolutely decisive. If, after examination of X, I and my friends say that X is tough-looking, and someone else says that he is not, it need not be the case that the last-mentioned person is wrong or doesn't know the language; he may for example be impressed by some dissimilarity between X and standard tough customers, by which I and my friends are not impressed, in which case the dissident judgment may perhaps be described as eccentric, but not as wrong. In the light of this discussion one might say that such characteristics as being tough-looking are 'visually near-determinable'; and they might also be ranked as visually complex (in view of their dependence on visually determinable characteristics), though 'loosely complex' (in view of the non-existence of logically sufficient conditions of their presence).[1]

I should like to emphasise that I have not been trying to legislate upon the scope to be given to the notion of a visual characteristic, but have only been trying to provide materials for such legislation on the assumption that the special character of visual experience may be used to distinguish the sense of sight, thus allowing a relatively unguarded use of such words as 'look'.

Let us now for a moment turn our attention to suggestion (II), the idea that senses are to be distinguished by the special character of the

---

[1] The logical relations between the different sections of the determinability range and those of the simplicity-complexity range may need detailed examination. For instance, consider the statement 'The sound of the explosion came from my right' (or 'The explosion sounded as if it were on my right'). It may be impossible to specify anything about the way the explosion sounded which determined its sounding as if it were on my right, in which case by my criterion being on my right will qualify as an auditorily simple property. Yet certainly the explosion's sounding, even in the most favourable observational conditions, as if it was on my right is a secondary (inferior) test for the location of the explosion. So we would have an example of a property which is auditorily simple without being auditorily determinable. This may be of interest in view of the hesitation we may feel when asked if spatial characteristics can be auditory.

experiences which their exercise involves. Two fairly obvious difficulties might be raised. First, that such experiences (if experiences they be) as seeing and feeling seem to be, as it were, diaphanous: if we were asked to pay close attention, on a given occasion, to our seeing or feeling as distinct from what was being seen or felt, we should not know how to proceed; and the attempt to describe the differences between seeing and feeling seems to dissolve into a description of what we see and what we feel. How then can seeing and feeling have the special character which suggestion (II) requires them to have, if this character resists both inspection and description? The second difficulty is perhaps even more serious. If to see is to detect by means of a special kind of experience, will it not be just a contingent matter that the characteristics we detect by means of this kind of experience are such things as colour and shape? Might it not have been the case that we thus detected characteristic smells, either instead of or as well as colours and shapes? But it does not seem to be just a contingent fact that we do not see the smells of things. Suggestion (I) on the other hand seems to avoid both these difficulties; the first because the special character of the experiences connected with the various senses is not invoked, and the second because since the smell of a thing is not listed among the properties the (direct) detection of which counts as seeing, on this view it emerges as tautological that smells cannot be seen.

We seem now to have reached an impasse. Any attempt to make suggestion (I) work leads to difficulties which seem soluble only if we bring in suggestion (II), and suggestion (II) in its turn involves difficulties which seem avoidable only by adopting suggestion (I). Is it the case, then, that the two criteria should be combined; that is, is the right answer that, for anything to count as a case of seeing, two conditions must be fulfilled: first, that the properties detected should belong to a certain group, and second that the detection should involve a certain kind of experience? But this does not seem to be a satisfactory way out; for if it were, then it would be logically possible to detect smells by means of the type of experience characteristically involved in seeing, yet only to do this would not be to *see* smells, since a further condition (the property qualification) would be unfulfilled. But surely we object on logical grounds no less to the idea that we might detect smells through visual experiences than to the idea that we might see the smells of things: indeed the ideas seem to be the same. So perhaps the criteria mentioned in suggestions (I) and (II) are not distinguishable; yet they *seem* to be distinct.

Maybe all is not yet lost, for there still remains the possibility that something may be achieved by bringing into the discussion the third and fourth suggestions. Perhaps we might save suggestion (I), and thus eliminate suggestion (II), by combining the former with one or both of the last two suggestions. For if to see is to detect certain properties (from the visual list) by means of a certain sort of mechanism (internal or external or both), then the arguments previously advanced to show the need for importing suggestion (II) seem to lose their force. We can now differentiate between the case in which two coins look different in size but feel the same size and the case in which they feel different in size but look the same size: we shall say that in the first case by mechanism A (eyes and affection by light waves) we detect or seem to detect difference in size while by mechanism B (hands and pressure) we detect or seem to detect equality of size: whereas in the second case the mechanisms are transposed. We can also characterize the visual list of properties as those detectable by mechanism A, and deal analogously with other lists of properties. In this way the need to invoke suggestion (II) seems to be eliminated.

Promising as this approach may appear, I very much doubt if it succeeds in eliminating the need to appeal to the special character of experiences in order to distinguish the senses. Suppose that long-waited invasion of the Martians takes place, that they turn out to be friendly creatures and teach us their language. We get on all right, except that we find no verb in their language which unquestionably corresponds to our verb 'see'. Instead we find two verbs which we decide to render as 'x' and 'y': we find that (in their tongue) they speak of themselves as x-ing, and also as y-ing, things to be of this and that colour, size and shape. Further, in physical appearance they are more or less like ourselves, except that in their heads they have, one above the other, two pairs of organs, not perhaps exactly like one another, but each pair more or less like our eyes: each pair of organs is found to be sensitive to light waves. It turns out that for them x-ing is dependent on the operation of the upper organs, and y-ing on that of the lower organs. The question which it seems natural to ask is this: Are x-ing and y-ing both cases of seeing, the difference between them being that x-ing is seeing with the upper organs, and y-ing is seeing with the lower organs? Or alternatively, do one or both of these accomplishments constitute the exercise of a new sense, other than that of sight? If we adopt, to distinguish the senses, a combination of suggestion (I) with one or both of suggestions (III) or (IV), the answer seems clear: both x-ing and y-ing are seeing, with different pairs of organs. But *is* the question really to be settled so easily? Would we not in fact want to ask whether x-ing something to be round was like y-ing it to be round, or whether when something x-ed blue to them this was like or unlike its y-ing blue to them? If in answer to such questions as these they said, 'Oh no, there's all the difference in the world!' then I think we should be inclined to say that either x-ing or y-ing (if not both) must be something other than seeing: we might of course be quite unable to decide *which* (if either) was seeing.

(I am aware that here those whose approach is more Wittgensteinian than my own might complain that unless something more can be said about how the difference between x-ing and y-ing might 'come out' or show itself in publicly observable phenomena, then the claim by the supposed Martians that x-ing and y-ing are different would be one of which nothing could be made, which would leave one at a loss how to understand it. *First* I am not convinced of the need for 'introspectible' differences to show themselves in the way this approach demands (I shall not discuss this point further); *second* I think that if I *have* to meet this demand I can. One can suppose that one or more of these Martians acquired the use of the lower y-ing organs at some comparatively late date in their careers, and that at the same time (perhaps for experimental purposes) the operation of the upper x-ing organs was inhibited. One might now be ready to allow that a difference between x-ing and y-ing would have shown itself if in such a situation the creatures using their y-ing organs for the first time were unable straight away, without any learning process, to use their 'colour'-words fluently and correctly to describe what they detected through the use of those organs.)[1]

It might be argued at this point that we have not yet disposed of the idea that the senses can be distinguished by an amalgam of suggestions (I), (III) and (IV); for it is not clear that in the example of the Martians the condition imposed by suggestion (I) is fulfilled. The thesis, it might be said, is only upset if x-ing and y-ing are accepted as being the exercise of different senses; and if they are, then the Martians' colour-words could be said to have a concealed ambiguity. Much as 'sweet' in English may mean 'sweet-smelling' or 'sweet-tasting', so 'blue' in Martian may mean 'blue-x-ing' or 'blue-y-ing'. But if this is so, then the Martians after all do not detect by x-ing just those properties of things which they detect by y-ing. To this line of argument there are two replies:

(1) The defender of the thesis is in no position to use this argument; for he cannot start by making the question whether x-ing and y-ing are exercises of the same sense turn on the question (*inter alia*) whether or not a single group of characteristics is detected by both, and then make the question of individuation of the group turn on the question whether putative members of the group are detected by one, or by more than one sense. He would be saying in effect, 'Whether, in x-ing and y-ing, different senses are exercised depends (*inter alia*) on whether the same properties are detected by x-ing as by y-ing; but whether a certain x-ed property is the same as a certain y-ed property depends on whether x-ing and y-ing are or are not the exercise of a single sense'. This reply seems fatal. For the circularity could only be avoided by making the question whether 'blue' in Martian names a single property depend *either* on whether the kinds of experience involved in x-ing and y-ing are different, which would be to reintroduce suggestion (II), *or* on whether the mechanisms involved in x-ing and y-ing are different (in this case whether the upper organs are importantly unlike the lower organs): and to adopt this alternative would, I think, lead to

---

[1] Cf. the Molyneux problem.

treating the differentiation of the senses as being solely a matter of their mechanisms, thereby making suggestion (1) otiose.

(2) Independently of its legitimacy or illegitimacy in the present context, we must reject the idea that if it is accepted that in x-ing and y-ing different senses are being exercised, then Martian colour-words will be ambiguous. For *ex hypothesi* there will be a very close correlation between things x-ing blue and their y-ing blue, far closer than that between things smelling sweet and their tasting sweet. This being so, it is only to be expected that x-ing and y-ing should share the position of arbiters concerning the colour of things: that is, 'blue' would be the name of a single property, determinable equally by x-ing and y-ing. After all, is this not just like the actual position with regard to shape, which is doubly determinable, by sight and by touch?

While I would not wish to quarrel with the main terms of this second reply, I should like briefly to indicate why I think that this final quite natural comparison with the case of shape will not do. It is quite conceivable that the correlation between x-ing and y-ing, in the case supposed, might be close enough to ensure that Martian colour-words designated doubly determinable properties, and yet that this correlation should break down in a limited class of cases: for instance owing to some differences between the two pairs of organs, objects which transmitted light of a particular wave-length might (in standard conditions) x blue but y black. If this were so, then for these cases the conflict would render decision about the real colour of the objects in question impossible. (I ignore the possibility that the real colour might be made to depend on the wave-length of the light transmitted, which would involve depriving colour of its status as a purely sensibly determinable property.)

I am however very much inclined to think that a corresponding limited breakdown in the correlation between sight and touch with regard to shape is not conceivable. The nature of the correlation between sight and touch is far too complicated a question to be adequately treated within the compass of this paper; so I shall attempt only to indicate, in relation to two comparatively simple imaginary cases, the special intimacy of this correlation. Both cases involve medium-sized objects, which are those with regard to which we are most willing to accept the equality of the arbitraments of sight and touch. The question at issue in each case is whether we can coherently suppose both (*a*) that, in a world which in general exhibits the normal correlation between sight and touch, some isolated object should standardly feel round but standardly look square, and also (*b*) that it should be undecidable, as regards that object, whether preference should be given to the deliverance of sight or to that of touch.

Case A. In this case I do not attribute to the divergent object the power of temporarily upsetting the correlation of sight and touch with regard to other normal objects while they are in its vicinity. Suppose that, feeling in my pocket, I were to find an object which felt as if it were round and flat like a penny, I take it out of my pocket and throw it on the table, and am astonished to see what looks like a square flat object: I find, moreover, that when surveyed by myself (and others) from various points it continues to look as a square object should look. I now shut my eyes and 'frame' the object by running my finger round its edge; my finger feels to me as if it were moving in a circle. I then open my eyes, and, since we are supposing that other objects are not affected by the divergent one, my finger also feels to me as if it were tracing a circular path, but not, of course, as if it were 'framing' the visible outline of the object. One possibility is that my finger is seen to cut through the corners of the visible outline of the divergent object; and I think that such a lack of 'visual solidity' would be enough to make us say that the object is really round, in spite of its visual appearance. Another possibility is that the visible path of my finger should be a circle within which the visible outline of the object is inscribed, and that, if I try, I fail to establish visible contact between my finger and the object's outline, except at the corners of that outline. I suggest that if the object's outline were visually unapproachable in this kind of way, this would very strongly incline us to say that the object was really round; and I suspect that this inclination could be decisively reinforced by the application of further tests of a kind to be mentioned in connection with the second case.

Case B. In this case I do attribute to the object the power of 'infecting' at least some other objects, in particular my finger or (more strictly) the path traced by my finger. Suppose that, as before, when I trace the felt outline of the divergent object it feels to me as if my finger is describing a circle, and also that, as before, the object looks square; now, however, the visible path of my moving finger is not circular but square, framing the visible outline of the object. Suppose also that I find a further object which is indisputably round, the size of which feels equal to the size which the divergent object is felt as having, and which (we will suppose) is not infected by proximity to the divergent object; if I place this unproblematic object behind the divergent one, as I move my finger around the pair of objects it *feels* as if I am continuously in contact with the edges of both objects, but it *looks* as if I am in continuous contact with the divergent object, but in only occasional contact with the normal object. (I am taking the case in which the corners of the visible outline of the divergent object overlap the visible outline of the normal object.) Given this information alone, I think that it cannot be decided what the real shape of the divergent object is; but there are various further tests which I can make. One of these would be to put the two objects on the table, the divergent object being on top, to place my finger and thumb so that they are in felt contact with both objects but are visually in contact only with opposed corners of the visible outline of the divergent object, and then raise my hand; if thereby I lift both objects the divergent object is really round; if I lift only the divergent object, it is really square.

A test closely related to the foregoing would be to discover through what sorts of aperture the divergent object could be made to pass, on the general principle that it is square pegs which fit into square holes and round pegs which fit into round holes. For example, suppose I find an aperture the real shape and size of which is such that, according to tactual comparison, it ought to accommodate the divergent object, while according to visual comparison it ought not to do so; then (roughly speaking) if the object can be made to pass through the aperture it is really round; if it cannot, it is really square. It seems to me that the decisiveness of this test can be averted only if we make one of two suppositions. We might suppose our fantasy-world to be such that apertures of a suitable real shape are not available to us; for this supposition, however, to be of interest, it would have to amount to the supposition of a *general* breakdown of the correlation of sight and touch as regards shape, which is contrary to the terms of our discussion, which is concerned only with the possibility of a limited breakdown in this respect. Alternatively we might suppose that when we attempt to make the divergent object pass through a suitably chosen aperture which is really round, it feels as if the object passes through, but it looks as if the object fails to pass through. On this supposition there is some prospect that the real shape of the divergent object should remain undecidable. But we must consider the consequences of this supposition. What, for example, happens to my finger when it is pushing the divergent object tactually, though not visually, through the aperture? In order to keep the question of the real shape undecidable, I think we shall have to suppose that the finger tactually moves into the aperture, but visually remains outside. Given this assumption it seems reasonable to conclude that it will have become a practical possibility, with regard to any object whatsoever, or at least any movable object, to divorce its tactual location from its visual location. Imagine, for example, that the divergent object is just outside one end of a suitably selected cylinder, and is attached to my waist by a string which passes through the cylinder; now I set myself the task of drawing the object through the cylinder by walking away. If I do not tug too hard, I can ensure that tactually my body, together with any objects attached to it, will move away from the cylinder, while visually it will not. And one might add, where shall *I* be then?

I suggest, then, that given the existence of an object which, for the Martians, standardly x-ed blue but y-ed black (its real colour being undecidable), no conclusion could be drawn to the effect that other objects do, or could as a matter of practical possibility be made to, x one way and y another way either in respect of colour or in respect of some other feature within the joint province of x-ing and y-ing; given, on the other hand, the existence of an object which, for us, standardly felt one shape

and looked another, then *either* its real shape would be nonetheless decid-
able, or it would be practically possible to disrupt in the case of at least
some other objects the correlation between sight and touch as regards at
least one feature falling within their joint domain, namely spatial location; at least some objects could be made standardly to feel as if they
were in one place and standardly to look as if they were in another.
Whether such notions as those of a material object, of a person and of
human action could apply, without radical revision, to such a world, and
whether such a world could be coherently supposed to be governed by
any system of natural laws, however bizarre, are questions which I shall
not here pursue.

To return to the main topic, I hope that I have put up a fair case for
supposing that suggestion (II) cannot be eliminated. How then are we
to deal with the difficulties which seemed to lead us back from suggestion (II) to suggestion (I), with a consequent impasse? The first of these
was that such an alleged special experience as that supposedly involved
in seeing eluded inspection and description. I think that this objection
conceals an illegitimate demand. We are being asked to examine and
describe the experience we have when we see, quite without reference
to the properties we detect or think we detect when we see. But this is
impossible, for the description of the experiences we have when we see
involves the mention of properties we detect or seem to detect. More
fully, the way to describe our visual experiences is in terms of how things
look to us, and such a description obviously involves the employment of
property-words. But in addition to the specific differences between visual
experiences, signalized by the various property words employed, there is
a generic resemblance signalized by the use of the word 'look', which differentiates visual from non-visual sense-experience. This resemblance
can be noticed and labelled, but perhaps not further described. To object
that one cannot focus one's attention, in a given case, on the experience of seeing as distinct from the properties detected is perhaps like
complaining that one cannot focus one's attention on the colour of an
object, ignoring its particular colour. So the initial assumption of the
independence of suggestions (I) and (II) has broken down: how extensive the breakdown is could be determined only by going on to consider
how far differences in character between things reduces to differences
between the experiences which people have or would have in certain
circumstances. This would involve a discussion of traditional theories of
perception for which at the moment I have neither time nor heart.

The second difficulty is that of explaining why, if sight is to be distinguished from other senses by the special character of the experiences
involved in seeing, there is a logical objection to the idea that we might
detect (say) the smells of things by means of experience of the visual
type. Why can we not see the smell of a rose? Well, in a sense we can; a
rose can (or at any rate conceivably might) look fragrant. But perhaps the
objector wants us to explain why a rose cannot look fragrant in the same

sense of 'look' in which it may look red. The answer here is presumably that had nature provided a closer correlation between the senses of sight and smell than in fact obtains, the word 'fragrant' might have been used to denote a doubly determinable property: in which case roses could have been said to look fragrant in just the sense of 'look' in which they now look red. But of course the current rules for the word 'fragrant' are adapted to the situation actually obtaining. If, however, the objector is asking us to explain why, on our view, given that fragrance is *merely* an olfactorily determinable property, it is not also at the same time a visually determinable property, then perhaps we may be excused from replying.

Note: It has been properly objected against me that, in comparing (on pages 148–152) the possibility of a limited breakdown in the correlation between x-ing and y-ing with the possibility of a corresponding limited breakdown in the correlation between sight and touch, I have cheated. For whereas I consider the possibility that a certain *class* of objects might x blue but y black, I consider only the possibility that a certain *isolated* object should standardly feel round but look square: I have failed to consider the possibility that, for example, all objects of a particular felt size which feel round should look square and that there should therefore be no normal holes to use for testing divergent objects.

I can here do no more than indicate the lines on which this objection should be met. (1) The supposed limited breakdown cannot be restricted to objects of particular shapes, since the dimensions of objects and of holes can be measured both tactually and visually by measuring rods: and what happens when a divergent measuring rod is bent double? (2) Any shape-divergent object would be tolerated tactually but not visually (or vice versa) by normal holes (if available) of more than one specifically different size. Consequently, since we are ruling out a *general* breakdown of the correlation between sight and touch as regards the shapes in question, there must be *at least some* normal holes which will tolerate tactually but not visually (or vice versa) *at least some* divergent objects: and this is enough for my purpose.

I owe this objection and the direction of part of the reply to Mr. G. Nozick of Princeton University.

5

Distinguishing the Senses

J. W. Roxbee Cox

I

I wish to consider two closely related questions. (1) By what criteria are the senses distinguished from one another? (2) How is it that, when one sees something, one is able to say that one *sees* it, as opposed to hearing or feeling it, for example, that when one hears something one is able to say that one hears it, etc? These questions (which I shall refer to as 'Question (1)' and 'Question (2)') have seldom been directly discussed. The absence of discussions of Question (2) is not easily explained; the failure to discuss Question (1) may be due to the fact that certain answers have seemed to different people so obvious that they did not need to be supported by argument. Thus one familiar type of answer to Question (1) is that certain physiological processes, involving certain parts of the body with which we are familiar, make an instance of perception a case of sight; the functioning of other processes, involving other familiar parts of the body, make it a case of hearing, etc. This may be called the 'Sense Organ' view ('SO' view for short). Another familiar answer is that there are characteristic experiences that are essential to seeing, feeling, etc.—the 'Characteristic Experience' view. A third answer is that seeing is perceiving colours, light and shade, shapes, etc.; while feeling is perceiving warmth, pressure, shape, etc., etc. This may be called the 'Characteristic Properties' view ('CP' view).[1]

I shall argue that the last of these approaches is on the right lines, although in need of improvement. The improved version I shall propose will be called a 'Key Feature' ('KF') account. After elaborating a Key Feature account in Sections VI to VIII, I shall qualify it, in order to accommodate what I think is the element of correctness in the SO account, presenting finally a 'Modified Key Feature' account (Section IX), which can answer Questions (1) and (2) satisfactorily. Much of the interest of

J. W. Roxbee Cox "Distinguishing the Senses", *Mind*, New Series, Volume 79, No. 316, pp. 530–550, 1970. (Reproduced with permission of Oxford Journals.)

---

[1] H. P. Grice has discussed these questions in "Some remarks about the senses" (in R. J. Butler (ed.), *Analytical Philosophy* (Oxford, 1962)). References to Grice are to that paper. [This volume chapter 4.].

the discussion attaches to the case of the sense of feeling. In the earlier sections the only kinds of feeling that I shall consider will be those covered by the description 'feeling things by touch'. This will simplify the discussion and prepare the way for a fuller treatment of the varieties of perception that we call feeling in Sections VII and VIII.

I shall begin by considering and rejecting the three answers to Question (1) that I have listed. This will help to justify the fuller treatment of the KF account; and the discussion of these views will also draw attention to some of the conditions that have to be met by any successful answer to the two Questions.

II. *THE SENSE ORGAN ACCOUNT*

Two distinct but not incompatible interpretations are possible of the Sense Organ view in its 'common sense' formulation.

Interpretation A: Physiological. When people talk of sense organs what we think of, at least at first, are the eyes, ears, nose, etc. On further thought however we may be inclined to extend our interpretation of the notion to include the physiological system whose functioning is necessary for the eyes, ears, nose, etc., to function in perception. We may call this the 'physiological' interpretation of the notion. On this interpretation, there are two ways in which the different sense organs might be distinguished from each other; (i) 'The eyes', as used in this context, or 'the organs of sight', might be taken to refer to the physiological system identifiable by the fact that it includes the eyes. Similarly for 'the ears', etc. (ii) 'The eyes', in this context, or 'the organs of sight', might be taken to refer to a physiological system distinguished from others by some such character as being sensitive to a certain kind of stimulus. The objection to the latter of course is that people who will be prepared to distinguish the different sense organs may be rather hazy about the physiological and physical factors in their functioning, especially when senses other than sight and hearing are taken into account. Thus (i) seems the more plausible way of understanding 'sense organ' on this physiological interpretation.

Interpretation B: Practical. A second way of interpreting the notion of a sense organ might be elicited from those who favour a Sense Organ account. Here we would take the sense organs, again exemplified by the eyes, ears, nose, etc., to be solely those parts of the body that we can use, or at least control, in the various kinds of perception; parts of the body that we direct, position, etc., or that we can close, block or avoid using, in order to perceive or in order not to perceive things. The problem of the precise identification of the organs of sight is avoided on this view, as our knowledge of the organs of sight will be manifested partly in our ability to use certain parts of our body—including parts about which we know nothing—in perceiving things. Referring to the sense organs as, *e.g.* 'the eyes' will merely be referring by its most easily distinguished element to the part of the body that we use for a certain kind of perception.

Since the eyes, ears, etc., are the most obvious elements in the sense organs on both the physiological and the practical interpretations, no inconsistency need result from combining the two. This is perhaps what usually happens when a Sense Organ view is proposed. Whichever interpretation is followed, the SO account appears open to serious objections. The two main ones are these. First, unless interpretation $A(ii)$ is followed and I have suggested this is implausible—a Sense Organ account will have difficulty in distinguishing between, *e.g.* seeing something with the use of the eyes and feeling something with the eyes. If the $A(i)$ view is followed, 'the organs of sight' means 'the system that includes the eyes'. We now have to distinguish two systems including the eyes, corresponding to seeing and feeling with the eyes. If we are not to fall back on the implausible $A(ii)$, we must make use of some further distinguishing feature. We might for example fall back on saying that these two cases involved different experiences, or that the properties characteristically perceived in these cases were different; that is, we would be falling back on the rival accounts of the criterion for distinguishing the senses. The practical interpretation, B, would have to be similarly amended, to distinguish the parts of the body, of which the eyes are the obvious feature, that we use when we see, from the parts, of which an eye is one feature, that we use, or at least can control, when we are feeling something with or in the eye. Once the SO account has been made to include features from the rival accounts, it loses much of its attractiveness. I shall be considering a composite account in Section IX.

The second objection is more decisive. What is the principle for classing together certain parts of the body as being the organs of sight, other parts as organs of hearing, etc.? Scientists might be interested in classifying the physiological processes involved, or the variety of stimuli, but there is no reason to think that such a concern underlies the use and value of the distinctions as they are ordinarily made. Why is the familiar classification not arbitrary, whereas a classification that grouped together the left eye, the left hand and the left ear as the organs of a certain kind of perception would seem arbitrary and absurd? Presumably there is some element common to the members of the groups of parts of the body that we call organs of sight, feeling, etc., that is not shared by the members of the group of 'left-hand organs'. To find such a feature, we shall again have to fall back on such considerations as the character of the experience, or the properties perceived, that are associated with the functioning of the various organs.

I may anticipate here a possible misunderstanding of the arguments of this Section. Although I have argued that the distinctions *between* the senses cannot be made by reference to the SO account, I do not wish to suggest that the senses, taken together, cannot be distinguished from other sources of beliefs by reference to the sense organs. A causal account of perception, for instance, might contrast those parts of the body which, when affected in a certain way by something outside the body, gave rise to an awareness of the presence of what was affecting it, with those others, of whose being affected we will normally be quite unaware.

III. *THE CHARACTERISTIC EXPERIENCE ACCOUNT*

I give reasons here, not so much for rejecting the Characteristic Experience account, as for not discussing it. First, my main reason for avoiding a discussion of it is that the onus would appear to lie on its supporters to show that the description 'the special character of the experience of seeing' has any application—if descriptions of what is actually perceived are not counted as descriptions of the experience. As Grice, who does however view this approach with some favour, says, echoing Moore, these experiences seem to be 'as it were, diaphanous: if we were asked to pay close attention, on a given occasion, to our seeing or feeling as distinct from what was being seen or felt, we should not know how to proceed' (p. 144 [this volume p. 93]). Secondly, supposing that one were sympathetic to a Characteristic Experience account, an elaboration of it would require a full discussion of various other matters with far-reaching implications. For example, the Characteristic Experience account seems to have to allow for the following possibility. The visual experience, that is, the one that normally accompanies our perception of, for example, colours, might on some occasion accompany the perception of sounds, and we should have the situation of sounds being seen. If such an eventuality is to be describable, the visual experience must itself be identifiable other than as whatever experience one has when one sees. This raises difficulties of a familiar kind. In this case there is also the special difficulty of showing people who claim not to be aware of such an experience that they do in fact continually have it. The discussion of such questions as these in connexion with a Characteristic Experience account may well await a full elaboration of such an account by a supporter or sympathizer.

IV. *DIRECT PERCEPTION*

In order to present and discuss the Characteristic Properties account satisfactorily, it will be necessary to introduce the notion I shall call 'direct perception'. (This notion of 'direct perception' will be seen to be closely related to Grice's notion of a property being 'visually simple' (p. 142 [this volume p. 91]).) The need for it is suggested by an obvious objection that might be made to the CP account as I formulated it in the opening paragraph: 'seeing is perceiving colours, light and shade, shapes, etc.; feeling is perceiving warmth, pressure, shape, etc.' If this is interpreted as it is natural to interpret it, as saying that when I perceive something to be warm, I am feeling it to be warm, the objection may be made that we often *see* things to be warm. Again one may be able to see that a noise is loud, through seeing children covering their ears, and so on. The CP theorist will no doubt be impatient with such objections. He might naturally say that we cannot strictly speaking *see* that something is warm or loud, in the way that we can see things to be red and round, feel things to be warm and hear things to be loud. The CP theorist is relying here on rather imprecise terms, 'strictly speaking', and 'seeing things the way we can see things to be red'. The following account of direct perception attempts to put more precisely the sort of point being made here. The notion will also be crucial for the discussion of the Key Feature account.

We may consider possible answers to the question, 'How did you tell that it is...?' asked of someone who is known to be, say, looking at or listening to the things in question.

Case 1. One kind of answer would be that he was able to tell because he saw or heard that the thing had certain other features. He could tell that the car was not new *by* the spots of rust; he could tell *from* the character of the orchestration that the work was by Prokofiev. He could indicate to others how to recognize what he was able to tell about these things, by drawing their attention to these features.

Case 2. A second kind of answer would be that he could just *see* that the car was not new, or that he could just *tell* that the work was by Prokofiev; that he did not particularly notice certain features and conclude from their presence that the car was not new or the work of Prokofiev. Nevertheless, he would agree, he could still pick out the significant features, in order to show others how to recognize the used car or the work of Prokofiev.

In this case, where the man has not gone through any process of inference, it is still true that these indicating features have been perceived by him. We can confidently say this, despite the fact that he might have some difficulty in isolating them.

Case 3. I now wish to distinguish a third case, where a man's answer to the question 'How did you tell that it is...?' is that (*a*) he did not tell *by* anything (this part of the answer is the same as in Case 2); and further that (*b*) he could not pick out any significant features in order, *e.g.* to explain to someone else how he recognized such a state of affairs. His perception that the thing has a certain property or feature, or that a certain state of affairs exists, does not involve his perceiving that it has other properties which he would recognize as indicating the presence of the first property, feature or state of affairs. It is this that I call a case of direct perception.

The man who says that, strictly speaking, we cannot see things to be warm or loud, no doubt has such a special kind of case of seeing in mind. What seems to be true, although it may stand in need of explanation, is that a man will be able to say in such a case that the presence of a property or feature, or the existence of a state of affairs, that he can perceive, does *not* involve his perceiving that it has other properties that he would recognize as indicating the presence of the first.

Examples of direct perception are provided by the most common kinds of case where we perceive something to be red, or perceive something to be loud; where we can say that our perception that the thing has this property takes place without our perceiving that it has other properties that we recognize as indicating the first. We may naturally talk in such cases of 'directly seeing', etc.

V. *THE CHARACTERISTIC PROPERTIES ACCOUNT*

The CP account may now be formulated with the help of the terminology of direct perception. According to this account, seeing is just perceiving that involves directly perceiving that things have colours, light and shade, shape, size, surface texture, spatial relations, etc.; hearing is perceiving that involves directly perceiving that things have pitch, timbre, loudness, etc. This position has the merit of giving a straightforward answer to Question (2). If we directly perceive something to have certain properties, we will, if the CP account is correct, thereby know which sense is involved.

Unfortunately, in this unqualified form, the CP account is fundamentally incoherent. When it is said of seeing, for example, that it involves directly perceiving things to have colours, shapes, etc., are we to understand that if I directly perceive something to be red, then I see it? We shall be inclined surely to answer 'Yes'. Then if I directly perceive something to be smooth, I see it? Clearly not. I may be able to *feel* that it is smooth, and may not see it at all. It seems that we must interpret the list 'colours, light and shade, shape, size, etc.', not as a disjunction, as at first seemed natural, but as a conjunction. Only if you directly perceive the thing to be smooth, *and* to have colour or character of light and shade, *and* to have other properties on the list, will it be a case of seeing it to be smooth. But even this interpretation of the CP account is unsatisfactory. I might directly perceive the thing to be smooth by feeling it, while directly perceiving it to be red and to have other properties on the list by seeing it to have them. Thus the conjunctive interpretation of the requirement for *seeing* it to be smooth would be satisfied; whereas in fact I would be *feeling* it to be smooth.

The CP theorist would seem to have to say that the very same perception, or 'act of perceiving' or 'experience of perceiving' is involved in directly perceiving that it is red and that it is smooth, when we see it to be both red and smooth; while when we see it to be red and feel it to be smooth, two different perceptions are involved. If such a suggestion is to be made out, the CP theorist must be able to explain what it is that makes directly perceiving it to be red and directly perceiving it to be smooth just *one* perception or act or experience in the first case, but two perceptions, etc, in the second. Until this task has been performed, the CP account remains incoherent relying as it must on an unexplained but very crucial interpretation of the word 'and' in its formulation.

Grice offers a striking illustration of the weakness of the CP account (pp. 137–138 [this volume p. 87]). "Suppose a man to be resting a half-crown on the palm of one hand and a penny on the palm of the other; he might (perhaps truthfully) say, 'The half-crown looks to me larger than the penny, though they feel the same size.'" Grice points out that if we apply the criteria suggested by what I have called the CP account, the man has said four things. (We may take Grice's use of 'direct' here to be equivalent for our purposes to my use of it.)

"(1) The coins directly seem to have certain spatial and colour properties.
(2) The coins directly seem to have certain properties drawn from the 'tactual' list.
(3) The half-crown directly seems larger than the penny.
(4) The coins directly seem to be of the same size.

But there is nothing in this statement of the facts to tell us whether the coins *look* different in size but *feel* the same size, or alternatively *feel* different in size but *look* the same size."

This is clearly an illustration of the general objection that I have just stated. I quote it for the further reason that it will provide a test for the Key Feature account that I wish now to propose.

VI. *THE KEY FEATURE ACCOUNT*

It is convenient to regard this view as arising out of the attempt to improve the CP account. We saw that according to the natural interpretation of that view, we shall expect its supporters to say, at least at first, that if I directly perceive a thing to be red, I see it to be red. We may expect them to become hesitant about saying this however, once it becomes clear that the corresponding claim cannot be maintained for the case where I directly perceive something to be *smooth*. The CP account seems to assume that the different characteristic properties are all of equal standing. At this point however one might naturally single out colour, light and shade from the other visible properties, and hold that (*a*) if one's perception involves directly perceiving that a thing has a certain colour or light property, then one sees that thing; and (*b*) if one's perception that a thing has a certain other property involves directly perceiving that it has some colour or light property, then one sees that it has that other property. In the case of sight, having some colour property may appropriately be called a '*key feature*' of what is perceived, accounting

also for our *seeing* that the thing has other properties, such as smoothness, roundness, etc. When we perceive something to have a property
that appears in more than one of the lists of characteristic properties, the
property will be one the perception of which on any occasion requires
the direct perception of one or other of the special properties I am calling key features.

The key feature for sight, which I have so far referred to above as
'some colour or light property', is, as Aristotle remarked, not easily indicated by a short phrase. We may perceive that a thing is illuminated, is
lighter than something else, that it is shiny, or that there is some variety
of light and shade, dullness or brilliance, that it has some particular hue,
is phosphorescent, etc. It will be convenient to refer to a thing's having
some selection of these properties as its *having some colour property*.

The key features for the other senses appear to be these. For hearing,
having some loudness and timbre; for taste, having some taste; and for
smell, having some odour. The case of feeling is more complex, and will
be fully discussed in Sections VII and VIII. In order to illustrate the
application of the KF account, I shall assume as a simplification in this
Section that there is a key feature for feeling things by touch, namely,
having some feel to the touch. That this is an oversimplification, although
harmless here, will become clear in the following Sections.

Comparing the KF account with the CP account, it might be objected
that the new account has merely replaced the crucial 'and'-relation in the
list of characteristic properties by the relation of 'involving' or 'requiring' which holds between a key feature on the one hand and the other
characteristic properties perceptible by the sense in question on the
other, and that this does not really make much difference.

It is true that the move from the CP account to the KF account has
this form; but the difference is still a substantial one. The force of the
'involving' or 'requiring' relation may be brought out by considering the
example of shape.

There are two ways in which we may perceive the shape of a thing,
by sight and by touch. If we perceive the shape by sight, this requires
us to directly perceive that the thing has some colour property; if we
perceive it by touch, this requires us to directly perceive that it has some
feel to the touch. To suppose that we perceived the shape of a thing, and
neither perceived the thing to have some colour property nor perceived
it to have some feel to the touch is to suppose something inconsistent
with our actual experience of perception. It is of course conceivable that
we should be able to perceive shapes in other ways, through hearing
perhaps, or through some quite novel sense. As a matter of fact however,
there are just these two ways.

It is therefore quite natural to say that the perception of shape *involves*
or *requires* the direct perception of one or other of these properties, or
even to say that the perception of shape *must* involve the direct perception of one of these. This does not mean that it is logically impossible

that things should have been otherwise, as I have just pointed out. On the other hand, it means more than that the perception of shape is always accompanied by the direct perception of one of them. The difference may be brought out by considering a world in which the seeing of some colour was always accompanied by the seeing of determinate shape. It would not be the case even so that the perception of colour required the perception of shape. One would not perceive the colour *through* perceiving the shape. I am suggesting, however, that we perceive shapes through directly perceiving the presence of some colour property or through directly perceiving something to have some feel to the touch.

The KF account can answer Question (2) quite easily. In any but the most abnormal circumstances, one will be able to answer the question, Does your perception of the shape involve the direct perception of some colour property or the direct perception of some feel to the touch? If the first is correct, it is a case of seeing, if the second is a case of feeling. We may of course expect to be able to elicit from a person the information about the direct perception of the key feature, without having to use any but the simplest language, as is shown by the introduction of the terminology of direct perception in Section III.

The satisfactoriness of the KF account may be illustrated with Grice's case of the coins, which the CP account cannot deal with. The KF account can link the first proposition with the third in Grice's list, and the second with the fourth. Thus what the man says is equivalent to: (1) the half-crown seems larger than the penny, and (3) the seeming-perception of this relationship involves the direct perception that the coins have some colour property; while (2) the half-crown and the penny seem equal in size, and (4) the seeming-perception of this relationship involves the direct perception that the coins have some feel to the touch.

In contrast to the SO and the CP accounts, the KF account is not open to an accusation of arbitrariness. I suggested earlier that the SO account provides no principle for grouping together as organs of a single sense a certain set of sense organs. Similarly, there is, as Grice remarks, a certain arbitrariness about the CP account. "To say that colour is a visual property would seem to amount to no more than saying that colour is a member of a group of properties the others of which are.... This leaves membership of the group as an apparently arbitrary matter" (p. 140 [this volume p. 89]). The KF account will group properties together as visual properties according to a principle giving a central position to the property of having some colour, as was indicated in the first paragraph of this section.

A final point for the understanding of the KF acount is this. It is not being claimed that whenever we see anything, then we directly perceive something to have some specific colour property; that we directly perceive something to be a dark shade of brown, or brilliantly glowing. It is required only that we directly perceive that something has some colour property or other. We may not notice at all *what* colour property it has. A rather extreme example will illustrate this point. Suppose one is reading something written in a variety of coloured inks on paper of variegated colour, in shifting multicoloured lighting conditions. Seeing a particular word will involve directly perceiving that what one sees has some colour property, but we need not notice what colour property it actually has.

VII. *FEELING: ONE SENSE OR MANY?*

Some of the examples considered so far have been taken from the field of perceiving things by touch, but we have not yet considered at all any of the other varieties of perception that we group together with this as feeling: feeling warm, feeling a room to be warm, feeling a pill go down the throat, feeling the dampness of a towel, the dryness of the air, etc. It is by no means obvious that these kinds of perception must form a single sense in the way in which sight, hearing, taste and smell have been seen to. We must allow for the possibility that feeling is a kind of rag-bag sense, or strictly a number of senses, the word feeling being used to cover perceiving that does not fall neatly into certain other categories. This view was suggested by W. C. Kneale in "Sensation and the physical world" (*Philosophical Quarterly*, vol. i (1950–51), p. 116). It appears to be supported by the great variety of kinds of feeling that can be distinguished. We may begin by noticing that there does not appear to be a property of what is felt that can fill the role of key feature in all the different kinds of case. I list some of the varieties of feeling below. I shall call cases (1) 'contact feeling' and cases (2)-(4) 'non-contact feeling'. Case (5) will be found to be more closely related to the latter category.

(1) The feature of directly perceiving something touching one is perhaps the most obvious candidate for the key feature role—either pressing hard or lightly touching, or somewhere in between. But the following cases of feeling do not involve the direct perception of something touching one.

(2) There are the familiar cases of feeling the air or a room to be warm, and feeling the warmth of something that radiates heat, where nothing need be perceived to be touching one. Feeling a breeze or the wind will perhaps always involve this kind of feeling of warmth or coolness, often together with the perception of other things such as the movement of the hair of the head or on the arms. Feeling a high wind, or feeling the water to be cool or warm when we are immersed falls into this category, although most often no doubt it is accompanied by the direct perception of something touching. Although it is accompanied by this perception of something touching, we do not feel the warmth or the coolness *by* feeling something touching. So even here there is not a shared key feature.

(3) We may be able to feel that there is some chemical adulterating the atmosphere, or that onions have been chopped, or that the atmosphere is rather dry, with the eyes or with the nose, where no direct perception of something touching is involved.

(4) One may perceive something to be live (electrically), without directly perceiving anything touching one.

(5) In the case of things that we feel going on inside our bodies, it is true that some involve the direct perception of some pressure or of some contact, as with swallowing a pill; and some may involve the direct perception of two parts of the body being in contact, as in some pulsations. But it would be difficult to maintain that such contact is always directly perceived, or even, as D. M. Armstrong claims in *Bodily Sensations* (London, 1962, pp. 36–37), that "Except for heat and cold, the properties of our body immediately perceived by [feeling] are purely spatial properties". Chemical properties seem just as likely objects of such perception. I shall not discuss this kind of feeling separately in what follows. I suggest later that it can for our present purpose be treated as if it were a case of non-contact feeling.

Thus the most obvious candidate for the role of key feature, the feature of *something touching one*, is not satisfactory. The only other candidate likely to suggest itself, I think, would be the property of having some degree of warmth or coolness. However, what plausibility this suggestion may have will vanish once we remember that the direct perception of the key feature must not merely accompany the perception of other properties; these other properties must be perceived through the direct perception of the key feature. The other properties that we feel things to have are not perceived through the direct perception that something is warm or cool.

In the absence of a single key feature it is natural to conclude that a 'Many Senses' view of feeling is correct. However, once we incline to this view, certain questions will have to be answered; and I shall in fact suggest that when they are answered, we will have good reasons for favouring a 'Single Sense' view.

First, if the perception verb 'feel' is to be understood as equivalent to a disjunction 'feel something to touch one, or feel the warmth of something around one, or feel the dryness of the air, etc.', then the answer given by the KF account to Question (2) will seem rather implausible in the case of feeling. We are able to say that we are feeling something in one way or another, the Many Senses view seems to suggest, through recognizing that we are perceiving in a way that involves the direct perception of a certain one of the key features that correspond to the various 'sub-senses', as we may call them, of feeling. However, even supposing— what is far from obvious—that we are all familiar with the membership of the list of sub-senses of feeling and their key features, the fact is that we seem more certain that particular cases of perception are instances of feeling *of some kind or other* than we are about what specific kinds of feeling they are. Thus we do not seem to use such a disjunctive list. Rather we seem to have a general idea of what will make an instance of perception a case of feeling. A point that I shall argue is closely connected with this is the following. It is not difficult to imagine cases where a new kind of perception would be classified quite readily as 'feeling'. This readiness suggests that there is a rationale behind the grouping together of these apparently distinct senses. This brings us to the second question that must be faced if we are inclined to accept a Many Senses view of feeling. What is it that causes us to group these allegedly distinct senses together as a single one, for ordinary purposes?

It is easy to see roughly the sort of thing they have in common. In all these cases, our perceiving something happening, some state of affairs, or some thing, involves the perception of some part of the body. The part of the body that we say we feel it with or in is included in what is perceived. We may ask therefore how, more exactly, a part of the body is involved in what is perceived in the case of feeling, and in what way it is involved here in which it is not in the case of sight, for example.

We may say that we can feel a lump in the mattress, the vibration of a machine, the warmth of a room, the dryness of the air, a process of digestion. But when we feel the lump, we will feel it with the hand or the back; we will feel the vibration in the legs; we will feel the warmth in the face, or all over; the dryness with the eyes, etc. This suggests that a feature common to *all* cases of feeling is just that (still speaking loosely) what we perceive will include something about how some part of the body is *being affected by* something else. The lump is pressing against the hand or the back; the machine is producing a sensation in the legs, etc.

While it will be agreed that feeling always involves perceiving something affecting a part of the body, it remains to be shown that this provides us with a feature to distinguish feeling from the other senses, since we frequently see, hear, taste and smell things having to do with and affecting the body. It may be pointed out that just as we feel something about a part of the body when we feel a dog brush past us, so we may see our eyes in a mirror, when a mirror is part of the scene before us. The way in which the perception of something affecting a part of the body is essential to the case of feeling may be brought out by comparing the following examples.

I may see a scene which includes my eyes reflected in a mirror on the end of my field of vision. A description of what is seen will include a reference to my body, in particular the eyes. We may also describe a related scene, where we see the same except that the eyes are no longer visible, the part of the mirror in which they could be seen being no longer visible. The rest of what we perceive may be exactly the same. Compare now something that I may feel: a dog brushing past my leg. A description of what I feel will include a reference to my body, in particular my leg. But we cannot describe a related scene, where everything is the same except that nothing about a part of the body enters into the description of what is perceived—unless of course we suppose that we perceive it with a different sense, and *e.g.* see the dog nearly brush my leg. In the case of sight it was not necessary to suppose that the second description was of a scene perceived with a different sense.

The key feature for feeling, treated as a single sense, may be indicated as follows. An instance of perceiving will be a case of feeling when (*a*) a description of what is directly perceived includes a mention of a part of the body being affected in some way by something else that is being perceived, and (*b*) this direct perception of a fact about a part of the body is necessary for the perception of the remainder of what is perceived. It is condition (*b*) that distinguishes a case of feeling from a case of sight such as the example just considered. We may say for brevity that an instance of perceiving is a case of feeling when the perception 'essentially involves our perceiving a part of the body'.

We may illustrate the role of this key feature for feeling, taking the case of things being in contact with the body. There are two, or perhaps three, ways in which we may perceive something touch our body. Sight, which requires that we directly perceive what is perceived to have some colour property. Perhaps also hearing, which requires that we directly perceive what we perceive to have some timbre and loudness. And feeling, which requires that our perception essentially involves the perception of a part of the body. In any particular case we can normally say which of these key features is involved. 'Was your perception of the dog's touching your leg such that, if you had not perceived something about a part of your body, then the rest of what you perceived would have been different in other respects also?' One answer might be, 'No: apart from there being no contact between the dog and my leg, the rest could have been the same.' This would have been consistent with its being sight or hearing, but not with its being feeling. In the case of feeling the answer would be something like this. 'Yes. If I hadn't directly perceived that something was happening to some part of my body, I would not have perceived some of the other things I perceived—for example, the dampness of the dog's fur.'

We can now answer the first of the two questions suggested by the Many Senses view of feeling earlier in this Section. The existence of a shared key feature for all cases of feeling explains how they can be grouped together and distinguished from the other senses (except, as we shall see later, taste). It thus suggests an answer to Question (2) for the case of feeling. Our ability to say that we are feeling, in one way or another, reflects the presence of this feature shared by all the different kinds of feeling, rather than any clear awareness on our part of the character of the different sub-senses that the Many Senses view requires us to be able to recognize. This shared key feature also explains the ease with which we may agree that certain imaginable kinds of novel perception would be (or would not be) classified as kinds of feeling. The test we use is, would the perception of something in this way essentially involve our perceiving some part of our body?

We may after all therefore be inclined to treat feeling as a single sense, with a single key feature; although in this case the key feature is less a feature of what is perceived than of the perceiving as a whole. The second question raised earlier still remains however. Granted that the various kinds of feeling *can* be grouped together as a single sense, why should we, in our ordinary thinking at least, tend actually to group them together? I wish to suggest that at least part of the answer may be supplied if we notice two purposes that are served by our distinguishing the senses. These functions will be performed if we talk of a single sense, feeling, just as well as if we distinguished a multitude of sub-senses in this area. In the case of one exception to this general claim—taste—we actually do distinguish a separate sense; while in the case of some *apparent* exceptions we shall see that these functions will in fact normally be performed even if we do not distinguish separate senses.

VIII. *TWO MAIN FUNCTIONS*

Among the useful purposes served by the existence of the words corresponding to the different senses, we may single out two whose importance will not be doubted. First, to mention the specific sense involved in an instance of perception will indicate what properties or features of what is perceived we may expect the perceiver to be in a position to notice if they are present. We may call this the function of indicating 'complementary features', or 'CF' function for short. Thus if I say that I saw a dog brush past me, you may expect me to be able to tell you, *e.g.* its size, colouring, the shape of its ears, what it is doing, whether it looks fierce, what is written on its collar, etc. If I say that I felt a dog brush past my leg, you might again expect me to be able to say a little about what it was doing or what it was like, its speed, its dampness or dryness, whether its fur is soft or wiry, etc. Clearly the list of complementary features will include the characteristic properties for a certain sense, but as the illustrations show, many other properties and features of a situation may be included also.

Secondly, mention of what sense is involved will indicate to us what we should have to do—to look, to listen to or for something, etc.—if we wish to perceive the same thing or happening and the same features of it for ourselves. We may call this the function of guiding 'further observation' or 'FO' function. When this function is performed we shall of course also be shown what we should do if we wish to perceive the same thing in an independent way, as a check on someone else's judgement for example. If I say that I can hear a woodpecker, and you wish to perceive what I do in the same way, you must listen; if you wish to perceive the alleged woodpecker, but to do so in a way that will provide an independent check, you will know that you should for example use your eyes.

It is obvious that if I had used only a general word like 'perceive', 'observe', 'tell', instead of 'see' and 'feel' in these examples, the two functions would not have been performed. Of course the same information can be given in other ways in certain situations. Sometimes we explicitly mention a key feature and indicate that we directly perceived it to be present; sometimes general knowledge will be a safe guide to what key feature is involved. This latter possibility will turn out to be of some importance in explaining why we do not distinguish certain sub-senses of feeling as separate senses in the way that we distinguish taste.

I wish now to argue that the CF and FO functions will be served if we group all the various kinds of feeling together, just as adequately as if we use the expressions that indicate the separate sub-senses of feeling. To show this, I shall first suggest why taste, which would qualify as a case of feeling according to the overall key feature criterion, is nevertheless singled out as a distinct sense, and then show how other apparent candidates for being singled out in the same way lack some of the features of taste and thus need not be so distinguished.

To see why taste is singled out, we must consider how adequately or inadequately the CF and FO functions would be performed if the verb 'taste' were replaced in its occurrences by 'feel'. The question has two main parts. We must consider the effect of using 'feel' where we now use 'taste'; and also the effect of using 'feel' where we now use 'feel', in a situation in which it can also be used where we would now use 'taste'. It will be convenient to consider contact feeling and non-contact feeling as separate cases.

Suppose, first, that we use 'feel' to talk about tasting; 'feeling garlic in the stew', 'feeling something peculiar about the orange', etc. For contact feeling the CF function will be served. We shall expect to be able to tell equally about such things as the hardness or softness, shape, size and texture of the mouthful of stew or the orange. Will non-contact feeling properties be felt if present? Radiant warmth from a part of the thing not in contact could be felt. Similarly any electric charge of a part of the body not in contact, if it were such as to affect us without contact, could be felt while we tasted it. So the CF function seems to be served for both classes of felt feature. On the other hand the FO function is obviously not performed. We cannot use just any of the parts of the body with which we can feel in order to observe further the flavour of the orange: only the tongue will do.

Suppose, next, that we are using 'feel' where we now use 'feel', in a situation where we can also use it where we now use 'taste'. The complementary features for what is felt will now include flavours: but we cannot expect to perceive the flavour a thing may have if we merely hold it in our hands or have it in front of us. Thus neither for contact feeling nor for non-contact feeling will the CF function be performed. What of the FO function? Consider first contact feeling. Feeling with the mouth and tongue will tell us something about the hardness, shape, size, surface texture, etc., of a thing just as feeling with other parts of the body will. The FO function will be performed here. Turning to non-contact feeling, we find that the FO function will be performed in some cases, such as radiated warmth, but not for others, such as the dryness of the air. Not any part of the body with which we feel or taste will enable us to tell that the air is dry.

These considerations show that the performance of the CF and FO functions requires that we have a separate word for the sense of taste. The argument also suggests a further problem however. Not only are there good reasons for distinguishing taste as a sense distinct from feeling; there appear to be equally good reasons for distinguishing, for example, contact feeling and non-contact feeling as separate senses. Again, should we not distinguish between the varieties of non-contact feeling as well? Thus arguments like those just used would seem available to show that the sub-sense for feeling the dryness or adulteration of the air should be distinguished from the sub-sense for feeling radiated warmth. There are however certain special features of these other kinds of feeling that explain why it is not necessary to distinguish separate senses for each case.

There are three points to notice here. (i) The class of things that we feel, and so can tell to have various properties, by contact feeling does not overlap the class of things that we can feel to have various properties by non-contact feeling—with the exception of feeling things to be warm, cool, etc., which I shall discuss separately below. Thus we can feel a towel, and feel it is dry, by contact feeling; and we can feel that the air is dry by non-contact feeling. By contact feeling we may feel bodies, and liquids and certain of their properties and relations; while by non-contact feeling we can perceive things outside this class to have certain properties. The properties may be common to the two kinds of feeling; but the things that have the properties are different.

(ii) In the case of non-contact feeling, when we say that someone can feel something, we shall normally mention the property whose possession by the thing is felt and the thing that has the property. We shall say that we feel that the air is dry, that we can feel a draught (of air).

Taking points (i) and (ii) together it is clear that when someone is reported to feel something, where the feeling is non-contact feeling, the report will indicate the thing that has the property (point (ii)); and since the classes of things felt in these two ways do not overlap (point (i)), we shall thus know whether contact or non-contact feeling is involved. Further, (iii) where non-contact feeling is involved, mention of the property felt will be enough to indicate the specific sub-sense and thus will also indicate complementary features and lines of further observation. If for example we are said to feel how dry the air is, the complementary features will include any adulteration and noticeable warmth or coolness of the air, and any slight motion, such as a breeze. Further observation of the situation as perceived will have to be with those parts of the body sensitive to the dryness of the air—for most people the eyes and the nose. It will also be seen that points (i) to (iii) apply to the case of feeling things inside us.

Thus, if we exclude the case of warmth, we see that the CF and FO functions will in fact be performed in the case of feeling, even if we do not actually use separate perception verbs for the various sub-senses. We must now consider the special case of warmth, which may be perceived both by contact and by non-contact feeling. The point (i) above does not apply in this case. Many things can be felt to be warm in both ways: food, domestic radiators, hot liquids, etc. A quite separate consideration must be noticed in order to explain how in many of these cases, but not all, the CF and FO functions may be performed.

I may be able to feel that a radiator is hot either by contact or by non-contact feeling, and a report that I can tell it is on does not indicate which. Such cases are exceptional, however. For many cases, the mention of the *degree* of warmth or heat attributed, together with the mention of the thing to which it is attributed, will in fact perform these functions. To feel that a heating stove is quite warm, I must touch it. The complementary features will be those available to one who touches such a thing, which will not necessarily be all those that would be available to one who felt and handled it. They will probably include stickiness and surface texture, for example, but not overall shape or size. To feel that a stove is very hot indeed, I may either hold my hands or cheek quite close, or I may touch it. In either case the complementary features will in fact be those for the non-contact feeling of warmth—probably none at all. Even if I touch the hot stove I cannot press hard enough against it normally to gather more than that it is very hot indeed.

The same considerations will account for the performance of the FO function. Whether a thing is not warm enough for us to tell that it is warm without having to touch it, or whether it is too hot to touch, will determine the line of further observation for someone who wishes to perceive the same features of the situation as we have.

These considerations explain how in many cases of the feeling of warmth the two functions will be performed. There will, however, be many cases where they will not be performed; cases of things that are quite hot but not too hot to touch, where contact feeling and non-contact feeling will both be possible. We may conclude then that normally, but not always, the CF and FO function, performed through the use of the separate sense verbs for seeing hearing, etc., will be performed in the various kinds of case of feeling without the use of separate verbs for the sub-senses. We thus have an answer to the question posed at the end of Section VII: granted that the various kinds of sub-sense of feeling could understandably be grouped either as a single sense or as several senses, why is it that we actually tend to treat them as a single sense? The answer is that the two important functions served by the use of separate sense verbs will still be performed even if we have only a single word for the variety of kinds of feeling. This answer should be taken in conjunction with the other important point mentioned in the penultimate paragraph of Section VII, that the Single Sense view makes it easy to see how Question (2) is to be answered.

IX. *THE MODIFIED KEY FEATURE ACCOUNT*

The following example suggests that a slight modification may be necessary of the KF account that has been elaborated in the last three sections. Consider the case of a man found by doctors to be, as we may say, medically blind; lacking the physiological equipment that normal people have, and lacking anything similar but, for example, differently situated. Suppose that this man is able nevertheless to do and understand all those things for which sight is taken to be necessary. He is even able to contrast the case where a shape is discriminable through the variety of colour properties that are directly perceptible with the case where a shape is discriminable through features directly perceptible by feeling. If the KF requirement is taken to provide the complete criterion for sight, then this man must be said to be able to see things. However, it is not clear that we will in fact wish to say this, or that we will wish to deny it. It looks as if our concept of sight includes some such condition as that the direct perception of the key feature should take place 'by means of the eyes or organs sufficiently like them'. I shall suggest the implications of this for the KF account.

Let us suppose that the criterion of sight were in fact composite in the way just suggested. The SO element could not be the fundamental one, since a composite criterion in which it was fundamental would be open to the objections brought against the simple SO criterion. Furthermore, if we suppose it to be the fundamental element, it must still be allowed that the KF element is crucially important, since it will normally be our knowledge of what key feature is directly perceived that tells us which sense organs are involved in the perception of something. It seems reasonable therefore to take the KF element as the fundamental one.

It may be noticed here that someone able to understand and inclined to favour the Characteristic Experience view might wish to argue that a similar role, at least a subordinate one, should be allowed to the experience characteristic of seeing. If the experience of perception were very different, even though the KF criterion was satisfied, we might be unsure whether to call the perception seeing or not. This suggests that the requirement that the eyes or something sufficiently like them should be involved in seeing is just one instance of a more general requirement that to be a clear case of sight, an instance of perception must not only satisfy the KF criterion, but also have the sorts of characteristic that are normally associated with perception that satisfies the criterion. The modification that must be made to the KF criterion is thus only a minor one.

The example of the medically blind but visually capable man can be paralleled for the case of hearing. The case of feeling does not appear to present this problem however. There is nothing especially puzzling about the supposition that a man might be able to feel things with parts of the body that are not in our experience sensitive, such as the hair. The cases of smell and taste are probably to be classified with sight and hearing in this connexion. Although the specific role of the SO element in the criterion is different in the different cases, the general formulation of the criterion remains the same. The sense involved in an instance of perception is determined by the direct perception of the appropriate key feature, together with the presence of the kinds of circumstance that are known normally to accompany cases of perception involving the direct perception of that key feature.

6

The Senses of Martians

C. A. J. Coady

I have a bone to pick with certain inhabitants of outer space who owe their existence to Professor H. P. Grice. The objectionable creatures are Martians and they make their appearance in Grice's article "Some Remarks about the Senses"[1] where their existence and conversation offer crucial support to Grice's account of the criteria by which we might decide to discriminate different perceptual senses.

Grice suggests that there seem to be four different and apparently independent ways of distinguishing the senses:

(I) The special features detected (or seemingly detected) by the operation of the senses.

(II) The "special introspectible character of the experiences" of the different senses.

(III) The external physical conditions upon which the senses depend.

(IV) The character of the putative sense organs and their modes of connection with the brain.

He further suggests that these may not be exclusive criteria and then devotes a major part of the article to defending the claim that criterion (II) "cannot be eliminated" in favor of (I) or some combination of the other criteria. It is to support this claim that he calls upon the Martians who are so arranged that if we went by (I), (III), and (IV) we would have to say that they had the same senses as we whereas if we invoke (II) we must say that they possess a sixth sense. Grice argues that, as described, "we should be inclined to say" that they do possess a new sense.

---

[1] In *Analytical Philosophy*, Series I, ed. by R. J. Butler (Oxford, 1962 [and this volume, chapter 4]). Bracketed page references in my text refer to this edition. Grice raises many important and complex issues in the course of his discussion and I make no pretense of dealing with them all.

The Case of the Friendly Martians goes as follows. On invading earth they amicably teach us their language, and our only problem is that we find no verb in their language which unquestionably corresponds to our verb "see." Instead, we find two verbs which we decide to render as "x" and "y" and which function in such a way that the Martians speak of themselves as x-ing and y-ing things to be of certain colors, sizes, and shapes. Further, they are similar to Earthmen in appearance except that in their heads they have, one above another, two pairs of organs "not perhaps exactly like one another but each pair more or less like our eyes: each pair of organs is found to be sensitive to light waves" (p. 146 [this volume p. 94]). It seems that x-ing is dependent upon the operations of the upper organs and y-ing on that of the lower organs. Grice poses the question: are x-ing and y-ing both cases of seeing or do one or both of them constitute the exercise of a sense other than sight? His reply is that on criteria (I), (III), and (IV) combined—or even on criteria (I) and (III) combined or (I) and (IV) combined—the Martians should be said to see with an extra set of eyes, but he does not think that this settles the matter because criterion (II) may decide the question the other way. He says: "Would we not in fact want to ask whether x-ing something to be round was like y-ing it to be round, or whether when something x-ed blue to them this was like or unlike its y-ing blue to them? If in answer to such questions as these they said, 'Oh no, there's all the difference in the world!' then I think we should be inclined to say that either x-ing or y-ing (if not both) must be something other than seeing; we might of course be quite unable to decide *which* (if either) was seeing" (p. 146 [this volume p. 94]).

I want to begin by drawing attention to the fact that Grice's claim that criterion (II) is ineliminable has implications for the idea that it is independent of suggestion (I) and/or the other criteria. Grice is not explicit about the sense of his notions of elimination, independence, and criteria, but if we take the ineliminability of (II) to require at least that there be possible cases which we would evaluate one way by consulting (II) and quite a different way by consulting (I) or a combination of (I), (III), and (IV), then it seems clear that the ineliminability of a criterion implies some degree of independence from those other criteria in favor of which it cannot be eliminated. In the Martian example, for instance, if the test of introspectible experience were not somehow independent of the property criterion, then Grice could not use it in the way he wants. Hence it is not surprising that Grice says of criteria (I) and (II) that "they seem to be distinct" (p. 145 [this volume p. 93]) and are "seemingly independent" (p. 135 [this volume p. 85]), although at the end of his article he claims that "the initial assumption of the independence of suggestions (I) and (II) has broken down" (p. 152 [this volume p. 99]). This conclusion is forced on him by consideration of the difficulty that the alleged special sensory experiences elude inspection and description except in terms of the properties involved in criterion (I). He hastens to add, however, that it is a further question as to just how extensive this breakdown is. He does not pursue this line of thought, but the idea seems to be that there is some dependence of (II) upon (I) but also some degree of independence. Just what such a claim amounts to is none too clear, but I shall not discuss it directly. I shall merely assume, what Grice seems both to allow and require, that criterial ineliminability involves *at least* some degree of criterial independence.

UNWELCOME IMPLICATIONS

According to Grice, what the Martians say makes it likely that one or both of x-ing and y-ing must be other than seeing and "we might be quite unable to decide which (if either) was seeing" (p. 146 [this volume p. 94]). It is a condition of this being true that if the Martians had in fact had only one set of these eye-like organs—suppose they were the y-organs—then it must have been possible that the y-sense was not the sense of sight. Grice must therefore consider it a possibility that creatures could have light-sensitive, eye-like organs which enabled them to distinguish the visually determinable properties of things but that they not have visual experience—indeed, that they have some very different sensory experience which is sufficient to constitute their performance of the exercise of a quite different sense. But presumably, there is nothing that such creatures could say which would give us any reason to suspect that this was so. They cannot talk about "all the difference in the world" between their experience and ours since they do not have access to ours. This is, to say the least, an awkward consequence for any putative criterion for distinguishing the senses since it means that there is a class of cases where there is no way of knowing whether or not this criterion is fulfilled. Moreover, it seems there is an even more alarming consequence to face since we do not need the Martians for such a situation. We daily confront it among ourselves.

Since we have no direct access to the nature of the sensory experiences of one another (for these are, on Grice's showing, introspectible characteristics) then perhaps there are as many varied sensory experiences going on behind the outward unanimity of eyes, stimuli, color reports, and so on as there are people. Consequently, if it is possible that we are all having radically different sensory experience in connection with the exercise of outwardly similar organs, and so forth, then it is also possible that we do not have the same senses. And if this is so, then Grice's investigation could hardly begin, since its starting point surely has to be one's knowledge that Smith, Jones, Brown, and oneself all have the same senses and that, for instance, all share such a paradigm sense as vision.

It might be thought that Grice could at this point claim that we can at any rate distinguish personally between the senses that each of us possesses, and in so doing we would use the criterion of different introspectible characteristics. This is of course a retreat from the original

question (how can *we* determine that others—for example, Martians—
have a sense different from our own?) and seems to bring an answer to
it no nearer. Furthermore, in such a situation, the idea that I am distinguishing my senses *as* sight, touch, taste, and so forth is endangered,
these terms of the common language being open to the possibility of
radical ambiguity in the light of Grice's approach. For Grice, the beetle
of sensory experience is at least partly constitutive of the sensory box.

A line of escape might be sought in some form of argument from analogy. In the context of general doubts about other minds, this argument
is beset with problems, and here Grice's position aggravates the usual
difficulties since the analogy would have to rest upon just those characteristics with respect to which (II) is supposed to be ineliminable and, at
least to some degree, independent. As we have noted, Grice is not explicit
about how we are to understand his notions of elimination, dependence,
and criterion but the ineliminability and independence in question must
be epistemological or "criterial" rather than ontological, so it is hard to
see how (II) can have this status if, in the paradigm cases such as human
sight, it can only be employed at the evidential behest of (I), (III), and
(IV). How can the analogical evidence of (I), (III), and (IV) determine
(II) without eliminating the need to appeal to (II) at all? Criterion (II)
seems simply superfluous where its status is decided by such analogies
and unavailable otherwise except where special circumstances allow for
remarks about "all the difference in the world." Hence, in the central cases
of sense differentiation, criterion (II) is either quite unavailable (though
crucially relevant) or else eliminable. If the former, then we humans have
no way of knowing that we share the same senses, and if the latter, then
the contribution of (II) in the rarefied Martian example is surely suspect.
This contribution there purports to be available on grounds of testimony
rather than analogy since analogy would settle the matter in favor of the
x-and y-organs being a superabundance of eyes.[2]

The status of this testimony will be examined shortly but it is worth
noting here that the Martian example is not as extreme as Grice's position would allow; after all, the Martians do have *two* sets of paired
organs which are "not perhaps exactly like one another but each pair
more or less like our eyes" (p. 146 [this volume p. 94]) and an envisaged
breakdown in x and y correlations is attributed by Grice to "differences
between the two pairs of organs." These differences are, of course, not
such as are intended to throw any weight on the scales but one wonders
what there is to prevent Grice from simplifying the example so that
the x and y senses operate through the one mechanism. Let us call the
shared organs z-organs. Now the intriguing question arises: how do these

---

[2] Further difficulties will arise for a Gricean view from the fact that we commonly
attribute sight, touch, hearing, etc. to dumb animals and here we not only make no use of
criterion (II) but there seems to be no way in which we could.

different sensory experiences actually occur to a Martian? And how does the vocabulary of x-ing and y-ing get going in such circumstances?

The second question seems unanswerable on the assumption that Martians just find themselves x-ing and y-ing. The Martians could say that in the course of detecting colors by the operation of the z-organs, they sometimes had one experience and at other times another and, if they all said this sort of thing, then they could use x-ing and y-ing for these experiences in such a way that they might become accustomed to accepting that whenever the z-organs were open they were either x-ing or y-ing. Individuals might even use "x-ing" to refer consistently to one of these kinds of experience and "y-ing" to the other (although even this might raise cries of "private language" in some philosophical quarters) but they would have no way of knowing even by an Argument from Analogy—with all its difficulties—that every Martian was using these words to refer to generically the same experiences. In such a situation they could hardly use "x-ing" or "y-ing" in anything like the way we use "seeing" or "smelling" so that their claim that there is "all the difference in the world" between "x-ing" and "y-ing" is barely of interest for the question of differentiating senses.

Furthermore, the question of how they get x-experience rather than y-experience throws light upon a feature of our use of sensory verbs like "look," "feel," "taste," and "smell."[3] Grice tends to treat these words in such a way as to obscure the fact that they are very frequently used to refer to publicly observable operations by persons; his stress is much more upon their role in referring to what he takes to be (at least partly) the psychological effects of the action of material things upon us. He emphasizes the way we speak of things looking red to us, smelling fragrant, and so on, but he underplays the way we speak of looking at a red rose, feeling the outline of a box, and smelling a flower. These are performances that we can request others to do. This active element in perception is very important and bears on the often neglected fact that perceiving is not a mere registering of psychological states but is something that involves the exercise of a certain range of abilities. For this reason I cannot see how we should ever accept anything as a kind of *sensory* experience if it were open to no voluntary control or supervision *at all*. We can control to some extent what we see, hear, smell, taste, and feel (and this is why we can investigate the world and not merely be struck by it) and the existence of the operations whereby we achieve this is connected with our having movable sense organs and with the actual logical grammar of our sensory vocabulary. With the x and y experiences, as we are now considering them, there is no such possibility of control except that the Martians can put themselves in the way of either x-ing

---

[3] Certain qualifications need to be made about the verbs "hear" and "listen" but I will not discuss these here.

or y-ing by opening their z-organs and can cut both off by closing them. Of course, if we restrict the case in such a way that the Martians get *both* x and y experiences *whenever* their z-organs are open, then they come closer to having the required sort of control; they can be sure of, say, x-ing whenever they have their z-organs open. Whether this supposition of constant co-presence is ultimately coherent need not concern us here, although it is worth remarking that it would provide no way of answering the vocabulary question raised earlier. What is important is that the point about control forces us to restrict the example in this way.

It is possible that some of the difficulties raised so far could be avoided by making the requirements for ineliminability less stringent than Grice's in the Martian example. One might, for instance, make the x and y organs significantly different in some way and try to play off a combination of criteria (II) and (IV) against a combination of criteria (I) and (III). This tactic would run counter to the letter, and perhaps even the spirit, of Grice's project (compare pp. 145–148 [this volume pp. 93–96]) and so, rather than discuss it in detail, I shall only sketch briefly the kind of obstacles it would have to overcome. To begin with, unless an independent account is provided of what it is to have a relevant difference of sense mechanism, there is a real danger that the satisfaction of (IV) will be wholly determined by the verdict of (II), thus rendering the supposed combination of criteria quite spurious. On the other hand, a genuinely independent specification of (IV) is liable to make an appeal to (II) superfluous; indeed, unless it does, it would seem possible to construct cases in which an appeal to (II) would be logically unavailable and yet—in combination with (IV)—crucially relevant to differentiating the senses, and this brings us back to some of the very difficulties raised above for Grice's own position. Of course, the combination tactic will also be heavily reliant upon testimony of the kind given by Grice's Martians.

THE STATUS OF THE MARTIAN TESTIMONY

This brings us to the question of the status of the Martian claim that there is all the difference in the world between x-ing something to be blue and y-ing it to be blue. Grice thinks we should be *very* struck by this remark but it seems to me an insubstantial foundation for the edifice he builds upon it.

To begin with, the remark may presumably be expanded into something like: "X-experiences are different from y-experiences in the kind of way in which taste experiences are different from smell experiences—namely, in the kind of way that differentiates experiences associated with different senses." And here one is committed to maintaining an important similarity between the x and y experiences—namely, that they both belong to the same range as the experiences of taste, smell, and so forth, and so can be contrasted within the range.

Further, the Martian utterance seems to be the sort of claim about psychological states that philosophers call "avowals" and perhaps some of the respect one is supposed to give it seems from claims about the incorrigibility or overriding authority of such remarks. It should be clear, however, that this avowal is far removed from such paradigms as the sincere claim to have a bad headache, a claim it would normally be absurd to dispute. The gist of the Martian's claim is a complex comparison of rather special psychological states. That it is a comparison does not rule it out as a genuine avowal, but I hope to show that the more we explore it the less decisive and the more peculiar the remark appears.

Certainly we can usefully refer to sensory experience in some technical discussions, but the Martians seem to be making this notion do a kind of work for which it is very poorly equipped by any of its more acceptable uses. X-experiences are supposed to differ from y-experiences in *the kind of way* that taste experiences differ from smell experiences, *but* this "kind of way" is to be understood without reference to differences of organ, medium, or properties. It is therefore required that there be neat differences on the side of pure sensation discernible in these cases to which the difference between x and y experiences can be assimilated.

The critical problem with the comparison of neat experience, however, is that the questions of identity and difference have been cut completely loose from their normal moorings in the public world. We can see the force of this difficulty by considering a nonsensory example. There is an obvious difference between the feelings of languor and exhaustion as matters presently stand, but our confident discrimination of this difference is not a simple matter of the introspectible contrast of one kind of feeling with another. The feeling of languor is very different from the feeling of exhaustion though they are both (roughly) kinds of tiredness (compare: the smell experience is very different from the taste experience although they are kinds of sensuousness). If someone were to say that feelings of languor and exhaustion were identical, we would not disabuse him by asking him to look inward but by pointing to the public circumstances which surround the correct application of these words. The languid are dreamy and apathetic about action, they are not tired by too much action but are simply incapable of initiating any demanding action at all; whereas the exhausted are normally active, and even activist, but as a result of too much activity and pressure they are temporarily incapacitated for further action. Obviously the causal factors leading up to each state are very different as is the characteristic behavior exhibited. Onlookers respond differently to each state. If, somehow, these circumstances and behavior were removed altogether, or if they were identical with each feeling as is the case with the x and y sensations, it can hardly be imagined that we could speak confidently about the differences between languor and exhaustion considered simply as neat feelings.

How do matters stand with sensory experience? Here the characteristic behavior and circumstances are those connected with gaining a certain kind of information about our environment and being enabled to cope with it in a specific way. If we were asked to describe the difference between the introspectible "feels" of smelling and tasting we could only reply by talking about the differences between odors and flavors (which Grice admits) and by showing the different possibilities of achievement created by the ability to discriminate such properties (something to which Grice does not advert). We would probably refer as well to the differences of organ. In short, our response would be similar to the response in the languor-exhaustion case. If the sensations of taste and smell "revealed" exactly the same sensory properties by the same organ and medium, then there would not only be no way of expanding the claim that they were quite different experiences in terms of publicly agreed and accessible differences, but there might no longer be any way of convincing *oneself* that there were two different, much less quite different, experiences.

The complexity and peculiarity of the Martian's claim can be further exhibited by looking more closely at the same claim as a remark about the differences between our present experiences of tasting and smelling. If we were to say, "There is all the difference in the world between the experiences of tasting *A* and smelling *A*," we might very well be wrong. Scientists investigating the senses maintain that what we think of as *the* experience of taste is frequently an amalgam of sensory experience in which smelling is an important ingredient. The taste of apple, for example, appears to be very different from the taste of a raw potato and we can distinguish them with ease, but if the nose is blocked and we have to distinguish a piece of apple from a piece of potato purely by the taste buds in the tongue, then the task is an impossible one—both are faintly sweet and that is all.[4] If we can actually fail to identify an olfactory experience as such when it is side by side with a taste experience, then perhaps "all the difference in the world" fares badly as a piece of testimony in this area. Similarly with taste and touch. Empirical investigation seems to show that there is a strong *tactile* element in what most of us take to be the *strong* or *hot* flavor of, for example, English mustard. Tactile impressions also play an important part in such characteristic dry tastes as unripe persimmon. Now it might be argued with regard to the first case that the empirical evidence shows only that the tongue is not the sole organ of taste and that the nasal passage plays a role in the production of some tastes. One might thus seek to salvage the subject's privileged ability to discriminate between his sensory experiences (and a similar shift could be adopted for the mustard and the persimmon cases) but not only does this move seem implausible (for surely, in the event

---

[4] Lorus and Margery Milne, *The Senses of Animals and Men* (London, 1963), p. 141.

of English mustard being found to sting the eyes in a way reminiscent of something about its taste, we would not say that the eye could taste some flavors); it is, more importantly, an admission that there is room for argument on the basis of public tests about whether some claim to have a specific sensory experience will stand up.

It might be worth noting at this stage that the very idea that introspection delivers an unequivocal testimony as to the *existence* of different kinds of neat sensory experience is itself by no means beyond dispute. Indeed, the alleged difference of kind of experience involved in exercises of the different senses has been denied by as eminent a theorist on the senses as H. H. Price who says, "[T]here are not different kinds of sensing. Visual sensing will simply be the acquaintance with colour-patches, auditory sensing the acquaintance with sounds, and so on; the acquaintance being the same in each case."[5] Price's divergence from Grice here is all the more interesting in that he agrees that there is in the perceptual situation a pervasive characteristic that is "obvious on inspection but it cannot be described" and he calls this "sensuousness."[6] He seems to think that it is a property of color patches, sounds, and so on. I do not want to defend (or attack) Price's theory; I merely draw attention to its existence since it shows the kind of vulnerability that attaches to the avowal of "all the difference in the world" as testimony. We can hardly settle the dispute between Price and Grice by seeking to determine whose credit as an introspecting witness is better.

It may be objected at this point, however, that there are two relevant features of Grice's example which I have so far ignored. These are: (*a*) the fact that the Martian testimony is plural and (*b*) the fact that Grice suggests a possible public test of the Martian claim. Space precludes a full treatment of these two issues, but I shall briefly indicate how such a treatment would proceed.

Concerning (*a*), the crucial question is whether a plurality of Martian testifiers fares any better than a single avower in the face of the objections already urged. Whatever we say in general about the cumulative weight of avowal testimony, the *kind* of judgment involved in Grice's example is essentially problematic whether made by one or many. In the case of taste and smell discussed above, it seemed clearly possible to have a mass misjudgment of just this kind.

---

[5] H. H. Price, *Perception* (London, 1932), p. 5.

[6] *Op. cit.*, p. 4. It is interesting that Grice speaks of the particular sensory experiences as "diaphanous" to indicate that they can be described only in terms of the properties they "present." Curiously enough, however, this term has a historically notable use in this connection to uphold something more like the view being maintained by Price. I refer to Moore's use of "diaphanous" in "The Refutation of Idealism." The similarity between Moore and Price comes out even more clearly in a companion piece on "The Status of Sense-Data"; cf. pp. 25 and 176, respectively, of G. E. Moore's *Philosophical Studies* (London, 1922).

Concerning (*b*), Grice suggests, on analogy with the Molyneux problem, that a difference between *x*-ing and *y*-ing would be shown if Martians who acquired the use of *y*-organs late in life had trouble detecting colors through these organs when the operation of the *x*-organs was inhibited. Grice, stating that he is not convinced of the need for introspectible differences to be publicly exhibitable, offers this test only in a brief aside and it is not clear how much importance he attaches to it. My view is that it is not a public test of the kind required for the following reasons.

(1) Difficulty in operating restored or repaired bodily mechanisms may show only that we need time to adjust to the *use* of such mechanisms. Patients are reported to have such difficulties in coping with recovery of function in impaired senses and limbs that had once been fully operational. Imagine a man blind from birth in his right eye who regains the use of that organ at a later stage. If we inhibit the use of his normal left eye, *he* may have trouble using color words fluently and correctly to describe what he detects through his right eye. This would hardly provide evidence that we operate two different senses through our right and left eyes.

(2) In any event, the Molyneux experiment is irrelevant to Grice's claims. For Berkeley, the patients' difficulties were evidence that visual properties were quite different from tactile properties even in the case where we have a common vocabulary for them—for example, size and shape. Indeed, the Molyneux comparison looks as if it supports Grice only because we already know that sight and touch *are* different senses and can understand what is meant by saying that they provide different introspectible experiences. But suppose the patient identified shapes and sizes fluently immediately he was made to see. Would this have any tendency to show that the introspectible experience of seeing cubes is the same as that of touching cubes?

DOUBLE DETERMINABILITY AND FRAGRANCE

Mention of the Molyneux problem brings us to the issue of double determinability, an issue that is crucial to Grice's presentation of the Martian example. In rebuttal of an objection to the Martian example, Grice says that color words would be, for the Martians, the names of single properties "determinable equally by *x*-ing and *y*-ing. After all, is this not just like the actual position with regard to shape, which is doubly determinable, by sight and by touch" (p. 148 [this volume p. 96]). It is true that later he modifies the analogy of *x* and *y* with sight and touch, but the present existence of properties that are doubly determined is very important for the setting up of the example. By itself, however, the analogy is not persuasive since there are a number of striking dissimilarities between the two cases which, in the absence of a general account of double determinability, must cast doubt upon extrapolation from the case of shape. Most notably, shape is doubly determinable by senses which singly determine a range of other unshared properties, whereas the x and y senses detect nothing but doubly determinable properties. (In Aristotelian terminology, they have no proper sensibles but only common sensibles.) Furthermore, unlike color, our present paradigms of double determinability, such as shape and size, seem to be structural properties which are essentially amenable to mathematical treatment. It is significant that the sort of properties listed by Aristotle as common sensibles (that is, movement, rest, number, figure, magnitude[7]) gained philosophical currency as *primary* qualities with the rise of the modern mathematical sciences. It may well be that this structuralism is closely related to the fact that properties like shape are detected by senses which, unlike the x and y senses, also detect other singly determined properties, so that such properties as shape are not, as it were, side by side with visual properties like color but are revealed in and structurally essential to the perception of color. All of this is a far cry from the sort of double determinability claimed for the x and y senses.

Yet if the comparison with shape is unconvincing, it may still be possible to argue for Gricean double determinability by way of a more general position about the connection of sensory experience with sensory properties. And indeed Grice does hold such a position. He notes (pp. 144–145 [this volume pp. 92–93]) that the use of criterion (II) as a distinct test makes it seem "just a contingent matter" that we detect certain characteristics by means of certain experiences, and this is problematic since it does not seem contingent that we see colors and do not see smells. In reply, Grice urges (p. 153 [this volume pp. 99–100]) that had things been different we might well have been able to see smells. His view is that if Nature had only provided a more extensive correlation between the senses of sight and smell, then fragrance, for instance, would have been a doubly determinable property and things would have looked fragrant in just the way that they look red. It is clear from what Grice says of fragrance and from his earlier remarks about sight and touch and the x and y senses that the notion of extensive correlation is crucial to his understanding of double determinability. He does not, however, provide us with a detailed account of this idea of correlation. Presumably (as his remarks on the x-y correlations indicate) double determinability arises when there are two senses that are equal courts of appeal. Nonetheless, it appears from his approach to the question of seeing fragrance that there is no sharp break of kind between doubly determinable properties and those properties which are specific to one sense but can be reliably

---

[7] *De Anima*, 418a18 [c.f. this volume chapter 2, p. 48]. The list is slightly different in *De Sensu et Sensibili*, 442b5–10, where he mentions roughness, smoothness, sharpness, and bluntness. Clearly they could be understood as common if they were taken in a mathematical way and not, e.g., as referring to textural properties.

indicated to another; properties like shape are merely higher up on the same scale as properties like warmth.

Is this really plausible? If the correlation between sight and smell were such that we could almost invariably tell that flowers were fragrant simply by looking, would this mean that we literally *saw* fragrance? This conclusion is repugnant on a number of grounds. First, no matter how unerringly we detect the presence of fragrance we surely feel a resistance to the suggestion that we might *experience* it with full immediacy when our nose is blocked by a very heavy cold or otherwise out of action. It might, however, be objected that this repugnance comes merely from the present logic of our sensory words and this, *ex hypothesi*, is different in the situation envisaged. Let us therefore pass on to a second objection which might be seen as a more sophisticated version of the first. Is there really double *determinability* in the sense of equal authority between the two senses? In the event of a disagreement between the deliverances of the two senses with respect to fragrance, would we be simply unable to give a decision on the matter (as is, Grice supposes, the case with a clash between *x*-ing and *y*-ing)? Surely not. In such circumstances the verdict of the sense of smell would have the final authority provided that there were no hallucinatory elements or anything of the kind involved. After all, the high correlation is between a certain smell and a certain standard arrangement of colors so that we could describe the breakdown simply as the discovery that some flowers of a certain color pattern which normally indicated fragrance were in fact odorless or malodorous or whatever. In the sort of world supposed by Grice this would no doubt be a very surprising discovery but it is surely quite intelligible.

The third difficulty is a development of the second and it involves the dimension of sensory simplicity or complexity. Grice unearths this dimension in seeking to determine what is a properly visual characteristic, but he does not commit himself on the precise role this dimension might play in such legislation. He holds that P is a visually simple characteristic if there is no answer to the question: "What is it about the way that M looks that makes it look P?" Visual complexity need not concern us in detail but by contrast with both simplicity and complexity a property P is merely visually indicable if there *is* an answer to the above question in terms of visually determinable properties "the presence of which indicates more or less reliably that M is P." An example of visual simplicity is blueness, and of visual indicability warmth.

There are a number of difficulties about the relation of the simplicity/complexity tests to the determinability tests but it is clear that if some property is visually indicable there is, as Grice claims, a strong case for eliminating it as a properly visual characteristic. Furthermore, a property's being visually indicable requires some degree of correlation to hold between the determinations of two senses, and it is hard to see how merely increasing the degree of correlation is going to transform a property from the category of the visually indicable to that of the visually determinable and/or visually simple. However high we place the correlation that Nature is imagined to provide between sight and smell on this matter, fragrance will still be no more than visually indicable since we can ask what it is about the look of a flower that constitutes its looking fragrant and a reply must surely be available in terms of some standard arrangement of shapes and colors. There is, of course, no question but that fragrance is an olfactorily simple characteristic.

Even in the face of these considerations, however, it might be urged that within the situation envisaged there *is* no answer to the question of what it is about the look of something which makes it look fragrant—in these circumstances, fragrance just is, like red, a simple, visual characteristic. This may well be *said*, but only, I suspect, at the cost of removing the suggestion of double determinability from the realm of comprehension. It would certainly involve a concession that talk of Nature providing correlations had no explanatory value but was a mere blind for the bare assertion that fragrance could be a simple visual characteristic. It seems then that there is more to the idea of a doubly determinable property than a correlation account will allow. Hence the notion of correlation will not serve to legitimate the appeal to such properties required by the Martian example.

CONCLUDING REMARKS

I conclude that Grice's Martians do not possess a further sense or senses and that their existence does nothing to further his claims on behalf of criterion (II). Of course, I do not deny the existence of something that may be characterized as sensory experience nor do I maintain that it has *no* bearing on a philosophical discussion of perception or the senses. I should also add that although my aim in this paper has been largely destructive, my criticisms are intended as a positive contribution to the important discussion initiated by Grice. I will therefore end on a constructive note by briefly indicating another direction in which a search for criteria might proceed.

Now it is an interesting fact about the Martian example that it invites us to accept a situation in which creatures possess a distinct sense, the *activities* of which are simply a duplication of another sense. Since the x and y senses have no differentiating achievements by way of detecting properties, some of which are available *only* to x and others of which are available *only* to y then one of them, considered *as* a distinct sense modality, is simply superfluous. It offers no specific style of orientation to the organism; it does not supplement the Martian's understanding of his environment in even the fairly minimal way that taste does. Grice tells us nothing about the functioning of the x and y organs, but even if they were so placed that the x organs (being, for instance, on the top of their heads) could give supplementary information about colors and situations not at the time available to the y organs, this could be equally consistent with both x-ing and y-ing being the operation of a single sense. The kind of supplementary contribution made available by a different sense is not just of the kind that advantageous position makes possible. It certainly seems to be the case that an important criterion for the possession of a separate perceptual sense, a criterion ignored by Grice, is that the operation in question must have some specific contribution to make to the task of being orientated toward and enabled to deal with one's environment, a contribution which involves *achievements* that are distinct in kind from the achievements of the other senses.

Imagine a congenitally blind community who encounter sighted explorers for the first time. No doubt, the idea of attributing a difference of sense will begin with the recognition of significant vocabulary differences which concern, at least in part, the attribution of new properties to those familiar things and events with which the deprived are already acquainted. These linguistic differences are important but not all-important since not only do we require some way of knowing whether these claims are all they seem but we are prepared to speak of sense-possession in the case of nonhuman animals who possess no language. What is crucial, of course, is some indication that the alleged properties really belong in the common world of things and events. The superior achievements of the explorers in dealing with the common environment provide such a test for the blind community. The explorers, for instance, are able to tell where all sorts of things are and what is happening to them before the blind can determine the matter by, say, tactile exploration, and they are able to warn of dangers and obstacles in an equally "prescient" way. It is precisely these sorts of achievement that the explorers account for in terms of mysterious words like "look," "glimpse," "glitter," "see," "red," and so forth. In addition, the blind could observe in a suitably structured experiment that the explorers are able to discover certain facts *solely* from considerations of color. Suppose, for example, that there are certain poisonous yellow berries which have an identical shape, taste, texture, and smell to certain nonpoisonous green berries. The blind must determine which berries are which by doing such things as cutting them open, but the explorers need no such tests.

Now such successes would surely convince the blind community that the explorers were detecting properties which they could not sense, but it might still be an open question whether these successes should be attributed to the specially developed powers of some sense that the blind already have—for example, hearing. (I here ignore the special problems raised by any suggestion of magical powers or the use of instruments.) After all, some animals can detect a much greater range of sounds than we, and even humans under conditions of stress can greatly improve their auditory abilities.

The first difficulty for such a suggestion would reside in the recalcitrant fact that the language of the explorers does not accommodate it since they cannot understand the proposition that colors can be heard and they regard the claim, for instance, that they hear the size of a nearby mountain as at least false. Yet perhaps the explorers are either lying or have drawn their conceptual distinctions in the wrong place. Against this, however, it is significant that the explorers are not superior (indeed they are likely to be inferior) to the blind in detecting undisputed sounds. This tends to discredit the idea that the superior achievements are due to auditory acuity. Nonetheless, it could be urged that we should not discount the possibility that the sighted have *dull* hearing in comparison with the blind within the range of hearing that is shared but possess additional hearing powers beyond that range. The implausibility of this maneuver may be somewhat lessened, for us, by calling upon an analogy such as the contrast of long-sighted with normal or short-sighted vision.[8] But even if this sort of tactic were successful, the explorers' successes seem to be different in kind from those of hearing.

To recognize this we need to realize first that the blind community cannot employ *hearing* as effectively as sighted people or the blind who live among and are reared by the sighted. This inferiority in the use of hearing arises from there being fewer ways for the blind community to establish the systematic connections of sounds with things and their nonaudible properties that possession of sight so facilitates. It may be that the auditory detection of a few such properties, such as direction at close quarters, is somehow direct but it seems obvious that, here, exception proves the rule. The blind community's auditory identifications (other than of particular *sounds*) are primarily dependent on their tactile identifications, but touch is not a distance sense nor a very rapid or comprehensive one. Nor does hearing, by itself, provide a continuous or stable assemblage of ordered impressions that might form anything analogous to the visual field. On the other hand, the explorers' superior achievements consist, in part, in reporting unhesitatingly ("at a glance") the shapes, sizes, relative distances, and position of faraway unmoving things. For the blind community this represents a feat far beyond anything achievable by hearing a greater range of sounds.[9]

Furthermore, the difference in kind of achievement is related to Grice's criterion (IV) because the superior achievements of the explorers can readily be related to certain parts of their bodies. The blind community can determine that the bodily organs which promote the

---

[8] The analogy limps in certain important respects because, for instance, the long-sighted do not *fail* to perceive by sight at close range but merely get a blurred visual impression, whereas the explorers do not hear certain soft a subtle sounds at all.

[9] Complications might be introduced by considering such radar feats as are achieved by bats and porpoises with what appear to be auditory powers. Much is, however, unclear about the nature of such powers. Although in some respects the resulting achievements are like those of vision, in many ways they are radically dissimilar. If any new structure is erected in an area familiar to them the bats invariably collide (often fatally) with it and migratory bats are notoriously prone to collision with tall buildings and radio towers.

explorers' superiority are very different from ears and that the way in which they are affected is also very different. This discovery would most naturally come about through attempts to inhibit the superior skill of the explorers.

I have tried to illustrate the sort of differences of achievement that would count for difference of sense rather than sensory extension and in so doing I have, I hope, made the role of achievement clearer. The story would need adapting to deal with the peculiarities of senses other than sight and hearing.

Finally, awareness of the importance of the achievement criterion can bring other problems in its wake. I have before me a scientific book in which occur the following seriously intended applications of the concept of a sense: sense of weight, sense of weather, sense of balance, sense of direction, sense of rhythm, sense of dreaming, sense of security, sense of sex, sense of hunger, "sense organs in the brain itself (which) respond to slight changes in the temperature of the blood,"[10] and so on. No doubt we should be prepared to extend or revise the traditional five senses if the evidence requires it, but the above proliferation, resulting from the stress on achievement, is highly suspicious. It is likely that Gricean criteria would help us economize; the organ criterion, for instance, is scarcely applicable to some of the examples. More generally, the fact, mentioned earlier, that the senses are typically modes of *investigation*, and hence necessarily under some degree of control, should serve to restrict the tendency to multiply senses. How does one employ the sense of balance or the sense "organs" in the brain or the sense of dreaming to discover a range of properties in the environment? (The idea of a range seems to be an important corollary of criterion [I].) Many such examples allow no room for a question form parallel to "Why didn't you look/listen/sniff...?" Where such a question does make sense there will, of course, be further issues such as whether the putative sense is an extension or special operation of a familiar sense and here each case would have to be looked at individually.

C. A. J. Coady
University of Melbourne

---

[10] Milne, *op. cit.*, p. 5.

7

The Senses, excerpt from
Perception and Cognition

John Heil

PRELIMINARIES

"Perceiving" is a general term, a technical—or, at any rate, quasi-technical—expression covering what one does with one's senses. To perceive something is, at the very least, to *sense* it in one way or another: to see it, hear it, feel it, taste it, or smell it.[1] In putting the matter this way, I do not mean to suggest that these are the only "sensory modalities." They are simply the most familiar. An explication of the senses, a determination of what constitutes a sensory mode must, it seems, occupy a position of central importance in any theory of perception. It might turn out, for example, that differences among various senses are so great as to frustrate any attempt to erect a simple, unified account of perception that is, at the same time, interesting. What holds for sight may not hold for hearing or touch. What is true of taste and smell may not be true of vision.

Regrettably, philosophers have had little to say about what distinguishes the senses from one another. It is generally acknowledged that hearing, for instance, is not at all similar to sight, or smell, or to any of the other sensory modes, but the significance of these differences for theories of perception is not well appreciated. This fact, I think, places in jeopardy the longstanding philosophical dependence on vision as the primary source of data for perceptual theories. In the absence of an account of how the senses are to be distinguished, an account of what *constitutes* a sense, it is

John Heil "The Senses", Chapter 1 from his *Perception and Cognition*, Berkeley and Los Angeles: University of California Press, 1983. (Copyright, 1994, John Heil. Republished by permission of John Heil.)

---

[1] To do one of these or in some other way "sensorily to apprehend it." If this is so, then the expression "extrasensory perception" is, strictly, a misnomer. There may well be perceptual modes other than those familiarly discussed, but if they are perceptual, they must, perforce, be sensory.

by no means clear that conclusions reached about visual perception can be taken to show very much at all about perceptions of other sorts.

This difficulty is, in the present context, particularly acute. First, I shall want to avail myself of the fruits of philosophical tradition in what follows and concentrate on vision. It cannot be merely accidental that we find it most natural to discuss perception largely in terms of sight. My hope, however, is that I shall be able to show that I am entitled to do this by showing that differences among the senses, although genuine and important, cannot materially affect the conclusions I wish to draw. Second, the view of perception that I shall recommend ties perceiving to the acquiring of beliefs. Not every instance of belief-acquisition, however, is an instance of perception. Roughly, my suggestion is that in perception we gain beliefs by way of the senses. And this way of putting the matter obliges me to offer some independent account of the senses. This is the goal of the present chapter.

SENSORY MODALITIES

What is it, then, that distinguishes the several senses? How many senses are there? Might there be creatures with senses other than those with which we are familiar? What constitutes a "sensory modality?"

Grice (1962, pp. 135 ff. [this volume pp. 85 ff.]) has provided an inventory of ways in which these and similar questions might be answered. There are, he contends, at least four distinct criteria to which one might appeal.

(i)   The senses might perhaps be distinguished by reference to the "features that we become aware of by means of them." Thus one becomes aware of colors, for instance, by means of sight, of sounds by means of hearing, of odors by way of one's sense of smell. (Such a view may be traced back at least to Aristotle; see *De Anima*, bk. ii [this volume chapter 2].)

(ii) It might be the case that each sense has a characteristic *experience* associated with it: certainly the experience of seeing something differs enormously from the experience of feeling or hearing it. And it seems possible that such differences afford a means of identifying and distinguishing sensory modes.

(iii) One could, instead, focus on the "differing general features of the external physical conditions on which the various modes of perceiving depend, to differences in 'stimuli' connected with different senses: the sense of touch is activated by contact, sight by light rays, hearing by sound waves, and so on" (Grice, 1962, p. 135 [this volume p. 85]).

(iv) Finally, one might wish to identify senses by reference to the organs involved. Seeing is what is done with eyes, hearing is accomplished by means of ears, smelling requires a nose.

I shall not here attempt to elucidate the view that emerges in Grice's discussion. I wish instead to offer an alternative account, one that avoids both the pitfalls and the inevitable complexities of views that attempt (as Grice's ultimately does) to distinguish among the senses by reference to some set of *internal* features of perceptual experiences or qualia.

The notion that the senses are to be defined and distinguished by reference to the phenomenal characteristics of sensory experiences—sensations—has a long and honorable history (one rehearsed admirably in Boring, 1942). Implicit in such views has been the belief that the senses comprise *pathways* (or "channels") that culminate in the production of sensations. The latter are, according to some theorists, specific to pathways: sensations arising from stimulation of the visual pathway differ phenomenally from those produced when the auditory pathway is activated (see Müller, 1838).[2] Awareness of sensations has been thought in this way to mediate perception of things and events outside the body. Perception, as distinguished from sensation, turns out on such a view to be always indirect, inferential.

Theories of this sort, however, theories that peg differences in sensory modes to characteristics of sensations or experiences (one may call them *internal feature* theories), are burdened with two major, and a host of minor, liabilities. In the first place, they are obliged to produce some *non-circular* account of those components of perceptual experiences or qualia that mark them off as experiences or qualia of one particular sense rather than another. This task (as Grice's paper attests) is by no means a simple one.

Second, an internal feature theory must provide a characterization of perceptual experiences that is suitably *universal*. Preanalytically it seems not unreasonable to suppose, for example, that both honeybees and human beings may correctly be said to *see* various features of the world. It is far from obvious, however, that we should want to say that a honeybee's visual experiences are very much like our own, or that the qualia encountered by a honeybee resemble the visual qualia with which we are familiar. More dramatically, there is nothing obviously wrong with the supposition that another person (or, if that seems implausible, a Martian) might, in seeing something, have the sorts of experience we have when we hear something. In any case, it would be disturbing to *begin* theorizing about the senses on the assumption that such things are impossible. The question seems largely (though perhaps not exclusively) an empirical one.

Further, the Aristotelian notion—embodied in Grice's first suggestion—that the senses are to be distinguished by differences in (as he says) "features that we become aware of by means of them," runs afoul

---

[2] If such a view were correct, it would be possible, perhaps, to conflate Grice's methods (ii) and (iv): commonalities and differences among sensory qualia would be accounted for by reference to biological features of perceivers.

of the evident fact that one may become aware of some one property in utterly different ways. Thus one may tell by feeling an object or by looking at it that it is warm or smooth. Difficulties here lead one back to the notion of distinctive internal features of sensory experiences.[3]

It might, at first glance, appear more promising to pursue the notion that the senses are to be distinguished by reference to their respective "organs." Seeing, on this view, is what one does with one's eyes, hearing requires the use of ears. This is, of course, indisputably correct, though for the purposes at hand it is largely unhelpful. It is a matter of contingent empirical fact that most of the creatures with which we are familiar have eyes and ears with certain definite anatomical features. Even here, however, there are difficulties. The compound eye of a honeybee, to take but one example, is in most ways unlike the eye of a human being.

It is surely imaginable, in any case, that there are creatures elsewhere in the universe who (we should wish to say) see and hear perfectly well, yet who lack anything physiologically similar to the eyes and ears of terrestrial species. Confronted with a race of such creatures, the most natural course for a scientific investigator to take would be to decide which anatomical bits are to be counted as eyes, which might be called ears, by determining, first, which portions of the creatures' anatomy enabled them to see and which enabled them to hear. And this requires that an investigator begin with some independent idea of what seeing and hearing are and how they are different.

CHARACTERISTICS OF "STIMULI"

There is reason, then, to regard with suspicion Grice's options (i), (ii), and (iv), that is, to resist theories that attempt to identify senses by reference to properties of objects perceived, to internal features of sensory experiences, or to anatomical characteristics of perceptual organs. What of option (iii)? Might the senses be identified and distinguished by reference to "the differing general features of the external physical conditions on which the various modes of perceiving depend," might they, that is, be distinguished by tracing out their connections to certain sorts of "proximal" stimulus?

Curiously, Grice spends little time exploring this possibility. It seems to me, however, at least if I understand rightly what Grice means by "stimuli" here, that this option affords a key to the solution of the problem.

---

[3] In fact the route back to perceptual experiences is more tortuous than this way of putting it suggests. Roxbee Cox (1970 [this volume chapter 5]) has attempted to construct a theory in which the senses are distinguished by reference to certain "directly" apprehended "key features" of perceived states of affairs. I shall not discuss this possibility here (though see below). The view I shall offer appears to account for the facts cited in support of the notion of key features and to do so in a much simpler, less ad hoc way.

Very roughly, what I should like to suggest is that sensory modalities are to be identified and distinguished (insofar as this is possible) by reference to the kinds of "physical stimulation" from which a sentient creature extracts information about its surroundings.

On this account, seeing involves the activity of extracting information from light radiation; hearing occurs when a creature gains information from pressure waves of certain sorts; smell and taste involve the extraction of information from chemical features of the environment (the former from features borne through the creature's medium—the air or water through which it moves—the latter from chemical features of things ingested); touch incorporates the capacity to obtain information about things via mechanical contact of some sort.

I do not, I hasten to add, wish to defend the view that the senses can, in all cases, be distinguished *sharply* from one another. I want rather to suggest that to the extent that the senses can be distinguished at all, they are best distinguished by reference to characteristics of the physical stimuli that affect them, their respective sources of information.

Before taking things further, there are a number of features of the suggested taxonomy that are worth mentioning. First, it is a relatively simple matter to move from this way of talking about the senses to a classification of sensory "organs" or "receptors." An eye, for example, is a collection of receptors sensitive to light, an ear, one sensitive to vibration in the medium.

Second, it is clear that there may be a variety of ways to "build" receptors sensitive to the sorts of stimulation mentioned. What creatures that see have in common is the capacity to respond to and make intelligent use of a particular source of stimulation—light. What they need not have in common is a particular anatomical doodad nor, it seems, a particular sort of experience.

Third, I do not mean to imply that it is a necessary truth that seeing involves a creature's sorting through electromagnetic radiation. It may be that present-day theories of light propagation are false. I do, however, want to advance the notion that seeing, whatever else it is, is a matter of information-extraction from available light. It is the task of the physicist to determine what light is. I do not know whether the claim that seeing involves the picking up of information in the light, if true, is a necessary truth. It is, at least, a promising conceptual hypothesis.

These same points are meant to apply, of course, to the other senses. That hearing, for example, is the extracting of information from pressure waves transmitted through the medium, that smell is the picking up of information borne by chemicals dispersing through the same medium; these are partly empirical claims, partly something more. The empirical part concerns one's characterization of the physical stimuli and one's account of the receptors (and deeper-lying mechanisms) that make information contained in the stimuli available to the perceiver. The remaining part concerns the less straightforwardly empirical notion that the senses are a creature's means of finding out about its world. Information about that world transmitted in the light is picked up by way of devices we call eyes; information transmitted by pressure waves rippling through the medium is extracted by means of ears; and so on.

This approach provides an answer to a question sometimes posed by philosophical skeptics (and others) with certain theoretical axes to grind: "Couldn't one imagine a being able to see with its ears, hear with its eyes?" If one characterizes an eye as a bank of receptors used to extract information from light radiation, then any organ that allows for this *is* an eye. And, of course, there are (presumably) very good physiological reasons why one cannot do this with one's ears (or perform the opposite feat with one's eyes). If, in contrast, the questioner is in doubt about the sorts of experience perceivers might conceivably have when they look about themselves or listen, then, if I am right, his question is badly put. Seeing need not be distinguished from hearing by reference to features of the respective experiences. I suspect that there are solid empirical reasons for adopting the view of common sense here. Thus it seems somehow *likely* that the particular character of a creature's perceptual experience is a function of the character of its sensory receptors and their associated mechanisms. It seems correspondingly unlikely that two creatures, physiologically very similar, might experience the world in thoroughly different ways.

I cannot prove this, of course, but I do not need to. On the view endorsed here, the peculiar flavor of the experiences had by perceivers is just irrelevant to the question at hand. We are entitled to day that S and T see the same thing without committing ourselves to any theory at all about the internal character of their respective experiences. We may say that a visual experience is one arising from the process of extracting information from available light; an auditory experience is one brought about when information is obtained from the oscillating medium. I shall say more about the nature of perceptual experience in chapters IV and VI, below.

GIBSON'S ACCOUNT

The view I have begun sketching here owes much to the work of J. J. Gibson (see e.g., Gibson, 1966, 1979; Schiffman, 1976). Gibson's fundamental notion is that perceiving is the picking up of information about the world made available to the perceiver by various sorts of physical stimulation. Such an approach is, I am convinced, essentially correct. I wish for the moment, however, to align myself with Gibson in just two respects. First, although Gibson does not directly appeal to characteristics of perceptual stimuli in constructing a taxonomy of the senses, such an account seems implicit in much of what he says (see for example, Gibson, 1966, chap. 3). Second, Gibson's characterization of perceiving as the picking up of information seems sound. I have tried already to make a case for the first point; now I should like to say a word about the second.

I have spoken repeatedly of the senses as devices (or, to use Gibson's term, "systems") enabling creatures to "extract information" about the world from various sorts of stimulation. This way of talking may offend some, but I think it need not. The information that a creature picks up may, in general, be characterized propositionally: that a certain object is green or rectangular, that it is loud or coarse, that it is sweet or warm. To say that a creature has picked up information describable in this way comes very close to saying that it has acquired a belief similarly describable.

I am not, I should say, suggesting that Gibson means by "information" what one ordinarily means by "belief." Information in the present context is a feature of a mode of stimulation; it may be picked up, or overlooked or ignored altogether. Information, in this sense, is "in the world," not (as a belief surely is) "in the perceiver." Nevertheless it seems right to say that the *picking up* of information is so close as to be indistinguishable from what I should prefer to call the acquiring of belief. Very crudely: we are able to acquire the beliefs we do about the world because the world is the way it is and because we are the way we are.

This way of putting the point is apt to seem spectacularly uninformative, but for all that it may be right. If light, for example, behaved differently from the way it does, it would *not* provide us with reliable information about such things as colors and shapes. Our visual apparatus, not surprisingly, evolved to take advantage of the information-providing characteristics of light: that light reflected from a smooth surface has different properties from light reflected from a rough surface; that light reflected by a tomato differs in systematic ways from that reflected by a cucumber. (The concept of information, what it might mean to say, for example, that light *carries* information, will be discussed in greater detail in chapter III.)

It is not, of course, that one perceives light radiation or pressure waves rather than tomatoes and thunderclaps. When one looks about the world, for instance, *what* one sees are objects and events illuminated by (or, in some cases, emitting) light. The notion that one might see *light* (a notion once fostered by impressionist painters) is, I am inclined to think, something very close to a category mistake.

Gibson's suggestion is that "ambient light" is structured by the objects and events it illuminates in such a way that it affords a creature, suitably equipped, with information about its surroundings. Light so structured at a "point of observation" (a point that may or may not be occupied) is labeled by Gibson the "optic array" (see Gibson, 1979, chap. 5). The latter may be thought of as embodying information about the objects and events that determine its structure. My suggestion is that the extraction of such information may usefully be regarded as a matter of

belief-acquisition. The idea is that a creature's senses enable it to discover properties of its surroundings by way of such information-bearing
stimuli as light radiation and pressure waves.

It is perhaps worth emphasizing that, for Gibson, it is not simply a
range of stimulation (light radiation, pressure waves, and the like) that
conveys information, but *structured* stimulation. Unstructured light
results in a luminous fog or *Ganzfeld* (Metzger, 1930) that is visually
impenetrable, unstructured sound in so-called white noise.

Concentrating for the moment on vision, it may noted that the structure of the "optic array"

> ...can be described in terms of visual solid angles with a common apex
> at the point of observation. They are angles of intercept, that is, they are
> determined by the persisting environment. And they are nested, like the
> components of the environment itself. (Gibson, 1979, p. 92)

As a perceiver explores his environment, the point of observation changes
and the visual solid angles comprising the optic array are transformed.
The systematic character of the resulting transformations "specifies" an
underlying pattern of permanence.

The details of all this may be found in Gibson's writings (in e.g.,
Gibson, 1966, 1979), and I shall not take the time to rehearse them here.
For our purposes the point to be emphasized is that it is structured stimulation, over time, that produces in us reliable perceptual beliefs about
our surroundings. Earlier, I volunteered somewhat unhelpfully that we
discover properties of our environment "by way of" structured stimuli.
I am now suggesting that one take "by way of" in a causal sense: structured stimuli *produce* certain beliefs in (suitably equipped) perceivers.

EXPERIMENTAL SUPPORT: "TACTILE VISION"

Perhaps all this can be brought into focus by considering a recent development in the applied psychology of perception. It is a virtue, I think, of
the sort of view I have been advancing that it allows one to take account
of the phenomenon I shall describe, and to do so in a way that seems
perfectly natural.

In a paper entitled (in my view, perspicuously) "Seeing with the skin"
(White, et al, 1970; see also Guarniero, 1974; Morgan, 1977; Reed and
Jones, 1978), a group of researchers discusses a device characterized as
a "tactile visual substitution system" (TVSS). The device consists of a
television camera (its "eye") coupled to a mechanism that converts the
visual image produced by the camera into an "isomorphic cutaneous
display" in the form of a pattern of vibration produced by a collection
of tiny vibrating pins arranged in a grid and brought into contact with
the skin (usually on the back or the stomach) of experimental subjects.
Practice in the use of this device enables persons who are blind to detect

reasonably fine differences among objects and events that appear in front of the camera.

The details of this experimental work are fascinating, but this is not the place to go into them (see above for references). I wish only to raise the question of how we are to describe such cases. My suggestion is that a person making intelligent use of a TVSS may be said to be *seeing* (though perhaps only dimly) features of his environment. This, surely, is what we should say were we to discover a creature whose "visual system" turned out to be a biological analogue of the mechanism described.

Let us call a person armed with a TVSS (or a creature biologically equipped with such a system) a *T-perceiver*. On my view it would be proper to say that a T-perceiver *sees* his surroundings because the T-perceiver makes use of information contained in reflected light.

There are two matters worth noting here. First, T-perceivers will enjoy a range of capacities and limitations thoroughly analogous to the capacities and limitations attributable to ordinary sighted creatures. Thus, for example, both ordinary sighted observers and T-perceivers will be able to describe the shapes and orientation of things without having to touch them, both will find it difficult to make out objects and events that are dimly illuminated.

Second, although T-perceivers and persons with ordinary eyesight may well describe what they see (or "T-perceive") in the same way, it is unlikely that we should want to attribute to them the same sorts of experience. If a T-perceiver were sufficiently practiced and well equipped, the fact (if indeed it is a fact) that his perceptual experiences were different from those of an ordinary perceiver would not necessarily be detectable from the ways in which he described his perceptions. Indeed a T-perceiver might well be at a loss to describe the character of his "visual experiences" without simply describing what he T-perceived.

In this regard at least, a T-perceiver would be no different from an ordinary (sighted) perceiver. As Grice puts it,

> ... such experiences (if experiences they be) as seeing and feeling seem to be, as it were, diaphanous: if we were asked to pay close attention, on a given occasion, to our seeing or feeling as distinct from what was being seen or felt, we should not know how to proceed; and the attempt to describe the differences between seeing and feeling seems to dissolve into a description of what we see and what we feel. (Grice, 1962, p. 144 [this volume p. 93])

The view I have set out here appears to provide one with a way of accounting for this difficulty; more, it leads one precisely to *expect* it. The point of perceptual talk is to describe things perceived, not to describe experiences of things perceived. It makes clear, in addition, just why the character of perceptual experiences—sensations—seems so often beside the point.

It is interesting to compare these musings with the testimony of one who has himself employed a TVSS, a living, breathing T-perceiver. G. Guarniero, a graduate student (in philosophy!) who had been blind from birth, was given a three-week training session in the use of the device. He recounts his impressions in a paper entitled "Experience of tactile vision" (Guarniero, 1974).

It is perhaps significant that Guarniero himself elects to describe what he has learned to do as *seeing*, rather than as feeling things. "Only when I first used the system did the sensations seem as if they were on my back" (p. 101). Later he came to be aware, as it were, not of vibrations, but of objects existing apart from himself.

> Very soon after I had learned how to scan, the sensations no longer felt as if they were located on my back, and I became less and less aware that vibrating pins were making contact with my skin. By this time objects had come to have a top and a bottom; a right side and a left.... (p. 104)

These observations again make clear a difficulty inherent in attempts to describe perceptual experiences without simply describing characteristics of objects perceived. They provide, as well, a certain amount of support for the "information pickup" view of perception advocated by Gibson. The function of sensory systems is to extract information from some particular stimulatory source (in the case of vision, from ambient light radiation), not to create distinct experiences, sensations or internal models of what is perceived. Given suitable equipment and proper training, evidently one can learn to extract visual information by way of the skin.[4]

I concede that it is, to an extent, misleading to describe a TVSS-user as *seeing* in an unqualified sense. Such a person, one might say, is employing a device that *enhances* or *extends* his senses. But *which* sense is thereby enhanced or extended? That will be determined, on the view defended here, by the character of the "intervening stimulation" sampled.

In putting it this way, it may appear that I have missed a crucial point. After all, one deploying a TVSS seems to be making use of *two* sorts of physical stimulation—the light radiation that reaches the lens of the apparatus and the vibration of pins against his skin. One might thus suppose that, given the tenets of my view, I ought to describe the case as one comprised of both touch and vision.[5]

This, I think, is partly correct, but, insofar as it *is* correct, it is perfectly unobjectionable. To the extent that one wishes to describe a TVSS-user as availing himself of his sense of touch, the *objects* felt are not those in front of the television camera, but the vibrating pins put in contact with his skin. If, in contrast, one takes the objects of his sensing to be those scanned by the camera, it is more plausible, surely, to describe them as (in some sense) seen, the beliefs thus acquired as (in some sense) visual.

It should be noted that a device such as a TVSS is workable chiefly because it establishes a partial isomorphism between an "optic array"

---

[4] Further, cases such as these suggest difficulties for theories that tie modes of sensing to particular psychological or physiological "channels" (see below).

[5] I owe this observation to Gary Monnard.

and a gridwork of vibrating pins, *not* one between the scanned items and the gridwork.[6] It is the optic array as sampled by the television camera that determines the character of the vibrations. This is why the former may be taken as, in a certain sense, primary, and *this* is why it seems not altogether unnatural to describe a person employing a TVSS as *seeing*.

If I am right about this, then another interesting conclusion appears to follow. As was earlier noted, the notion that particular senses depend on particular neural pathways or mechanisms is a longstanding one (see Müller, 1838). Thus vision has been associated not only with retinal occurrences, but in addition with goings-on in the optic nerve and the visual cortex. This seems, however, unnecessarily restrictive. Not only does it appear to rule out—unreasonably—the possibility that creatures built in ways different from us might properly be said to see (or hear, or taste, or smell) their environment, it confuses as well questions about the ways in which sensory mechanisms are in fact realized with questions about how they might be realized—what is essential to a certain mode of sensing.

This confusion is associated by Gibson with the doctrine of "specific nerve energies" formulated in the nineteenth century by Johannes Müller (see Müller, 1838; Gibson, 1979, pp. 33 ff.). If the function of perception is, as I have suggested, to produce in the perceiver certain cognitive or doxastic states, and if the senses are distinguished chiefly by features of the world that produce these states, then particular characteristics of the internal mechanisms that mediate this process are strictly inessential. Perception may depend upon a causal process, but it is important to be clear about what is and what is not intrinsic to that process. This requires, among other things, a specification of its beginning and end states. My suggestion is that the process begins with physical stimulation structured by objects and events in the environment, and ends with the production of a belief (or belief-like cognitive state). Different senses are distinguished by differences in one of these boundary states, not by differences in neural pathways or by differences in the sorts of sensation generated by the activation of these.

THE POSSIBILITY OF DIFFERENT SENSES

Before going on to discuss particular sensory modalities, it will be useful to ask how many senses there might be. I have spoken of vision,

---

[6] Properties of the optic array are determined by, but are not identical to, properties of illuminated objects and events. An object in motion relative to an observer, for example, may systematically transform the array without itself changing. Thus, an approaching object will "loom large," an object moving away will eventually "vanish." According to Gibson, visual information is conveyed largely by means of these and similar *transformations* of the optic array that occur as the perceiver observes, moves about in, and manipulates his environment.

hearing, smell, taste, and touch. In the section that follows, I shall discuss "proprioception," the awareness of one's own bodily disposition and movements. But what of the feats of bats, dolphins, and other creatures that seem able, through the use of sonarlike devices, to discover features of the world that we detect, if at all, in other ways? On the view I am recommending, the question of whether a creature is endowed with an entirely *different* sense will hinge on the extent to which the creature is equipped to pick up information of a sort that we are "blind" to. Creatures sensitive in certain ways to X-rays or to radio waves might be thus describable.

It is useful in this regard to distinguish creatures equipped with what I should call *extended* senses from those employing new or entirely *different* senses. (I am well aware that this distinction may turn out to be more a matter of degree than kind. My claim, however, is not that it is *sharp*, merely that it is *useful*.) Thus, many terrestrial creatures are equipped to detect light radiation or sounds that human beings are insensitive to. Given that, for such creatures, the sort of information picked up is *continuous* with that which we human beings extract from our surroundings, it is perhaps best to regard them as employing senses merely extended relative to our own. Spot responds to a whistle that we cannot hear. It is not that Spot has a special sense that we lack, but that he can hear more (or better) than we can.

What of bats, dolphins, and other creatures said to be capable of using sounds to discover things about their environments in ways analogous to our use of sight? Do we want to say that such creatures possess a sense different from any of ours? Perhaps not. A human being may be taught to use a sonar device that will enable him to probe his surroundings in ways comparable to the methods employed by bats and dolphins. Here it seems better to say that such creatures, in common with blind persons capable of detecting large obstacles "echoically," have developed more sophisticated and discriminatory ways of picking up information from sound waves that reach them through their respective media.[7] Other creatures have come to possess more highly developed chemical detection systems. Spot's nose enables him to make use of information that we are ill-equipped to detect, but which is not different in kind from what we encounter when we stroll past the bakery.

To make a case for an entirely different sense, one would want to show that its possessor is able to respond to information of a sort for which we have no receptors, hence *cannot* pick up. I have suggested that

---

[7] Such creatures, of course, exhibit a capacity to *enrich* the auditory information available to them, as well, by emitting certain noises. This activity on their part is analogous to our carrying a flashlight to help us see our way about at night and in dark places where there is little natural light. Sensory enrichment of this sort is often relied upon by the blind in employing so-called "facial vision" (a misnomer—see e.g., Gibson, 1966, p. 2). An interesting first-person account of this phenomenon may be found in Mehta, 1982.

a creature able to detect radio waves, or one capable of responding to X-rays, might be said to enjoy a novel sense. If pigeons are equipped, as has been claimed, to discriminate features of the earth's magnetic field (or rather to use information in that field to discover something—heaven knows what—about their location), then this capacity, too, might begin to look like a genuinely novel sense.

Such cases are, at any rate, importantly different from a fanciful one discussed by Grice (pp. 146 ff. [this volume pp. 94 ff.]). Grice imagines that we are visited by friendly, intelligent Martians who teach us their language. At length we discover that there is no simple translation into Martian of the English verb "to see":

> Instead we find two verbs which we decide to render as "x" and "y": we find that (in their tongue) they speak of themselves as x-ing and also as y-ing, things to be of this and that color, size and shape. Further, in physical appearance they are more or less like ourselves, except that in their heads they have, one above the other, two pairs of organs, not perhaps exactly like one another, but each pair more or less like our eyes: each pair of organs is found to be sensitive to light waves. Grice (pp. 146 ff. [this volume p. 94])

As it happens, "x-ing" is accomplished by means of the upper organs, "y-ing" by means of the lower set.

Now should we say that "x-ing" and "y-ing" are both cases of seeing? Or is it that one or both of these constitutes "a new sense other than sight"? Grice's contention is that, before we can settle this question, we should have to determine whether the experiences of "x-ing" and "y-ing" were alike.

> Would we not in fact want to ask whether x-ing something to be round was like y-ing it to be round, or whether when something x-ed blue to them it was like or unlike its y-ing blue to them? If in answer to such questions as these they said, "Oh no, there's all the difference in the world!" then I think we should be inclined to say that either x-ing or y-ing (if not both) must be something other than seeing: we might of course be quite unable to decide *which* (if either) was seeing. Grice (pp. 146 ff. [this volume p. 94])

This, I have wanted to suggest, is not so. If both "x-ing" and "y-ing" involve the extraction of information from the available light, then it seems best to regard them both as forms of seeing. If the organs are different, perhaps they are sensitive to different wavelengths of light. If that were so (the question would have to be settled experimentally), it would scarcely be surprising that "there's all the difference in the world" between "x-ing" and "y-ing." But if we insist on that account that both "x-ing" and "y-ing" could not be cases of seeing, then we should have to say that honeybees and houseflies do not see either. Such a view has, for me anyway, little intuitive appeal.

Surely it is both useful and correct to mark off what it is that honeybees and human beings do when they make use of their eyes, despite obvious and important differences, as the exercise of the sense of sight, and to distinguish this from what goes on when we listen to, taste, touch, or sniff about our respective habitats. Such distinctions can be made, and made in an altogether natural way, I have suggested, if one considers the character of the "information source," the physical stimuli probed by the creature in the process of getting about in the world.

It is now possible to see why attempts to distinguish the senses by reference to properties of objects *simpliciter* seem bound to fail. In the first place, not just any property will do. Smoothness, for example, or roundness may be both seen and felt. Roxbee Cox (1970) has attempted to overcome this difficulty by arguing that there are certain "key features" of objects that can be detected "directly" only by a single sense. Color, for example, might be such a feature. Colors may, it seems, be apprehended "directly" only by means of sight. If this were so, one might be able to construct a taxonomy of the senses by reference to commonsense properties of things perceived, and not have to bother with light radiation and similar exotica.

A fundamental obstacle faced by any such account is that it seems possible to imagine importantly different ways in which creatures could become aware of *any* feature of ordinary objects and events. Thus, even if it could be shown that the "direct" detection of color is, for a human being, limited to our sense of sight, it is anything but obvious that colors could not be "directly" sensed in radically different ways—via sonar devices, for example. A creature equipped in this way might, I am suggesting, best be described as *hearing* the colors of objects. Such creatures might be able to report on colors even in total darkness, but experience difficulty in doing so in a noisy room. Similar cases could be multiplied indefinitely. Admittedly, it may be possible to amend one's account of key features so as to cover each new possibility, but such a move appears suspiciously ad hoc.

If, in contrast, one adopts a taxonomy of the senses founded on kinds of stimulation sampled, difficulties of this sort are neatly avoided. It will, in addition, be possible to find a place for the intuition (appealed to earlier) that distinct senses possess distinctive liabilities and advantages: these are a function of particular characteristics of various sorts of stimuli. If touch, for example, requires mechanical contact, then objects touched must be contiguous—or, at any rate, mechanically connected—to a perceiver. If sight depends on light radiation, then factors affecting light—opaque barriers, for instance, or mirrors or lenses—will result in familiar deficits or enhancements of visual capacities.

Finally, the view I am recommending provides a relatively simple explanation of the data to which Roxbee Cox appeals. One can understand why it is that, for a human being, the apprehension of color, for instance, depends on sight: the stimulation that produces in us ("directly") beliefs about colors is structured light radiation. It is not that colors can only be seen, but that colors can only be seen by *us*. That colors are detectable "directly" only by sight is—at best—a contingent fact, not a necessary truth about vision.

To establish the presence of a sensory modality, of course, one must do more than simply locate receptors with appropriate ranges of sensitivity. The latter must be coupled, as well, to the production of the right sorts of cognitive state. Thus receptors must enable their possessor to extract information about the environment that is carried in the stimulatory source, not merely be sensitive to it.[8] A sensory mode requires not only the presence of receptive faculties, but the capacity as well to employ these in such a way that they provide their possessor with a source of information about how things stand in the world. In this regard, cameras and photocells—and eyeballs—are blind.

I conclude that a taxonomy of the senses must be founded on distinctions among physical stimuli. To the extent that these are vague, to the extent that they run together, to that extent our taxonomy of sensory modes must be vague and indeterminant. This, however, can hardly be reckoned a flaw unless one has some argument to show that the boundaries between the several senses are, despite appearances to the contrary, sharp and firm. I am skeptical that such an argument can be produced.

A PRELIMINARY TAXONOMY OF THE SENSES

The classification that follows is meant to be illustrative only. Its purpose is merely to draw together the various strands of the present chapter.

• Vision

The sensory capacity of sight allows its possessor to extract information about objects and events from ambient light radiation. If one prefers, a clause may be added specifying that the radiation must be of a certain sort or fall into a certain range, roughly that comprising those wavelengths and intensities to which human beings are sensitive "and adjacent wavelengths and intensities" (to allow for the vision of honeybees and similar creatures).

• Audition

An auditory system is one enabling a creature to extract information from pressure waves rippling through its particular medium (in the case of terrestrial animals, air, in the case of aquatic species, water). Again, one may attach a proviso restricting the range of such stimulation to

---

[8] The latter, to be sure, is part of the environment, hence one may, it seems, imagine creatures equipped to pick up information about it, about light radiation, for example, as distinct from information *borne* by it about separate objects and events. I shall discuss this distinction in chapter II, below.

those frequencies roughly continuous with frequencies to which human beings are auditorily sensitive.

• Touch

A creature's "haptic" system enables it to acquire information about objects and events via mechanical contact with those objects and events. This contact may be "direct" (as when one explores an object with one's hands) or "indirect" (as when one probes with a stick). There are, as always, borderline cases. Does a child who has learned to detect an approaching train by putting his ear to the rail hear or feel the train? This will depend on details of the case. (For some relevant considerations, see below.)

Both hearing and touch are *mechanical* senses, although the information afforded by sound is exclusively vibratory. Certain vibrations, of course, may be detected haptically, as when one feels a distant explosion "through the soles of one's feet." When the volume on a phonograph is excessive, the result can be both heard and felt.[9]

• Smell and Taste

A sense of smell incorporates a capacity to extract chemical information about objects and events that is dispersed through the medium, information pertaining to *volatile* sources. Like smell, taste is a chemical sense, though one associates it with things ingested rather than with things sniffed. Because the character of the physical stimuli are so similar, one may be inclined to lump the two senses together under the rubric "chemical senses." There is no objection to one's holding to the traditional distinction, provided that in doing so one realizes that the line between tasting and smelling seems impossible to draw with any precision. This, of course, is not a special problem for my account of the senses, it simply reflects a commonly recognized fact about taste and smell.

• "Kinesthesis"

It is not obvious what one should say about the knowledge one evidently has concerning motions and dispositions of one's body and its parts. It is far from clear, for example, that one is obliged to regard such knowledge as *perceptual*. One knows without, as it were, having to look, that one's hand is resting in one's lap. Is this something one perceives?

In common parlance, the notion of perception seems restricted to the detection of goings-on "in the world," things and events *outside* one's

---

[9] These somewhat cavalier remarks about touch conceal a great many interesting and important distinctions. See e. g., Gibson, 1966, chaps. 6 and 7 for a more detailed and informative discussion.

body. There are no special perceptual verbs for the activity of detecting bodily states and occurrences. One does, it is true, speak of *feeling* one's hand to be in one's lap, but this seems only a way of indicating that one can tell this without having to look at or touch anything, in particular without having to look at or touch one's hand.

It is doubtful, in any case, that there is a special perceptual mode of "feeling" that is brought into play here. Feeling one's hand in one's lap is not like feeling the edge of a table or feeling a spider scuttle across one's arm; feeling one's body to be upright is not like feeling a doorknob in the dark. Further, there seem to be no special receptors designed exclusively for the picking up of kinesthetic or, as I shall designate it (following Gibson, 1966), *proprioceptive* information. In fact, such information apparently comes from a variety of distinct sources including occurrences in the inner ear, happenings in the muscles and joints, and from ordinary visual perception (as when one suffers the illusion of motion in a stationary railway carriage when another carriage passes on an adjacent track). Such considerations suggest that it would be a mistake to regard proprioception as a distinctive sensory mode (see Gibson, 1966, pp. 33 ff.).

One consideration that, historically, has had considerable influence on this matter strikes me as wrongheaded. It has occasionally been pointed out that there are no distinctive proprioceptive *sensations*. This was hinted at above when it was noted that the proprioceptive use of "feeling" differs from its use in haptic contexts. I have suggested, however, that it is wise to distinguish sensation and perception. It is not altogether clear, for example, that there are distinctive visual or auditory *sensations*, yet vision and audition are paradigmatically perceptual modes (see Gibson, 1966). The fact, then, if it is a fact, that there are no simply identifiable proprioceptive sensations (or, if there are such, their seeming not to form a natural class) is neither here nor there so far as the matter at hand is concerned.

A further source of confusion springs from the circumstance that the notion of perception has a technical employment that does not, in every case, sit comfortably with our ordinary ways of talking about the senses. This technical or specialized application is traceable, perhaps, to certain vaguely epistemological concerns of philosophers and psychologists. There is a professional interest in our knowledge of the world, that is, *empirical* knowledge, its sources and its warranting conditions. From this point of view, beliefs about one's own body are on all fours epistemologically with beliefs about spatially discontinuous states of affairs.

This is not to say that the notion of proprioception is exclusively a technical one, that concern with proprioception is entirely absent from ordinary discourse. On the contrary, it seems rather to be taken for granted. Beliefs about one's own bodily dispositions and movements seem so often to be true, that questions concerning their evidence or warrant may tend to be regarded as out of place, superfluous. Because my aim here is not to chronicle ordinary usage but to elucidate the quasi-technical notion of perception, I shall not want to exclude proprioception from the list of perceptual modalities solely because it differs in many ways (physiologically and phenomenologically) from other perceptual categories.

There is, however, a residual problem. I have recommended that the senses be distinguished by reference to features of physical stimuli. In the present case, unfortunately, the stimuli in question appear to be extremely diverse, ranging from occurrences in muscles, joints, and inner ears, to optic arrays undergoing certain sorts of global transformation. How, then, can one speak sensibly of a single proprioceptive modality?

I concede that this way of speaking is improper, indeed that it is, in some respects, positively misleading, but I shall argue that this fact is, for present purposes, beside the point. It is not my intention to produce here an exhaustive taxonomy of the senses—that, after all, is, on my view, an empirical task—but to indicate, first, a logic for such a classification and, second, to show how this logic fits even our ordinary commonsensical classifications reasonably well.

It may be, then, that what is called proprioceptive information is in fact determined by a variety of disparate physical stimuli. If this is so, then proprioception may be reducible to some combination of sensory modes. The use of a single expression here comes, I suspect, mainly from an implicit theory of sensory classification, one that encourages us, roughly, to lump together information-sources because they all provide information about a single subject matter, in this case one's bodily dispositions and movements. Proprioceptive information (as distinct from, say, visual or auditory information) is typically classified by reference to its *content*, rather than by reference to its source.

I doubt, then, that it can be very useful to regard proprioception as *a* sensory mode. Rather, there seem to be several proprioceptive modalities. I shall use this term merely to stand for whichever of these modalities remain (if any) when one subtracts those discussed already (vision, touch, and the like). Thus, if some proprioceptive information is gleaned from goings-on in the muscles and joints, then such goings-on may form the basis of *a* proprioceptive mode. To the extent that these goings-on differ from vistibular occurrences in the inner ear, we may wish to regard the latter as a second proprioceptive mode. Again, such matters cannot be decided in advance; they are, in the broadest sense, empirical. It is, for that reason, pointless for me to speculate on them here.

I shall use the term "proprioception," then, as a cover for my empirical ignorance. In fact, of course, this point can be extended to what I have said about *all* the senses. I have not sought an exhaustive listing. Indeed, I could not set out to do that given my suggested classificatory technique. The number of possible sensory modes depends upon the number of possible information sources, and there is no obvious way to specify these in advance. My goal, however, is not to legislate for the physiologist, but merely to pave the way for a general account of perception. Such an account must, I have insisted, be defined over all the senses, all *possible* senses.

Intuitively, the conditions that must be satisfied in order for it to be the case that S sees something may not be very much like the conditions that must be satisfied in order for it to be true that S feels or hears something. My hope is that I can provide a characterization of perception that can be completed for any sensory modality by "plugging in" the special conditions associated with that modality. This seems to me the proper route to take even though it may be impossible to say in advance much about those special conditions. Certainly it is preferable to the elaboration of an extremely general characterization of perception applicable without modification to any sensory mode. Even if such a broad account were feasible, something one may easily doubt, its very generality would serve to obscure more than it would illuminate.

My strategy will be to follow tradition and focus in most of what follows on visual perception. It is hoped, however, that the present chapter provides at least an inkling of how claims founded on characteristics of one modality may (or, in some cases, may not) be extended to others. I begin with vision, not because I regard visual perception as in any epistemological sense privileged. Rather it is just that vision seems, for whatever reason, both more interesting and simpler to talk about. A discussion of perception that takes off in this way from features of a single modality would, in most cases, merit suspicion. In providing a principled way of distinguishing the senses, however, one provides (in principle, anyway) a technique for generalizing across modalities. This, perhaps, is as close as one can reasonably expect to come to a thoroughly general or neutral characterization of perception.[10]

References

Boring, E. G. 1942. *Sensation and Perception in the History of Experimental Psychology*. New York: Appleton-Century.

Gibson, J. J. 1966. *The Senses Considered as Perceptual Systems*. Boston: Houghton Mifflin.

———. 1979. *The Ecological Approach to Visual Perception*. Boston: Houghton Mifflin.

Grice, H. P. 1962. Some Remarks about the Senses. In *Analytical Philosophy*, 1st ser., ed. R. J. Butler. Oxford: Blackwell.

Guarniero, G. 1974. Experience of Tactile Vision. *Perception* 3: 101–104.

---

[10] I have deliberately left aside discussion of our awareness of "bodily sensations," such things as pains, tickles, itches, and (perhaps) afterimages. These are, it seems, *had* rather than perceived. Later (chiefly in chapter IV) I shall argue that perception is best regarded as "epistemic," that in perceiving a thing we come to have beliefs about it. In contrast to this, one's having a bodily sensation, B, seems not to depend on one's having any beliefs at all about B, in particular, not on one's having the belief about B that it is a B-type sensation.

Mehta, V. 1982. Personal History. *New Yorker* (Nov. 15): 51–155.

Metzinger, W. 1930. Optische in Ganzfeld II. *Psychologische Forschung* 13: 6–29.

Morgan, M. J. 1977. *Molyneux's Question*. New York: Cambridge University Press.

Müller, J. 1838. On Specific Energies of Nerves. In *A Sourcebook in the History of Psychology*, ed. R. J. Herrnstein and E. G. Boring. Cambridge, Mass.: Harvard University Press, 1965.

Reed, E. S., and R. K. Jones. 1978. Gibson's Theory of Perception: A Case of Hasty Epistemologizing? *Philosophy of Science* 45: 519–30.

Roxbee Cox, J. W. 1970. Distinguishing the Senses. *Mind* 79: 530–50.

Schiffman, H. R. 1976. *Sensation and Perception*, New York: Wiley.

White, B. W., F. A. Saunders, L. Scadden, P. Bach-y-Rita, and C. C. Collins, 1970. Seeing with the Skin. *Perception and Psychophysics* 7: 23–27.

8

Characterising the Senses*

Mark Leon

What distinguishes the senses? The answer, I think, essentially involves reference to the character of experience. I will argue that the character of experience is ineliminable; in particular it is not eliminable in favour of some suitably circumscribed cognitive feature—perceiving is not definable in terms of believing. This is not to suggest that experience is non-cognitive or non-epistemic. On the contrary I think it is cognitive or epistemic. The point is rather that this feature does not exhaust its nature. Nor is it to suggest that the feature of character is akin to the intrinsic quality—the qualia—of sensations. In a way which points away from this assimilation, experiences are diaphanous, unlike sensations, which might be thought of (by contrast) as opaque. One can think of the difference this way: When we describe our experience we do so by reference to what the experience is of, or apparently of—we describe it representationally, in terms of what it represents. So the redness we appeal to in characterising our experience is not a property of the experience itself—the experience is not red—but a feature of what we see or appear to see. By contrast—and here I present without endorsing the position—it would seem that when we describe our sensations we do so by reference to their own intrinsic non-representational properties. In characterising a sensation as throbbing, we ascribe a property to the sensation itself. The sensation is throbbing. If experience is diaphanous in being characterisable in terms of what it represents, the sensation is opaque in being replete with intrinsic non-representational character. (For more on this difference, see Leon 1987). But neither of these aspects will feature centrally here.

My objective in the first part of this paper is partly to clear the ground for laying out the thesis to be examined in the second; partly it is to anticipate some of the objections to that thesis; but partly it is to look at a certain strategy of understanding sense experience which is more

Mark Leon "Characterising the Senses", *Mind and Language*, Volume 3, No. 4, pp. 243-270, 1988. (Reproduced with permission of Blackwell Publishing Ltd.)

---

* I would like to thank the editor and some anonymous referees for helpful comments and suggestions.

general than that embodied in the cognitive thesis. Though much of the argument will be negative, the idea is to indicate what aspects or elements must be found in a more adequate account. In the second part I confront the radical thesis more directly.

But first a qualification. It is clear that one could ask what it is that distinguishes and characterises the senses and expect or receive different answers. There is, for example, the interest one might have in the physical phenomena which activate the different senses; or there might be an interest in the internal mechanisms on which the various senses depend, whether in terms of the (apparently) computational processes involved, as in the work of Marr on vision (Marr 1982), or in terms of—if these differ—the psychological processes involved, or in terms of the underlying physiology. As the interests vary so the answers will vary. My interest is at a more general level; the objective is to uncover those features which a sense *must* possess in order to be the sense it is. This is not to suggest as it might seem, a disinterest in the empirical facts of the operation of the senses. What is more correct is that the account is not always tied to those facts. For it might turn out that the senses can survive certain variations in their operation at some of the foregoing levels. If so that throws light on the essential features of a sense. Of course it could turn out that the general and more specific interests do not diverge. That is not my position. But irrespective of the substantive conclusion—that will be a function of the argument and evidence considered—I hope at least to exhibit the point of the more general interest.

PART ONE   SENSE AND EXPERIENCE

I

What is it that distinguishes the various senses? Pre-reflectively one might be inclined to say the character of the experiences associated with their operation. There seems to be a qualitative difference between seeing an object and feeling an object; seeing an object as square seems different from feeling an object as square. And this difference seems more radical than that between seeing an object as square and seeing an object as round. Not only are the objects different as it would be natural to claim, but the experiences themselves appear to be different. Since one is focussing on the phenomenology of an experience to couch this claim in such terms as 'it seems that there is a difference in character' might appear to be superfluous. If the experiences appear different then there is a difference in appearance, as it were.

Sympathetic as I am to this response it is nevertheless too fast. Crucially the notion of a difference in experience is not unproblematic. When we describe our experience we do so in terms of what we perceive or seem to perceive. This being so what appears to be a difference in experience might on closer examination turn out to be a difference accountable for in other ways. If we describe our experiences in terms of the objects or properties we perceive or seem to perceive, is the difference not merely in the objects and properties we perceive or seem to perceive? If it is, reference to a difference in character of the experience is otiose. The differences are entirely in what is perceived. Still, there is a temptation to say that the experiences themselves are different. In seeing an object as square and feeling that object as square, though the same property is detected it seems to be 'filtered through' different modes of presentation. The trouble is it is not clear how we are to characterise that difference further without making reference to what we seem to perceive. Alternatively, as some have claimed, that difference is further describable, not in terms of the ordinary objects and properties perceived, but in terms of special objects or properties perceived. It might be held that when we describe our experience what we describe are special objects of the various senses, objects accordingly peculiar to these senses. On this account then, shape turns out to be divisible at least into visual and tactile shape. The appearance of there being a common property perceived being merely illusory. This is not a line I will pursue here.

The experiential account is not unproblematic. Putting it aside there are three others which taken alone or in combination have been suggested. They focus on 'external' features of perception. (The division I follow is made by Grice in his marvellous paper 'Some remarks about the senses' (Grice, 1962 [this volume, chapter 4])).[1] The first is the property account (for a version and defence see Roxbee Cox, 1970 [this volume, chapter 5]) according to

---

[1] In the ensuing discussion I assume that in practice one can treat the senses as fairly discrete systems 'associated with' particular properties (or sets of properties), activating mechanisms and physiological processes. This is a somewhat idealised assumption. For it is clear that there are various linkages between the senses. The McGurk illusion is one such illustration. (See McGurk and Macdonald 1976—more on this later in this section.) There is also the phenomenon of synaesthesia in which a stimulus associated with one modality apparently yields an experience characteristic of another. An example is that of so-called 'coloured hearing' where an aural stimulus, a vowel sound, or a musical note, evokes a sensation or image of colour. However, such synaesthetic experiences are rare (Marks 1987, p. 384) and the underlying mechanism and the significance not well understood (Marks 1975, p. 315; Marks 1987, p. 393). For example, it is not clear whether the aural stimulus actually produces the visual experience, or whether what is operative is some form of association. Marks tends to take synaesthesia as exhibiting some 'communality of structure' of the various senses, as he puts it '...synaesthetic relations appear to express correspondences between dimensions of sensory experience that are fundamental to sensation in general'. (Marks 1975, p. 316). Either way it would seem that the phenomenon though highly interesting is fairly peripheral, and I don't think it undermines the assumption of this paper (and that standardly made elsewhere in the literature) that the senses can be viewed as modular systems with certain distinctive features; that, for example, the visual system is one characterised by a certain sort of experience which, because elicited by light which is structured in a certain way partly as a function of certain properties of objects, gives a representation of those properties. Of course though the senses in practice have certain distinctive features, as I try to argue in this paper, not all those features are essential in characterising the senses. (I think it is more open as to the degree to which perceptual systems are 'informationally encapsulated' (and so modular in that sense). Obviously not just any bit of background information affects how we perceive things; but maybe more can than Fodor allows (see Fodor 1983). (For a critical discussion of some questions relevant to this issue, see Leon 1986.))

which the senses are distinguished in terms of the properties detected by means of them, for example, sight by shape and colour. Assuming some common perceptual term, seeing would be perceiving something as having a certain colour and shape. The second account appeals to the 'mechanisms' which activate the different senses or on which the senses depend for their operation, for example, light in the case of sight; seeing would be having a perception brought about by light. The third account focuses on the internal mechanisms associated with the different senses, for example, taking sight once again, seeing would be perceiving with the eyes and perhaps the whole physiological system underlying vision.

In this first section I will be examining the property criterion for distinguishing the senses (taken independently of a reductive claim which can be associated with it); in the second section I examine the 'activating' mechanism criterion; and in the third I examine the sense organ one. In the fourth section I return to the experiential criterion, firstly in order to determine whether, or in what way, it is independent of the others, and secondly in order to consider whether it is a plausible criterion for distinguishing the senses in terms of whether it is necessary or sufficient or both.

Do the non-experiential criteria taken singly or in combination suffice? Consider the property criterion first. Is it, in the first place, the case that the various senses are associated neatly with distinctive properties? There seem to be two problems; the first, a hurdle which must be overcome; the second, deeper lying. We do associate different sets of properties with the different senses; colour, for example, is taken to be a visual characteristic that is a property accessible to sight, and say, fragrance, an olfactory property, one accessible to smell. And yet at times we describe ourselves as seeing the fragrance of a plant; or seeing the warmth (a tactile property) of an object. Fragrance and warmth would not appear on the visual list, yet we seem able to perceive or detect them visually. One way of reconciling this would be by differentiating between properties directly detectable and hence perceptible by a sense, and properties only indirectly detectable and hence (perhaps) only in an extended, metaphorical sense, perceptible by a sense.

Roxbee Cox, following a suggestion of Grice, proposes that we define direct perception in terms of 'not perceiving that (an item) has other properties which (a percipient) could recognise as indicating the presence of the first property, feature or state of affairs'. (Roxbee Cox 1970, p. 535 [this volume, p. 105].) This seems correct. We recognise that a plant is fragrant by seeing that it has certain visual properties associated with and hence indicative of its being fragrant. And we recognise that a stove is hot by associating the plate's being a particular colour and its being independently determinable as hot. Crucially in telling that a plant is fragrant or that a plate is hot, we go mainly on the basis of colour. There seems to be a clear difference between telling that an object has these properties visually, and seeing those properties. Telling that an object has them is seeing that the object has certain visual properties which *indicate* through association that the object possesses the non-visual properties.

This intuitively satisfactory account runs, however, into further problems. Some have argued that we perceive shape by perceiving the colour of an object (or if not colour in the sense of a chromatic hue, then as Berkeley too allowed, by perceiving or being aware of 'different proportions of light and shade' (Berkeley 1975, p. 54), or as we might put it more perspicuously, brightness contrast).[2] But then it would look as if shape is only indirectly 'perceived' and so not a visual characteristic at all. But clearly this is not the case. We need a further refinement to allow us to represent the difference between fragrance as a visually indicable property, and shape as a visually determinable, and so visual property.

A possible refinement is to adopt a causal account: in a world in which we lacked a sense of smell, all other things being equal, we could not tell by visual means that objects were fragrant, certainly not just by looking at them. Yet if we only had a visual sense we would still be able to tell the shape of objects. What we appeal to then is the 'causal efficacy' of shape on our visual system and the lack of it in the case of fragrance. How an object structures light is at least partially a function of its shape not its fragrance. So a property on this account would be directly perceived just in case it was causally efficacious with respect to a particular perceptual modality. This is a tentative suggestion, requiring refinement and certainly not without problems; for there are properties which are causally efficacious and yet which we do not take as visual, for example, having a certain atomic structure; and there are higher order properties, noncolour and non-spatial properties, which in our normal commerce with the world, we take ourselves as having visual access to, which, because in some sense supervenient on colour and shape properties, seem only to 'derive' their causal efficacy from that relation. Bearing this in mind, we are at least in a position to examine the property account directly.

Is it the case that whenever certain properties are perceived which fall under one list, then they are perceived by the modality standardly associated with that list? And is it the case that if these properties are not perceived, then it is not a case of sight in operation? I will try to show that there is at least a prima facie case against this suggestion.

The first difficulty with this account arises out of doubly-determinable properties. Shape, for example, features on both the visual and tactile

---

[2] That shape is perceived through colour is a thesis associated with Berkeley. It might seem to be contradicted by the contemporary emphasis on brightness contrast as the key feature in shape perception; for without brightness contrast, at isoluminance, certain characteristics of shape perception fall away, like stereopsis or depth; and with such a contrast there can be shape perception even without colour differentiation in the sense of a differentiation of the chromatic hues. But I am not sure that this contradicts the thesis. Berkeley's point was that shape perception is through colour or variations of light. Further to the point brightness is often referred to as one of the dimensions (together with saturation and hue) in terms of which colour is characterised. So either way, the point remains that shape is perceived in a sense through something else.

lists. So that the shape of an object is perceived does not tell us whether it is perceived by sight or touch. Admittedly, in certain circumstances, if we only perceive shape and other properties featuring on the visual list, that would be indicative of its being perceived by sight. But this will not always be the case. Grice illustrates the problem by considering a case in which one object looks larger than another while feels to be the same size as the other (Grice 1962, p. 137 [this volume, p. 87]). How could such a case be represented on the property account? For what we have is that we both directly perceive the discrepancy in size, and directly perceive the equality in size, and directly perceive certain properties featuring on the visual list (apart from shape) and directly perceive certain properties on the tactile list (apart from the shape). However, that is not enough to tell us whether the objects look different in size or feel different.

Roxbee Cox has a suggestion in response to this. He argues for a modification of the property account—his key feature account. He isolates for each sense what is termed a primary or key property; so that if one's perception involves directly perceiving that a thing has that property, then one's perception belongs to the appropriate modality for that property. For example, in the case of sight, he takes colour to be such a key feature. So if one's perception of an object's shape involves a perception of the object's colour, then one sees rather than feels the shape. Accordingly, in the problematic case if one's seeming perception of the difference in size is through colour, then the size is seen; and if one's seeming perception is through 'feel', then the size is felt to be the same.

Less than a resolution of the problem, this key feature account highlights shortcomings with this strategy. Firstly, the notion of perceiving a property through the perception of another is problematic. Even in his own terms this would suggest that Roxbee Cox would have to allow that fragrance and warmth are visual properties, which even if not damaging to the endeavour to differentiate the senses—since sight and smell presumably could still be distinguished in terms of what other properties are perceived, or primarily perceived—seems straightforwardly wrong as things stand. Secondly, it is not clear on his account what perceiving one property through another comes to and such that we will have a resolution of Grice's dilemma.

What is it for one property to be perceived through another? Within the limits of the key feature account, it at least involves the co-detection of the two properties. In a case in which only properties appearing on one list are perceived, we might also say that the one property would not be perceived if the other were not perceived; but not vice versa. Perhaps we cannot perceive shape without perceiving colour, while we can perceive colour without perceiving shape. This seems to be more than co-detection. But does it suffice for Grice's example? I think not. In that case there are additional properties perceived, and most importantly the same property perceived by more than one sense. It is entirely possible that one would discover that when one no longer perceives colour, one no longer perceives inequality in size. And that would be reason for thinking that the one object looked larger than the other. But as Grice himself points out, this reasonable inference is not strong enough (Grice 1962, p. 139 [this volume, p. 88]). For it might be the case that perceived difference or equality of size was in part a function of the operation of another sense. (For an illustration of how the operation of one sense can be affected by another, consider the McGurk Illusion (See McGurk and Macdonald 1976). What McGurk and Macdonald showed was that the way sounds are heard can be affected by visual cues, like lip movements. They showed that the utterance of one sound could be misheard if presented with visual information for another. When the countermanding visual information is absent, the experience reverts back to what would be expected going on the auditory stimulus alone). So that certain tactile properties are perceived and that equality of size is perceived, does not imply that prior to the elimination of the visual sense, the size of the objects was felt to be equal. In the context where there are properties from different though overlapping lists, short of switching to another criterion we cannot make use of the notion of perceiving one property through another other than in this unsatisfactory way. For while it might be true that the inequality and equality of size are perceived through other properties, so long as we cannot say which is perceived through which property, we cannot tell whether the perception is visual or tactile.

The heroic course for one who holds the key feature account would be to admit that in certain extreme cases we could not *tell* by which sense the equality or inequality of size was perceived, but still hold that since there is a *determinate* answer even if we lack it, the key feature account still suffices; if the inequality is perceived through colour then it is seen; if through 'feel' then it is felt. So let us take this course and see whether there are not additional problems with it.

We are counselled to specify the operation of one sense rather than another in virtue of one property or set of properties being perceived rather than another. But what determines whether a property falls onto the respective lists? What makes a property visual or tactile and so on? One answer is that these are the properties which, as it happens, we do perceive by means of the various senses. Of course, this is correct, but it is troublesome. For are the senses not being defined by reference to contingent conditions—conditions which do obtain but which *need* not?

There are two sorts of problems. Shape is a doubly determinable property; might it not be for all we know through some unknown sense triply determinable? Could there perhaps not even be some different sense by means of which just those properties which appear, say, on the visual list are perceived? This indeed supposes not only a qualitative difference in perception, but also that that difference, if radical enough, would count as the operation of a different sense. Here we play on two points; that a property might be accessible to more than one sense; and that the 'perceptions' of that property might be different as, say, shape as felt and as seen appear different. And that, in turn leads us to suppose that there might be a different—qualitatively different—sense by means of which just the same properties as belonging to one known modality are perceived.

This first problem focuses on the apparent contingency of the neat correlation between sense modalities and sets of properties; while single properties feature on more than one list, whole sets of properties do not, as it happens, overlap. The second problem I wish to raise concerns the apparent contingency of the association of sets of properties and perceptual modalities as we at present distinguish them. Could we not imagine that the properties featuring on the one list come to cause types of perceptions of the 'wrong' modality? Couldn't visual properties come to cause aural type experiences; and aural properties come to cause visual type experiences?[3] In so far as the appropriate properties are not constituted by the having of the appropriate experiences, this does seem to be a genuine possibility. And in so far as the various properties are constituted by the having of the appropriate experiences, the property account falls away.[4] One cannot distinguish the senses by reference to the properties perceived, and then distinguish the properties by reference to the experiences which constitute them. (Peacocke also points out that the failure of such a realism undermines accounts of the senses which do not make reference to (unreduced) experiences. He goes on to argue (as I do not here) that this realism cannot be sustained. (See Peacocke 1983)).

Taking the property view seriously entails taking the possibility of causal switches seriously. But then both the necessity and sufficiency is undermined; for visual type perceptions could be brought about by non-visual properties—and would this not be to see the properties on that list? And properties featuring on the visual list could be perceived by means of non-visual perceptions—would that still be to see those properties? At the heart of the account there seems to be a dilemma; take the properties to be wholly independent of the experiences or perceptions which they cause, in which case the account lacks the appropriate necessity required of a general specification of the senses—any set of properties could come to cause any set of experiences in suitable conditions; or take the properties to be constituted by our experiences or perceptions in which case they lack the appropriate independence required for a vindication of the account as a property account.

---

[3] Here, as elsewhere in this paper, I am indebted to Malcolm Budd. He first drew my attention to the 'possibility' of a switch in experience. My argument was developed in the light of that consideration. This possibility is also mooted by Colin McGinn (McGinn 1980, p. 43) and by Lloyd Kaufman who introduces it interestingly as an extension of Johannes Muller's doctrine of specific nerve energies. (Lloyd Kaufman 1979, p. 70.)

[4] This is an overstatement. The property account does not fall away but it would no longer be basic. We would be able to distinguish the senses in terms of the properties perceived by means of them, only because these, or more properly, some of these properties were in part constituted by the experiences 'they give rise to'.

II

What about the suggestion that we define the senses by reference to the mechanisms which activate them or the external physical conditions which make them possible? So to see would be to have a perception brought about by the effect of light on the percipient, and so on.

Could we not see in the absence of light? Could we not imagine the possibility at least of coming to have visual experiences which matched an array of objects at a certain location in as systematic a way as our ordinary visual experience does, and yet where it is not light which activates the perceptions? Would this not be to see those objects? Consider: could it not turn out that contrary to what we believe light was not really, but only apparently, the operative activating mechanism of sight in our case? Could there not be some other as yet unknown mechanism at work? Under these conditions would we concede that after all we lacked sight of objects? I think not. I think that we would rather take ourselves to have been wrong about the importance of light in sight. And similarly, even if light were the mechanism for sight in our case, that ought not to preclude the possibility of creatures who could see despite the fact that their visual experiences were not activated by light. (Dretske too would seem to moot the possibility of sight without activation by light. (See Dretske 1969, pp. 50–51)).

Similarly, the sufficiency could be challenged. Just as we could come to imagine certain properties causing in us experiences of an abnormal type, could we not imagine, say, light coming to cause in us experiences of an aural kind, and, say, sound waves, vibrations in the air, coming to cause in us experiences of a visual kind? That it was light or vibrations in the air that activated or brought about the perceptions would not suffice to show that it was correspondingly a case of seeing or hearing.

(There are those who contest this claim, citing in support a less fanciful sort of example involving the operation of what has come to be called the Tactile Vision Substitution System—the TVSS. (For an account of the case see Bach-y-Rita et al 1969, White et al 1970, and for a personalised view, Guarniero 1974). In brief, the device comprises a television camera connected to a set of vibrators acting on the skin (normally the back) of a subject, by which means an optical array is transformed into a 'tactile' image. What is clear from the example is that a subject is enabled to glean certain spatial information, normally associated with vision, from the optical array, but crucially not by having a visual experience. This aspect is of some importance. The experience the subject enjoys is akin, at least at first, to a tactile one. This is to be expected for the vibrators are acting on the skin. But the experience is of a very unusual kind:

> 'Very soon after I had learned how to scan, the sensations no longer felt as if they were located on my back, and I became less and less aware that

vibrating pins were making contact with my skin. By this time objects had come to have a top and a bottom; a right side and a left; but no depth— they existed in an ordered two-dimensional space, the precise location of which had not yet been determined'. (Guarniero 1974, p. 104).

Is this a case of 'seeing' with the skin as is claimed somewhat cautiously by Guarniero (Guarniero 1974, p. 101) or is it a straightforward case of see- ing as is claimed by Heil (Heil 1983, pp. 13–18 [this volume, chapter 7]) and by White and his co-authors (White et al 1970, especially p. 27)?

I don't think the TVSS enables sight. As described the example is not persuasive. It is no more persuasive than the suggestion that we would hear sounds and various of their properties by means of the eyes, simply because we observe an optical transformation of an aural input by using say, an oscilloscope. In this latter case I take it that we perceive (clearly visually) certain configurations on a screen; we observe the effects of the aural input. This access to sounds is indirect. The same, I think, is true in the case of the TVSS. The access to the light is indirect. The access is mediated by the vibrating pins, which because isomorphic with the optical array, produces an experience by means of which certain spatial information is available. Just as the aural input acts on something we see, the oscilloscope, so the light acts on something we feel, the pins on the back. This is not to say there are no differences between the two cases. There are. Most importantly as seen the experience produced by the TVSS is not exactly alike the standard sort of tactile experience (though that is a function of the unusual tactile stimulus—the arrangement of vibrating pins). And it also seems to be the case that with time and prac- tice the subject comes to 'see through' the experience—the experience seems to give awareness of spatial relations 'out there' rather than of sen- sations on the back. These are significant points; but for an account like this which focuses on the activating mechanism hardly relevant.

One could modify the example in the attempt to get rid of the prob- lematic feature. The ground of my rejection was the reasonably neutral claim that the information acquired is indirectly acquired. So sup- pose, instead, that the mechanism were 'internalised'. What would be required is a photo-sensitive device (either part of or connected to the body), and an internal mechanism connecting the device to a centre able to produce the relevant sort of experience. (One could use the eye as the relevant photo-sensitive device, though in this use it would be hooked up to a system producing the different sort of experience.) The trouble is that by this modification we arrive back at a variation of the switch in experience—this time a tactile experience produced by the activity of light. (It is a notable fact that not only would the experience produced be of the wrong kind, but the properties it gave us access to would be of the wrong range. Crucially colour is left out. These two points are not of course disconnected; though as seen they are not connected in a way that lends comfort to the property account)).

Before leaving the activating mechanism account, there is a complication that needs to be dealt with. In the discussion so far I have treated the property criterion and the activating mechanism criterion as if they were wholly independent. But are they? The objects of hearing are sounds or various properties of sounds; and the activating mechanism of hearing consists in sound waves. The situation with sight is not quite the same, but there are parallels. Though we seldom take light to be the object of sight, we sometimes do. We at least sometimes see lightness and darkness; yet these are modifications of light, and so properties of light. But then light, too, can be both object of sight and activating mechanism. Think also of colour. A realist about colour is likely to identify the colour of an object with a modification of light reflected by an object. Objects, we might say, are coloured, but their having colour, and having certain colours consist in their modifying light in certain ways. Once again the property criterion and the activating criterion are closely related. (This thesis, of course, needs qualification. What colour an object looks to have is not just a function of the wavelength of light reflected by the object. There are two major points of complication: not everything that looks the same in colour has the same physical property—different properties can enable the production of similar colour experiences; and not everything with the same property necessarily looks to have the same colour, for other factors can intrude, like background contrast, the state of adaptation of the eye and even higher-order factors like how the object is seen—as what. (See Land 1959, and Land 1977)).[5]

If the foregoing account of colour is correct, would it follow that it would be impossible to have a world in which colours of objects were seen, or lightness and brightness were seen, and yet where the perception was not by means of light, that is, where the perception was not brought about by the effect of light on the percipient? Would it follow that one's matching visual experiences in our original case could not be taken to constitute seeings of the objects at the matching location because the perceptions were not brought about by light? I think not. We would still need to distinguish the fact that the properties apparently perceived involved light essentially, and the fact that the activating mechanism did not. Could it not be that light was the object of the perception but not the medium of the perception or the activating mechanism? What these considerations tend to show is that light might enter into the story (in so far as the identification of colour with wavelength of light reflected was correct) but not that it needs to enter the story at the level of activating mechanism. If it were possible for light to be the cause of, but not the mechanism of, the perception, then that would suffice to show that colour could be perceived by means of visual experiences without

---

[5] I simplify, for given my interest, the presence of the mechanism is more important than the details, and more significantly the simplified account is stronger than I need, but as strong as an opponent needs. (See the earlier discussion of the property account.)

those experiences being activated by light. Similarly, if sounds were the cause of, but not the mechanism of, perceptions of an aural kind, then sounds could be heard even though one's perceptions were not activated by sound waves impinging on the ears.

Consider, for example, the following case. Assume that a creature has gone blind, because of a malfunctioning in the nerve pathways beyond the eye. Could we not imagine overcoming this blindness by inserting a radio device which conserved function between the severed nerves? Now imagine a creature whose malfunctioning is in the eye. Could we not imagine a radio device which connected his afferent nerves of sight beyond the eye to some other individual's eye such that once again functioning is conserved—the individual would have more or less the same experience that his benefactor had. Now let us imagine the benefactor goes to Paris. Radio devices are powerful mechanisms. We could quite easily imagine that while our 'blind' creature languishes in Johannesburg, he could yet enjoy the visual experience enjoyed by his benefactor while touring the Louvre. Does he not see the paintings housed there? For after all, combining the examples, we can imagine the benefactor himself to possess a device of a similar kind connecting up severed nerves. Clearly of him we would still say he sees, so why not the other? Just because the radio waves have a greater path to travel?

Some might object that this is not properly a case of seeing where the mechanism which activates it is not light or not light of a wavelength we are normally sensitive to; for does the first step not involve light impinging on eyes? Perhaps this is so—one's intuitions become clouded as the cases become more unusual. Still one can see in continuing this development of unusual cases how even that might become possible. I am persuaded that any system which could deliver matching visual experiences even if not by means of light would not only be a visual system but one which under the right conditions, would allow us to see the objects so matched.

III

The last criterion which needs to be looked at is that which appeals to the sense-organs in distinguishing the senses. Interestingly enough this is the one which pre-reflectively we are as likely to use as we are the experiential one. Yet it would seem to be by far the most unsatisfactory. The general idea is that seeing would be perceiving by means of the eyes; hearing, perceiving by means of the ears, and so on.

A number of problems have been posed for this account. There are just two that I will concentrate on. The first and minor one is that we can both see and feel with our eyes—the eye is both visually and tactually sensitive. Given that it can serve these two functions, how could we differentiate purely in terms of 'sense-organs' whether we are seeing with our eyes or feeling with them?

The second and I think fatal problem arises out of the fact that this criterion is either too specific or it is too general to be of use. It is too specific if by the sense-organs we pick out only our sense-organs with their underlying physiological structure. For we ought to allow for the possibility of creatures with sense-organs exhibiting a totally different structure, which nonetheless we would have no hesitation in claiming would allow these creatures to have just the perceptions which we have. In fact, we do not have to take into account other creatures. Simply think of the progressive sophistication of prosthetic devices. Clearly more and more of our sensory organs could be replaced by devices which conserved or created anew just those functions which our organs happen to realize. In this sense it is not even a truth, let alone a necessary truth, that we see with our eyes—if, of course, by 'eye' we mean anything having the same structure, whatever that is, which our eye has. But if we liberalise the notion of a sense-organ to take in these possibilities, reference to sense-organs as differentiating the senses would be completely otiose. For now we would be identifying an organ, as, say, an organ of sight, in virtue of something else—either a sensitivity to certain properties or activating mechanisms, or its delivering certain matching experiences, that is, experiences which match an already identified sensory modality.

In short, if we mean by 'eye' that physiological mechanism which we possess, then eyes are not necessary for sight; any prosthetic or functionally equivalent device will suffice. But if we mean by 'eye' some device which subserves a certain function, then eyes will be necessary for sight, but we then have no way of specifying when an item is an eye without appealing to something other than the nature or structure of that item. We would have had to have distinguished the senses prior to determining whether an item was an eye or not.

IV

The difficulties facing the non-experiential criteria lead us back to the experiential one. It is this that I will defend. I will argue that in order to characterise and distinguish the senses we need to make reference to the character of, and differences in, experience. But my immediate objective will be something less than a thorough statement and defence of this position. Here I wish to accomplish two things: on the positive side to sketch the experiential position in order to defuse certain primary criticisms and in so doing clarify what is being claimed; and on the negative side argue against an account which might be thought to promise a way out of our problems by attempting to give a reductive analysis of experience in terms of a set of characteristic beliefs. In short I hope to show that reference to experience is both necessary and basic. Two central problems have been noted with the experiential criterion. The first arises out of the apparent diaphanous character of experience. When asked to describe our experience we do so in terms of what we perceive or appear to perceive. We make reference to the *properties* or objects that our experience appears to give access to. But then to what extent is the experiential criterion independent of the property one? And where does that leave the claim that the senses differ in the character of their experience? The second, highlighted by Grice, focuses on an apparent unacceptable consequence of the account. If the account is correct to perceive in a modality is to detect certain properties by means of a modality-specific experience. That suggests in turn that it is a contingent fact that certain properties are detected by certain senses. 'But it does not seem to be just a contingent fact that we do not (for example) see the smell of things.' (Grice 1962, p. 145 [this volume, p. 93]).

Consider the first difficulty. That experience is diaphanous suggests the experiential criterion is not logically independent of the property one. For how else are we to account for our being directed to the properties we perceive or appear to perceive in describing our experience? There is, I think, something to the thought that the criterion is not logically independent of the property one; but it is crucial to get clear on the sense in which this might be so. What is not in question is the possibility of experience obtaining in the absence of those objects and properties it normally gives us access to—not all experiences are veridical experiences of objects. In this respect experiences are independent of objects. For the moment I will also assume (without argument) that the world could be propertied as it is in the absence of perceivers and so experiences. (This realism across the board is more than I need, and more than I accept, but it is a useful starting point, not only because of the wider agreement it might allow, but also for the distinctions it enables one to draw which hold even if the thesis is not true in full generality.) What this realism allows for is the possibility of experience of one kind being brought about by properties drawn from an alien list.[6]

The worry that arises about the logical independence of the experiential criterion from the property one, has its proper source in the way we characterise experience; when we describe our experience we do so in terms of what is experienced. To characterise or represent the differences—phenomenological differences—between the various senses we appeal to differences in what is perceived or apparently perceived. Given the apparent independence of experiences and properties this might seem problematic. Why is experience not describable intrinsically

---

[6] An interesting question is what would happen if the reversal of mechanism and experience were to take place. One only needs to think of Kohler's experiments with inverted lenses to recognise the empirical possibility of a re-inversion occurring. If that were to happen it would demonstrate a point I am trying to indicate, that certain experiences and certain properties are made for each other. Or better still, certain experiences are *made* for certain properties.

especially if there is, as alleged, an intrinsic difference in the various senses?

I suggest this feature is less a problem, more a way of highlighting (what I claim is) the nature of experience. In the first place what is exhibited is that experience has a representational content; veridical or not, our experience represents the world as being a particular way. More importantly, and this is what the diaphanous character points to, that representational content of an experience is not a mere extrinsic feature of it. The experience is intrinsically representational. This is a substantive point about experience over which there is much disagreement. The thesis, if correct, suggests it is not an accidental feature about our experience that we so describe it; it is not an accidental feature about our experience that it represents what it does—in the visual case a spatial and coloured world. This contrasts strongly with accounts suggesting the intrinsic character of experience has nothing to do with its representational content; that were the causes of the experience different, its representational content would be different. (See for example Paul Churchland (Churchland 1979) who argues that our sensations are mere 'causal middlemen' whose representational content is not a function of their intrinsic character. On the other side, Roger N. Shepard (Shepard 1984, p. 432) in highlighting the importance of intrinsic features, makes the point that if the environment had been different—if the causes had been different—then a different intrinsic (perceptual) structure would have evolved.) In addition to a content specifiable by reference to the objects or properties of objects the experience represents, an experience also has a character. If experiences can overlap in content they differ in character (think again of the difference between seeing and feeling something to be round). That character can be described at least as visual or aural and so on. What is disturbing, however, is that it seems not to be significantly further describable. Almost any description of our experience is a description of what it represents rather than of how it is in itself. There are exceptions. Blurredness (as opposed to clarity) is a property of an experience in itself; and so is its location within the temporal order. But with these two features of experience noted, I return to the main discussion. (For more on these features, see Leon 1987.)

If the first problem is concerned with what makes an experience belong to a particular modality, the second is concerned with what makes a property belong to a particular modality. Consider this second problem now. The property criterion taken alone seems inadequate for defining a sense. And the experiential criterion brings in reference to properties perceived. For an experience to be visual it must have a certain content specified by reference to the properties it represents. This suggests that we combine the two criteria. The idea would be that one sees just in case one enjoys a certain experience and one detects certain properties. Accordingly, it would be logically possible to detect, say, smells by means of visual experiences and yet not to see smells. The experiential criterion is satisfied but not the property one. But Grice takes this suggestion to be unsatisfactory: '…surely we object on logical grounds no less to the idea that we might detect smells through visual experience than to the idea that we might see smells; indeed the ideas seem to be the same'. (Grice 1962, p. 145 [this volume, p. 93].)

Putting aside the question whether the suggestion is satisfactory or not this rejection is puzzling. The problem is that the notion of 'detection' is ambiguous. On the one hand we might be using it to indicate that we can determine something has a certain smell by looking at it as when we tell that a rose in full bloom is fragrant; while on the other we might be claiming not only that we detect the smell in this—extended—sense, but that we actually see it. Grice himself draws a similar distinction between characteristics which are visually determinable and so can correctly be said to be seen; and characteristics which are merely visually indicable like fragrance and warmth. So there does seem to be a sense in which we can detect smells through a visual experience and yet not see them.

But perhaps Grice has a slightly different example in mind. When we say that we see the fragrance of a plant we know that the property does not stimulate our visual system; fragrance is merely correlated with that which does—colour. But now imagine that smells come to cause in us visual experiences. Would we still be able to distinguish between detecting smells through a visual experience and seeing smells—given that the distinction could no longer be made in terms of the causal efficacy of that property?

Grice seems to want to reject this possibility. There might be two motivations for this; firstly he seems to accept that it is an analytic truth that smells cannot be seen; and connected with this he seems to deny, what is necessary for the possibility, that the property criterion is entirely independent of the experiential criterion. His exact position and so the connection between these ideas is somewhat obscure. If one denies the (full) independence of the property criterion from the experiential one, then doubly determinable properties are going to be problematic. If it is the case that we determine what property is perceived in part by reference to the type of experience had, and if the different senses are associated with different experiences, then how can a property be doubly determinable? Grice seems to suggest that this involves a correlation between the experiences, reflected in agreement as to when an object has that property by the two senses (Grice 1962, p. 148 [this volume, p. 96]). But it is difficult to see how any amount of correlation could make a property doubly determinable without presupposing what has to be established, that it is the same property showing up in both sets of perceptions. Ex-hypothesis that seems to be ruled out, if the properties are (in part) constituted by the experience. If this were so we could object on logical grounds to the idea of seeing smells; smells if constituted by certain non-visual experiences cannot be seen by means of visual experiences. And we could not allow the possibility of smells being detected visually. For smells would lack the independence the thought experiment requires, namely, a realism with respect to the various properties.

The trouble is that Grice seems to waver in his acceptance or rejection of realism with respect to the various properties. While apparently accepting it with respect to shape, he seems to reject it with respect to colour. He takes colour to be a sensible property—the best way of determining that an object has it is by looking (Grice 1962, p. 149 [this volume, p. 96])—while still talking of correlations in the case of shape (a non-realist interpretation) and even moots in the case of colour and other such secondary properties the possibility of their being doubly determinable (which once again suggests realism).

Are the ideas of detecting a smell through a visual experience, that is, through 'sight', and seeing smells the same? There is one sense in which they are not—as when we tell the fragrance of a plant through its colour. But could we make out a case for holding that while we might detect smells through a visual experience, if smells caused in us that experience, still that would not be to see them? Under this causal interpretation where the plants being fragrant causes us to have the visual experience we do have, can we drive a wedge between the ideas of detecting and seeing smells? In general can we distinguish between (causally) detecting and perceiving a property?

Perhaps we can. Assume the background of realism. The idea that we might visually detect a property like a smell at least involves the idea of that property causing a visual experience. The idea that we might see a smell goes beyond this in a way in which I will indicate here only metaphorically and analogically. For a property to be seen not only must it cause an experience it must also 'show up' in the experience in the way in which middle-sized objects show themselves. This metaphor can be bolstered by analogy for there is a parallel in our current situation; though an object's atomic structure is causally responsible for our having the experiences we do, we do not take ourselves to see that structure. If causation is necessary it is not sufficient to make a property perceptible. Significantly, if I am correct, constraints on perceptibility issue from the nature of the experience involved. In this way by combining the two criteria, without appeal to analyticity, we could exhibit why smells do not fall on the visual list. And even if, as it may later turn out, there is a stronger impediment to smells being seen, or more generally, to secondary properties being doubly determinable, we at least have an indication that there is a difference between (causally) detecting and perceiving a property and an indication of what that difference comes to. (This distinction between detection and perception is akin to that between inference and perception. Part of the point here is that what is causally unmediated (as is the smell in the imagined case which contrasts with our current 'visual' access to smell) *need* not be uninferred. Similarly I would argue what is causally mediated *need* not be inferred. (Our access to spatial and colour properties of objects is causally mediated by light and much besides. Still I think that access is not inferential.) (For more on the question of inference see Leon 1986)).

PART TWO   EXPERIENCE AND BELIEF

What makes an experience visual? Earlier I rejected accounts suggesting that visual experiences can be defined and distinguished by reference to their special sensory objects. In turn I suggested that the distinguishing feature of an experience is on the one side its having a content and on the other, a character. The account is not unproblematic. We have yet to examine the notion of content at work, and the feature of character is puzzling. Given this, one might be inclined to look for an alternative account. One beckons which in clarifying the notion of content promises to eliminate serious reference to character. The account is the radical belief thesis. It is associated with D. M. Armstrong, J. W. Roxbee Cox and G. Pitcher (Armstrong 1968; Roxbee Cox 1971; Pitcher 1971). The account reflects that current and often fruitful tendency of viewing matters from an evolutionary and functional point of view. The function of perception is to acquire information. That function is subserved by our experience having a certain representational content. Taking these two aspects together, the account suggests that perceptual states are informational states or (more perspicuously) beliefs—with a certain content. The content of experience goes over to the content of belief; to perceive is to acquire certain beliefs in a specified way. The feature of character is—if the account is correct—eliminable; to see is to acquire a certain *distinctive* set of beliefs in a specified way. This is an echo of an earlier answer. Visual experiences are defined and distinguished by reference to their objects; not by reference to a special set of 'internal' objects, but by reference to an ordinary set of 'external' objects. What makes a state a visual experience is that it is a belief of a kind 'related to' certain (properties of) objects.

In the following my focus will be on this radical reductive thesis. It has two components. The first is the claim that there is no irreducibly sensory, subjective, phenomenological or qualitative character to experience. Whatever the experiential criterion purported to discern is explained away. We specify the distinctive features of experiences and modality specified experiences by selecting the appropriate set of beliefs that constitute them. This thesis is distinct from and more radical than that which suggests perceivings are beliefs *with* a sensuous character. The second component of the thesis is the claim that the relevant cognitive component in terms of which experiences are to be defined is that of belief—as opposed to, say (unasserted) thought. I deal with only the first of these claims in the following.

I

The thesis, I think, is false. Seeing is, if believing, not merely believing. Seeing involves being in a state with a certain phenomenological or qualitative character. There is something that it is like to be in that state. For any belief one wishes to specify it seems possible to have that belief and yet not be in a visual state. Similarly for any visual state there seems more to being in it than there is to being in a belief state with a certain content. That informally is the way prereflective thought would take us. By examining the resources available to the belief thesis I will try to show that that is the way we should go on reflection too.

The belief thesis has a more general and a more specific objective. The general one is to specify which beliefs are perceptual beliefs, which constitute perceivings. The specific one is to specify amongst these, which correspond to or constitute the 'experiences' of the specific modalities—which, for example, are seeings. These objectives correspond to defining a sense in general and specifying the species specific properties of the various senses. My discussion follows the course of these endeavours.

According to the thesis, to perceive is to perceive that something is the case (or questions of veridicality aside) to acquire the belief that something is the case. However, not all beliefs, not even all the beliefs that we acquire through the senses, could constitute the class of beliefs in terms of which experiences or perceivings are to be defined. We learn of things by being told about them, by means of representations of them, by means of their effects or traces, and by means of their perceptually indicable even if not determinable properties. These are all perceptually acquired beliefs but not perceivings. So which perceptually acquired beliefs are perceivings?

The problematic cases carry within them the seeds of a solution. These beliefs were, if not inferential, at least indirectly acquired. Accordingly the solution involves taking the relevant perceptual beliefs to be those acquired directly, those not acquired by first acquiring others.

This modification is on the right track. However, it is not clear that it does or can go far enough. One problem, that I pass over here, is the contention that inference in perception reaches much further than this response assumes, that ordinary beliefs about external objects are inferred from sensory stimulation. I have argued against this elsewhere (see Leon 1986). The more serious problem turns on the possibility of acquiring the right set of beliefs non-inferentially or directly, but where we would not wish to consider these the appropriate set of perceptual beliefs (in terms of which perceivings are to be defined).

There are two sorts of problematic cases: firstly, specific instances of non-inferential beliefs which do not appear to be experiences; and secondly, the general possibility of a specified set of non-inferential beliefs which don't appear to be seeings. The first problem expresses doubt as to whether the account can distinguish non-inferential visual beliefs and non-inferential visual experiences; the second expresses doubt as to whether the account can specify (in the first place) which beliefs are visual and which not. I lead up to these two points in turn.

If perceptual beliefs are non-inferentially acquired beliefs, how are the sensory modalities to be distinguished? As a first step, the modalities can be distinguished in terms of the content of their respective beliefs. Visual beliefs are those beliefs which represent (in the first place) spatial and colour properties of objects. When I see an object I at least see it as having a certain shape or colour. More than this can form the content of a visual experience (and so belief); but it is at least because this much forms the content that the rest does.

Now for the first problem. Could I not acquire a belief with a content appropriate for comprising a visual experience which was not a visual experience? For consider. At present I believe that there is a typewriter (of somewhat antique provenance) in front of me. I believe that because I am seeing it. But assume further that I presently take a break, perhaps start dozing, only to suffer the ceiling above me falling on my head; and assume (still further) that that disturbance so jars my brain as to bring it about on waking that I believe that there is a typewriter in front of me. I have, it would seem, a belief with the same content as before but one which does not comprise an experience. As the example is set up, the belief is not one acquired inferentially, so how is it to be excluded either from the class of perceptual beliefs—beliefs comprising experiences—or from the more specific class of visual beliefs—beliefs comprising visual experiences?

Try this. The notable feature of this belief is its deviant ancestry. It is acquired non-standardly. So why not appeal to this feature in order to exclude it from the domain of perceptual beliefs or visual beliefs? Perceptual beliefs would then be beliefs with a certain content acquired in a certain way.

Informally the idea is that the belief is not perceptual or visual for not being acquired by means of the senses or by means of the eyes. I pass over the problem of whether we can specify on this account a sense other than by reference to a mechanism for acquiring beliefs non-inferentially, and I postpone discussion of the specific visual case. Still the account won't do, for either it appeals 'problematically' to an already given distinction in cases or it fails to distinguish two sorts of cases. This is the problem. Not only might we acquire (or suffer) non-experiential beliefs in non-standard sort of ways, we could also acquire (or suffer) experiential beliefs in a non-standard sort of way. Consider for example hallucinations. These are experiential beliefs non-standardly caused. So how do we include these within the domain of the perceptual? The answer calls on an analogy. Think of forged coins. These are of a type produced by the authorised mint. But being forged they are of course not so produced. Similarly consider hallucinations. These are beliefs of a type produced in a certain sort of way; but being hallucinations they were not so produced. Now for the distinction. Whereas hallucinations are beliefs of a kind brought about in normal conditions in a certain sort of way, non-experiential believings are not. But of course it is just this which is problematic (if not circular); for given that both sorts of states are aberrantly caused (depart from the standard model) we would have had to distinguish them beforehand in order to align hallucinatory states with the right set and so exclude the non-experiential ones. But how could we do that if not intrinsically?

Even if we accept, as is not my wont, the terms of this response from the belief thesis—recognising that there are non-inferential beliefs with the same content some of which are visual and some not—we are led to the next and general problem of specifying extrinsically which beliefs are the visual beliefs, comprise visual experiences.

The objective of the extrinsically motivated account is to show that any belief state of a certain kind, normally brought about in a certain way would be visual. By 'state of a certain kind' is meant state with a certain content and genesis. Is it possible to connect up being a belief state with a certain content and genesis to being visual?

Consider the features we can appeal to in specifying an extrinsic genesis for visual beliefs. We can appeal to sense organs, activating mechanism and the properties responsible for such states. We might say that visual beliefs are those beliefs with a certain content which are acquired by means of the relevant sense-organ, the eye; or by means of a certain activating mechanism, that is, light reflected by objects; or by means of the action of certain properties, namely, those which satisfy the content of one's beliefs.

Here I rehearse the previous arguments to indicate the inadequacy of these positions. The sense organ account can be dismissed for being too discriminative, that is, excluding sight in creatures with functionally equivalent but distinct organs. Similarly reference to light won't do because as I have suggested before, were we to enjoy the same set of states produced by a different activating mechanism that too would count as sight (so long as the end states were, whatever this means, qualitatively identical to our visual states) and so matched (whatever that means) what our visual states match. That leaves the property criterion. It would seem more promising for the reason that there seems to be a non-accidental connection between our beliefs having a certain content and their being satisfied by a certain set of objects or properties. If content can be tied to a certain genesis *then* couldn't being visual be tied to a certain content?

Promising as this might be, it won't work. Even if content could be tied to a certain sort of genesis in which reference is essentially made to the properties responsible for states of a certain kind, the account will not do. At best it would motivate a functionalist specification of the senses but it would not be an eliminative account of the character of sensory experience; it might treat that character as inessential but not eliminable. Here is the argument. According to the thesis, what makes a belief visual is that it has a certain content and its having a certain content is its being of a kind normally brought about by the impact of certain properties—colour and spatial properties. These properties are one thing; the states of belief (or believing) are another. But then would it not be possible, if there were, say, a switch in the afferent nerves of sight and sound, for the one set of properties, the visual ones, to bring about a different set of states, say, those previously comprising aural ones, and vice versa?

If the switch is possible, we face a dilemma. Either we concede this is an instance in which visual beliefs are produced by aural properties, so contradicting the claim that to be visual just is to have a certain sort of (even typical) genesis; or we take this to be an instance in which our beliefs come to have a switch in content with the switch in the afferent nerves. This latter supposition is not exactly implausible given that because of the new causal network there could be information available in the one sort of experience about the, until then, alien set of properties. However, even this will not help the account for at best it recognises the irrelevance, if you like, of character or difference in character of the sense modalities. But it does not eliminate reference to character. Making content parasitic is not to make character disappear.

Is there then a way of avoiding the first horn? Here is one response. Might it not be argued that a switch in experience poses no problems. For consider: on the account for a state to have a certain content and so be of a certain character, say visual, it would have to be of a kind normally brought about in some appropriate way. However what the switch in experience contravenes is this requirement of appropriateness. So though an aural experience might be brought about by a set of properties, acting by means of the medium of light, say, on the sensory system, that would not make the experience have the corresponding content to make it eligible for being visual (in character).

But this won't do. Either the specification of the 'appropriate path' will be too general not appealing to specific routes as the process is enacted in us—it specifies, like Peacocke's excellent suggestion in terms of differential explanation, non-accidental causal connections (Peacocke 1979, p. 63) in which case it fails to block a systematic change of the kind described; or it will appeal to such specific details of the process as it is enacted in us, a form of theoretical identification of 'appropriate mode' with mode of causation in us, but then we exclude from the domain of sight creatures who have, as we would say, the same experience as us, but whose physiology differs.

The problem with this account at its most general is this: either states can match in content without matching in character—they are intrinsically different—in which case their character cannot be a function of content; or to block this it would have to be held that states cannot match in content while diverging in character, but that would be so only if content was at least partially a function of character and not vice versa. Either way the account fails. Appeals to content fail to individuate; or appeals to content are not basic in a way in which an eliminative extrinsic theory requires.

(A similar line is taken by Hamlyn. Consider his criticism of Gibson: '...vision is not just a system for obtaining information about the world but a system for obtaining *visual* information about it'; and his going on to deny that the term 'visual' can be 'cashed in terms of the function of light as a stimulus for the optical system'. (Hamlyn 1977b, p. 10.) His point is that the different modalities are in part differentiated by their 'sensations'; though this is not to say that sensations are to be thought of as sense-data, rather '...they give a kind of character to the form of awareness of the object...' (Hamlyn 1977a, p. 210). These two points (taking them now in reverse order) are important; that the differentiation of the senses requires more than reference to the information acquired (even together with a certain mode of arousal); and that what more is required involves reference to the character—however we are to take that—of the senses.)

Now for diagnosis. The belief account is problematic in the way in which it attempts to handle both the specific and general problem. To exclude non-inferential believings which aren't experiences from the domain of the visual it appeals to states of a kind having certain extrinsic characteristics; and to select amongst believings those which are visual as opposed, say, to aural, it appeals once again to certain extrinsic features. But this is surely misguided; we can tell the difference between (merely) believing there is an object in front of us of a certain kind, and if you like visually believing that, without looking at the distinct geneses of the two states; and we can tell the difference between having a visual and aural experience without making reference to their mode of arousal. Even if (not that I grant it), this way we fix the notion of content, we don't this way fix the notion of character. The relevant differences between mere beliefs and experiences and between modality specific experiences are intrinsic and so far the belief account fails to make allowance for that.

If my diagnosis is correct an adequate account needs to locate an intrinsic as opposed to extrinsic difference for the reason that there appears to be a phenomenological and introspectible difference between, say, seeing and hearing. There is one sort of account which at least recognises the need for some sort of intrinsic difference, yet which does not appeal to any unreduced sensory subjective or phenomenological character. The account focuses on a difference in the physical realisation of states. That difference is intrinsic even though physical. The claim is that two states might have the same representational *content;* while differing in the *mode* of representation. (For an account like this see Maloney 1985.)

What this type of account recognises is that there is no mental difference without a physical difference. What the account accordingly appeals to is that physical difference in differentiating the two mental states. So, if as I have claimed there is a difference between (non-inferentially) believing that there is an object in front of me with a certain (visual) property and being in the state of its looking to me as if there is an object in front of me with a certain (visual) property, then that difference must be reflected—to put it neutrally—in the physical make up of the two states. Accordingly, why not take that physical difference to constitute the sole distinguishing mark; identify visual experiences with those physical brain states that embody them. Visual experiences are beliefs with a certain distinguishable realisation. (One can develop the account further. The idea might be that to believe or to think is to be related to representations, where those representations are identified with brain states. So the difference then between perceptual and non-perceptual beliefs is held to be a difference not of content but of representation. One is related to distinct tokens in the two cases; that is, tokens different not in terms of what they represent but in how they represent—in themselves.)

There are two ways one can take this thesis. Understood one way it is, I think, more or less correct. Understood the other way, it merely involves digging in one's heels in the face of contrary evidence.

If the claim is that one difference between belief and perception is that they differ in mode of representation, that is, I think, correct. If the claim is as further interpreted, that whereas pure beliefs have no sensuous character, perceptual beliefs have such a character, then again I think this is correct though misleadingly put. And if the claim is that these representational and phenomenological differences are physically discernible, again it is difficult to demur.

But this is not the way I think it is intended. At least this is not the interpretation that concerns us here. The relevant interpretation in our context is that reference to phenomenological character or sensuous quality is definable in terms of or eliminable in favour of purely physical features. Visual experiences would not merely supervene on but would be identified with certain brain states (as would have to be the case in order for the thesis to have the full reductive force). Visual experiences would be beliefs comprising a natural physical kind. Presence or absence of phenomenology would mark a difference, but the difference marked would be physical. (To put it a different way: what we notice when we notice a difference between the two sorts of states is a physical difference. It is only misleadingly put to suggest the difference is phenomenological or whatever.)

The obvious response to this is that we know beforehand that were we to find creatures diverging in physical make up while apparently converging in experience, those creatures would (correctly) be taken to instantiate the same experiential states. They would see, or hear or touch . . . Accordingly it would be a merely contingent occurrence were it to be the case that all creatures, not only humans if even humans, instantiated the same physical states when instantiating the same experiential state. It would be an astonishing fact, but it would not follow that having an experience, and indeed a modality specific experience, would be identical with being in a certain physical (kind) of state. Being variously realisable—whether actually so realised or not—theoretical identification is excluded. It is precisely because physical differences can only record or correlate with psychological differences but not illuminate them that we need not await neurological research to discover whether our states of an experiential kind constitute a natural physical kind. (See Nagel 1974.) I would be surprised if there were not at least species specific commonalities. But that doesn't even make plausible the idea of some one physical kind underlying all qualitatively identical experiential states. After all it seems just a matter of time before any part of our brain be replaceable by some functionally identical but physically dissimilar component. (And even if this is technological utopianism it is not theoretically unsound.)

In the case of a natural kind like gold, we know that anything which was qualitatively identical to gold but which diverged in underlying constitution would not be gold (See Kripke 1972). And this holds whether or not there could be anything qualitatively identical to gold but lacking its constitution. In the case of experience we know that anything qualitatively identical to it would be an experience of the same type—at least holding fast on the antecedents of like experiences—even if it diverged in its realisation. This difference in the direction of judgement reflects, independently of rubbing intuitions about what is possible, the failure of this last attempt to secure a physicalist basis for distinguishing states of its looking a certain way to creatures and their having certain beliefs with the same content, or specifying what makes a belief with a certain content visual.

Now for a qualification. The account that I have been examining holds that what makes it true that a subject is in a state in which it looks to him as if he were seeing a certain sort of object is his being in a belief state with a certain content or with a certain genesis, or with a certain realisation. That I have argued against. But the criticisms I have given so far should not be taken as dismissing the possibility of creatures or devices possessing cognitive states playing a functional role in their system akin to our perceptual states yet where such creatures or devices lacked sensory experience.

This possibility is interesting for the light it throws on my thesis and argument so far, and indeed for the light it throws on a further thesis that has not yet come up for discussion, but on which this possibility seriously rests. So consider it for the moment.

We could imagine, with some plausibility, creatures in whom beliefs arose paralleling in some respects—not all—the beliefs we acquire in perception, but where those beliefs are not as I wish to put it, experience-based beliefs. One might take as a model here premonitions. These seem to be thoughts or beliefs which spring up without any *obvious* inferential source. Could we not imagine similar states arising more systematically in differently constituted creatures or devices? Two questions are raised by this. Could such beliefs have the right content? Would such beliefs be counted perceptual?

The answer to the first is qualified. Were we to find creatures who were sensitive to the same properties as we are in a causal sense and who were enabled by that sensitivity to operate as well as us within an environment, then that would be reason for supposing such creatures had beliefs about that environment. (By this I do not mean to suggest that just any capacity which allowed something to conduct itself round an environment would count as cognitive; I assumed a cognitive capacity and the question which then arose had to do with content). The qualification is that here we assume a realism of the secondary properties. If, however, such a realism cannot be sustained then there would be a limit on what could form part of the content of such a creature's states. In fact I think such a realism cannot be maintained, which gives further reason for supposing the belief account won't work—it can't set up the right content. But that I let pass here. (However, see Christopher Peacocke 1983, especially p. 50, for an explicit statement of such a criticism of the reductive belief account.)

The answer to the second question is also qualified. It all depends on what we take to be a perceptual device or mechanism, and on the importance which resides on the presence of a sensory experience. Arguably the notion of a sense has two components; the idea of a certain sensitivity—changes in the world being reflected in changes in our states—and the notion of a sensory quality. Perhaps a device which reflected the first feature—if such is possible without sensory experience—would be taken as perceptual despite the absence of the latter.

Why consider this possibility? Amongst other reasons I cite two. On the one hand there is the somewhat controversial phenomenon of 'blindsight' arguably—if we don't dig too deep—a way of acquiring beliefs without our normal experience. The latter of course indicates why the phenomenon fails as an effective refutation of the non-reductive view of experience. Blindsight is sight if at all *without experience;* the contrast is with normal vision which is sight with experience. If there is blindsight then perhaps there could be a cognitive process akin to perception exhibiting the appropriate sensitivity but lacking a sensory character. There would be belief but no experience. The second goes further. It allows for the possibility of creatures or devices who are in some respects capable like us of acquiring information about the world around them yet to whom we are not wont to ascribe experience. Consider computers especially those with sensors. Oddly we would probably be more tolerant with respect to cognition and the ascribing of beliefs to creatures or devices than we would be with respect to experience.

What this indicates is that the order of difficulty is the reverse of what is typically supposed. Belief is far more functionalist based than experience. Our readiness to ascribe beliefs to a creature or device depends to a large extent on the difference that would make to how we understand or explain their behaviour. It is not hard to imagine machines which could operate on their environment in ways which parallel our capacity. The more sophisticated their behaviour the more ready we would be to ascribe beliefs to them. Put another way, functionally isomorphic creatures might be ascribed the same beliefs, but not necessarily the same experience. Experience requires not just a functional characterisation but also an intrinsic one. Because of this seeing may be more difficult to bring about than believing. (Still, these remarks are offered by way of contrast rather than conviction. What I am committed to is the thesis about experience not belief.)

My focus in this paper has been on showing that experience is not 'merely' believing. As evidenced by the Müller-Lyer illusion, it is not quite believing either. The cognitive component in experience is not, or is not always, asserted thought. But that thesis I will not defend here.

References

Armstrong, D. M. 1968, *A Materialist Theory of the Mind*. London: Routledge and Kegan Paul.
Bach-y-Rita, P., Collins, C. C. Saunders, F., White, B. and Scadden, L. 1969: Vision Substitution by Tactile Image Projection. *Nature* 221: 963–964.
Berkeley, G. 1975: *Philosophical Works*. London: J. M. Dent. & Sons Ltd.
Churchland, P. 1979: *Scientific Realism and the Plasticity of Mind*. Cambridge: Cambridge University Press.
Dretske, F. I. 1969: *Seeing and Knowing*. Chicago: University of Chicago Press.
Fodor, J. A. 1983: *The Modularity of Mind*. Cambridge, Mass.: M.I.T. Press.
Grice, H. P. 1962: Some Remarks About the Senses. In *Analytical Philosophy* (First Series) Ed. R. J. Butler. Oxford: Basil Blackwell.
Guarniero, G. 1974: Experience of Tactile Vision. *Perception*. 3: 101–104.
Hamlyn, D. W. 1977a: Unconscious Inference and Judgement in Perception. In *Images, Perception and Knowledge*. Ed. J. M. Nicholas. Dordrecht: Reidel Publishing Company.
Hamlyn, D. W. 1977b: The Concept of Information in Gibson's theory of perception. *Journal for the Theory of Social Behaviour*, 7: 5–16.
Heil, J., 1983: *Perception and Cognition*. Berkeley: University of California Press.
Kaufman, L. 1979: *Perception: The World Transformed*. New York: Oxford University Press.
Kripke, S. 1972: Naming and Necessity. In *Semantics of Natural Language*. Ed D. Davidson and G. Harman. Dordrecht: Reidel. Publishing Company.
Land, E. H. 1959: Experiment in Colour Vision. *Scientific American*, 5: 84.
Land, E. H. 1977: The Retinex Theory of Colour Vision. *Scientific American*, 237: 108–128.
Leon, M. 1986. Interpreting Experience. *Philosophical Papers*, 15: 107–130.
Leon, M. 1987: Character, Content, and the Ontology of Experience. *Australasian Journal of Philosophy*, 65: 377–399.
Maloney, J. C. 1985: About Being a Bat. *Australasian Journal of Philosophy*, 63: 26–49.

Marks, L. E. 1975: On Colored-Hearing Synesthesia: Cross-model Translations of Sensory Dimensions. *Psychological Bulletin*, 82: 303–331.

Marks, L. E. 1987: On Cross-modal Similarity: Auditory-visual Interactions in Speeded Discrimination. *Journal of Experimental Psychology: Human Perception and Performance*, 13: 384–394.

Marr, J. 1982: *Vision: A Computational Investigation into the Human Representation and Processing of Visual Information*. San Fransisco: W. H. Freeman. and Company.

Mcginn, C. 1980: Functionalism and Phenomenalism: A Critical Note. *Australasian Journal of Philosophy*, 58: 35–46.

McGurk, H. and Macdonald, J. 1976: Hearing Lips and Seeing Voices. *Nature*, 264: 747–748.

Nagel, T. 1974: What is it Like to be a Bat? *Philosophical Review*, 83: 435–450

Peacocke, C. 1979: *Holistic Explanation: Action, Space, Interpretation*. Oxford Clarendon Press.

Peacocke, C. 1983: *Sense and Content: Experience, Thought and their Relations* Oxford: Clarendon Press.

Pitcher, G. 1971: *A Theory of Perception*. Princeton: Princeton University Press.

Roxbee Cox, J. W. 1970: Distinguishing the Senses. *Mind*, 79: 530–550.

Roxbee Cox, J. W. 1971: An Analysis of Perceiving in Terms of the Causation of Beliefs. In *Perception: A Philosophical Symposium*, Ed. F. N. Sibley London: Methuen.

Shepard, R. N. 1984: Ecological Constraints on Internal Representation: Resonant Kinematics of Perceiving, Imagining, Thinking and Dreaming *Psychological Review*, 91: 417–447.

White, B. W., Saunders, F. A., Scadden, L., Bach-y-Rita, P. and Collins, C. C. 1970: Seeing with the Skin. *Perception and Psychophysics*, 7: 23–27.

9

Categorising the Senses

Norton Nelkin

The perceptual issues to be considered are somewhat modest, but they have some intrinsic interest and the truths concerning them open up or close down avenues for resolving larger issues. The issues at hand concern our means of subdividing perception into the senses: visual, auditory, gustatory, olfactory, and tactile. There are really two sorts of questions involved, although they are often conflated: (i) By what means have people discovered the senses and come to the belief that there are five of them? That is, where did we get our concepts of the senses from in the first place? (ii) Having recognised the senses, by what defining criteria should the senses be distinguished? The means by which we come to have concepts of them are, at least in principle, independent of their defining criteria, just as the means by which we first picked out gold (the colour, shininess, malleableness, and so forth) are not directly involved in the defining criteria for gold (the atomic structure).

The two questions are importantly different sorts of questions. The first question is a factual question: It asks how we, in fact, discovered and distinguished the senses. The second question is a theoretical question: It asks how we should define the senses so as to make them scientifically useful concepts. More metaphysically, the second question asks what is the *real* nature of the senses. We can go a long way toward answering both the first and second question. Section I will consider the first question, while Section II will deal with the second question.

I

1. How do we discover the senses? One possibility is that each of the senses is differentiated by the kind of external property to which it is especially sensitive. While this claim may have some truth to it (see note 11), it is hard to figure out exactly what that truth is. The main

Norton Nelkin "Categorising the Senses", *Mind and Language*, Volume 5, No. 2, pp. 149-64, 1990. (Reproduced with permission of Blackwell Publishing Ltd.)

problem is that some properties affect more than one sense. For instance, the primary qualities are perceivable by both sight and touch.[1] Moreover, at least some properties—distance, for example—are perceivable by both of these and by hearing as well. If different senses are sensitive to the same properties, then these properties cannot be used to distinguish the senses from each other.

Two replies to this objection can be made, but neither is convincing. (i) 'It may be true that these shared properties do not distinguish the senses from each other; but there are others, the secondary qualities, by which we distinguish the senses, for each of the secondary qualities is available only to a single sense.' Even if this claim be true, it would still leave unexplained how we distinguish visually processing the primary qualities from tactilely processing them, auditorily processing how far away something is from visually or tactilely processing the distance, and the like. Moreover, it would leave unexplained how we can *feel* more than one secondary quality. In ordinary parlance, we say we feel such diverse properties as hardness, heat, and squishiness. Since there is more than one secondary quality which we ascribe to the tactile sense, there is the unanswered question of why we have individuated only one sense here rather than several.

(ii) 'The objection that the primary qualities are shared between visual and tactile processes (and perhaps, in part, with auditory processes as well), relies on too gross a distinction. There are properties of those properties that are not themselves shared among the senses. The reflectance properties of the primary qualities account for their being visually processed. Other sorts of properties of the primary qualities account for their being tactilely processed.' But this reply, too, fails to account for the undifferentiated lumping of properties we say are felt. That we feel heat, texture, motion, and hardness, just to consider a few properties, does not seem to be the result of any common property or properties shared among these in the way the reflectance properties of an object might account for our categorisation of visual processes. Once more, we do not seem to generate any explanation of why we talk about one 'feeling' sense rather than several. Perhaps it is yet more telling that the reply does not solve the problem even for visual processing. Reflectance properties can also affect how we *feel*, as anyone who has felt the heat of the sun knows. So this reply is not very helpful.

2. A second possibility for the desired criterion is that we divide perception into the senses because different parts of the body are differentially

---

[1] The primary qualities are generally taken by philosophers to include extension, size, shape, position, motion, and sometimes solidity (or impenetrability), texture, and hardness. The secondary qualities are then made to include colour, sound, taste, smell, heat and cold. Texture and hardness are most usually included among the secondary qualities. I am not defending the distinction, only spelling out moves that have been made in philosophical literature about the senses.

affected. Because we separate out the eyes from the ears as sense organs, we distinguish seeing from hearing. Because we conceive of the skin surface and underlying flesh as a single organ, we say we *feel* heat, texture, hardness, and motion. If the eyes, ears, nose, mouth, and skin were not such distinguishable parts of the body, we would never have distinguished the different senses.

Whatever truths are contained in the organ criterion, it surely does not explain why we believe there to be more than one sense. There are lots of distinguishable parts of the body—hands, feet, legs, knees, torsos, backs, hair, and so on—none of which we take to be sense organs. There must be some further criterion by which we distinguish those parts of the body which we designate as sense organs from those which we do not so designate. But this further criterion is surely the criterion we were after in the first place, for this distinction is just the original distinction in a new guise.

3. Well, how and why do we distinguish sense organs in general and one sense organ from another? Consider facing an object with one's eyes open and with one's eyes closed. What difference results in our believing the eyes to be a sense organ? Surely when our eyes are open we are aware of different effects. Which effects? One answer might be that when we have our eyes open we generally have phenomenological sensations of a kind we do not have if our eyes are closed.[2] Moreover, these sensations are also quite different in kind from the sensations we are deprived of if our ears are stopped up or if patches of skin are desensitised or if our noses are stopped up with a cold or if our tongues are damaged or removed. It is because of these very different typings of sensations that we differentiate the kinds of sense organ we have and ultimately divide perception into the senses. Our criterion for such division lies in this difference among sensations.

This sensation criterion gives rise to a couple of correlative points that I find congenial (with some important reservations): (i) It would explain why we talk of 'visual experiences' even when sense organs are not being stimulated, as in hallucinations. The internal processes, the sensations, distinguish these experiences as visual. If we want to explain human behavior, then, Behaviorists aside, we will not want to explain it partly on the basis of what is going on 'inside' the organism. And if we want to use a term like 'seeing' as an epistemological success verb, as much

---

[2] I realise that the word 'sensation' has different uses and that philosophers and psychologists often use the term differently. The modifier 'phenomenological' is intended to emphasise that I mean the term in the way that most philosophers have meant it, as an experience with the property of phenomenologicality, the kind of experience we have in a conscious seeing or conscious hearing (or conscious pain, for that matter). Philosophers sometimes talk about 'qualia' instead of 'sensations', but I think there are reasons to stick to the latter. When I use the word 'sensation', even without the modifier, I mean it in this philosophers' sense.

recent literature treats it—and there might be good reasons to do so—then it would be well to have a term like 'visual experience' or 'visual process' to name the sense as that sense enters psychological explanation. Such a term would be wider in extension than 'seeing', not carrying the weight of epistemological success; but the wider term will allow us to understand that similar behaviors result from similar internal events.[3] (ii) Another apparent advantage of this criterion is that it would allow us to solve this problem of our discovery of the senses even if skepticism turns out to be correct and there are no grounds for believing that external objects, including sense organs, exist. We need not beg any questions against skepticism in our solution. If we, in fact, distinguish the senses by the different sorts of sensations we experience, then we do so on a basis that makes no prior commitment to perceptual realism.

Despite these advantages, the sensation criterion is not adequate either. Very different sorts of sensations are felt. As with the previously proposed criteria, we have the problem of why instead of one tactile sense there are not several recognized.[4] Think how different the sensations one has in feeling heat are from those one has in feeling squishiness. Like those previously proposed criteria, the sensation criterion does not seem able to solve that problem.[5]

4. When we ascribe the senses to other organisms, species or individuals, we make these ascriptions on the basis of the organism's behavior but not because we think the behavior provides evidence for the organism's sensations. Instead, behavior provides evidence for the organism's beliefs, irrespective of its sensations. So perhaps kinds of beliefs distinguish one sense from another. This belief criterion would be apt in that it would preserve the two correlative points raised earlier: It would put the criterion for distinguishing the senses inside our psychological selves and it would not presuppose the falsity of skepticism. Besides, there is good reason to think that the senses evolved because they provided the organism with mostly correct beliefs about the world. So if it turns out that we do distinguish the senses on the basis of beliefs, it ought not to

---

[3] That is, what I have in mind is that the statement 'A sees an x' entails the statement 'A has a visual process as of an x' (where the best reading of 'as of' will become clearer later in the paper), but not *vice versa*. For reasons that will also come clearer later on, I will use 'visual process', 'auditory process', and so on as terms to name the senses rather than 'visual experience', and so forth.

[4] It is true that now some people would like to distinguish different senses among those that have been labeled 'tactile'. But why we ever did otherwise is still a question that has to be answered.

[5] Mark Leon 1988 [this volume chapter 8], and perhaps John Searle 1983, want to distinguish phenomenological properties from phenomenal ones (qualia). I will have more to say about this distinction in a later part of the paper. But it is germane to point out that the question of why only one 'feeling' sense is distinguished remains the same problem for that view. It is significant that Leon, who is otherwise very thorough (and who defends something like a sensation criterion), never considers this problem.

be too surprising. Finally, while it is true that beliefs about the primary qualities are formed both in visual and tactile processing, it is arguable that the sorts of beliefs formed are really different from each other: For example, with the visual sense we form beliefs about objects at a distance, which we do not form through the tactile sense, and so on.

Despite these reasons in favor of accepting the belief criterion, it also fails to explain why we think there are five senses—or any senses at all, for that matter. Why would we have divided the different beliefs as constituting, or deriving from, different senses? Granted we have beliefs about colours, tastes, sounds, smells, and so forth, but why should that fact commit us to a different sense for each? After all, we also have beliefs about colours, shapes, and sizes; but that fact does not commit us to believing that there must be a different sense corresponding to each sort of belief. The belief criterion is unable to get us off the ground.

5. Every proposed criterion has failed to explain how people divide up the senses. So how do people do it? There are at least three possible accounts, any of which would explain our dividing the senses as we do; and each account is worthy of comment. We will have to consider whether there is any way of deciding which among the accounts is the actual one.

6. One possibility is that we divide perception into the senses because we combine the sensation criterion with something like the organ criterion. We discover that certain kinds of sensations correlate with what we take to be stimulations of particular parts of the body. Undoubtedly we come to have beliefs about these correlations because of our beliefs about what happens when that part of the body is made inoperative in some way—when our eyes are shut, or our ears are stopped up, or the like. We learn that the sensations we get when the eyes are stimulated are quite different from those we get when the ears are stimulated, and so forth. Thus, we come to take the visual sense as one kind of process, the auditory sense as another, and similarly for the gustatory, olfactory, and tactile senses. When these criteria are combined, not only can we understand our identification of sense organs, we can also understand how the senses are constrained to five. Although, in the case of feeling, different sorts of sensations are experienced, the organ that correlates with these different sensations is the same.

But what about the possibility that different beings may have different sensations correlated with their beliefs in different organic origins? That possibility creates no problem. The senses would still be differentiated by each organism equally as long as there is a strong correlation between the set of sensations in one being (whatever those sensations are) and the belief that the eye, say, accounts for that set. If the sensation-types that correlate with my eye stimulations are different from the sensation-types that correlate with yours, we will equally, despite this difference, distinguish a visual sense. But would we have the same sense in that case? That is an important question, but it is a question about the real nature of the senses (*i.e.* our second question), not a question of how we come to recognise the existence of the senses.

Does this combination of criteria preserve the desiderata of putting the senses inside us and of not begging questions against perceptual skepticism? Let us consider these questions in reverse order, for our answer to the second will enable us to answer the first. Do we not beg the question against skepticism since we seem committed to the existence of sense organs? No. What has been presented is not quite the organ criterion. We have put things in terms of our beliefs about organ stimulation, organ deprivation, and the like. One can believe one has eyes even when one does not have them. Beliefs can be false. This answer to the skepticism question shows that we have clearly put the senses in ourselves: Beliefs, like sensations, are internal states. We infer from our sensations and from our beliefs about how those sensations originate that we have different organs of sense, *i.e.* different senses.

7. But there is a second possible account about how we come to divide perception into the senses; and it, perhaps somewhat surprisingly, omits any mention of sensations. It says we distinguish the senses on the basis of a combination of the belief criterion and the organ criterion as previously modified. Could a creature that experienced no sensations have ever arrived at the idea of sense organs? At the idea of five senses? I think so.

For starters, there really do seem to be differences among the kinds of beliefs generated by each of the sense organs. We come to believe that our beliefs about colours are by and large correlated with and originally made possible by our eyes' being open. We find that persons without eyes or with damaged eyes do not come to have the appropriate range of beliefs about colours. One may doubt that anyone could have colour beliefs without having colour sensations, but there is evidence from experiments on monkeys whose visual cortex has been severed that exactly this kind of thing can and does happen (Keating 1979). These visual-cortex-severed (VCS) monkeys can be taught to discriminate colours. Evidence from human blindsight patients (Weiskrantz 1977) indicates that blindsight discriminations occur without any sort of relevant phenomenal, or phenomenological, conscious experience.[6] Thus, there seems no *a priori* reason why creatures resembling VCS monkeys

---

[6] I put *visual* in shudder quotes here only temporarily, so as not to beg any questions. Later, I will argue that there are good reasons to remove the shudder quotes. I do not mean to imply that human blindsight patients have made colour discriminations. As far as I know, they have not.

could not have acquired the concept of colours or of a visual sense, although the creatures resembling VCS monkeys had no visual sensations whatsoever.[7]

Moreover, we believe that many of the sorts of beliefs about the primary qualities are also made available to us only through our eyes. We believe that if we did not have our eyes open, we would not acquire these other sorts of beliefs. People without eyes or with damaged eyes are unable to form these beliefs. On the other hand, blindsight experiments (Weiskrantz 1977) and split-brain experiments (Gazzaniga 1970; Gazzaniga and LeDoux 1981) lend support to the idea that creatures can acquire 'visual' beliefs about the primary qualities without having visual sensations.[8] Weiskrantz had patients, for instance, who consistently discriminated X's from O's in their 'blind' area. It is true that such patients are not conscious that they are making such discriminations, and so perceivers like *them* would not acquire the concept of visual shape from these discriminations. But that these patients are not conscious of their discriminations is an added fact about their situation. There seems no *a priori* reason why the patients *must* be unaware. VCS cats and monkeys, after a period of adjustment, act as if they *are* conscious of their discriminations. Moreover, most of the beliefs we *are* conscious of don't seem tied in any direct way to sensations. One may be conscious that one believes tomorrow is Wednesday, but there is no set of *sensations* required for that consciousness (see Nelkin 1987b, 1989a). As with the eyes, so for the other organs. If there be a correlation between types of beliefs about one's external environment and the beliefs about how those belief-types originated, then an organism might well come to make just the same sorts of distinctions among the senses we make. That is, it is plausible that we are such organisms.

Even though sometimes the same belief-type can originate from different senses (for instance, 'There is a chair in front of me'), the fact is that we often believe of a token of this type that we would not have held it if our eyes, say, had been closed. And that fact distinguishes this belief

---

[7] Larry Hardin 1988 has argued persuasively that there are no objective colours (actually, he says this only for hues). He concludes that there is only hue-experience, and hue-experience is to be identified with qualia. Even if he is correct about there being no objective hues, he is wrong to identify hue-experience with qualia. Moreover, his arguments do not show that there are no objective hues: What the arguments show is that, if there are objective hues, they are not scientifically useful natural kinds. These issues are much too large to be dealt with in this paper, but see Nelkin 1987a, 1989b.

[8] One might argue that split-brain cases do not show that the patients do not have sensations, only that they cannot talk about them. But this claim overstates its case. It is true that the cases do not entail that split-brain patients sometimes perceive without having sensations. But the patients do *deny* having sensations, and their denial is of a kind with the denial of hemianopic patients. Second, split-brain patients *do* talk about some sensations whose cause is left-body stimulation: For instance, such patients will tell you they have a pain in their left arm when the arm is stuck with a pin, say. So their denial in the other 'sensory' cases seems to carry some weight.

as visual.[9] We do have second-order beliefs about how our belief-tokens about the external world originate; and this fact, in combination with the fact that many beliefs about the external world type uniquely in correlation with a particular organ, could well account for our typing of the senses. There is no reason in principle why this belief/modified-organ-criterion combination does not account for our discovery of the senses as well as a sensation/modified-organ-criterion combination does.

8. The third possible account simply combines the first two accounts. The sensation-organ[10] correlation reinforces and is reinforced by the belief-type/organ and belief-token/organ correlations. For instance, our belief that a certain colour is before us is correlated with our believing that our eyes are open and that we would not have had this belief if they were not; and these beliefs, in turn, correlate with given kinds of sensation that occur most often in just these situations.

9. So which of these three accounts correctly explains how we originate our beliefs in the senses? I do not know. But any of them would work. And that fact perhaps explains the diversity of the criteria reviewed previously, the truth contained in them, and their inadequacy when taken alone. Each criterion by itself might explain part of the truth; none by itself explains the whole truth. We somehow combine the originally proposed criteria. By means of some such combination or other we differentiate the senses. My guess is that the third account is the likely one, but that is only a guess.

Defenders of one account or the other will probably find such agnosticism disconcerting even if they cannot say exactly why. But one origin of their unease is their conflating this question of how our beliefs in the senses arise with the second question mentioned in the introduction: However it is that we come to our beliefs in the senses, how should we understand or define the senses? In so far as this latter question is equivalent to 'What is the *real* nature of the senses?' it is this question that philosophers most usually want answered. And agnosticism about it is less satisfying.

---

[9] The story is somewhat more complicated than this, but only somewhat. If I am both looking at and feeling the outline at the same time, it might be true that I would have the belief, 'There is a chair in front of me', even if my eyes were closed. But I realise at that time that I have acquired that belief both through my eyes and my touch, as illustrated by several other higher-order beliefs I also have (even if not explicitly represented): 'If my eyes were closed, I would still have this belief because I am also feeling the chair', 'If my skin were insensitive, I would still have this belief because my eyes are open', 'If both my eyes were closed and my skin insensitive, I would not have this belief', and so forth.

[10] Of course, this should be 'belief about...', *etc.* I use 'organ' here for short only. I will use 'organ' in a similar fashion in combination with beliefs about the external world. And I will, in turn, abbreviate 'belief about the external world' by 'belief'. I am hopeful that such abbreviations, here and elsewhere in the paper, do not cause confusion. They sure save a lot of writing.

II

10. When we consider the plausible answers to the first sort of question, we find that all three share in common our beliefs about organ stimulation. So perhaps the best way of defining the senses, of answering our second sort of question, is according to organ stimulation: The visual sense is having the eyes stimulated; the auditory sense, the ears; and so forth. But at least two sorts of considerations, closely connected, militate against this sort of identification.

(i) Suppose there are organisms quite different looking from ourselves. If we accept the organ criterion as the defining criterion, how could we decide whether they see or not? Obviously in order to do so, we would have to decide whether they had eyes. But it seems as if our only criterion for making this decision would be whether some part of the organism's body looks like a human eye. Surely such a criterion is inadequate, both in principle and in practice. The 'ears' of eared owls, for instance, are not ears at all. They just look like ears. Perhaps there is a way around this objection that does not involve a redescription of the criterion—for instance, in terms of how the organs are structured—but the motivation behind this objection also underlies the second objection. So let us turn to it.

(ii) An organ can be stimulated and yet sensing be absent. For instance, some blindness cases are the result of cortical damage. In such cases the blind person's eyes are intact and can be stimulated in just the way a sighted person's can be. But blind people have no visual sense.

What these objections show is that any division into the senses needs to involve more than proximal stimulation of the organ. A sense involves this proximal stimulation but only in so far as the proximal stimulation is involved in a larger causal chain. There must be a larger set of causal events embedding the organ stimulation—or initiated by the organ stimulated—and it is that larger set we should use to define a particular sense. What are the bounds of this chain? Suppose we take organ stimulation as one boundary, what should be regarded as the other bound?[11]

The only plausible candidates for the second boundary are the resultant sensations or the resultant beliefs. Any attempt to stop prior to one of these mental states (for instance, at the kinds of nerve endings stimulated) seems destined to be compatible with the lack of a sense, just as eye stimulation by itself is compatible with blindness. So our real

---

[11] Actually, the first boundary probably should involve the kind of stimulation received by the organ, not just the organ that is stimulated (it matters whether light affects eyes or whether the eyes are touched instead). It is this truth that seems to motivate the external property criterion. I will skip over this possible complication because I am more interested in the other boundary, though undoubtedly a full typing of the senses would have to take this boundary into serious account. Also involved might be the sorts of nerve cells stimulated, how they are structured, and so on. Again, because of my focus in this paper, I will skip over these physiological considerations.

choice is to identify a sense with a state of affairs in which a sensation-type results from (particular sorts of) stimulation of an organ (whichever organ it is) or to identify a sense with a state of affairs in which a belief-type (about the external world) is fixed by a particular kind of causal chain that is initiated by that organ's being stimulated. Given such a choice, there are overwhelming reasons to pick the latter.

(i) Consider the following two sorts of cases. (a) Suppose there were people whose eyes seemed to be in working order. When their eyes are appropriately stimulated, they have all the 'wrong' sensations (*i.e.* sensations quite different from ordinary human beings), but all of their beliefs about the world track ours almost exactly and they have the same success in getting about in the world that we do. (b) Suppose again people whose eyes seem to be in working order. When their eyes are stimulated, they have just the sorts of sensations we would expect them to have but they have all the wrong beliefs, such that they fail to believe that there are colours, they run into objects, and so forth. It seems natural to call the first people sighted and the second people blind. This result is magnified if we think that the first sort have no sensations but the right beliefs while the second have the 'right' sensations but no beliefs. It would seem that beliefs are essential to the sightedness-blindness distinction in a way that sensations are not. Granted that sightedness, which involves success of a certain kind, is not to be identified simply with the having of a visual process. Still there is an intimate relation between the having of a visual process and sightedness, with the latter depending in some way on the former. I want to emphasise this connection. Any good account of the senses will maintain this connection: Something that sees (hears, and so on) does so only when its visual (auditory, and so on) sense is activated. That this connection should be maintained in a theory of the senses is a presupposition that underlies all the remaining remarks and arguments. If this dependence of seeing on the visual sense exists, it would seem to be the beliefs that result from stimulation of the eye that are an essential feature of visual processes. The sensations are not essential.

(ii) A second reason to accept this conclusion is that there is evidence that differences in neural structure mean differences in sensations. Some people who have been made colour blind by trauma (accident or disease) can have their colour vision restored by the implantation of tinted lenses. Such people often complain that colours look different to them, even though they are able once again to make colour discriminations similar to those they made before their accidents (Hurvich 1981, p. 257). These people seem to mean that their colour *sensations* are different. And one gathers that it is a neurological difference that accounts for this sensation difference. Nonhuman animals, such as certain freshwater fish, make hue discriminations very similar to ones human beings make—despite the fact that the visual system of these fish is radically different from our own (Hurvich 1981). Thus, there may be good reason to think that other species of organism have sensations very different from our own when they see. Indeed, there is enough variation in normal human brains to make one wonder whether human 'visual' sensations, say, are very much alike.[12] Given this variation, if we insist on the sensation criterion, then we might be forced to say that only human beings have a visual sense (and therefore *see*); or worse, each of us might be forced to say that only he or she has a visual sense (and therefore sees).

However, if 'visual sense' is to have explanatory force in psychology, then it would be odd to restrict it in this way. For other organisms (including other human beings!) whose eyes are open seem to believe in ways that largely overlap each of our own. What we seem to share are beliefs, not necessarily sensations. Our common *beliefs* shape our common behaviors. What seems essential to visual (or other perceptual-type) processes in explanations of behavior is kinds of beliefs, not kinds of sensations.

(iii) This point is reinforced by thinking about how we ascribe visual or auditory or so forth processes to others. We do it on the basis of their common behaviors. And it is because we think those behaviors exemplify shared beliefs, not shared sensations. We might be surprised, even disconcerted, to discover that their sensations were different even though their behavior was similar to ours. But we would be totally baffled if the beliefs turned out to be different (presuming a sameness of other propositional attitudes such as desires). In fact, finding out the beliefs really were different would probably compel us to redescribe the behaviors, so that they came out as different also.

(iv) Something like evolutionary considerations enter also. Our sensations will be what they are when a person carrying a shining metal object is running toward us. But our survival may depend on our believing that this object is a knife. If there is an evolutionary reason why senses exist, then again the essential feature of such processes seems to be the beliefs, not the sensations.

(v) There is at least some reason to think that there are cases of unconscious seeing, hearing, and so forth—as in cases of blindsight, split brains, and subliminal perception. If we want seeing conceptually tied to the visual sense, then it is more plausible to think of the visual sense as essentially involving belief rather than as involving sensation. For it seems to be more understandable that there are unconscious beliefs than that there are unconscious sensations.[13] One could say that such 'perceivers' do not really perceive, or that while they perceive they nevertheless lack perceptual senses (thus, thoroughly separating 'seeing' and 'visual sensing'). Both moves are arbitrary. Blindsight patients and VCS

---

[12] See Nelkin 1986, 1987a, 1989b for more detailed considerations of these cases.

[13] I am not sure the notion of unconscious sensations really is so farfetched (see Nelkin 1989c). But even if it is not, there being such events will not help provide an objection to my remarks here—especially given the other reasons for taking beliefs as essential to individuating the senses and the reasons for saying that there are unconscious sensations.

monkeys and cats would not make the discriminations they make unless their eyes were open, and so forth. And the discriminations they make, even if impaired to some degree, are of a like *kind* to those we make when we *see* and *visually sense*. Why be committed to two theories of vision when one will do nicely? Seeing is one thing; being conscious that one is seeing is another. But the important thing is to consider seeing itself as only *one* thing.

The beliefs, not the sensations, really do seem essential to the senses. Even if we first discover the senses (partly) because of differences in sensations we experience, there are reasons for believing that sensations are only contingently connected to those senses we thereby discover. The senses are best defined by combining belief-types with an account of how those beliefs originated (through the eyes, through the ears, and so forth).[14]

11. Before closing, let me consider some objections against this criterion for the senses. One objection to the criterion goes as follows: Suppose there is a creature who has beliefs about sounds, but these beliefs originate through the eyes. On the proposed criterion would one not have to say that this creature *visually* processed sounds? Even if we say yes, what is the objection? We, in fact, tactilely process very different sorts of properties. There is no *a priori* reason to think that a creature might not visually process properties additional to those we, in fact, process.

But perhaps this is too facile a reply or too facile a spelling out of the objection. Suppose that the creature through its eyes gets beliefs about sounds; through its nose, beliefs about colours, shapes, sizes, and so on. That is, in general, this creature has a systematic correlation between sorts of beliefs and organ of sense but that this systematic correlation is also systematically different from our own. What should we say in this case?

It depends. If the creature is sufficiently different from us, we should suspect that we have misidentified its eyes, ears, and other organs. What looks like an eye might not be an eye. As already noted, the 'ears' of eared owls are not ears. But what if this creature is otherwise just like a human being, even born of human beings? Should we say the creature sees sounds or hears through its eyes? For reasons already given, we cannot answer this question by appealing to the organ criterion alone or to the belief criterion alone. If such creatures arise, and especially if they become at all common, then our concepts of the individual senses will probably become less and less scientifically useful, needing to be eliminated or radically revised. But all that result shows is that

---

[14] My position on these issues is closely aligned to those of Armstrong 1968, Pitcher 1971, and Smart 1962, though their positions on differentiating the senses are mostly implicit in their general theories of perception.

our concepts really do run up against the world. And the world is a contingent place.[15]

A second objection is that the given analysis of the senses makes the senses to be conceptual and cognitive apparatuses of far too great complexity and sophistication. While the analysis may be persuasive when human beings are thought of, it loses more and more of its plausibility as one goes lower and lower down the phylogenetic scale. Consider an extreme case of a 'sensor', that of an electric 'eye' on a grocery store door. Surely, it is plausible to think of its sensing but not of its having beliefs.

A first obvious reply is that electric 'eyes' are eyes or sensors only by analogy. However, despite the fact that such a reply is 'obvious'—and probably true—it is preferable not to avail oneself of it; for it is possible that the sensors of some organisms are not all that different from the door opener. So the problem needs to be faced head on.

Before replying, it is worth pointing out that to whatever degree the objection weighs against building beliefs into the concept of a sense, this same objection also weighs against building in sensations. That electric 'eyes' do not have sensations seems perfectly obvious. Nor is it likely that creatures such as oysters have sensations either.

But I would argue that there is a minimal notion of belief such that electric 'eye' mechanisms and oysters, as well as we, may be said to have beliefs in so far as each has sensors. Because the electric 'eye' is sensitive to a certain kind of information, it causes the door to open. I grant that this sensor is sensitive to very minimal information, but information is information. And information is propositional. Following Fodor 1983 and Dretske 1981, I would be willing to refrain from calling such a state a belief state. Call it, as Fodor does, a subdoxastic state (or as Leon 1988 [this volume chapter 8] does, a representational state). But subdoxastic states are propositional-attitude states, and propositional-attitude states need not be conscious. Both Dretske (1981, 1986) and Fodor (1983, 1987) would seem to agree with me about each of these last two points. Without ascribing such a propositional-attitude state to the electric 'eye', it is difficult to explain why we think of it as a sensor. Perhaps oysters really do differ from electric 'eyes' in that oysters, but not electric 'eyes', *represent* the world's information, and because of that fact, electric 'eyes' are not really sensors. And if oysters do not have the appropriate propositional-attitude—representational—states either, then neither do *oysters* sense. If a thing does not obtain and represent information (or misinformation) from its environment, it is hard to understand in what regard it has senses. It is that very fact that motivates the 'belief' criterion.[16]

---

[15] For these kinds of cases to occur an awful lot of our science would have to be wrong. Eyes seem to be the wrong kinds of structures for processing sound waves, and so forth for the other senses. So there are good scientific, if not *a priori*, reasons to think such cases cannot occur.

[16] The shudder quotes reflect my willingness to think of this propositional-attitude state as subdoxastic rather than as fully doxastic.

One might maintain, as Leon 1988 (this volume chapter 8) does, that while representation is important to categorising the senses, there is something distinctively phenomenological to the sort of representation that takes place in conscious perception. At the same time, Leon agrees that there is nothing distinctively phenomenal in such experiences, that the phenomenological quality of perceptual experience is not that of sensations *per se*. As I have written elsewhere (1987b, 1989a, 1989c), my attitude toward nonphenomenal, phenomenological states is very much like Hume's toward a self: I do not find any such states in myself. If all that is meant by the claim that there are such states is that people can introspect the existence of at least some of their own representational states, then we should agree that people can. But phenomenological properties are not a necessary condition for introspection of representational states. Some (perhaps even all: Nelkin 1989c) of our perceptual states have phenomenological (phenomenal!) qualities, but we need to separate out the representational properties of such states from the phenomenology of these states. In the sense of 'conscious' implicit in Leon's paper, conscious perceptual states have the same representational properties as unconscious ones such as blindsight. Having previously argued these points in other papers,[17] I will not do so again here. Yet, it is possible that phenomenological (phenomenal—qualia) properties, although we need to discriminate them from representational properties in principle, may *in fact* play an integral role in the kind of perceptual representation we perform. But even if phenomenological (phenomenal) properties play an integral role in some types of representation, that role is independent of what Leon calls 'experience'.[18] What matters is the *representation* itself, and the representation is primarily a 'cognitive', not a phenomenological, state. Moreover, one can be in such a state, although—in Leon's sense of 'experience'—there is no experience in which there is something it is like for one to be in that state (see especially Nelkin 1987b, 1989a, 1989c). Positing nonphenomenal, phenomenological properties is the last resort of a British Empiricist philosophy that has had its claims for the importance of phenomenal properties deflated (as Wittgenstein 1953 does).

A third objection to the view defended in this paper is raised in the following question: Has not the analysis presented begged the question against skepticism after all, for does not the analysis presuppose the existence of sense organs? Yes. But doing so just illustrates the large difference between the two kinds of questions this essay has been considering. There are good reasons not to beg any questions against skepticism when we are trying to answer the first sort of query, *i.e.* how we discover senses in the first place. But the second query—how we should define the senses if we are to make them useful in psychological explanation—*requires* that we disregard any

---

[17] In every one of my papers listed in the bibliography.
[18] What in my previous papers I called a 'C2' state.

thoroughgoing philosophical skepticism. One cannot have science without such disregard. Of course, the theory presented will be false if there are no sense organs, no material objects. But, in that case, no interesting theory about the senses will be true. If the proposed theory is correct, brains in the vat have no senses. At best, they only think they do.

But this last remark points up an oddity in the proposed delineation of the senses and leads to a further objection: There could be two experiences that are exactly alike but one of them be sensory and one of them not. Moreover, both experiences would lead to similar behaviors, yet one experience be labeled 'a visual experience' and the other not. The obvious case is that of hallucinations. In hallucinations one has beliefs about the external world in a very similar way to how one has such beliefs in what the proposed theory would label a 'sense' experience. Moreover, hallucinators try to behave in just the same ways they would if they were having what the theory would label 'sense' experiences. The proposed theory, despite my intentions for it, seems to have turned visual (auditory, and so on) sensing into seeing (hearing, and so on), and to have thereby lost the senses as powerful *internal* explainers of behavior.

Of all the objections, this one is the most bothersome; but, in the end, the objection does not cut as deeply as it first appears to. *Pace* its last claim, *seeing* and *visual sensing* are still distinguished. In visual sensing *false* beliefs can be formed. We usually label such false beliefs as *mis*seeing (or *mis*hearing, or the like). Thus, seeing is not the same as visual sensing itself, but, instead, is identical to successful visual sensing. Visual sensing is different from seeing. But so is it different from hallucinating. Pure hallucinations involve neither seeing nor misseeing. So the last claim of the objection can be defused; however, the remainder of the objection needs to be dealt with.

As the objection itself seems to recognise, the problem concerns labeling. In calling one of these experiences 'sensory' but denying that label to the other, we are emphasising the differing origins of the beliefs that constitute the experiences. And that difference in labeling by difference in origin hardly seems worth spilling much blood over. If one wants to call hallucinations 'visual' (or 'auditory', or the like) experiences, that is all right with me, as long as one keeps in mind that in doing so, one is saying that these experiences are *like* the ones an organism sometimes has when it visually (auditorily, *etc.*) senses.

If such a reply seems at all inadequate, it is because the objection has in its grasp a very important truth: When it comes to explaining behavior, what matters is the beliefs. But the objection adds: How those beliefs originated is irrelevant for psychological explanation. Perhaps so. And if so, *the senses* will not serve as a natural kind in psychology.[19] Still, it is hard to believe that the origins of our beliefs will not matter in psychological

---

[19] Perhaps this conclusion is entailed by Fodor's methodological solipsism (Fodor 1981).

explanation. Sensing seems to have a different psychological import from hallucinating. Perhaps for explaining some behaviors either sensing or hallucinating would do equally as well. But, for other behaviors, surely the difference in origin matters. Contemporary psychology contains lots of 'transducer' talk. It is hard to believe that it is all a waste of time.

III

12. In sum, we may distinguish that we have five senses because there is a systematic correlation between our sorts of sensations and our beliefs about their organic origins or because of a systematic correlation between our sorts of beliefs and our beliefs about *their* organic origins, or a combination of the first two combinations. But it was emphasised that once we have discovered the senses, the means by which we come to this realisation may not be the criteria by which the senses are to be individuated and defined. In the second part of this paper it was argued that combining sorts of beliefs about the external world with the correlated origins of those beliefs is best for individuating the senses. Finally, it was pointed out that the scientific usefulness of 'the senses' is a contingent matter. While dividing perception into the senses may be scientifically useful in fact, that fact depends upon certain strong, but contingent, correlations, which we take to reflect underlying causal connections. But this contingent usefulness of a scientific concept hardly seems unusual.

While the project of this paper is modest, if the things said about sense individuation are essentially correct, then there are consequences for a larger theory of perception. One consequence is that any proposed theory of perception that does not give a central place to 'belief'-fixation, while giving a more peripheral place to sensations, cannot be a good theory of perception. By giving 'belief'-fixation a central place in perceptual theory, I do not mean to imply that phenomenal qualities and, more especially, image-like representation do not have roles—even important roles—to play. But there have been attempts at perceptual theories that concentrated almost wholly on these latter, considering 'belief'-fixation to occur only after perception has taken place. If what I have argued for is correct, then 'belief'-fixation is no mere sequel to perception. It plays a, if not *the*, central role in perception. And that is no small consequence of this otherwise modest proposal.[20]

Department of Philosophy
University of New Orleans
New Orleans, LA 70148

---

[20] This paper would not have seen the light of day without the critical care given to it, and the encouragement given to me, by Radu Bogdan, Graeme Forbes, and Carolyn Morillo. I would also like to thank Larry Hardin for some good advice as to how to improve the paper.

References

Armstrong, D. M. 1968: *A Materialist Theory of Mind*. London: Routledge and Kegan Paul.

Dretske, Fred I. 1981: *Knowledge and the Flow of Information*. Cambridge, MA.: MIT Press.

Dretske, Fred I. 1986: Reasons and Causes. Unpublished paper read at Chapel Hill Colloquium.

Fodor, Jerry A. 1981: Methodological Solipsism Considered as a Research Strategy in Cognitive Psychology. In *Representations*: Cambridge, MA.: MIT Press, 225–53.

Fodor, Jerry A. 1983: *The Modularity of Mind*. Cambridge, MA.: MIT Press.

Fodor, Jerry A. 1987: *Psychosemantics: The Problem of Meaning in the Philosophy of Mind*. Cambridge, MA.: MIT Press.

Gazzaniga, Michael S. 1970: *The Bisected Brain*. New York: Appleton-Century-Crofts.

Gazzaniga, Michael S. and Ledoux, Joseph E. 1978: *The Integrated Mind*. New York: Plenum Press.

Hardin, C.L. 1988: *Color for Philosophers: Unweaving the Rainbow*. Indianapolis: Hackett.

Hurvich, Leo M. 1981. *Color Vision*. Sunderland, MA.: Sinauer Associates.

Keating, E. C. 1979: Rudimentary Color Vision in the Monkey after Removal of Striate and Preoccipital Cortex. *Brain Research* 179; 379–84.

Leon, Mark 1988: Characterising the Senses. *Mind and Language*, 3; 243–70.

Nelkin, Norton 1986: Pains and Pain Sensations. *Journal of Philosophy*, 83; 129–48.

Nelkin, Norton 1987a: How Sensations Get Their Names. *Philosophical Studies*, 51; 325–39.

Nelkin, Norton 1987b: What is It Like to Be a Person? *Mind and Language* 2; 220–41.

Nelkin, Norton 1989a: Propositional Attitudes and Consciousness. *Philosophy and Phenomenological Research* 49; 413–30.

Nelkin, Norton 1989b: Reid's View of Sensations Vindicated. In Eric Matthews and Melyin Dalgarno (eds.) *The Philosophy of Thomas Reid*. Dordrecht: Kluwer 65–77.

Nelkin, Norton 1989c: Unconscious Sensations. *Philosophical Psychology*, 2: 129–41.

Pitcher, George 1971: *A Theory of Perception*. Princeton: Princeton University Press.

Searle, John R. 1983: *Intentionality: An Essay in the Philosophy of Mind*. Cambridge: Cambridge University Press.

Smart, J. J. C. 1962: Sensations and Brain Processes. In V. C. Chappell (ed.) *The Philosophy of Mind*. Englewood Cliffs: Prentice-Hall, 160–72.

Weiskrantz, Larry 1977: Trying to Bridge Some Neuropsychological Gaps Between Monkey and Man. *British Journal of Psychology*, 68: 431–45.

Wittgenstein, Ludwig 1953: *Philosophical Investigations*. Oxford: Blackwell.

10

Sight and Touch

M. G. F. Martin

We can tell what the shape or size of an object is by either sight or touch. These two senses are very different in character, not only in the mechanisms of perception—the physical media, the physiological organs of sense and possibly the psychological processing involved—but also in their phenomenological character, what it is like to see and to feel.

This can lead one to ask how it is that the same properties can be perceived by the two senses, and the issues that surround this question have been discussed by both philosophers and psychologists over the centuries.[1] But a converse question also arises, namely, given that the same properties are perceived, where does the difference between the senses lie? Is this phenomenological difference really a difference in spatial perception between the senses? That is the topic of this paper.

The commonest treatment of these issues fails to offer any satisfactory answer. It suggests that we can look for one in two places: in the different properties of things in the world that are perceptible by each of the senses; or in the different subjective qualities of perceptual experiences.[2] Since we are concerned with the differences between senses with respect to perceiving the same properties, the former approach is not applicable. But the latter approach fails to offer any illuminating answer to the question. For it simply posits some introspectible difference between the senses without saying any more about it. Indeed it is common to suppose that this difference is just ineffable: no more can be said about it than that one can just tell which sense one perceives by.

---

[1] This is the issue surrounding Molyneux's Question, as raised by Locke (1689, II, ix, 8).

[2] See Grice 1962 [this volume, chapter 4]. Grice mentions four criteria for distinguishing the senses. Two come out under what I have called mechanical differences, the other two are as mentioned here. Grice himself argues for the indispensability of an introspectible quality as the criterion of difference.

A way out of this impasse is suggested by Berkeley.[3] This is to find what one might think of as a structural difference between the experiences. Implicit in his discussion of vision and touch is such a structural difference; while he assumes that there is a field of visual sensation internal to the mind, he supposes no such thing for touch. A modern proponent of this approach is Brian O'Shaughnessy. In his striking and suggestive account of touch he writes:

> There is in touch no analogue of the visual field of visual sensations – in touch a body investigates bodies as one body amongst others. (O'Shaughnessy 1989, p. 38)

These distinctions are ones that are clearly intended to reflect a difference in what the experiences are like, and at the same time they are anything but ineffable. But in making the distinction between the senses in this way, Berkeley and O'Shaughnessy commit one to a particular view of sight, to the idea of a private visual field as posited by a sense-datum theory of perception. So it might appear as if one can only make such a distinction between sight and touch if one endorses this theory. Indeed, such seems to be Gareth Evans' (Evans 1985b) assumption in his discussion of spatial perception where he argues as if the motivation for contrasting visual and tactual spatial perception must depend on an adherence to such a theory.

Following Berkeley and especially O'Shaughnessy,[4] I want to pursue the idea of there being such a structural difference between sight and touch. However I want to argue for this solely in terms of the phenomenological character of these experiences, remaining neutral between different theories of perception. The contrast that I shall argue for is not quite O'Shaughnessy's, that vision has a visual field which touch does not. Instead I shall argue that the visual field plays a role in sight which is not played by any sense field in touch. Touch is dependent on bodily awareness and if, or where, that involves a sense field, it does so in a strikingly different way from that in which visual experience involves the visual field.[5]

The rest of this paper divides into four parts. In part I, I introduce the idea of a visual field or space which is independent of any sense-datum theory of perception, offering a preliminary contrast with some cases of touch. In part II, I discuss our awareness of our bodies and argue

---

[3] See Berkeley 1709, pp. 1–59.

[4] In addition to the article mentioned, O'Shaughnessy 1980, volume 1, chapters 5–7 are highly germane to this discussion. Anyone acquainted with O'Shaughnessy's work will recognise the debt this discussion owes.

[5] But this is not to deny that there is some further qualitative difference between the senses. One might, for instance, be inclined to suppose that the TVSS examples of touch-based perception discussed by Bach-y-Rita 1972 involve a sense field akin to the visual field and yet is not vision.

that touch is dependent on this awareness;[6] and in part III, I then draw as a consequence of this the contrast suggested above between sight and touch. In the final part I conclude that these differences between the senses should make us sceptical as to whether there can be a single theory of spatial perception to apply equally to all of the senses.

I

Philosophers often use the term 'visual field' only when discussing sense-datum theories of vision. In such a context the visual field is taken to be some array of colour patches internal to the perceiver's mind; it is a two-dimensional mosaic of which the perceiver is aware and only through which she comes to see objects in the physical world.[7] Its use here is not intended to evoke this theory and picture of perception. Rather the visual field and visual space are taken to be features of the phenomenology of visual experience, aspects which can be identified independent of a commitment to any specific theory of perception. On the view of the visual field presented here, we should think of the colour-mosaic of the sense-datum theory as an attempt to explain this feature of the phenomenology. Rejecting the *explanans* should not be equated with rejecting the *explanandum*.

What features of visual experience do I mean? Normal vision can afford us experience of more than one object simultaneously. Distinct objects are experienced as at distinct locations, and as spatially related to each other. There is also a sense in which the space within which the objects are experienced as located is itself a part of, or the form of, the experience. One is aware of the location of visual objects not only relative to other visually experienced objects, but also to other regions of the spatial array—regions where nothing is experienced, but where something potentially could be.

Consider the case of looking at a ring-shaped object, a Polo mint, for instance, head on. One is aware of the various white parts of the mint arranged in a circle, and aware of how they are related to each other. One is also aware of the hole in the middle of the mint, and that that hole is there in the middle. If one was not aware of the hole one would not see the mint to be a ring-shape rather than a circle. Nothing need be perceived to be within the hole. One is aware of the hole as a place

---

[6]The first two parts overlap with my 'Sense modalities and spatial perception' (forthcoming) which concerns the contrast between the visual field and the spatial aspects of bodily awareness but which offers a more detailed discussion of some of these issues.

[7] See, for instance, Moore 1965, Price 1932, Jackson 1977; and as suggested above, O'Shaughnessy 1980, volume 1, chapter 6. Note that both Price and Jackson deny that the field of sensations is two-dimensional.

where something potentially could be seen, not as where something is actually seen to be.

So we can think of normal visual experience as experience not only of objects which are located in some space, but as of a space within which they are located. The space is part of the experience in as much as one is aware of the region as a potential location for objects of vision. This is not to say that one can actually experience all sub-regions of a visual space at one time—the fronts of objects obscure their backs, objects occlude each other. The occluded areas of the visual scene count as part of visual space in the sense that one could come to be aware of something at that location without altering the limits of the visual field provided by the angle of vision at that time. An area can come into view simply by a re-arrangement of things within the field, rather than by changing the field itself.

It is this idea of a visual field or space as part of visual experience itself which is intended. There is no obvious connection between this and some private object of attention such as an internal colour-mosaic. We can think of this visual space as simply a region of public space containing the objects currently seen. So the notion is genuinely independent of such a sense-datum theory. At the same time it should not be thought to be entirely innocuous. Although this picture of a visual space fits well with what normal visual experience is like, it doesn't seem appropriate in the same way for many other examples of spatial perception.

Indeed it seems to fail to fit many examples of touch. Think of the fairly simple case of determining the shape of a glass by running one's fingertip around its rim. In doing this one can tell whether the glass is circular. Nothing like the visual field appears to be involved. At any one time one only has contact with one point on the surface of the glass, so there does not seem to be at any time an awareness of the relations between many points in space. Rather the perception is sequential, essentially involving tracing a path around the rim.[8]

But I don't mean to imply that the difference here is merely a matter of the one perception being sequential and the other simultaneous. Take a case of simultaneous touch, as when one discovers the shape of the glass by grasping it in one hand. Like the last example, this is a way in which one can tell whether or not the glass is circular. Such perception is spatial perception, but in this case it is not sequential perception. Can we think of this example of touch as akin to the case of seeing the Polo mint to be ring-shaped?

When one grasps the rim one comes into contact with it at only five points, where one's fingertips touch it. Nevertheless one comes to be aware that the glass as a whole is circular. In being tactually aware in this way, is one aware of the parts of the rim in between the points of

---

[8] Some of the empirical research on these matters suggests that we are in fact very bad at discerning the shape of things by such tracing. See Klatzky et al. 1991.

contact in the same way as one is aware of those points, and is one aware of the region of space lying inside the rim? The answer would appear to be not: one comes to be aware of the glass by being aware of the parts one touches. In this it contrasts with the Polo mint, since one is aware both of the ring-surface and of the hole in the same way.

We noted in the visual case that things could fall within visual space without being experienced, if they were obscured. So one might ask whether points on the rim of the glass with which one has no contact nevertheless fall within a tactual space. If this is to be analogous to the visual case this must mean we are to ask whether these points are themselves potentially points which can be felt as the tactual field stands. For the visual case we could determine this by asking whether if objects were re-arranged within the limits of the angle of vision one could come to experience that point. So in the tactual case we may ask what the limits of the tactual field would be, and why one is aware only of the five points. To this there appears to be no obvious answer.

It is just this which makes the idea of applying the notion of a tactual field to these examples of touch so puzzling. We know in each case that there is definite felt contact with a number of points, one or five, and we know that the perception results in an awareness of the spatial properties of objects in space. But there is no clear sense of what would be the limits to a tactual sense field in which (potentially) objects would be felt to be. If there is one, then we would have to think of it as somehow being boundless. The re-arrangement of objects within it would just be the re-arrangement of objects in space. At the same time there seems to be no possible explanation analogous to occlusion in the visual case to explain why one fails to tactually perceive all of this tactual field. The alternative is to see the lack of any obvious limits to a tactual space as evidence that there is no such analogue in touch to the visual field. This is what we shall go on to argue, once we have seen the dependence of touch on bodily awareness.

II

In talking about bodily awareness, or body sense, I mean to group together some of the various ways in which we are aware of our own bodies. At present I am aware of my posture, orientation in space, the position of my limbs; I have some sense of the shape and size of my body, and within and on it I am aware of various goings on—itches, aches, patches of warmth. What is interesting about these kinds of ways of being aware of oneself as opposed to seeing, hearing or touching oneself is that one is aware of one's body in a way that one is aware of nothing else in the world. One might grandly say that the world of bodily awareness is restricted to one's own body. But there is an important sense for us in which that is false: in our awareness of ourselves we are aware of ourselves as being an object in a world which potentially can contain many other objects. We are aware of ourselves as bounded and limited within a world that extends beyond us.

One's own body is the proper object of such awareness in that anything which one feels in this way is taken to be part of one's body. There is no case, for instance, of feeling someone's legs to be crossed and then determining from how it feels whether the legs are one's own or someone else's. What marks out a felt limb as one's own is not some special quality that it has, but simply that one feels it in this way. Likewise when one feels a bodily sensation to have a location there is no issue over whose body it appears to belong to (see O'Shaughnessy 1980, volume 1, p. 162). Rather in as much as it feels to have a location, it feels to be within one's own body.[9]

Note that neither of these things commits us to saying that in fact one can only feel limbs to be where one's body actually is, or feel sensations to be located within the actual limits of one's body. Both claims are false, as the incidence of phantom limb illusions and cases of projected sensation into prosthetic devices show. The claim is rather that whatever one feels, feels to belong to one's body whether or not it does.[10] This is not because the feelings have some special quality by which one identifies the felt object as belonging to one, rather a limb or a sensation count as apparently belonging to one's body simply by being felt.[11]

In addition to this there is also in such an awareness some sense of an other, a world which extends beyond this proper object of awareness. One's sensations, for instance, feel to be within one's body. This is not some special quality each one has which it might lack, for then we could imagine the case of a bodily sensation which felt to be completely external to the body. Contrary to that, every sensation which feels to be located feels to be located within the body. For there to be a contrast with being external to the body, there must be a contrast between where it is possible to feel sensation, the apparent limits of the body, and where one could not be feeling a sensation, that which lies outside the body.

A similar point applies to position sense. If one is aware of the position of one's hands relative to each other when one's arms are stretched out ahead of one, the space between the hands is occupied by no part

---

[9] This is not to deny the possibility of bodily sensations which don't feel to be located at all. For an example of such sensation resulting from damage see Volpe et al. 1979.

[10] There are examples of what are called 'extra-somatic sensations' which may be thought to contradict the claims here made, see von Békésy 1967, pp. 220–226. However, as von Békésy himself notes, these cases are akin to the phenomenon of projected sensation, and in such cases one's body appears to extend with the projection. For examples of the plasticity of the body schema see Lackner 1988.

[11] Wittgenstein 1958, pp. 49–52, seems to think that it is merely a contingent fact that I can't feel sensations in your body or the position of your limbs as I can my own. This seems wrong, since, where one feels a limb to be, one feels one's own body to be: it would 'add another joint' to our concept of bodily awareness, as Wittgenstein might put it, to make room for a distinction between self and other in such awareness.

of one's body. But it is not true that one feels one's hands in space only related as through parts of one's body: one feels them to be a certain distance apart in space extending beyond the body. Similarly one feels oneself to have a certain shape and size in a space which contains one and extends beyond one. This space, which extends beyond one's body, cannot be a place where one feels a limb or sensation to be since then it would no longer appear to be somewhere which falls outside of one's body but would come to appear to be a part of it.

In the case of bodily awareness there is a candidate to be an analogue of the visual field with limits analogous to it. We thought of the visual field as a spatial region within which visual awareness was possible. A bodily space would be a region within which bodily awareness was possible. The candidate would then be the apparent body itself, since the apparent limits of the body are the apparent limits of possible sensation. In the visual case one is aware of an object's spatial properties as occupying that visual space, so in the bodily case one might suppose one came to be aware of the spatial properties of something as it occupies bodily space.

However, it is clear that many of the spatial properties of bodily awareness indicated above cannot be thought of as experienced in this way. In order for a sensation to feel to be inner, we need some contrast with outer, so we need to think of it as located relative to a space which extends beyond the limits of possible sensation. If my thumb hurts I am aware of where the sensation is, the place where it hurts, as at a location relative to my mouth. This awareness is reflected in my knowledge of how I would have to move the thumb in order to suck away the pain. But that path between thumb and mouth appears to fall outside the limits of the body, so that the felt spatial relation between thumb and mouth is not one which could be given within the limits of a field of bodily awareness.

That suggests that we cannot think of much of the spatial character of bodily awareness as akin to our visual awareness of the spatial properties of things as located within a visual field. The spatial character of bodily awareness will force on us an alternative conception of spatial experience. Central to it will be this contrast between the sense of that which falls within the limits of experience and things feeling to be within a space which extends beyond those limits.

This feature of bodily awareness, the contrast between inner and outer, provides what we need for a sense of touch. The model of touch here is that of the body as template. We are embodied in a world which contains potentially many other bodies. We can come into contact with other bodies, and they can impede our movement and distort our shape. Such physical impingement on us is reflected in the awareness we have of our bodies. One is aware when one's movement is impeded, and when one's skin is in contact with objects or is distended by them. In being aware of one's body, sensing how it is disposed, where it can and can't move, and where one has sensations, one can attend to the objects in virtue of which these are true. One measures the properties of objects in the world around one against one's body. So in having an awareness of one's body, one has a sense of touch.[12]

The best way of arguing for these claims is just to see how they fit the examples of touch which we mentioned earlier. When contrasted with visual experience, these common cases of touch appeared strange and puzzling. By contrast, I suggest, when we understand them as deriving from bodily awareness, any such mystery disappears. How exactly is bodily awareness supposed to provide a sense of touch?

Thomas Reid, in his discussion of touch in the *Inquiry*, noted that in tactual perception there were two elements to which a perceiver could attend: a subjective sensation internal to the mind, and an objective perception of the properties of the felt object (Reid 1785). In noting the presence of sensation in touch Reid is undoubtedly correct. Think again of the case of running one's finger around the rim of a glass. When one touches the glass one does feel a sensation in one's finger, something that one does not normally attend to as such, but which is nevertheless present. However, where Reid surely goes wrong is in describing this sensation as nothing more than a subjective sign, internal to the mind, to be contrasted with full-blown perception. For the sensation one feels in one's fingertip has as much claim to be concerned with a feature of the objective world as does one's tactual perception. The sensation itself has a felt location, and that is not some metaphorical location 'internal to the mind'—it is felt to be at some location internal to one's body. The sensation feels to be within one's fingertip, and one's finger is every bit as much a part of the physical world as the glass it touches.

Recognising this feature of the sensation suggests a different description of the phenomena Reid identifies. The sensation one feels in one's fingertip feels to be within one's body and at the limits of one's body, at the skin. One also feels one's fingertip to be pressing against an object, one which resists the further movement of one's finger down through the rim. The place where one feels the sensation to be shares certain spatial properties with the object which impedes one's movement; it is in the same place in space. So the spatial location that the sensation feels to have can provide an awareness of the spatial location of the point on the rim which keeps the fingertip there. We should think of this case not as one in which we have two distinct states of mind, a bodily sensation and a tactual perception, both of which can be attended to; but instead simply one state of mind, which can be attended to in different ways. One can attend to it as a bodily sensation—in which case its spatial character reveals the location of sensation—or attend to it as tactual perception of something lying beyond the body but in contact with it, so that the

---

[12] Cf. Sanford 1983, who stresses the role of the boundaries of the body in touch perception.

spatial character is that of the location of whatever it is which connects with and impedes the movement of one's body.

Sensation has a role in touch not, as Reid thought, simply as a subjective precursor to objective perception, but as a form of bodily awareness which provides for the sense of touch. One's awareness of one's body gives one an awareness of it as an inner realm located within a wider world. Where its limits connect with the surfaces of other objects in that world, a sense of one's own limits can also be a sense of those objects' surfaces. A sense of one's own spatial organisation can become a sense of the spatial order of things around one: the body is a template to measure things in the world.

With this in mind we can explain the sequential nature of our original example of touch without introducing any mysteries. Some accounts of tactual perception seem to suggest that such sequential perception comes to have a spatial aspect only as a result of some temporal construction of a perception out of momentary sensations which themselves have no spatial significance.[13] It would indeed be mysterious how nonspatial sensation could generate spatial perception simply on the basis of qualitative variations over time. But the sensations involved in touch do not lack spatial aspects. Rather each sensation is one which feels to have a location, either as bodily sensation a location in the body, or as tactual perception an awareness of the position of a point on the rim in space relative to one's hand. The sequential nature of the perception does not introduce the spatial element as such, rather it introduces a way of determining the spatial relations between points felt.

In feeling a sensation in one's finger one is aware of the position of one's finger relative to the other parts of one's body, other fingers and one's wrist, for instance. In moving the finger, one is aware of it as moving. The finger traces out a circular path, relative to the rest of one's hand, and one is aware of it as doing so. In attending to the rim of the glass, one is aware of the rim as not moving relative to one's finger. So as one's finger moves one can attend to that motion as revealing the shape of the rim. One's movement mirrors that shape; in being aware of the movement one comes to be aware of the shape. This is an example of perception of spatial relations which does not depend on being aware of things as related in a space all experienced at once.

A similar explanation can be given of the second example of touch. When one grasps the glass one has to arrange one's fingers into a shape that mirrors that of the glass. In so arranging one's fingers one is aware of their positions relative to each other, that they are arranged in a circle. In coming into contact with the glass one is aware that the glass fits the shape of one's grasp. In being aware of the shape of one's grasp one can

---

[13] Cf. here Evans' discussions of theories of touch which involve a successive concept of space versus those which involve a simultaneous: Evans 1985b, pp. 368–369.

attend to it as the shape of the rim of the glass, both being coincident. The arrangement of one's body mirrors that of the object touched; in being aware of the former one can attend to the latter.

A sense of one's own body as an object in a space extending beyond it is sufficient for one to have a sense of touch. When one comes into contact with another body one comes to be aware that there is somewhere that one's own body cannot be, and so can attend to the fact that something is there. The two examples of touch which we started with can be explained by just this model, where assimilating them to the model of visual experience would make them mysterious or puzzling.

We noted above that one's awareness of the location of parts of one's body relative to each other can't be a matter of being aware of them as positioned within a sensory field or space. For the notion of a visual field we introduced was that of a region of space within which experience of an object was possible given the current limits of that field. Any such sense field of the body would restrict its limits to the limits that one's body appears to have, but one's awareness of the distance between one's thumb and mouth was an awareness of them as located in a region of space extending beyond the apparent limits of the body. We can only do justice to the spatial character of bodily awareness by denying that spatial experience is necessarily experience of objects in a sensory field.

A consequence of this is that cases of touch which depend on such bodily awareness do not involve a sense field either. We have already noted that we cannot easily model such cases of touch on the idea of a visual field. The above account of touch shows us why we need not do so. When one's finger touches the rim, one is aware of the location of one's fingertip relative to one's wrist. This is an awareness of how they are related in a space which extends beyond the apparent limits of one's body. This is not awareness of them as in a sensory field. It is this very spatial aspect of the bodily sensation which one then attends to as the location of the rim of the glass, when using one's awareness of one's finger and its movements to discern the shape of the glass. Just as feeling one's finger to be in a certain position doesn't require a sense field, feeling the glass in contact with one's finger to be in that position doesn't require a sense field either.[14]

Normal visual experience of the world involves a visual field or space in the neutral sense of simply being aware of objects as within a region of space where one can potentially be experiencing other objects. This is a distinctive feature of the experience in as much as other examples of spatial experience can lack such a sensory field. An example of this was bodily awareness, and now we have seen that at least some examples of

---

[14] Both of these examples are cases of 'active touch'. Psychologists such as Gibson (1968, chapters 6 & 7) have emphasised the importance of active exploration; but others have questioned whether it is simply the role of kinaesthesia (or position sense) which is distinctive of this kind of touch. In Part III we turn to examples of so-called passive touch.

touch fit this model as well. We have a contrast between normal visual experience as involving a visual field and common examples of tactual experience which lack such a field.

III

This returns us to the issue of what distinguishes (phenomenologically) visual and tactual spatial perception. Given the examples we have discussed it might be tempting to suppose, with O'Shaughnessy, that the difference lies in whether a sense field is present or absent in experience. Visual experience has a sense field where touch does not.

But the contrast cannot be as simple as that. It cannot be claimed that all vision involves the presence of a visual field. We can imagine very limited kinds of vision, extreme tunnel vision, for instance. Such visual experience would appear to have no intrinsic spatial character, much less a sensory field. Nevertheless it would be possible to exploit such experience in discerning the shape of things in a way analogous to tracing the rim of a glass. One might trace out a pattern of light by moving one's head so as to trace the outline of stimulation: here one's sense of the position and movement of one's head would provide one with an awareness of the spatial organisation of the pattern, just as one's awareness of the position and movement of one's finger does with respect to the rim of the glass.[15]

The claim would have to be that no touch can involve a sense field, and this also seems far from uncontentious. For one's skin offers an extended area of sensitivity, which might suggest that one could be aware of an area of skin as an area of possible locations of stimulation. One could feel things to be located at positions on it relative to other potential areas of sensation; much as one can be visually aware of something relative to a potential location of a visible object.

For instance, one's fingertips do not just give point sensations; one is sensitive to a pattern as pressed against or brushed by the fingertip. One also has a certain amount of sensitivity in the palm of one's hand, and across regions of skin such as the thigh and back. It is plausible to think of these regions of skin as offering one a two-dimensional field in which one can feel shapes to be located. One might imagine someone who could tell from having a coin pressed against their skin whether it was a 50-pence or 10-pence piece. In learning braille, someone will come to recognise the different arrangements of point stimulation against their fingertip.

---

[15] Cf. the experiments on limited vision through an aperture in Loomis et al. forthcoming.

It is tempting to think of these as experiences which involve sense fields analogous to the visual field. In being aware of a braille pattern, one is aware not only of points of stimulation and how they are related, but also how they are related to points on the skin where no stimulation is felt but could potentially be felt. So this just suggests that the skin is a sense field for touch analogous to the visual field.

It would be extremely difficult to deny that this is so on the basis of the etiolated notion of a sense field which we have been employing. One might have phenomenological grounds for denying that anyone's tactual experience in fact had this character, that anyone really can distinguish a 10-pence piece from a 50-pence;[16] but this would only be relevant if it could be shown not simply to be a limitation of the acuity of sensation. There seems no phenomenological basis for such a claim.

O'Shaughnessy does deny that there is any such cutaneous sense field. But he does not do so on strictly phenomenological grounds. Rather, he accepts a point which commits him to a sense field in our sense:

> the sensation must in the first place come to consciousness *as* determinately located amidst an actual or merely potential array of sensations that comprise a continuum that is at least akin to a sense field. (O'Shaughnessy 1980, volume 1, p. 207)

He refuses to admit that there is a sense field of the skin only because he understands more by the epithet 'sense field' than we do. According to him a sense field just is the spatial arrangement of sensation within a private, psychological space. He is led to deny that there is any such thing present in bodily awareness or touch because this would be to make such awareness mediated where he claims it to be immediate. One can only adopt O'Shaughnessy's position here if like him one adopts a sense-datum theory of vision, and accepts his arguments for the immediacy of one's sense of one's body.

We cannot then simply distinguish the structure of visual experience from that of tactual experience by claiming that the former involves a visual field for which there is no analogue in the latter. But there is still a contrast between them arising from the role of bodily awareness in touch for which there is no analogue in sight, and this I suggest forces a different role on any sensory field in touch from that the visual field occupies.

The putative examples of tactual sense fields are cases of cutaneous sense fields. As such they are further examples of our earlier contention that touch depends on bodily awareness. To feel an object pressing against one's skin is to feel one's skin to be a certain way such that one can feel the object which presses against it. Consider the case of feeling a warmed coin against one's palm. One feels a warm extended area of a

---

[16] Loomis and Lederman (1986) discusses pattern recognition of tactile displays; this suggests that we are not always as poor at it as this line of objection needs to claim.

sort which one can feel as simply a warm area of skin. Just such a pattern of warmth could be produced simply by the rays of the sun and attended to as such. Since one also feels that there is something pressing against that area one can attend through the patch of warmth to the object which is warm. As before, bodily awareness, this time of an extended area of skin, provides for the attention to that which lies against it, outside the limits of the body.

A consequence of this is that the experience is only experience of tactual objects in as much as it feels to be the limits of the body, such that one can attend to that which lies outside these limits but presses against it. The spatial character of the experience has to be taken as itself located within a space extending beyond what can be given in the sense field. For the sensations can only feel to be internal to the body where one has a sense of a space extending beyond possible locations of sensation and hence beyond any such sensory field. If the sensations cannot feel to be internal then there is no sense of a contrast with that which is outside of what is felt, and there is nothing to attend to as the boundary between inside and outside which can reveal the form of that which presses from outside into the body. The result is that the cutaneous sense field is only a tactual field containing objects of touch in as much as it is embedded within a space which extends beyond any such field.

In contrast to this, our visual experiences are of objects as located within a visual space. There is no sense of these objects being experienced as internal to one's body, nor is one aware of physical objects in space as lying outside the limits of this visual space. Indeed this may be made vivid by imagining what visual experience would have to be like in order to be analogous to tactual experience.

For instance, we might imagine visual experiences as being sensations of stimulation to the retina. When one shuts one's eyes and faces the sun, one has a sensation of warmth on one's eyelids. One also often has a visual experience of an indeterminately extending red wash, which appears to have no determinate location. If one had sensations of the retina, one could imagine such experience being of how one's retina was, that it was currently red. Location of bodily sensation is reflected in our dispositions towards the felt location of a sensation; so we might imagine having such dispositions towards our retinas when having visual experiences.

A more extreme example would be to imagine the retina to be like some extendible membrane which one could press against the surface of objects in one's environs. The membrane would take on the shape of objects it pressed against and their surface colours. In visual experience one would be immediately aware of the surface of the membrane and its colour and shape, and only come to be aware of the physical objects it is in contact with as lying behind it and responsible for its present shape.

These are fanciful stories and very far from what visual experience is phenomenologically like for us. There is no contrast in visual experience when taken as experience of objects in physical space between the experienced objects and objects lying outside of one's body. There is no role in such experience for the limits of the experience; one cannot think of it as a template.

Here we have found an essential phenomenological difference between sight and touch. The former is experience of objects external to one as arranged in physical space. The latter is experience of objects as they come into contact with one's body; one is aware of one's body and its limits and so aware of objects coming into contact with one's body as they discernibly affect those limits. Normal visual experience is essentially experience of objects as they fall within the visual field; tactual experience is essentially experience of objects as they press from the outside onto the limits of a felt sensory field.

IV

We have now articulated differences between sight and touch which are phenomenological in character and independent of a commitment to any specific theory of perception. Anyone struck by these differences might find themselves sceptical as to whether one can give one general theory of what perception is, and in particular what it is to perceive the spatial properties of objects. In this concluding section, we shall pursue just this sceptical line of thought. In the first half I shall give reason for concurring with Berkeley and O'Shaughnessy that a sense-datum theory of vision cannot be extended to the case of touch. In the second half I then express reservations as to whether intentional theories of perception can explain or accommodate the differences between the senses.

A sense-datum theory of vision claims that one's visual experiences are constituted by an awareness of some mosaic of colour patches which are mind-dependent and located within a non-physical, psychological space. According to such theories one perceives physical objects through, and only through, being aware of the mental array of colour.[17]

It cannot be claimed that such an array of mental entities is obvious to one in introspecting one's visual experiences, even though a sense-datum theory claims that this array must be an object of awareness for the perceiver. Rather we can see the motivation for introducing the mosaic as arising from the problems of perceptual error. A visual hallucination, for instance, may be indistinguishable from a veridical perception; so it is not unnatural to assume that such an hallucination would share the same phenomenological character as the perception. An account of the

---

[17] As noted above, a recent proponent of such a view besides O'Shaughnessy is Frank Jackson (1977). Unusually, however, he takes visual sense data to be located in physical space.

phenomenological character of visual perception must then also satisfy as an account of visual hallucination.

When one hallucinates, the physical scene before one need not match how things look, and even if it does one is not aware of it. The sense-datum theory offers us a surrogate for that physical scene in explaining the phenomenological character of one's visual experience. That is, it claims that there must be some visual array actually experienced, and since there is no appropriate physical scene to match how things look, it offers us a mental stand-in. Since the very same type of experience is assumed to occur when one perceives, the conclusion is that the surrogate is present even when there is such an appropriate physical scene.

Two points are worth stressing about this progression. First, the colour mosaic is introduced as a feature of what is experienced, and only as what is experienced; it is not normally taken to extend beyond the limits of the visual field. Second, in being introduced in this way, it is taken to stand in for the physical scene perceived, as the material object of awareness.

Whether or not one is attracted to such a theory of vision, it is at least worthy of note whether a similar theory can be applied to touch, to ask whether there is the same motivation and whether one can make any sense of such a theory. Berkeley appears not to think so, since it offers no analogue to the visual field in his account of touch; while O'Shaughnessy, as we have seen, denies that there can be any such thing as a tactual field.

The justification for such conclusions lies in the phenomenological features we outlined in earlier sections, and principally derives from the claimed dependence of touch on bodily awareness. Tactual hallucination must depend at least partly on bodily illusions or hallucinations. Imagine a case in which it feels to you as if there is a coin in your hand when there is none. Is it possible to have such a tactual hallucination, without some element of illusion in body sense? If so, then one should be able to be aware that nothing is pressing against the skin, and there is nothing to prevent one from clasping one's fist as tightly as possible. How can the appearance of the coin survive the awareness of these facts? Or take a case in which it supposedly feels as if there is a flat surface which one is brushing one's fingertips across. As suggested earlier, that involves an element of resistance; it must appear to the subject as if she can't move her fingers straight through the surface. Suppose now that there is no such kinaesthetic misinformation: how can it still feel to one as if there is a surface present, when it also feels as if there is nothing to prevent the movement of one's body through it?

One can have tactual hallucinations deriving simply from illusions about one's body and how it can move: one can set up cases in which it feels as if there is something present, when nothing is there, and all that one needs to explain the appearance are certain elements of the bodily experiences involved. Suppose that you lay your hand flat out in front of you and it feels as if the palm can move no further, there is a feeling of the skin of the palm being flattened and distended and there are corresponding sensations across the palm. There is some sense of resistance to moving the hand forward, and it feels as if one cannot do so. This is a case of tactual hallucination: it feels as if one's palm is resting against a surface. Yet there is no surface present. Neither a physical surface, nor some mental surrogate for one.

Indeed the introduction of such a mental object would be otiose. A physical object comes to be an object of tactual attention through occupying a certain causal role. Were we to suppose that some mental surrogate were present we would have to suppose it to play a similar role to one's apparent body, as if it resisted the movement of one's body. This is close to ascribing to such entities causal powers. In addition, the sense-datum theory of vision only posits entities existing within a visual space in as much as they are experienced by the subject, falling within the limits of a visual field. But the suggested analogue for touch would be positing objects which fall outside any such sense field (since they are felt as that which is outside the body) and which are therefore not directly experienced. As extravagant as the metaphysics of a sense-datum theory of vision may appear to be, the metaphysics of a sense-datum theory of touch would be far greater.

This difference between sight and touch simply derives from the differences as noted above in the structure of visual and tactual experience. Visual experience presents an array of objects, and it is this array which the sense-datum theory claims must be accounted for in terms of some internal surrogate. Tactual experience presents things as through the felt limits of the body. So as long as the body feels as if it is restrained by things in the way it is when touching them, then it will appear as if there are objects felt through touch. The sense-datum theory at best has an argument which requires the seen or felt elements of experience to be explained by some internal aspect of the experience. While the objects of sight are seen, the objects of touch are those things which are not felt in bodily awareness, but are just adjacent to the objects of such awareness.

Since sense-datum theories of perception do not now generally command acceptance, the conclusion that one cannot offer a sense-datum theory of perception for the senses in general might be accepted with equanimity. However, the differences between sight and touch are also likely to cause problems for the most commonly discussed alternatives to a sense-datum theory, intentional theories of perception.[18]

An intentional theory of perception claims that perceptual states are states with an intentional content, analogous to propositional attitudes

---

[18] For a robust defence of a purely intentional theory of perception see Harman 1989. Evans (1985b) appears to adopt an intentional theory of the spatial aspects of perception.

such as belief and desire. When it looks to me as if there is an elephant in front of me, my visual experience has an intentional content which represents that there is an elephant in front of me. Such an approach to perceptual experience has no problems with examples of perceptual error: one can believe things which are false, so too things can appear to one to be a way that they are not.

Such a theory may seem appropriate to the problem example of touch. Believing that something is round hardly requires that there is some spatial field for beliefs, so why should its appearing to one as if there is something round itself require some such spatial field? The fact that such experiences have a spatial content would be reflected in the perceiver's responses to them, that the experiences in question prompt and make appropriate actions directed onto the spatially ordered world around the perceiver. Indeed, in the face of the kind of problems a sense-datum theory of touch engenders, avoiding any reference to sensory fields or spaces will seem to be a positive advantage.

As capable as an intentional theory of perception might be at explaining the spatial aspects of touch, a sense which does not locate its objects within a sense field, one must surely be sceptical whether the theory can explain spatial perception equally involving and spatial perception lacking a sensory field. Consider again the case of holding a glass in one's grasp. One touches five points on the rim, and has some sense of them. One is also aware that the glass is circular. According to an intentional theory of perception, these facts are to be understood as one's experience having an intentional or informational content that the rim is circular.

If we take this as a general theory of spatial perception we must think of a visual experience of such a circular shape as also having an intentional content that the rim is circular. In the tactual case one has an awareness of the five points of contact of a sort one does not have with any other part of the rim. In the visual case one perceives all parts of the rim indifferently; furthermore in the visual case one is aware of the rim as located within a visually perceived space, one is aware of it as positioned relative to many other points which could potentially contain other visually experienced objects. In the tactual case, there is no such analogue of this visual field. One is aware of tactual objects as located in a space beyond any such experienced spatial region; this is what put paid to any sense-datum theory of touch.

Since there are such obvious phenomenological differences between the two kinds of spatial perception, an intentional theory can only hope to be adequate if it has the resources to explain these differences. It is at this point that one must surely be sceptical. The best the theory could hope for is to claim that the presence or absence of a sensory field is to be explained in terms of an experience's being more or less replete with information about the world. This is unlikely to succeed, though, for it does not seem to be essential to the visual field that it should provide more spatial information than touch. A region of visual space could be a potential position of a visually experienced object without one thereby being aware either that something definitely is there or that nothing is: as when a region is occluded by other things or when one is seeing in a thick fog.

There does not as yet appear to be much consensus on what the correct account of perception is, or even what it should look like. The problems discussed above suggest that things are even more complicated in that there is no reason to think that any theory adequate to one sense should be adequate to all. So Reid's objection to a representative theory of perception, that it could not sensibly be applied to touch, is not a good argument against applying it to sight (this is not to say that there are not many other such good reasons); nor can one assume simply because one's theory works well for one sense that there should be no problem generalising it to others.

At the beginning of the paper we noted that a traditional approach to the differences between the senses was unable to offer us any illuminating answer to our questions, the phenomenological difference being reduced simply to some ineffable quality of the experiences. We might now conclude that this is no accident: if one attempts to offer a general theory of perception applicable to all senses, then one has inadequate resources to account for the phenomenological differences between sight and touch. Correspondingly, once one does focus on these differences, one is left with the conclusion that there is no reason to think that we can offer a single theory to account for the different ways in which we perceive the world.[19]

References

Bach-y-Rita, P. (1972) *Sensory Substitution*. New York: Academic Press.

Berkeley, George (1709) *An Essay Towards a New Theory of Vision in Philosophical Works*, edited by M. R. Ayers, London: J. M. Dent, 1975.

Evans, Gareth (1985b) 'Molyneux's Question', in *Collected Papers*, Oxford: Clarendon Press, 364–400.

Gibson J. J. (1968) *The Senses Considered as Perceptual Systems*, London: George Allen & Unwin.

Grice, H. P. (1962) 'Some Remarks about the Senses', in *Analytical Philosophy, First Series*, edited by R. J. Butler: Oxford: Oxford University Press.

Jackson, Frank (1977) *Perception: a Representative Theory*, Cambridge: Cambridge University Press.

Klatzky, R. L., Lederman, S.J. and Balakrishnan. J. D. (1991) Task-Driven Extraction of Object Contour by Human Haptics: I' *Robotica*, 9; 43–51.

---

[19] Earlier versions of this paper were read at a conference on space and time in Dubrovnik; at the Wolfson Philosophy Society, Oxford; and at the Spatial Representation seminar, King's College Research Centre, Cambridge. I am most grateful to Bill Brewer, Justin Broackes, John Campbell, Naomi Eilan, Julie Jack, Tony Marcel, David Owens, Paul Snowdon and Peter Sullivan for comments on these papers and discussion of these issues.

Locke, John (1689) *An Essay Concerning Human Understanding*, edited by P. H. Nidditch. Oxford: Oxford University Press, 1975.
Loomis, J., Klatzky, R. L. and Lederman, S. J. (forthcoming) 'Similarity of Tactual and Visual Picture Recognition with a Limited Field of View', *Perception*.
Loomis, J. and Lederman. S.J. (1986) 'Tactual Perception', in *Handbook of Perception and Human Performance II*, edited by K. R. Boff, L. Kaufman and J. P. Thomas, New York: John Wiley, 311–314.
Moore, G. E. (1965) 'Visual Sense-Data', in *Perceiving, Sensing and Knowing*, edited by R. J. Schwartz, California: University of California Press, 130–137.
O'Shaughnessy, Brian (1980) *The Will: a Dual Aspect Theory* (2 volumes). Cambridge: Cambridge University Press.
(1989) 'The Sense of Touch', *Australasian Journal of Philosophy*, **67**; 37–58.
Price, H. H. (1932) *Perception*, London: Methuen.
Reid, Thomas (1785) *Essays on the Intellectual Powers of Man*, edited by Baruch Brody, Cambridge, Mass.: MIT Press, 1969.
Sanford, David (1983) 'The Perception of Shape', in *Knowledge and Mind*, edited by Carl Ginet and Sydney Shoemaker, Oxford; Oxford University Press, 130–158.
Volpe, B. T., Le Doux, J. E. and Gazzaniga, M. (1979) 'Spatially Oriented Movements in the Absence of Proprioception', *Neurology* **29**, 1309–1313.
von Békésy, G. (1967) *Sensory Inhibition*, Princeton, N.J.: Princeton University Press.
Wittgenstein, Ludwig (1958) *The Blue and Brown Books*, Oxford: Blackwell.

11

Making Sense of the Senses: Individuating Modalities in Humans and Other Animals *

Brian L. Keeley

One of the perhaps most striking phenomenological facts about the human perceptual experience of the world is that it seems to be divided into *modes*. Our perceptions of the world are delivered to us in distinct classes, those of the separate sensory modalities, such as vision, hearing, and touch. When confronted with, say, a horse after a ride on a hot summer's day, we experience vivid impressions of the animal in the form of how it looks (large and brown), how it sounds (loud, heavy breathing), how it feels to the touch (hot and slick with sweat), and so on. That these different modes of experience are, well, *different* seems beyond question. The existence of separate sensory modalities would seem to be a brute fact about perception, if ever there were one.

The apparent "bruteness" of this fact of human experience might explain why, throughout history, philosophers and perceptual scientists have had relatively little to say about the nature of this difference. Yet the apparent fact of this difference lay at the very foundation of philosophical and scientific questions about the senses. Its very centrality is what makes it simultaneously both a difficult and a crucial question: Exactly what is it that distinguishes the senses from one another?

Brian L. Keeley "Making Sense of the Senses: Individuating Modalities in Humans and Other Animals", *Journal of Philosophy*, Volume 99, No. 1, pp. 5–28, 2002. (Reprinted with the permission of the editors of the *Journal of Philosophy* and Brian L. Keeley.)

---

* I have received many useful suggestions on early drafts of this paper. In particular, I want to thank the following: Kathleen Akins, Eric Brown, Austen Clark, Carla Fehr, George Graham, Margaret Holland, Jim Lennox, Alva Noë, Peter Ross, Eric Saidel, David Sanford, and Virgil Whitmyer. Antecedents of this paper were presented at the 1999 meeting of the *Society for Philosophy and Psychology*, and at the 1999 Eastern Division meeting of the *American Philosophical Association*. At these meetings, I received thoughtful comments from my respondents, Tom Polger and Murat Aydede, respectively. Thanks go to audiences at the University of Northern Iowa, Iowa State, Duke University, Franklin and Marshall College, and the Center for the Ecological Study of Perception and Action at the University of Connecticut. During the writing of this article I was financially supported by the Philosophy/ Neuroscience/Psychology Program at Washington University in St. Louis and the McDonnell Project in Philosophy and the Neurosciences.

I. INTRODUCTION

My goal here is two-fold. First, I want to bring attention to this under-explored topic—to bring together much of what little has already been written on it and, in doing so, to encourage others to take up the challenge it represents. Second, I want to propose an answer to the question. The answer is based on the criteria used in neuroethology, one of the sciences that daily confronts issues related to distinguishing, comparing, and contrasting sensory modalities. Distinguishing the senses in a way useful to those sciences which study perception requires knowledge of several factors, including the categories of physics, as well as the neurobiology, evolutionary biology, and behavior of the organism whose senses are to be distinguished. On my account, to possess a genuine sensory modality is to possess an appropriately wired-up sense organ that is historically dedicated to facilitating behavior with respect to an identifiable physical class of energy. Perhaps the correct way to think about modality is best suggested by a definition of the term in *Webster's Ninth New Collegiate Dictionary*: "One of the main avenues of sensation (as vision)." Modality is an "avenue into" an organism. Question: What travels on an avenue? Answer: information about the physical state of the world exterior to the *central nervous system* (CNS). What constitutes an "avenue"? An evolutionary dedicated sense organ that converts energy into nerve impulses and conveys those impulses to the CNS. This captures the original sense of the term: the different senses are different "modes" of perceptual interaction with the world.

I shall leave further discussion of my proposed answer to sections II (where I discuss how to set up the problem of distinguishing the senses) and III (where I present my proposal in detail). Perhaps surprisingly, I shall argue that the distinct experiential qualities of perception—the qualia—so central to the common-sense understanding of perception are simply nonstarters for a scientific understanding. I draw a similar conclusion about the most venerable theory of the senses: Aristotle's account of the senses in terms of the "proper objects of sensation." In section IV, I shall turn my attention to these prima facie plausible proposals in order to show how they fail to provide a firm foundation for an empirically adequate account of sensory differentiation.

Both the Aristotelian and the qualia-based approaches are best thought of as representing common-sense accounts of the senses. Although they may well be adequate for this purpose, this is not my goal. To the contrary, I offer what might be termed a "thoroughly naturalized" approach to distinguishing the senses—one that proposes to make sense of the problem as it presents itself to the perceptual sciences. Therefore, one way of looking at what I do here is to provide an eliminative materialist theory of the sensory differentiation as an alternative to common-sense theories.

Before proceeding to the answers, however, I need to explain a little more fully what the *philosophical* question is here. What is it about the question of how we ought to differentiate the senses from one another which should draw the interest of philosophers? Further, what is the philosophical payoff?

Let us get the somewhat facetious answer out of the way first. If one defines philosophical problems as those questions which actual philosophers find important enough to grapple with, then the issue of distinguishing the senses would seem to qualify as sufficiently philosophical. Although, as I note above, the topic has received relatively little philosophical interest, it has nonetheless drawn the interest of philosophers as varied as Aristotle, H. P. Grice, David M. Armstrong, and Nelson Goodman. Introducing his take on the issue, John Heil[1] observes: "Regrettably, philosophers have had little to say about what distinguishes the senses from one another" (*ibid.*, p. 3 [this volume, p. 136]). That situation may be changing, however, as evidenced by a number of recent papers.[2]

Surely, we can say more about the source of this interest. Turning again to Heil: "An explication of the senses, a determination of what constitutes a sensory mode must, it seems, occupy a position of central importance in any theory of perception" (*op. cit.*, p. 3 [this volume, p. 136]). Perceptual psychology, sensory biology, neuroethology, and numerous other sciences make foundational use of the notion of separate senses without much discussion of the details. Such sciences typically just assume the existence of different senses. One sees this reflected in the textbooks used in undergraduate psychology and neuroscience curricula. These textbooks are often divided into chapters covering the various separate senses, but it is rare to see an explanation for what makes the separate senses separate. (Not that this is a feature unique to scientific theorizing. Philosophical theories of perception likewise tend to start from an unexplicated foundation of differentiated senses. Those which do explicate such a foundation typically do so in terms of the approaches I shall criticize in section IV.)

I agree with Norton Nelkin: the question of differentiating the senses "asks how we should define the senses so as to make them scientifically useful concepts. More metaphysically, [it] asks what is the *real* nature of the senses" (*op. cit.*, p. 149 [this volume, p. 184]). That is, the issue engages philosophy of psychology in both of its emphases. To the extent that philosophy of psychology is a branch of philosophy of science, the notion of the senses as differentiated from one another is a core notion in perceptual sciences;

---

[1] *Perception and Cognition* (Berkeley: California UP, 1983 [this volume, chapter 7]).

[2] Norton Nelkin, "Categorising the Senses," *Mind and Language*, v (1990): 149–65 [this volume, chapter 9]; Dominic M. McIver Lopes, "What Is It Like to See with Your Ears? The Representational Theory of Mind," *Philosophy and Phenomenological Research*, LX (2000): 439–53; Peter W. Ross, "Qualia and the Senses," *Philosophical Quarterly*, LI (2001): 495–511; Alva Noë, "On What We See," *Pacific Philosophical Quarterly*, LXXXIII (in press).

a scientific assumption requiring philosophical justification. Philosophy of psychology also has a foot in philosophy of mind, and Nelkin's "more metaphysical" aspect of the issue invokes that connection. Part of what is required in spelling out this fundamental aspect of perception involves explicating exactly what sort of metaphysical entity a sensory modality is.

In discussing this topic with colleagues, I have discovered a surprising amount of unrecognized disagreement among individuals. Some believe that the problem is intimately tied up with qualitative experience, to the extent that a "nonconscious sensory modality" is seen as an oxymoron. To have a sense is to have a unique set of experiences—qualia—associated with that sense. But others see the issue as much more related to the sorts of things in the world which can affect behavior, regardless of whether we are ever consciously aware of such influence. For example, they feel that we would be right to posit a human magnetic sense if people could be shown to respond behaviorally to magnetic stimuli in a systematic fashion regardless of whether we experience "magnetic qualia." Still others insist that the senses are strictly related to sense *organs*; for example, refusing to accept the existence of a genuine "vestibular sense" until informed of the existence of the semicircular canals and associated cranial nerves. "No organ, no sense" seems to be their rule.

These differing intuitions agree on Aristotle's five senses, so people tend not to notice their different intuitions. Such apparently widespread agreement reinforces the strength with which these intuitions are held. After echoing the sentiment that the differentiation of the senses have "seldom been directly discussed," J. W. Roxbee Cox[3] goes on to diagnosis this curious condition by supposing that it may be "due to the fact that certain answers have seemed to different people so obvious that they did not need to be supported by argument" (*ibid.*, p. 530 [this volume, p. 101]). The disagreement among individuals begins to become clear once we start considering potential senses in addition to Aristotle's five, examples of which I shall be discussing below. What makes the problem of discriminating the senses philosophically interesting is that the intuitions here are *fundamental*, *firm*, and generally *unrecognized* by the people who hold them. When one finds a disagreement with these three qualities, it is a clarion call for philosophical inquiry.

That I shall argue that qualia are *not* central to differentiating the senses indicates one important philosophical payoff from the topic under discussion here. The legitimacy of the concept of qualia in our scientific understanding of the mind is a matter of ongoing controversy. One line of argument might run thus:

P1: QUALIA are essential to the project of differentiating the senses; one cannot make sense of different modalities except by reference to the qualitative character of perceptual experience.

---

[3] "Distinguishing the Senses," *Mind*, LXXIX (1970): 530–50 [this volume, chapter 5].

P2: DIFFERENTIATING the senses is an essential component of any science of perception, such as perceptual psychology or sensory biology.

∴ C: Qualia are an essential component of any science of perception.

I fully accept P2. In offering my "qualia-free" account of sense differentiation, however, I will be attacking P1—an attack that, if successful, can only undermine one of the primary purposes for which qualia could be useful. But if the account I defend here is wrong, and qualia are essential to differentiating the senses, then this would represent a powerful, new argument for the scientific legitimacy, nay the scientific *necessity*, of qualia.

For these reasons, I suggest that it is clear that the problem of how to differentiate the sensory modalities is an interesting and important philosophical topic. I shall return to the topic of philosophical implications in the final section. That said, assuming I have adequately justified the legitimacy of the topic, I shall consider in the next section how to address the question and consider what form the answer should take.

II. HOW TO THINK OF THE QUESTION AND THE FORM OF ITS ANSWER

Aristotle famously counted five human sensory modalities: vision, hearing, taste, smell, and touch. Since then, his list has been expanded to include such potentially novel modalities as proprioception (our sense of the relative location of our limbs) and the vestibular sense (the sense of one's orientation with respect to gravity). So, Aristotle undercounted, but by how many? Reviewing the human sensory literature, Robert Rivlin and Karen Gravelle[4] opine: "Five [is] obviously just not enough to account for the huge range of sensory possibilities of which the human species is capable; *seventeen* senses is probably a more accurate count" (*ibid.*, p. 17; my emphasis).

Lurking behind the empirical seeming question of the number of modalities, we find a philosophical question of *how we ought to count them*. By what criterion (or set of criteria) should we count individual senses? I believe it is wise to recognize two different versions of this problem. The first version I call *Aristotle's problem*: How many modalities do humans have and how ought we decide the issue? This version of the problem is rather hoary, and I do not believe I need to introduce it further.

The same problem arises again, in a slightly different guise, in animal sensory biology. Aristotle not only counted a total of five *human* senses, he thought that was the number found in the entire animal kingdom. We also

---

[4] *Deciphering the Senses: The Expanding World of Human Perception* (New York: Simon and Schuster, 1984).

have good reason to believe, however, that he underestimated the sensory skills of other species. The animal kingdom is full of all sorts of wonderful ways of detecting the world. Certain snakes and boas use special pits below their eyes to sense infrared.[5] It has been proposed that certain fish, such as shad, can hear in the ultrasonic frequency range,[6] as can bats.[7]

While all these examples are interesting, one might argue that they are not genuinely different from human sensory capacities. If our ears or eyes, say, were built just a little differently, then we too could hear in the ultrasonic range or see in the infrared. Nonetheless, there are animals with sensory capacities that are extremely alien with respect to human capacities. Sharks are apparently capable of sensing magnetic fields.[8] There are also animals, including several species of fish, capable of perceiving electric potential.[9]

Consider, for a moment, the star-nosed mole. Perhaps the most striking thing about this animal is the structure that gives the animal its name: a fleshy, tendriled nose. Casual observation quickly reveals that its star-shaped nose is most likely a sense organ. The mole constantly jabs it against the ground when exploring the environment. For the sensory biologist, a question arises: Given that the nose is a sense organ, what modality is involved? Is the nose a tactile receptor, a chemoreceptor, or perhaps even an electroreceptor? These questions have been a topic of recent debate in biology. In 1993, scientists[10] at the Smithsonian Institution published experiments suggesting that the star-nosed mole uses its nose for electroreception. Others[11] dispute this claim, and the recent work of Kenneth C. Catania and Jon H. Kaas[12] argues that the nose's modality is most likely tactile in nature.

---

[5] Theodore H. Bullock and Raymond B. Cowles, "Physiology of an Infrared Receptor: The Facial Pit of the Pit Viper," *Science*, CXV (1952): 541–43; reprinted in T. H. Bullock, *How Do Brains Work? Papers of a Comparative Neurophysiologist* (Boston: Birkhäuser, 1993), pp. 138–39.

[6] D. A. Mann, Z. Lu, M. C. Hastings, and A. N. Popper, "Detection of Ultrasonic Tones and Simulated Dolphin Echolocation Clicks by a Teleost Fish, the American Shad (*Alosa sapidissima*)," *Journal of the Acoustical Society of America*, CIV (1998): 562–68.

[7] Donald R. Griffin and Robert Galambos, "The Sensory Basis of Obstacle Avoidance by Flying Bats," *Journal of Experimental Zoology*, LXXXVI (1941): 481–506; reprinted in L. D. Houck and L. C. Drickamer, eds., *Foundations of Animal Behavior: Classic Papers with Commentaries* (Chicago: University Press, 1996), pp. 553–78.

[8] A. J. Kalmijn, "Electric and Magnetic Field Detection in Elasmobranch Fishes," *Science*, CCXVIII (1982): 916–18.

[9] See my "Fixing Content and Function in Neurobiological Systems: The Neuroethology of Electroreception," *Biology and Philosophy*, XIV (1999): 395–430; and "Shocking Lessons from Electric Fish: The Theory and Practice of Multiple Realization," *Philosophy of Science*, LXVII (2000): 444–65.

[10] E. Gould, W. McShea, and T. Grand, "Function of the Star in the Star-nosed Mole, *Condylura cristata*," *Journal of Mammalogy*, LXXIV (1993): 108–16.

[11] P. A. Schlegel and P. B. Richard, "Behavioral Evidence against Possible Sub-aquatic Electrosensitivity in the Pyrenean Desman *Galemys pyrenaicus* (Talpidae, mammalia)," *Mammalia*, LVI (1992): 527–32.

[12] "The Organization of the Somatosensory Cortex of the Star-nosed Mole," *Journal of Comparative Neurology*, CCCLI (1995): 536–48; "The Unusual Nose and Brain of the Star-nosed Mole: A Star in the Brain," *BioScience*, XLVI (1996): 578–86.

What I shall call the *star-nosed mole problem* is the general philosophical problem raised by this type of scientific controversy. On what philosophical grounds should we decide which organisms possess which modalities? When scientists claim to have discovered a new sensory modality, what is the theoretical content of this claim? If philosophers have paid relatively little attention to Aristotle's problem, they have almost completely ignored this related problem.

The above discussion gives some feel for what I take the *question* to be. But before continuing, I shall say a little more about my assumptions concerning the appropriate form of the *answer*. I introduced the topic by proposing that we should think of the sensory modalities as "avenues" into the organism for information about the physical state of the external world. Further, I draw the boundary at the edge of the CNS. At this point, three questions arise.

First, why draw a boundary at all? Central to the concept of perception is that there is a duality: a perceiver and a perceived. Senses do not exist *en vacua*; they are possessed by "sensers" and, at the most basic level of analysis, they act as some kind of informational connection between the world and the psychological entity that possesses them. A theory of perception must posit such a boundary between perceiver and perceived. The concept of modality would then refer to the different ways in which information about the world crosses that boundary.

Second, if we must draw such a boundary, is it not necessarily arbitrary? Why draw the boundary at one place versus another? My answer is that drawing the boundary at the CNS is not arbitrary if we keep in mind my initial starting point: I am here presenting a concept of sensory modality which is useful to sciences that deal with human and animal perception. Given an environment and some kind of psychological system under investigation—two things I am assuming here—a sensory modality is a potential mode by which information in the environment can pass through some boundary and enter into the psychological system. If we are materialists and believe that the central nervous system is somehow the locus of the mind, then it is not arbitrary to draw the boundary between the environment and the psychological system at the "world/CNS" junction.

Finally, I claim that the appropriate boundary surrounds the CNS and *not* the body in general. I do not have space to go into an example here, but I wish to leave open the possibility of "internal modalities"—for example, proprioception or our sense of thirst (mediated by hypothalamic blood osmotic pressure receptors). The point in these examples is that information about the world external to the CNS (in this case, the body) is passing across the conceptual boundary surrounding the CNS along a particular pathway that represents a mode of interaction different from other pathways.

III. FOUR PROPOSED CRITERIA FOR
INDIVIDUATING THE SENSES

So much for preamble. Now, I shall survey the four criteria that I believe, taken together, constitute the best account of modality differentiation. These criteria are, I propose, individually necessary and jointly sufficient. I shall discuss why each is a necessary component of a correct account, as well as what is insufficient about each taken on its own.

(1) *Physics*: the external physical conditions upon which the senses depend. That is, we might distinguish the senses by reference to the physical qualities of their respective stimuli: vision is the detection of differences in electromagnetic stimuli; olfaction is the detection of differences in concentrations of chemical stimuli.

Sensory systems operate by physiologically responding to different forms of energy in the environment. Independent of any psychological and biological concerns, physics provides us with an ontology of energy forms. According to our best physics, electromagnetic phenomena are just different from mechanical energy, both of which are different from chemical gradients. This ontology provides a foundation for a nonarbitrary sensory differentiation.

In providing an ontology of forms of energy, what physics provides is the space of *possible* modalities. Whether any animal on earth makes use of a magnetic modality or not, the fact that physics identifies magnetism as a type of energy raises the possibility of a magnetic modality. Although necessary, physics is not a sufficient criterion. By itself, physics tells us nothing about which modalities *actually* exist. Physics can give us magnetism as a form of energy, but in order for there to be a magnetic modality, there must be organisms capable of sensing this physical class of stimuli.

(2) *Neurobiology*: the character of the putative sense organs and their modes of connection with the brain.[13] For example, vision is what we do with our eyes; audition is what we do with our cochlea and associated auditory brain areas.

This would seem to be the additional "contribution of the organism" required by the discussion of (1). It also matches well with some of our naive notions of modality individuation; that is, we individuate our modalities in part on the basis of our sense organs. As Armstrong[14]

---

[13] Some of the felicitous wording of criteria 2 and 3 are due to C. A. J. Coady's "The Senses of Martians," *The Philosophical Review*, LXXXIII (1974): 107–25 [this volume, chapter 6], which is a commentary on Grice's "Some Remarks about the Senses," in R. J. Butler, ed., *Analytical Philosophy*, Series I (New York: Oxford, 1962); reprinted in Grice, *Studies in the Way of Words* (Cambridge: Harvard, 1989), pp. 248–68 (1989 printing cited here [this volume, chapter 4]).

[14] *A Materialist Theory of Mind* (London: Routledge, 1968).

points out, however, individuating sense organs is itself no mean problem. Following a suggestion by Anthony Kenny, Armstrong proposes (*ibid.*, pp. 211–13) that sense organs are bodily structures that we actively use to gain information about the world, as when we open and move our eyes to see or cock our head to hear. But he continues, this runs up against the problem that we do not actively move organs in *all* the putative cases of sense. For example, we do not *do* anything to gain vestibular information. It seems to be ever present (which might explain why Aristotle did not remark upon it). The use of an organ in active perception does not seem to be of help here.

My suggestion is to follow sensory neurobiology and look for physiological, anatomical, and morphological characteristics to individuate sense organs. A legitimate sense organ, I suggest, has three characteristics:

First, it has to be an organ that physiologically responds to a naturally occurring degree of physical stimulation.[15] If the organ in question is a genuinely magnetoreceptive organ, then it needs to respond to the presentation of appropriate amounts of magnetic stimulation.

Second, a sense organ needs to be innervated by neurons; in other words, something cannot be a sense organ unless it is "wired up" properly to the CNS. (Hence, the neurobiology criterion explicitly helps rule out vestigial sense organs.)

Third, we need to be able to identify an "end organ" of some type; the neurons leading to the CNS from the putative sense organ need to *start* there. This is to discount as sense organs the second, third, fourth, and so on neurons in the chain leading from the sensory periphery. A sense organ must contain cells that respond to energy in the environment, not another nerve cell. Most legitimate sense organs feature morphologically distinct end organs (for example, the rods and cones of the eye) that are physically so constituted as to transduce some class of energy (say, photons) into the electrochemical energy of neurons. But some senses seem to make use of so-called "free nerve endings" without any identifiable end *organ*. In these cases, however, the putative sensory cells still lie at the *beginning* of a chain of neurons leading to the CNS. In its usage here, the stress is on end rather than organ.

There is, of course, more to be said here, but suffice it to say, I think it is possible to deal with the issue of individuating sense organs. I said above that this criterion "helps" deal with the problem of vestigial organs. It does not completely rule them out, however, which indicates the insufficiency of this criterion. It is possible to conceive of an end organ which is wired up to the CNS, but which passes on information of which the animal never makes any use. To have a genuine modality, it is not enough to have an organ of a particular type wired up to the CNS;

---

[15] It must to respond to a *naturally occurring* degree of physical stimulation. The reason for this additional lemma will be discussed under criterion (4), dedication, below.

that organ has to allow you to do the right sorts of things. Hence, the next criterion:

(3) *Behavior*: the ability to discriminate behaviorally between stimuli that differ only in terms of a particular physical energy type.

Part of what it means to have a modality is to be able to make behavioral discriminations within that modality. Once again, the suggestion of this individuating criterion generates further individuation requirements. To wit, how ought we individuate "behaviors?" For example, it seems odd to identify tanning as a behavior. My plan here is simply to follow Fred Dretske[16] on this issue: "behavior. is endogenously produced movement, movement that has its causal origins within the system whose parts are moving" (*ibid.*, p. 2). Tanning is something that *happens to* a person, not something one does. On the other hand, pressing a button or vocalizing are paradigmatic behaviors.

The science that is arguably most invested in the study of the relationship between behavior and the senses is the science of psychophysics. In his *Sensory Qualities*, Austen Clark[17] wields the impressive conceptual and empirical framework of psychophysics to ground an account of qualitative appearances which is materialist in spirit and which answers a variety of philosophical questions concerning the nature of appearances. Furthermore, he proposes that psychophysics alone has the resources to individuate the sensory modalities. For this reason, I shall now go into that proposal in some detail to show why the behavior criterion taken alone is insufficient to differentiate the senses.

Central to Clark's account is the psychophysical concept of "matching" (taken originally from Goodman[18]). "Matching" is the relation between two stimuli that differ physically but are nonetheless in principle indiscriminable from one another. For example, two color patches might reflect slightly different wavelengths of light, but differ so minutely that any human subject would report that the two patches are perceptually identical. Perhaps surprisingly, it turns out that the matching relation is nontransitive: stimulus A may match stimulus B, and stimulus B match stimulus C, but stimulus A need not match stimulus C. Using this relationship, one can construct "matching spans" of stimuli in which each stimulus matches its immediate neighbors, but the ends of the spans are easily discriminable.[19] For example, we can construct such matching spans for color, creating a series of stimuli that vary infinitesimally by wavelength from red to green, say. A given observer, when presented with any two adjacent elements from this series, will be unable in principle

---

[16] *Explaining Behavior: Reasons in a World of Causes* (Cambridge: MIT, 1988).
[17] New York: Oxford, 1993.
[18] *The Structure of Appearance* (Boston: Reidel, 1977, 3rd edition).
[19] Clark, pp. 79–84.

to discriminate them, even though she can clearly distinguish red from green (the ends of the matching span).

This is only a tiny fraction of the story Clark tells, but it is all we need to understand his proposal for individuating modalities (also taken from Goodman):

> Facts about matching can individuate modalities. Sensations in a given modality are connected by the matching relation. From any sensation in the given modality, it is possible to reach any other by a sufficiently long series of matching steps. Distinct modalities are not so connected. One can get from red to green by a long series of intermediaries, each matching its neighbors; but no such route links red to C-sharp, (*op. cit.*, pp. 140–41).

There are two problems with Clark's proposal. First, on this account of modality individuation, we get many more modalities than we might have otherwise thought. Clark's account would entail breaking up the modalities into many submodalities, for not only can you not get from red to C-sharp (thus demarcating vision from audition), you also cannot get from red to "moving left to right across the visual field" (or however motion sensations ought to be described), nor from C-sharp to "darn that's as loud as a 747 engine from ten feet away" (or however auditory intensity sensations ought to be described). Lacking the appropriate matching relationships, there is no reason to class the "color" and "motion" submodalities of vision as both being submodalities *of vision*. We are left with an account that makes "color" and "motion" as distinct from one another as each is distinct from "pitch." Such an account fails to provide the resources for grouping together as "the same modality" sensory qualities that we would intuitively group together. All Clark has shown us is how to individuate submodalities.

Second, Clark's account attributes the wrong modalities to the wrong organisms. For example, using (3) alone, humans would have an electrical modality! Consider the following: humans are easily capable of discriminating fully charged nine-volt batteries from "dead" ones, simply by sticking them to the tongue. Nine volts is more than enough electricity to stimulate the sensory cells of the tongue. You could do all sorts of interesting psychophysical studies of human electrical discrimination. Yet it seems absurd to claim that humans have an electrical modality, at least not in the same sense as electric fish are thought to. Something more is needed than simply a capacity to discriminate behaviorally stimuli of a certain physical type. We need some acknowledgement of the function of the alleged sensory modality in the species under consideration.

(4) *Dedication*: the evolutionary or developmental importance of the putative sense to an organism. For example, we ought not attribute an electrical modality to an individual unless electrical properties of the world are part of the normal environment of that individual and to which the organism is attuned.

Dedication, a concept taken from the science of neuroethology,[20] is an attempt to make relevant what is biologically important to an organism. Just because a particular individual can behaviorally respond to a particular class of stimuli does not give us warrant to propose a modality for sensing that class of stimuli. In the example above, the reason why it is absurd to attribute an electrical modality to humans is that, as a species, we do not go around using this electrical capacity of our tongues to sense the electrical properties of the world. Electric fish, on the other hand, detect the electrical properties of their world all of the time. It allows them to navigate the nearly opaque environment of the tropical waterways in which they live. It allows them to carry out a nocturnal lifestyle, which in turn gives them a fitness advantage over nonelectroreceptive fish.[21]

Neuroethologists, neurobiologists who study the evolution and neural basis of animal behavior, make a distinction that is useful here. The suffix-*detection* is applied to any organism that is capable of responding, by any means, to the presence of a particular type of stimulation in the environment. The suffix-*reception* is reserved for those organisms which carry out such sensory discriminations through the use of a dedicated anatomical system of structures. So, they would say that whereas electric fish are capable of electro*reception*—they can behaviorally respond to electrical stimulation using structures that have evolved specifically to process electrical information about the world—at best, humans are capable of electro*detection*—humans detect electrical potential using the pain, taste, and tactile receptors on the tongue. By considering both the developmental history of an individual and the evolutionary history of its species, we can determine to what forms of energy in the world a putative sense organ has become dedicated.

To consider a concrete example, there are at least three different things that can stimulate a vertebrate eye: (1) photons, (2) mechanical distortion (as when you press the eyeball with a finger), and (3) a properly inserted stimulating electrode (as in a neurophysiological experiment). These are quite clearly three different forms of energy (electromagnetic, mechanical, and electrical, respectively) to which the eye qua sense organ is physiologically responsive (satisfying criteria (1) and (2)). All three types of stimulation can elicit behavior as required by criterion (3). What makes the eye part of a visual system, but not part of a mechanosensory or stimulating-electrode-receptive system, is the evolutionary history of those vertebrates which have eyes. It is this history which determines to what sense a putative sense organ is dedicated. Dedication, in turn, allows us to distinguish those animals which

---

[20] See my "Neuroethology and the Philosophy of Cognitive Science," *Philosophy of Science* (Proceedings), LXVII (2000): S404–17.
[21] See my "Fixing Content and Function in Neurobiological Systems: The Neuroethology of Electroreception."

genuinely possess a given sensory modality from those which have figured out a way of using some other sense to make occasional inferences about the world.

At this point, I can finally address an account that has likely bothered some readers by its absence in this discussion: ecological psychology. In *The Senses Considered as Perceptual Systems*, J. J. Gibson[22] offers a characterization of the senses at odds with many other accounts in psychology. As Heil points out (*op. cit.*, pp. 10–11 [this volume, pp. 140–142]), Gibson does not directly address Aristotle's and the star-nosed mole problems, but such an account seems implicit in his work (and I shall rely on Heil's explication here). According to Heil, "Gibson's fundamental notion is that perceiving is the picking up of information about the world made available to the perceiver by various sorts of physical stimulation" (*op. cit.*, p. 10 [this volume, p. 141]). The notion of "information" is critical to the Gibsonian account, and it is at the crux of why I part company with them. Gibsonians hold that it makes sense to attribute a sensory modality to any organism that can act on structured stimuli of a particular physical type *regardless of how that information is obtained by the organism*. Take the case of a blind person equipped with a video camera and mechanism that converts the visual image into an isomorphic pattern of vibrating pins placed against the skin, as in the 1970s experiments with "tactile visual substitution systems" (TVSS) made famous by the work of P. Bach-y-Rita.[23] On the ecological psychology account, therefore, it makes sense to say that TVSS-equipped persons can see (albeit poorly)—that they have a visual modality.

Given what I just said about the distinction between detection and reception, however, it should be clear why I disagree here. A TVSS-equipped, but otherwise blind, individual is capable of visual detection, not visual reception. Such persons should no more be said to have a visual modality than all of us should be said to have an electrical modality just because we can detect electricity with our tongues. It is true that they are getting visual information about the world, but they are getting that information via their tactile modality. Giving a blind person a TVSS system does not give them a modality they did not have before. Rather, it allows them to make better use of the modalities they already have. To the extent that ecological psychology fails to draw this distinction, it does not give us an adequate account of the senses.

The distinction at play here is that between the content of the senses and the mode of perceptual interaction between the organism and the world. Sensory modality is not simply an issue of what things in the external world can become the content of an individual's psychological

---

[22] Boston: Houghton Mifflin, 1966; see also *The Ecological Approach to Visual Perception* (Boston: Houghton Mifflin, 1979). Noë (*op. cit.*) also defends a Gibsonian account of the senses.

[23] *Brain Mechanisms in Sensory Substitution* (New York: Academic, 1972).

states, but rather the mode by which that content comes into the organism. It may well be the case that a blind person can come to have every propositional attitude a sighted person has. But such an individual is still blind; he lacks the modality of vision. He has one less modality than typical members of his species. He has just cleverly jury rigged a sensory system dedicated to the reception of mechanical distortion (his skin) into one capable of providing him with generally reliable information about the electromagnetic spectrum. But his perceptual mode of interaction with the "visual world" is tactile.

What this example shows is that there is more that we may wish to learn about perception than simply what modalities are at play. But an understanding of modalities will help us recognize an important way in which a TVSS-equipped blind person and others differ perceptually: one (the blind person) lacks a sensory system dedicated to the perception of electromagnetic stimuli which another person (a sighted one) has. One lacks a modality that the other one has, just as electric fish possess a modality (electroreception) that humans lack, although, thanks to our ingenuity, we can sometimes obtain information about the electrical world.

IV. TWO CRITERIA TO BE REJECTED

In the preceding section, I argued for the four criteria that I believe are necessary to differentiate the senses. Other criteria have been proposed. On my account, however, they are misapplied to Aristotle's and the star-nosed mole problems. Nonetheless, they are worth considering in some detail, if only because they have a great deal of intuitive plausibility.

In perhaps the twentieth century's most cited discussion of Aristotle's problem, Grice (*op. cit.*) discusses a set of four criteria for distinguishing the senses: proper objects, sensation, neurobiology, and physics. The bulk of Grice's paper, however, is *not* spent arguing for the adequacy of these four criteria, but rather discussing the relationship between the first two:

(5) *The proper objects of sensation*: the special features detectable by the operation of the senses; that is, by "the differing features that we become aware of by means of [the senses]" (*op. cit.*, p. 250 [this volume, p. 85]). For example, through vision, we become aware of colors; through audition, degrees of loudness.

(6) *Sensation*: "It might be suggested that two senses, for example seeing and smelling, are to be distinguished by *the special introspectible character* of the experiences of seeing and smelling; that is, disregarding the differences between the characteristics we learn about by sight and smell, we are entitled to say that seeing is itself different in character from smelling" (*op. cit.*, p. 250 [this volume, p. 85]).

Grice's first criterion (our (5)) is perhaps the most venerable approach to the issues at hand. This is the account to be found in Aristotle's *De Anima*, Book ii [this volume, chapter 2].[24] He points out that there are qualities, such as color, that are perceived only by a single sense. These are the "proper objects" of these senses, "the things to which the very being of each sense is naturally related" (*ibid.*, p. 3 [this volume, p. 65]). Aristotle goes on to contrast the proper objects with the "common sensibles"—number, shape, magnitude, motion, rest, and so on—which are qualities that are sensible by multiple modalities. Therefore, on this account, one first identifies the formal objects that are proper to only one sense, and based on that list we can derive a classification of the senses related to those objects.

In a sense, Aristotle's criterion can be seen as a primitive version of the physics criterion (1) in that a proper object account draws a strong connection between the categories of physics and those of our phenomenology. The categories of Aristotelian physics are the categories of common-sense physics. Of course, it is always open to us to reinterpret Aristotle's account in light of contemporary physics and argue, for instance, that "wavelength of electromagnetic energy" and not "color" is the *true* proper object of vision. But such a reinterpretation represents such a significant change to the common-sense nature of Aristotle's original proposal that it seems appropriate to identify it as a *different* proposal.[25]

Grice's[26] second criterion (our (6)) proposes to individuate modalities by reference to the *"special introspectible character,"* or what might be more commonly referred to as the distinct *sensations* or *qualia* asso-

---

[24] According to Richard Sorabji's reading of Aristotle, which I follow closely in this discussion—"Aristotle on Demarcating the Five Senses," *Philosophical Review*, LXXX (1971): 55–79 [this volume, chapter 3].

[25] At this point, I should mention two relatively recent approaches that are suggested improvements on Aristotle's "proper object" account. Both are attempts to spell out an account of the senses based on the content of perception; spelled out in terms of either "key features" (Roxbee Cox, *op. cit.*) or "primary objects" of perception (David H. Sanford, "The Primary Objects of Perception," *Mind*, LXXXV (1976): 189–208). In addition, Lopes (*op. cit.*) has recently endorsed a sensation-based account. He does not actively argue for it, however. Instead, he concentrates his attention on showing the inadequacies of Dretske's position (*Naturalizing the Mind* (Cambridge: MIT, 1995)) that we can make sense of the senses using an appropriate theory of content. At best, Lopes seems to ignore the possibility of unconscious sensory modalities. At worst, he rules them out by stipulation: "what it is like to perceive in one sense modality is different from what it is like to perceive in others—each has a unique 'phenomenal character'—and this is a fact which any theory of perception must take account" (*op. cit.*, p. 439). My disagreement with this claim should be clear from the discussion of criterion (6) below. (Cf. Dretske, "Reply to Lopes," *Philosophy and Phenomenological Research*, LX (2000): 455–59. See also Nelkin (*op. cit.*), and Ross (*op. cit.*) for related content-based approaches to the senses that regrettably I do not have space here to engage.)

[26] Grice does not use the terms 'proper objects of sensation' or 'sensation' or 'qualia' in his discussion of the senses. But what he says about each position seems to line up well with the common uses of these terms, so for pedagogical reasons, and to place Grice's discussion in a broader context, I shall use these terms to identify his criteria.

ciated with each given sensory modality. Since each sense has its own unique experiential quality, we can use these qualities to differentiate the senses. The second criterion would have us catalogue the different experiences we have, sorting them in terms of similarity and difference, and end up with several sets of related experiences that are the different modalities: the visual experiences, the olfactory experiences, and so on.

While these two criteria seem independent of one another, one of the central goals of Grice's article is to argue that they are not: any attempt to make suggestion (5) work leads to difficulties which seem soluble only if we bring in suggestion (6); yet suggestion (6) in turn involves difficulties which seem soluble only by adopting suggestion (5) (*op. cit.*, p. 259 [this volume, p. 93]). I do not wish to regurgitate Grice's clear, and to my mind correct, arguments for the interdependence of these criteria. But to motivate my critique of the sensation criterion below, let me present half of it—the dependence of proper objects on sensations.

Grice begins by following the suggestion of the proper objects criterion. He identifies a series of perceptual features of the world that are independent of the agent—for example, color, pitch, and temperature. This then allows us to individuate the senses using this list, without any reference to the way such features are experienced by a perceiver. At this point, a problem arises: "According to [the proper object criterion], certain properties are listed as visual properties, certain others as tactual properties, and so forth; and to say that color is a visual property would seem to amount to no more than saying that color is a member of a group of properties the others of which are...[*sic*]. This leaves membership of the group as an apparently arbitrary matter" (*op. cit.*, p. 255 [this volume, p. 89]). That is to say, relying on the proper objects of sense does not tell us by virtue of what these properties are the proper objects of *vision*, whereas those properties are the proper objects of *touch*. Of course, the obvious thing that classes these properties together is that we *see* the visual ones, and *tactually feel* the tactile ones. But to invoke this feature is to revert to the sensation criterion.

A second problem with the proper objects criterion is that it breaks down once you try to put it into practice. That color is a proper object of vision seems uncontroversial. But is warmth a proper object of the tactile sense? This seems correct until we realize that one can occasionally see the temperature of objects, as when the blacksmith sees that the red glowing metal bar next to the furnace is hot. The clear response to this worry is to draw a distinction between *directly* sensing temperature (as the tactile sense does) and *inferring* temperature (as we sometimes do with our visual senses). The *proper* objects of a sense are those which it directly senses. Grice demonstrates over several pages, however, that we cannot make sense of this suggested distinction without cashing out the notion of "directness" in terms of having a particular qualitative experience; for example, directly sensing warmth is to experience a sensation of warmth, something you get through the tactile sense and never through the visual sense (*op. cit.*, pp. 251–55 [this volume, pp. 86–91]). Once again, criterion (5) only makes sense by invoking criterion (6).

Given the above arguments, the cogency of criterion (5) rests on the foundation provided by criterion (6). How firm is this foundation? Grice argues that any account of the senses in terms of experiential character of sensation rests, in turn, on an account in terms of proper objects. I want to take a different tack. I accept that a proper object account rests on an account of sensation, but argue that we cannot use the experiential character of sensation to differentiate the senses. *Both* proper objects and sensations are nonstarters when it comes to solving Aristotle's and the star-nosed mole problems.[27]

What is wrong with using the experiential character of sensation as a criterion for individuating the senses? There are two problems with this approach. First, while potentially useful for solving Aristotle's problem, it is less clear what use it is in solving the star-nosed mole problem. Do we have to believe in the existence of electrical qualia, say, before we can sensibly talk of an electrical modality in electric fish or decide whether the star-nosed mole has an electrical modality? It seems to require that we be able to answer Thomas Nagel[28] type questions concerning what it is like to be an electric fish or star-nosed mole. This point echoes one made by Coady: "Further difficulties will arise for a Gricean view from the fact that we commonly attribute sight, touch, hearing, etc. to dumb animals and here we not only make no use of [the sensation criterion] but there seems to be no way in which we could" (*op. cit.*, p. 111 [this volume, p. 123]).

Of course, there is never a guarantee that philosophical analysis will make science easy (or even possible), and we might just have to accept that science cannot answer the star-nosed mole problem until it has overcome the worries raised by Nagel. I think, however, that there are other reasons for rejecting criterion (6) which render Nagel mute on the issue at hand. Grice's proposal runs into problems even with humans, because there is reason to believe that there are legitimate sensory modalities that *lack a special introspectible character altogether.*

Consider the case of the vomeronasal system. Admittedly, there is still controversy as to whether humans possess this modality, but over the past decade evidence in its favor has begun to mount. Furthermore, if we in fact possess this system, two things about it are striking: first, it plays a significant role in human behavior; and, second, we experience no sensations associated with this modality—there is no "special introspectible character" here, hence no basis to individuate this

---

[27] In addition to Grice, Mark Leon—"Characterising the Senses," *Mind and Language*, III (1988): 243–70 [this volume, chapter 8]—also argues for a sensation-based approach to differentiating the senses. But he is mainly concerned to counter the criticisms of Grice and to distinguish his account from belief-based approaches. He does not address the issues I raise here. Lopes (*op. cit.*) also endorses criterion (6), but see footnote 25 above.

[28] "What Is It Like to Be a Bat?" *The Philosophical Review*, LXXXIII (1974): 435–50.

modality from any other. It would appear to be a modality without sensory experiences.

In almost all vertebrates investigated, airborne chemicals are detected by multiple anatomical systems. One is the well-known system involving the olfactory epithelium within the nasal cavity containing chemosensory cells that project to the olfactory bulb. In humans, this is the system responsible for smell and taste experiences. In most animals, this system is primarily responsible for the detection and evaluation of food.

There is a second system, however, that is primarily social in function. The vomeronasal organ is located in a pair of pits on either side of the nasal septum. The vomeronasal system is primarily responsible for detecting pheromones, which in turn have been shown to play a central role in reproductive behavior.[29] For example, animals with lesioned vomeronasal organs typically exhibit greatly reduced sexual behavior. Similarly, artificially stimulating this organ and the nuclei to which it projects generally produces sexual behaviors in the animal so manipulated, even in the absence of appropriate conspecifics.

Do humans have a vomeronasal system? The textbook answer has traditionally been that while this system is present in human fetuses, it disappears during normal development.[30] In recent years, however, this received wisdom has been called into question.[31] In terms of anatomy— contrary to the textbooks—vomeronasal pits are present in most adult humans.[32] Furthermore, the pits are innervated by sensory neurons.[33]

Behaviorally, there is a growing list of findings in humans that closely resemble behaviors carried out by the vomeronasal system in other species. This, combined with the fact that these behaviors seem to have no conscious correlates, suggests the presence of a nonconscious modality in humans. First, it has been reported that individuals can detect the gender of another based on smelling the breath alone. Some women are reportedly able to identify the gender of a breather with an accuracy of ninety-five percent![34] Second, clinicians have observed that damage to the nerves in the nasal region is often, but not always, associated with a loss of interest in sex. (Because medical

---

[29] M. Halpern, "The Organization and Function of the Vomeronasal System," *Annual Review of Neuroscience*, X (1987): 325–62.

[30] Elizabeth C. Crosby and Tryphena Humphrey, "Studies of the Vertebrate Telencephalon," *Journal of Comparative Neurology*, LXXI (1939): 121–213, especially p. 121.

[31] Robert Taylor, "Brave New Nose: Sniffing Out Human Sexual Chemistry," *Journal of NIH Research*, VI (1994): 47–51.

[32] A. Johnson, R. Josephson, and M. Hawke, "Clinical and Histological Evidence for the Presence of the Vomeronasal (Jacobson's) Organ in Adult Humans," *Journal of Otolaryngology*, XIV (1985): 71–79.

[33] S. Takami, M. L. Getchell, Y. Chen, L. Monti-Bloch, D. L. Berliner, L. J. Stensaas, and T. V. Getchell, "Vomeronasal Epithelial Cells of the Adult Human Express Neuron-specific Molecules," *NeuroReport*, IV (1993): 375–78.

[34] Rivlin and Gravelle, p. 154.

students have typically been taught that humans do not have a vomer-onasal organ, however, nobody has pursued a study of naturally occur-ring lesions to the vomeronasal versus olfactory epithelial systems in humans. Therefore, to my knowledge, no attempt has been made to try to tease apart the functions of these two systems, as has been done in nonhuman animals.)

While the science is admittedly controversial here, the possibility of a human vomeronasal system stands as a potentially interesting case of a modality without a special introspectible experiential character. Women who can guess the gender of breath do not report that they experience "male" versus "female" qualia associated with the breaths. Indeed, sub-jects are generally surprised to be informed that they are so good at distinguishing the smells. Gender detection via the putative vomero-nasal sense seems akin to an olfactory version of blindsight.[35] And if it is a modality that lacks qualia, then criterion (6) cannot even begin to distinguish this modality from others.

Many will no doubt be surprised by the above arguments that the dif-ferentiation of the senses is independent of any appeal to the experiences associated with the senses. A commentator[36] on an early version of this article put it this way: "Much of the bad press over qualia is well-de-served; but if there is one place experiential qualities have a safe home, I would've thought it would be with the sense modalities." In response, I would say that experiential qualities do have a safe home in the modali-ties. Much of what we experience, we experience through the senses. My argument here is *not* that there is no such thing as sensory experi-ence, but rather that we should not use those experiences to differentiate the senses. Experience is often associated with the senses, but its nature does not define the difference between the individual senses.[37]

---

[35] L. Weiskrantz, *Blindsight: A Case Study and Implications* (New York: Oxford, 1986).
[36] Tom Polger made this comment at the 1999 *Society for Philosophy and Psychology* meeting in Palo Alto, California.
[37] For reasons of space, one issue I have not discussed here is the assumption that the senses are "fairly discrete systems," as Leon puts it (*op. cit.*, p. 245, footnote 1 [this volume, p. 158, footnote 1]). It is common to assume that the different senses are significantly sepa-rate and independent of one another. Indeed, this assumption motivates the questions dis-cussed here. To my knowledge, this ubiquitous assumption has received even less attention in the philosophical literature than the star-nosed mole and Aristotle problems; a curious observation given the existence of empirical phenomena that raise questions about it. I am thinking here of synesthesia: Richard E. Cytowic, *Synesthesia: A Union of the Senses* (New York: Springer, 1989), *The Man Who Tasted Shapes: A Bizarre Medical Mystery Offers Revolutionary Insights into Emotions, Reasoning and Consciousness* (New York: Putnam, 1993), and the McGurk effect—H. McGurk and J. MacDonald, "Hearing Lips and Seeing Voices," *Nature*, CCLXIV (1976): 747–48. In the neurological-condition synesthesia, the proper objects of one sense result in experiences in more than one modality—for example, "colored-hearing." In the McGurk effect, normal humans will literally hear the same audi-tory speech stimulus differently, depending on what they see (lip movements of one sort versus another). It is not clear what effect such interaction between senses has on the story I am telling here. Unfortunately, to explore the issue fully would require another article.

V. IMPLICATIONS: WHAT SENSES DO HUMANS AND OTHERS HAVE?

The proof, they say, is in the pudding, and I conclude by showing how my account deals with some actual cases by spelling out its philosophical implications. First, let us consider Aristotle's problem. On my account, vision, hearing, touch, smell, and taste come out as different senses. Each involves sense organs dedicated to the detection of a different class of physical stimulation. If future science pans out as I have described it above, humans should be said to have a vomeronasal modality as well. We also have a vestibular sense (based in the semicircular canals in our heads) as well as a proprioceptive system (based in the stretch receptors in our skeletal muscles).

At the same time, on my account, humans should not be said to have an electric sense because we have as yet discovered no organ that is dedicated to the processing of electrical information in our environment. As noted above, we can access electrical information through our tongues, but only by electrically stimulating sensory systems that are normally responsive to other physical properties—physical properties that are part of the normal human sensory environment. On the other hand, electric fish *should* be said to have an electrical sensory modality because these organisms have organs that have evolved specifically to process biologically meaningful electrical stimuli in their environments.

What about the star-nosed mole? On my account here, the nose of a star-nosed mole would seem to be best thought of as mediating a tactile sense. Although it is true that sensory cells in the nose of this animal can be stimulated by the presentation of electricity, as with the case of the human tongue, I realize that this fact does not settle the issue. All sensory cells, when blasted with enough electricity, can be made to respond. The question is whether there is any reason to believe that the amount of electricity required to stimulate the nose of a star-nosed mole is within the range that would make it likely that their noses had evolved this capacity. Is the detection of electricity a dedicated function of star-nosed mole noses? To date, such evidence has not been forthcoming. On the other hand, the work of Catania (*op. cit.*) indicates that these same sensory cells are responsive to tactile stimulation and, furthermore, that the range of mechanical stimulation required falls within an ecologically plausible range. With such a nose, a star-nosed mole is able to make all sorts of useful sensory discriminations of the texture, motion, and shape of objects that it places its nose upon. What is more, Catania has done careful comparative studies indicating that the sensory end organs on the nose of the star-nosed mole are likely modified versions of the tactile-sensing end organs found in related species of moles, which in turn are modified versions of the basic tactile-sensing end organs found in most mammals, including humans. All of these discoveries point to the conclusion that the nose of a star-nosed mole is properly thought of as a tactile-sensor.

The sort of story told about the star-nosed mole can be used as a template in the cases of all putative sensory modalities in nonhuman animals. If, for example, one wishes to argue for the presence of a magnetic sense in migratory birds or an electrical sense in the platypus, then the same set of evidence needs to be collected. One must characterize the target of the sense in physical terms (What range of magnetic stimulation? Exactly what electrical properties?). One must demonstrate via the organisms' behavior that the organisms in question can make use of the alleged sense. One must find a sense organ that can transduce this information from the environment to the CNS of the organism. Finally, one must demonstrate that this organ has the evolutionary or developmental function to carry out such sensory transductions. Only if you do all four of these things can you properly talk of the animal as having the sense in question.

Those are the scientific implications of my account. What of the philosophical ones? If the account that I have presented here is plausible, then it represents a strong, naturalized alternative to the more common-sense approaches to the issues typically favored by philosophers. For the purposes of the perceptual sciences, at least, distinguishing the senses from one another is not a matter of such folk-scientific entities as the proper objects of sensation or some specific qualitative feel of conscious perceptual experience. Strictly speaking, this is not to say that qualia do not exist, but rather that they do not have a role to play in this particular scientific story, however useful they may be to our folk understanding of ourselves. Defenders of qualia need to look elsewhere for scientific legitimacy.

If you are unconvinced with the positive story I have told here, I hope to have at least persuaded you that there are interesting philosophical and scientific questions yet to be answered concerning the differentiation of the senses in humans and other animals. At the same time, I believe I have shown that some of the more intuitive criteria for partitioning our senses run into problems, particularly when it comes to such potentially novel senses as proprioception and the vomeronasal sense, not to mention those of such exotic animals as star-nosed moles and electric fish. The principled extension of common-sense concepts into novel domains is a long-standing project in philosophy. I hope that this discussion has shown that there is still interesting contemporary work to be done on ancient problems.

Section II

NEW WORKS

12

On the Nature of the Senses

Richard Gray

1. INTRODUCTION

In his seminal discussion of the senses, H. P. Grice (1962/this volume, chapter 4) suggests that any one of four criteria—the *proper objects* criterion, the *character of experience* criterion, the *physical features* criterion, and the *sensory organ* criterion—might be used to distinguish two senses and therefore to determine whether a sense with which we are not already acquainted constitutes a new sense.[1] It is unclear whether Grice is describing or recommending a procedure for distinguishing the senses.[2] Indeed, it is unclear exactly how these criteria are supposed to be used. Before listing the criteria, he introduces them as "seemingly independent". After listing the criteria, he comments that they need not be regarded as mutually exclusive and remarks that there is likely to be "a multiplicity of criteria" rather than any one essential criterion for distinguishing the senses. In fact, at this point he suggests that the most desirable approach in difficult cases would be to examine "the applicability of the suggested criteria and their relative weights" (1962, 136/this volume, p. 85). Rather than continue with this suggestion, Grice moves on to the main theme of his discussion, namely, an examination of the

---

[1] Familiar proper objects that might be used to distinguish two senses would be the colors and sounds that are seen and heard, respectively. Familiar characters of experiences that might be used to do so would be those that colors and sounds typically cause. Familiar physical features that might be used to distinguish two senses would be the stimuli, such as electromagnetic radiation and sound waves that activate the distinct senses. Familiar sensory organs that might be used to do so would be the eyes and the ears. Unfamiliar proper objects, characters of experience, physical features, and sensory organs that might be used to distinguish a new sense would be novel instances of the kinds to which the preceding belong.

[2] Given that Grice framed the issue in terms of how one might recognize a new sense, it might be thought that he was thereby suggesting the criteria that *should* be employed in distinguishing the senses. He might, however, have been suggesting that we would just extrapolate from the criteria we actually use to distinguish the senses that we possess. For more on the distinction see Nelkin (1990/this volume, chapter 9).

independence of these criteria and in particular of the independence of the first two criteria.[3]

Much of the philosophical literature concerning the senses in the intervening half century has addressed the epistemological issues raised by Grice's suggestions about how we distinguish (or should distinguish) different senses, resulting in corresponding proposals about the nature of particular senses, with the more general question of the metaphysical nature of the senses remaining in the background.[4] However, the failure to satisfactorily resolve the issue of exactly how we identify the different senses has recently resulted in a closer focus on the more general question of the nature of a sense. This question has been thrown into particularly sharp focus by two starkly contrasting approaches to the senses.

On the one hand, Brian Keeley (2002/this volume, chapter 11) has argued that we can provide a better philosophical understanding of the senses if we take a lesson from how scientists, in particular neuroethologists, distinguish them. By looking at the grounds on which neuroethologists seem to identify the senses, Keeley proposes that we replace the common-sense conception of a sense with a scientific one by rejecting two of Grice's criteria (the proper objects criterion and the character of experience criterion) and adopting a set of four criteria drawn from the natural sciences constitutive of neuroethology. His project is, in essence, that of naturalizing the senses.[5] These criteria, Keeley goes on to claim, can be used to provide a set of individually necessary and jointly sufficient conditions for the differentiation of the senses in all animals. Hence, in an effort to resolve the issues surrounding how we identify the senses, Keeley sets out a scientific realist position regarding the nature of the senses.

On the other hand, Matthew Nudds (2003) has argued against the quest for any set of criteria that match the way in which we commonly distinguish our senses, let alone a set of criteria drawn from the natural sciences.[6] Rather, what we should be looking for is an explanation of *why* we ordinarily distinguish the senses in the way that we do. His own

---

[3] Grice did point out the difficulty of identifying distinct types of sensory organs or sensory mechanisms without reference to proper objects or physical stimuli, thereby indicating that at least one criterion could not serve as an independent criterion for individuating a novel sense. More controversial was his suggestion that the presence of a novel phenomenal character of experience might be sufficient for the individuation of a new sense. See Coady (1974/this volume, chapter 6) and Ross (2001) for critical responses.

[4] See, for example, Roxbee Cox (1970/this volume, chapter 5) for a defense of the *key features* condition, a more sophisticated version of the *proper objects* condition; Leon (1988/this volume, chapter 8) for a defense of a *phenomenal character* condition, although one distinct from that suggested by Grice; and Nelkin (1990/this volume, chapter 9) for a defense of the view that the senses should be distinguished in terms of the origins of beliefs.

[5] In acknowledging the physical features criterion Grice would seem to accept a role for science, although he does not make use of it in the way that Keeley does.

[6] Nudds comments (2003, 35) that such a revisionary view of the senses bears on our ordinary concept of a sense only when it can be shown that the latter incorporates "the kind of proto-scientific understanding of the senses which is liable to revision".

	ORDINARY CONCEPT	CRITERIAL APPROACH	REALISM
GRICE	✓	✓	
KEELEY	✗	✓	✓
NUDDS	✓	✗	✗

Figure 12.1 Contrasting views on the individuation of the senses

answer is that we want to know not merely *that* someone perceived something but also *how* they perceived it (i.e., we want to know not merely that someone perceived something but whether they saw it or touched it or otherwise perceived it). It is the usefulness of this additional information that explains the significance of our ordinarily distinguishing the senses in the way that we do. Such a story should precede any debate about criteria. Indeed, it should pre-empt it. For Nudds goes on to claim that our reasons for distinguishing the senses in the way that we do is, in large part, a conventional matter rather than a reflection of any real divisions in nature. Hence, in responding to the difficulty of articulating an account of how exactly we distinguish the senses, Nudds develops an anti-realist position regarding them.

Both of these proposals incorporate a number of interesting suggestions for thinking about the senses, all the more so in that they are in several significant respects diametrically opposed to each other. The former advocates the support of science; the latter eschews it. The latter rejects a criterial approach; the former reinforces it. However, most significantly for present purposes, the one leads to a robustly realist conclusion concerning the senses, while the other leads to an anti-realist conclusion concerning the senses. These various ways of thinking about the senses are summarized in figure 12.1.[7]

It is my view that one way of moving the discussion about the senses forward is to construe the issue of the senses in terms of a debate between realists and anti-realists. Here I mediate between the two positions. In the next section I set out Keeley's case for realism; I point out some problems that face his criterial approach to the individuation of the senses and that also face a criterial approach of a more minimal kind. In the subsequent section I outline Nudds's case for anti-realism; I argue that our intuitions regarding three test cases that he cites in support of it (novel senses, counterfactual cases, and non-paradigm sensory processes) can be equally well explained by realists and that his anti-realism regarding the paradigm senses is based on a controversial assumption of what a sense is. The view I advocate is what you arrive at when you

---

[7] Grice appears to assume a form of realism about the senses, as do most of those who have discussed them, but the commitment is seldom clarified.

acknowledge that an explanation is required for why we distinguish the senses in the way that we do and that our conception of a sense applies to the senses beyond those that we possess.

2. SCIENTIFIC REALISM AND THE SENSES

In providing accounts of how we distinguish the senses, Grice and others have drawn attention to some of the features that constitute a distinct sense. However, providing an account of how we distinguish one type of sense from another need not account for all the features that make a token sense an instance of a particular type of sense. The point should be uncontentious. The features that are discriminated when two types of things are discriminated are seldom sufficient to provide a full account of the constitution of those types of things. In as much, one might justifiably differentiate two tasks. There is the task of ascertaining what is required for us to distinguish between tokens of two types of sense, and then there is the task of ascertaining all that is required for a token sense to be a member of the type of sense of which it is a member.[8] However, putting matters this way assumes the independent reality of the senses. So one should distinguish a further task, namely that of ascertaining the general metaphysical nature of the senses. It is to that task that the present essay is primarily addressed. Nonetheless, it can be addressed only via the attempts to tackle the other two tasks.

Grice suggests criteria that we might use to distinguish a new type of sense. As such he is addressing the first issue noted above. Were such an account to be successful, it would have set out the conditions that are necessary and/or sufficient for distinguishing two senses. It would thereby have also provided at least a partial account of the constitution of the senses. As the subsequent literature testifies, Grice failed to provide an adequate account of what is required for us to be able to distinguish two types of senses, hence opening the door to the question of the metaphysical nature of the senses.[9] In the rest of this section, I set out and contest two of the most recent attempts to finesse a criterial account by drawing upon the resources of science.

2.1. Scientific Criteria

Keeley attempts to fill in some of the gaps in Grice's story. His proposal is explicitly stated in terms of individually necessary and jointly

---

[8] Nudds (2003, 33) similarly notes that an account has to be given not only of how the senses are distinguished from each other but also of what all of the perceptions of a single sense have in common.

[9] In the introduction to his article Grice provides some remarks about what constitutes a sense.

sufficient conditions for distinguishing the senses. If successful, it should enable us to distinguish between any two types of senses. However, it would be able to do more than this; it would also be able to tell us what is required for any putative instance of a sense to be a member of a particular type of sense and hence provide justification for the presupposition that there really are senses. In proposing such conditions Keeley defers to the way in which scientists distinguish the senses. The problem with his proposal is that it is not true with regard to the way scientists in fact distinguish the senses. It thereby fails to provide an adequate account of the constitution of the senses and vindication for realism.

Keeley's proposal, in brief, is that "to possess a genuine sensory modality is to possess an appropriately wired up sense organ that is historically dedicated to facilitating behavior with respect to an identifiable physical class of energy" (2002, 6/this volume, p. 221). He explicates this proposal by providing an ordered set of four independently necessary and jointly sufficient conditions drawn from the four sciences that compose neuroethology, which he claims can be used to distinguish the senses. They are in order as follows: (1) physics, (2) neurobiology, (3) the behavioral sciences, and (4) evolutionary biology. Physics, first and independently of the other sciences, identifies the classes of physical energy (*possible sensory spaces*, as Keeley calls them); neurobiology then ascertains which of the possible sensory spaces are actualized by identifying the appropriately wired-up sense organs that are sensitive to these classes of energy; the behavioral sciences are then required to confirm that the sense organs actually facilitate behavior (ruling out vestigial senses), and evolutionary biology bears out the fact that this stimulus is the one to which the sensory system was designed to respond (avoiding the unnecessary multiplication of senses). Keeley's procedure is intended to identify both the possible and the actual senses. In this respect, the senses are taken to exist prior to and independently of our classification of them. It is this that marks it out as a realist account of the senses and, since it employs the sciences constitutive of neuroethology, a scientific realist account. Using these four conditions in this way, Keeley claims, we will be able to individuate the senses that any creature possesses. However, there are two complementary counterexamples that demonstrate that his proposal is flawed.[10]

The *pit viper problem* is derived from the pit viper, which possesses two sets of sense organs (the pit viper has, below each of its eyes, a small pit) that are each receptive to non-overlapping ranges of electromagnetic radiation. On Keeley's proposal one should count only a single type of sense; a difference in the type of physical stimulus is necessary for a difference in the type of sense; therefore, sameness in the type of physical stimulus is sufficient for sameness of the type of sense. Yet

---

[10] See Gray (2005) for a fuller discussion of the two problems outlined here.

neuroethologists themselves standardly distinguish two senses: eyes are involved in seeing; pits are involved in thermal imaging. Hence, the pit viper problem demonstrates that scientists do not always start out by employing the physics condition, nor, more importantly, does the physics condition act as an independently necessary condition for differentiating the senses.

The *vampire bat problem* is the converse case. The vampire bat problem is derived from the vampire bat, which has an appropriately wired-up sense organ that is historically dedicated to facilitating behavior with respect to two identifiable physical classes of energy: kinetic energy and radiant energy.[11] On Keeley's proposal, if there are two types of physical stimulus, then there are two possible sensory spaces. There might be distinct senses, one of which is appropriately related only to kinetic energy and the other of which is appropriately related to radiant energy. Indeed, the thermal imaging sense of the pit viper seems to be an example of the latter. Thermoregulation might be an example of the former. However, the vampire bat problem demonstrates that this is not always the case. Here scientists do not distinguish two senses despite the presence of distinct physical stimuli. Yet, if the neurobiological condition is required to play a role in our individuating the senses, it is again unclear how the physics condition is supposed to act as an independently necessary condition for sensory differentiation.

The two problems arise with Keeley's proposal because of the particular role he gives to the physics condition in his treatment of the senses. He holds that this condition provides a starting point and an independently necessary condition for the "differentiation" of the senses. It is clear how the physics condition could be necessary yet insufficient for the *constitution* of a sense. A sense is not merely constituted by the physical stimuli to which it is sensitive; a sensory organ also has to have evolved to detect that type of stimuli. It is also clear why one should require some sort of external constraint in order to individuate the senses; as others have noted, how otherwise would one classify a sensory organ? However, on Keeley's account, if the physics condition is *independently* necessary, it should be all that is required for the *individuation* of one type of sense from another. Yet, as the two cases show, on certain occasions it is clearly the case that the physics condition does not play this role.

Both problems indicate that reference to the physics condition may be necessary but insufficient for the individuation of a sense. However, now that we have switched from regarding the neurobiological condition as a merely constitutive condition for a sense to regarding it as an individuation condition for certain types of senses, it is no longer clear

---

[11] I say that this *may* be the case because current research, as far as I am aware, has not determined what the vampire bat is receptive to. Nevertheless, many mammals, including humans, have heat receptors that are sensitive to both forms of energy. So the example needs to be addressed.

how we should regard Keeley's idea of possible sensory spaces as a strong constraint on the individuation of the senses, nor is it clear when exactly the neurobiological condition should play such an additional role. Hence, a realist view of the senses remains less than fully vindicated.

2.2. Minimal Criteria

In another recent response, Peter Ross (2008) provides a different challenge to Keeley's account. Ross argues that the behavioral condition (that for something to be a sensory system it has to facilitate behavioral responses with respect to a class of physical stimuli) can be made to work only if qualitative properties are presupposed. Therefore, qualitative properties cannot be eliminated from an account of the senses in the way in which Keeley proposes. Ross favors a common-sense conception of the senses that can nevertheless be informed by scientific data, whereby a distinct sense enables perceptual states characterizable by means of a distinctive qualitative determinable. Indeed, Ross claims that a *qualitative determinables* criterion (another descendent of Grice's proper objects criterion) is the only criterion the satisfaction of which is necessary for our distinguishing two senses (i.e., tokens of any two types of senses must differ with respect to the qualitative determinables they determine) and hence is sufficient for the identification of two token senses as members of the same type of sense (i.e., token senses determining the same qualitative determinable would be enough to qualify them as belonging to the same kind of sense). He thinks that the prospects for other necessary conditions or for providing sufficient conditions for our distinguishing a sense are poor. He cites the case of touch; even though touch is associated with a number of qualitative determinables, Ross notes that they have all been grouped together as the determinables determined by the sense of touch. In the case of touch, some further feature seems to be required for us to distinguish more than one sense.

One benefit of his view, according to Ross, is that the two problems that challenge Keeley's proposal can be resolved. In the case of the vampire bat problem, there is plausibly only a single qualitative determinable; therefore, there is only one sense. In the case of the pit viper problem, there are plausibly two qualitative determinables to which the pit viper could be perceptually sensitive: hotness and brightness. We do not know to which of the two qualitative determinables the pit viper *is* sensitive. However, if it is sensitive to brightness, then its sense would qualify as a visual sense, whereas if the pit viper is sensitive to hotness, then its sense would qualify as a touch sense. It all depends on what it is like to be a pit viper (in the relevant respect).

Ross claims that multidimensional scaling, which is used to explore the sensory spaces constituted by the determination of qualitative determinables, might be able to tell us whether the pit viper's sense is related to vision or to touch. This seems to me to be highly optimistic. However, even if it could provide a clue, it is arguable whether it would be enough. For Ross assumes a reductive externalist representationalist theory of perceptual experience in which the character of experience can be fully explained in terms of the properties (determinates of the qualitative determinables) represented by experience. Ross's reasoning is that if we can determine the character of thermal imaging, we can determine its content and thereby the sensory modality. However, unless a version of representationalism can provide an independently plausible explanation of which of the two properties is the one that the pit viper's sense represents, it remains unclear whether the character of the pit viper's experience is indeed constituted by the properties it represents. If we cannot ascertain independently which properties thermal imaging represents, we have no justification for identifying the sense in one way or another. None of the versions of content determination presently on offer seem obviously up to the job.[12]

Even were a plausible account of content determination to be provided that supported the view that the thermal-imaging sense determines brightness, it is not indisputable that the sense should be classified as a visual one. Should we not also take into account the way the pit viper's sense detects the emission of radiation from warm bodies in a way that vision does not? Similarly, were a plausible account of content determination to be provided that supports the view that the thermal-imaging sense determines heat, should we not also want to take into account the way the pit viper's sense detects the size, shape, and movement of objects in a way unlike that in which we sense heat by touch?

One might here suggest that it would be useful to draw a distinction between species and genera of senses. One might claim that the present case shows that there are two species of the genus vision or two species of the genus touch. However, saying that we might have two different species of visual senses here would significantly modify our understanding of what vision is. Similarly, saying that we might have two different species of touch here would significantly modify our understanding of what touch is. Besides, Ross notes the way in which we include a number

---

[12] See Gray (forthcoming) for further discussion. This case, it seems to me, provides a more realist and more serious challenge to representationalism than Grice's Martian thought experiment. Ross (2001) argues that Grice's Martian thought experiment, which involves a creature that has two sets of sensory organs sensitive to similar ranges of electromagnetic radiation and sees colors with both systems but has different characters of experience, can be explained without introducing qualia (intrinsic properties of experiences). Ross claims that the difference could be explained by the Martian's being sensitive to other qualitative properties to which we humans are perceptually insensitive. Let us grant that the phenomenology could be explained in both these ways. The matter comes down to whether additional qualitative properties are involved, a matter that would presumably be empirically ascertainable. Both alternatives seem possible (although both seem somewhat far fetched). Whether we would regard a sense that either determined color via a different character of experience or determined it along with other qualitative determinables as being distinct from vision is unclear, just as it is with other counterfactual and non-paradigm cases (see sections 3.2 and 3.3).

of qualitative determinables as those that are determined by the sense of touch; why should we not think of the visual perception of brightness and the imaging of hotness as being related in the same way? In general it is difficult to know just how to respond to Ross's suggestion until the broader metaphysical issue of the nature of the senses, upon which a minimalist approach is, by its own nature, silent, has been resolved.

3. ANTI-REALISM AND THE SENSES

The problems facing criterial accounts suggest the need for an alternative approach to the senses. Nudds (2003) provides such an approach: what is required is an *explanation* of why we ordinarily distinguish five senses in the first place, not a list of the criteria that might be used to identify them given that we have already made the distinctions that we have. What is most significant about his approach, in the present context, is that it leads to an anti-realist view of the senses.

For Nudds, it is significant that, when asked how many senses there are, ordinary folk will typically say five, but, when asked why they say this, they are unable to provide a good reason for saying so apart from the fact that they have been taught to. It is common knowledge that we have five senses, but, according to Nudds, this is only a piece of conventional wisdom.[13] In support of this, Nudds notes that "it is surprising, given the obviousness of the fact that we have five senses, that there should be so little agreement as to what account should be given of them" (2003, 31).

Following a rehearsal of the principal criterial accounts and the main objections to them, Nudds turns to what he takes to be the more fundamental issue.[14] Even if one could formulate an extensionally correct account of the way in which we distinguish the five senses in terms of

---

[13] The obviousness of the fact that we have five senses, even the possibility of this being a universal distinction among humans, might seem to be equally well explained by natural features. However, it would not decide the philosophical issue. Perhaps early proto-scientific theories, such as the Aristotelian view, were really based on conventional distinctions.

[14] Those who adopt the criterial approach might be uneasy at Nudds's quick rejection of it. In my view his objection to the proper objects criterion is unsatisfactory. He raises two difficulties: that of telling whether a property is perceived by one rather than another sense when it is simultaneously doubly determined and that of explaining how perception by a particular sense can occur without the key features that are supposed to individuate that sense. One response, as Grice seems to suggest in the case of seeing and feeling shape, is that we can tell that a property is perceived by a particular sense—without the presence of key features—when the spatial properties have different appearances due to the way in which they are differently positioned with respect to the distinct sense organs. Nevertheless, this does not challenge Nudds's main point about the significance of distinguishing the senses. Nor does it resolve the metaphysical issue, for simply endorsing a criterial account does not entail endorsing realism. One might even argue that one criterial account is the best way to identify the senses without endorsing their reality independently of our identification of them.

appropriate criteria, this would still not tell us why we make (or should make) the distinctions we do. Hence, so Nudds claims, a condition on any satisfactory account of the senses is that it should be able to tell us why we distinguish the five senses as we do.[15]

According to Nudds, our concepts of the five senses are core folk psychological concepts that are of use to us for our understanding of each other. It is of explanatory significance to us to know that someone is in a folk psychological state related to one sense rather than another because their being so will have consequences for their judgments and actions. We want to know not merely that someone perceives an object but also how they perceive that object—whether they are seeing it or touching it, for instance—because knowing that will produce a difference in our potential explanations and predictions. The basic idea here is that if people perceive an object in a certain way (i.e., via a certain sense), then they have information that they would not have were they to have perceived the object in another way. Hence, we can make inferences about their judgments and future behavior. In other words, the ways in which we distinguish between the senses should be spelled out in terms of the consequences of our so doing rather than in terms of pre-existing criteria. So the explanation for our distinguishing the senses is that it has explanatory significance.[16]

Nevertheless, this only seems to postpone the question of why we distinguish the number of senses that we do. Perhaps we distinguish the senses for the explanatory reasons suggested because distinct senses, which are to be characterized by certain properties, really exist. Ultimately, according to Nudds, the distinctions we make are conventional (2003, 48) and, to some degree, arbitrary. This claim has already received some motivation from the prior rebuttal of criterial accounts. However, central to the claim is the argument that our distinguishing five senses is only partly a consequence of the fact that we have the sensory mechanisms that we do. Although sensory mechanisms contribute to the differentiation of the senses, they do not play the role of criteria, nor can they be regarded as constituting the relevant type of natural kinds. None of this is to say that conventional divisions are not somehow constrained. There are pragmatic reasons for distinguishing

---

[15] Given that Nudds focuses on our five senses, an appraisal of the various criterial approaches in their own terms would be restricted to whether they are de facto accurate. However, some criterial accounts propose a view about the criteria that *should* be adopted, implying that there are reasons for distinguishing the senses in the way that they recommend. No doubt, such accounts are often not as explicit about their reasons as Nudds would like. Nevertheless, the criterial approach is not always a matter of fitting the theory to the data as Nudds seems to be suggesting. Indeed, to my mind, the main force of Nudds's position lies in his claim that criterial accounts invariably come up short.
[16] Roxbee Cox (1970/this volume, chapter 5) draws attention to the usefulness of our dividing up the senses, in particular touch, in the way that we do without explicating the metaphysical implications in this way.

the senses in the way that we do; the information thus provided is of benefit to us. Furthermore, once we have established the distinction in folk psychology, we can consolidate it by mutually acting on it. Nudds holds that the senses are, if anything, social psychological kinds. In this respect he endorses a form of anti-realism.

Nudds concludes that his approach to the individuation of the senses is not only able to explain why we distinguish the five senses that we ordinarily distinguish but also has the advantage of being able to explain our intuitions about three other types of cases: new senses, counterfactual cases, and non-paradigm sensory processes. In the rest of this section I argue that the realist can provide equally satisfactory explanations of our intuitions about all three cases. As it turns out, the case for anti-realism is best supported by the paradigm senses, but here Nudds assumes a model of what a sense would be that realists should reject.

3.1. Novel Senses

Since the senses that we distinguish depend upon our conventions and we have no conventions for senses that we do not possess, Nudds (2003, 50) holds that his anti-realist account has nothing to say about senses that we might newly possess. One difficulty with this response is that many people accept that other animals have senses that we do not (but could perhaps) possess, and people typically have intuitions about such senses. So any account of the senses should have something to say about new ones.

There seems to be no obvious restriction to our providing new conventions and thus being able to think of something as a new sense. All of the parties to the debate agree that we already possess the general concept of a sense as that which enables a distinctive way of perceiving. What remains at issue is how to construe such a concept and in particular whether such a concept enables us to recognize a new sense that exists prior to and independently of our conceptualization. It is not obvious that a consideration of novel senses speaks in favor of anti-realism without further consideration of putative examples of such novel senses. I return to this in the final section.

3.2. Perceiving and Possibility

Try to imagine a possible world in which sounds cause experiences that in the actual world are caused by colors. How would we classify such a sensory process?[17]

---

[17] I am not here describing a case of colored hearing synesthesia, in which additional experiences as of color are caused by sounds. That occurs in the actual world. Whether it is appropriately so named is another issue. I think that it is a case of hearing and that a construal of the use of the term *colored* can be provided.

Nudds explains our lack of any secure intuitions about how we would think about the counterfactual example by pointing out that the distinctions we make are governed by conventions that are meant to apply only to the actual world. This, however, hardly decides the issue. For the criterial approach also has a readily available explanation for why we should not have any secure intuitions about such cases. Drawing on Grice's common-sense criteria, one could say that the reason we would have no firm intuitions about how to classify the aforementioned case is that the criteria are here combined that might actually be used to distinguish two different senses (hearing and vision). The reason we have no firm intuitions about this and similar counterfactual cases is that the way we actually distinguish the senses with which we are familiar precludes it.

Keeley's criterial approach might seem to offer a different response. On his proposal we individuate the senses by reference to the physics condition since physics delimits all possible sensory spaces. So the present example would be a case of hearing. Intuitively, there seems to be something problematic about this. However, this is not all that Keeley's account requires; we also need to add a specification of the neurobiological condition if this is to be a case of a genuine sense. Now do we really have clear intuitions about the kind of sensory system that would have to have evolved so as to enable the possessors of such a system to respond experientially to the relevant stimuli in the stipulated fashion? If we do not, as seems plausible to me, we would have another explanation available, based on a realist standpoint, for why we have no secure intuitions about how we should think of the counterfactual case.

Other criterial views that give pre-eminence to a single criterion over the other criteria can be similarly problematic. Leon (1988/this volume, chapter 8) claims that distinguishing between the senses requires reference to the character of experience. He cites several modal examples in favor of this. For instance, he claims that the presence of light is not necessary for seeing: another phenomenon (e.g., sound) might enable us to see (have experiences with the appropriate *visual* phenomenal character) in the absence of light. Such modal intuitions are, to say the least, controversial, especially since we are given no indication of how they are supposed to be realized.[18]

---

[18] Kripke (1980, 130) raises precisely this possibility. There are a number of reasons to doubt that it is a genuine possibility. Could sound waves cause the appropriate events in the eye? Alternatively, could sounds cause events in the ear and brain that resulted in experiences qualitatively identical to actual visual experiences? Could the brain be wired in the appropriate way? Or would the character of experience in such a world still be constituted by the external sound properties? Perhaps all of these worries contribute to our uncertainty about what to make of these cases and thus make is hard to extend Kripke's account of natural kinds and natural kind terms to the senses and terms for the sensory modalities.

3.3. Non-Paradigm Sensory Processes

By way of further support for anti-realism, Nudds (2003, 50) explains the vagueness in our judgments about non-paradigm cases by claiming that our conventions do not provide us with clearly determined ways of thinking about them. Given that he distinguishes non-paradigm processes from both new senses and counterfactual cases (ibid.) and that he accepts the common-sense view that we possess five paradigm senses, what he might have in mind as an example of the way in which perceptions are produced in non-paradigmatic ways is the tactile-visual substitution system (TVSS).[19] One might well waver over classifying TVSS as a tactile or a visual sense because of the difficulty of deciding whether further explanation is to be gained by thinking of TVSS in one way or the other. Some advocates of a criterial approach have not seen any difficulties here; some hold this to be a clear case of touch, while others regard this as a case of vision.[20] Nevertheless, the presence of disagreement can itself be regarded as providing some support for the anti-realist view that there is no mind-independent fact of the matter about the case.

However, an alternative response might be made on behalf of the realist: a case such as TVSS, in which perceptions are produced in a non-paradigmatic manner, gives rise to a certain vagueness in our judgments because our concepts of distinct senses concern only normal sensory processes. Indeed, Keeley's realist account of the senses explicitly recognizes the way in which sensory systems have evolved to respond to specific stimuli.

3.4. Paradigm Senses

A better place to look for support for anti-realism, contrary to what one might have expected, turns out to be the putatively paradigm senses. By accepting the common-sense view that we have five senses, Nudds seems to be suggesting that they are all cases of paradigm senses; we have conventions that provide us with clearly determined ways of thinking about five senses. However, one might well differentiate between the five senses in this respect.

Distinguishing the senses, on Nudds's account, assumes the double determinacy of an object (ibid., 46).[21] Nudds holds that a folk psychological account of the senses assumes that there are distinct ways of

---

[19] See Bach-y-Rita et al. (1969).
[20] See Leon (1988/this volume, chapter 8) for a defense of the former view. See Heil (1983/this volume, chapter 7) for a defense of the latter view. Noë (2004, 106–17) claims that reference to sensorimotor contingencies should be used to distinguish the senses. Therefore, this should be regarded as visual-like given certain similarities of sensorimotor contingencies with visual perception.
[21] One assumes that the term *object* is used to cover more than just middle sized dry goods in the case of, for instance, taste.

determining the one object because this explains how different information about that object can be acquired. The most persuasive cases of distinct senses occur when double dissociation is manifested between the senses that doubly determine the same object. We can both see and hear the same object, but we can also see objects without hearing them and hear objects without seeing them. This, presumably, is one reason that it is so obvious to us that sight and hearing are distinct senses. Similarly, we can both see and touch the same object, but we can also see objects without touching them and touch objects without seeing them. Hence, it is uncontroversial that we distinguish vision, hearing, and touch.[22]

But does the same apply as obviously to smell and taste? Ordinary folk sometimes have more trouble responding to the question of whether taste and smell are really instances of distinct senses than they do when asked whether vision, hearing, and touch are instances of distinct senses. First, in knowing that someone tasted as opposed to smelled an object, how obvious is it that there is a difference in the information acquired? Second, taste and smell do not display double dissociation in such an obvious way; while it seems clear that we can smell things without tasting them, it is less clear whether the sense of taste does not depend in some way on the sense of smell.[23] Taste seems to be less paradigmatic than the other four senses. However, it is precisely this that lends some support to a conventionalist view. Despite the fact that the difference between taste and smell is less clear cut than that between the other senses, it is nonetheless sufficiently useful for us to draw a distinction between two senses. Perhaps it is useful for us to know that someone tasted something rather than smelled it because we would then also know that they would have learned how it felt. Conversely, perhaps it is useful for us to know that someone smelled something rather than tasted it because then they would not have the additional information. These, so it might be claimed, are the reasons that we distinguish two senses here.

This line of argument receives support from another case, that of heat perception, where, despite certain similarities to the preceding example, a distinction is not ordinarily drawn between touch and a heat sense. Smell and taste are, respectively, distal and proximal senses. We smell objects that can be at various distances from us, whereas objects can be tasted only if we are in contact with them. Similarly, objects can be

---

[22] No doubt such senses influence each other; vision contributes to the perception of the location of sounds. My point concerns the contribution to what is putatively distinctive about each sense. I view synesthesia, which involves additional characters of experience, as evidence for the distinction between the senses rather than evidence for the joining of the senses, as some have suggested. This is because the character of such experience is dependent on the distinct contents of normal experience.

[23] Interestingly, no cases of smell/taste synesthesia have been reported, suggesting that taste and smell are not such as to be suitable for synesthetic cross-modal associations in the way that hearing and vision are (e.g., colored hearing synesthesia).

touched only if we are in contact with them, yet we can sense the heat of objects at a distance from us. Despite this similarity between the cases and other reasons to distinguish two senses (i.e., the different objects of and characters of heat sensations), we do not ordinarily draw a distinction between touch and a heat sense. That is because there remains a significant difference between the two cases: it is of no explanatory use for us to draw a distinction between two senses in the case of touch and heat perception because we do not automatically learn anything extra in knowing that someone perceived something by means of heat perception as opposed to by touch. When we touch something, we can feel its heat, but when we feel the heat of something, we may or may not have perceived its tactile properties. Of course, there may be some use in drawing a distinction between feeling the heat of something with or without touching it. Nonetheless, this does not provide a reason for ordinarily drawing a distinction between heat perception and touch.[24]

Although one might draw a distinction between the five paradigm senses as a way of motivating anti-realism, this then leaves the anti-realist with the problem of accounting for the other paradigm senses. The way to deal with this is to draw a parallel between the five senses. Touch seems to be distinctive among the senses because it involves a number of distinct types of mechanisms (sensory receptors) that put us into contact with different properties (pressure and heat) and enable different kinds of sensations. For these reasons we seem to have some basis on which to think that there is no single, independently existing sensory modality in the case of touch. Since ordinarily we do not distinguish more than one sense, we should therefore conclude that the sense of touch, as we understand it, does not exist independently of our conceptualization of it. However, as Nudds argues (this volume, chapter 16), similar reasoning can be applied to vision and hearing. Psychologists have discovered that sight and audition, as we ordinarily think of them, both incorporate distinct sub-systems. According to Nudds, if realism were the correct view of the senses, then senses would be natural kinds, and the senses would be natural kinds only if they were each realized by one kind of system. Since sight and hearing are realized by a number of distinct sub-systems, Nudds concludes that not even the archetypical senses can be natural kinds.

However, this model of a sense is one that the realist should reject. To begin with, it is inappropriate to think of a sense in the way in which

---

[24] Roxbee Cox (1970/this volume, chapter 5) discusses the contrast in detail. Despite there being no obvious key feature that can be used to group together tactile and heat sensations, Roxbee Cox argues that all such cases involve feeling and essentially involve a part of the body with which we sense the world by feeling how the world affects the part of the body. He notes that we do not have separate sense verbs because our current linguistic practice (the way we employ the term *feel*) can adequately serve two functions that are elsewhere served by the use of separate sense verbs: it allows us to indicate properties of what is perceived that we may expect other perceivers to be able to notice and what another would have to do to perceive the same features.

one might think of a chemical natural kind (e.g., water or gold) or even a biological natural kind (e.g., tiger), where some item belongs to that kind only if it has a certain intrinsic nature. If a sense is to be regarded as a psychological natural kind, then it is more plausible to individuate it by reference to a broad function rather than a specific realization.[25] We do not withhold the attribution of vision to reptiles, fish, and even insects, for whom the underlying mechanisms that realize vision are without doubt different from those of human vision. Relatedly, it does not seem right to think of senses as first-order kinds; it would be better to think of them as higher-order kinds. It seems intuitively correct that particular senses come in a variety of forms. Human vision is just one kind of vision, and human hearing is just one kind of hearing.

4. THE REALITY OF THE SENSES

Insofar as Keeley's account of the senses is sensitive both to the essentially relational nature of the senses and to the variety of forms that we think distinct senses can take, his proposal seems to me to be closer to the mark. What is problematic about it, however, is the way in which it employs criteria to differentiate the senses. Here Nudds offers an appropriate corrective. Anyone seeking to account for the senses must explain why we distinguish the senses in the way that we do. For the realist, the explanation will have to lie not in how we may benefit by drawing the distinctions between the senses in the way that we do but in how the creature that possesses the putative senses is benefited by possessing them. All of the ingredients for such an explanation are already available in Keeley's account. Rather than applying them in the way that he does, my suggestion is that they should be used as the elements of an explanation of how and why the different senses have evolved.

Consider the case of thermal imaging. Following Keeley's proposal, since vision and thermal imaging both involve the detection of electromagnetic energy, we would not distinguish a different type of sense in this case but another species of visual perception. Yet scientists do distinguish thermal imaging from visual perception. Scientists typically regard this as a kind of sense that we do not possess. But why do they do so? Employing the kind of considerations that Nudds suggests, it might be useful for us to posit another sense because we might learn something about a pit viper by knowing that it detects an object by thermal imaging rather than by sight. For instance, we might learn that it is more likely to have detected a warm-blooded animal if it perceives it by thermal imaging rather than vision, for if it were using sight, it might have mistaken the object for a similarly sized inanimate object. However, scientists do

---

[25] An argument can also be given for thinking of modules as relationally individuated, psychological natural kinds. See Gray (2001).

not distinguish thermal imaging merely because it is useful for them to do so. They distinguish thermal imaging from vision because of what the snake itself learns from being able to perceive objects in this new way. The best explanation for snakes' being able to perceive objects in such a way is that they possess a distinct kind of sense, that is, there is a distinctly new way in which they come to learn about the world.

The distinctiveness of thermal imaging has a number of aspects. First, the thermal pits, which constitute apparently distinct sensory organs, turn out to form part of an anatomically distinct sensory system, albeit with connections to the visual system. Second, although thermal imaging functions in combination with visual perception, pit vipers are able to use thermal imaging where visual stimuli are impoverished or lacking altogether. Third, thermal imaging has an evolutionary origin distinct from that of vision. Relative to vision, thermal imaging is a recently evolved capacity in those snakes that possess it. It is not merely an evolutionary modification of an existing visual sense; it is the differentiation of a new kind of sense. Finally, although thermal imaging is sensitive to electromagnetic radiation, what is of more significance for the selection of thermal imaging is that it is thereby sensitive to particular properties and objects in its environment. For, although vision and thermal imaging are both sensitive to ranges of electromagnetic radiation, these non-overlapping ranges of radiation are each related to different properties and objects; vision is sensitive to the solar radiation that is reflected from objects, while thermal imaging is sensitive to the radiation that is emitted from certain terrestrial sources. All of these considerations contribute to differentiate thermal imaging from vision. However, thermal imaging is not distinguished from vision by applying a set of criteria. Rather, the considerations that Keeley notes are employed to explain how and why thermal imaging has evolved in distinction from visual perception. To conflate thermal imaging with vision would be to neglect these significant features that explain the presence of thermal imaging.

Explaining the evolutionary differentiation of the senses provides additional justification for the reality of paradigm senses, such as vision and hearing, and more unusual senses such as thermal imaging.[26] In my view, evolutionary considerations provide some support for the view that we also have a heat sense that has evolved independently from a tactile (or pressure) sense. However, it would be rash to claim that reference

---

[26] A sticking point should be noted here. Suppose vision has evolved independently on a number of occasions. I am suggesting that the evolution of thermal imaging is distinct from all of these instances of visual senses and their descendants. However, if thermal imaging in fact determined the emission of electromagnetic radiation, some might argue that it should be classified along with the other visual senses (recall Ross's suggestion). Given that how one classifies thermal imaging would seem to depend on what one's classificatory interests are, such considerations might be developed into another argument for anti-realism: scientific anti-realism. Of course, this worry would be alleviated somewhat if the case were to be made for the unique origin of the visual sense.

to evolutionary explanations resolves debate in all cases. For instance, consider how the tongue of the pit viper has evolved to capture airborne chemicals, which it then detects by means of an organ (Jacobson's organ) in the roof of its mouth. It is unclear to me whether this way of perceiving the world is by smell or by taste, but then I am still unsure whether smell and taste are really different senses in our own case.[27]

References

Bach-y-Rita, P., C. C. Collins, F. Saunders, B. White, and L. Scadden. 1969. Vision Substitution by Tactile Image Projection. *Nature* 221: 963–64.
Coady, C. A. J. 1974. The Senses of Martians. *Philosophical Review* 83: 107–25.
Gray, R. 2001. Cognitive Modules, Synaesthesia, and the Constitution of Psychological Natural Kinds. *Philosophical Psychology* 14: 65–82.
———. 2005. On the Concept of a Sense. *Synthese* 147: 461–75.
———. Forthcoming. An Argument for Non-Reductive Representationalism. *American Philosophical Quarterly*.
Grice, H. P. 1962/present volume. Some Remarks about the Senses. In *Analytical Philosophy*, series 1, ed. R. J. Butler. Oxford: Blackwell.
Heil, J. 1983. *Perception and Cognition*. Berkeley: University of California Press.
Keeley, B. F. 2002/present volume. Making Sense of the Senses: Individuating Modalities in Humans and Other Animals. *Journal of Philosophy* 94: 5–28.
Kripke, S. 1980. *Naming and Necessity*. Oxford: Blackwell.
Leon, M. 1988/present volume. Characterizing the Senses. *Mind and Language* 3: 243–70.
Nelkin, N. 1990/present volume. Categorizing the Senses. *Mind and Language* 5: 149–65.
Noë, A. 2004. *Action in Perception*. Cambridge, Mass.: MIT Press.
Nudds, M. 2003. The Significance of the Senses. *Proceedings of the Aristotelian Society* 104: 31–51.
———. Present volume. The Senses as Psychological Kinds.
Ross, P. W. 2001. Qualia and the Senses. *Philosophical Quarterly* 51: 495–511.
———.2008. Common Sense about Qualities and the Senses. *Philosophical Studies* 138: 299–316.
Roxbee Cox, J. W. 1970/present volume. Distinguishing the Senses. *Mind* 79: 530–50.

[27] I am grateful to a number of people for comments on earlier drafts and presentations. Alessandra Tanesini and Emma Tobin commented on an earlier draft. Members of the audience at the "Individuating the Senses" conference at the University of Glasgow provided a number of useful suggestions. However, I am especially indebted to Brian Keeley, Fiona Macpherson, and Peter Ross for their ongoing advice and suggestions.

13

Re-Imagining, *Re*-Viewing, and *Re*-Touching

Robert Hopkins

THE SENSES: A STRATEGY

How are we to individuate the senses? My strategy is to address this question by linking it to another. Sense experience is not the only mental state that divides into the various sensory modes. Sensory imagining does so, too. Just as we distinguish seeing a cube from touching one, so do we also distinguish visualizing a cube from imagining one in a tactual way. Again, to the sensory states of smelling coffee and tasting it correspond imaginative states of imagining both that smell and that taste. More generally, to each form of sense experience there corresponds an imaginative state. Just what this correspondence amounts to is a difficult question. Certainly we should be chary of assimilating a given imaginative state to its sensory analogue. However, we are on firmer ground in supposing that the differences between the various sensory imaginings correspond somehow to the differences between the various forms of sense experience. That supposition is enough for the strategy I propose. To the question about individuating the senses, we can add a question about individuating the sensory imaginings. The strategy is to pursue these questions in tandem. A satisfactory answer to either should also help answer the other.

The strategy will not appeal to everyone.[1] Defenders of some of the traditional attempts to individuate the senses may think it stacks the deck against them. Appeal, for instance, to the forms of energy to which the various senses are sensitive is unlikely to help with the various imaginings. Whether or not vision is essentially sensitivity to light, visualizing clearly does not require light and does not clearly require the subject even to have an idea of light. It is hard to see what other link we might draw between visual imagining and that form of energy. Appeals to the

---

[1] Matthew Nudds (2000) rejects the strategy for reasons other than those discussed later.

role of the body in perceiving are similarly handicapped. To imagine, say, in an auditory way, one need not use one's ears or indeed any sense organ; nor need one imagine doing so. A more robust appeal to the body might focus on sensory systems rather than organs. There is some empirical evidence that the same neurophysiological systems are at work in visualizing as in seeing and in auditory imagining as in hearing.[2] However, whether this holds for all of the sensory imaginings remains to be seen. Even if it does, it is quite another question whether such overlap is essential to imagining in a given mode. Perhaps the reuse of sensory systems in imagining is just a contingent fact, albeit an entrenched one, about actual imaginers.

A different source of antagonism lies in a certain conception of the imagination. Some take sensory imagining to be a higher-order activity, something along the lines of *thinking about* sense experience. Gilbert Ryle offered the classic statement of such a view, and the idea has found rather different expression in recent times.[3] Much depends on the details here, but there is at least the prospect that these positions will reject the strategy. If imagining simply embodies our everyday conception of sensing, there are two possible obstacles to learning about the various sensings by considering the various imaginings. To the extent that our everyday conception of the various senses might be wrong, the strategy will mislead. The correct way to individuate the senses will come apart from the way to individuate sensory imaginings. Furthermore, to the extent that we cannot imagine in a given sensory mode without already grasping whatever conception of that sense it involves, the strategy will be uninformative. The study of sensory imagining will only tell us what we already knew, (i.e., what our everyday conception of the senses is).

Of course, any tension with these views does not necessarily show the strategy to be misguided; the difficulty might be laid at their door. Nevertheless, it is possible to avoid some of the conflict here by focusing what we hope to use the strategy to achieve. The claim that the differences between the sensory imaginings reflect those between the various forms of sensing is most plausible as a claim about the phenomenology of two sorts of experiential state, sensory experiences, and sensory imaginings. So the two questions that are most naturally linked are these: What individuates the sensory imaginings? And what individuates the various forms of sense *experience?*[4] In addition, the answer we are naturally led to seek is one that individuates these experiential states by giving an account of their phenomenology. So formulated, the strategy does not clearly conflict with attempts to individuate the senses in terms of energies, or bodily systems. For such

---

[2] For a selection of recent evidence see Denis, Mellet, and Kosslyn (2004).

[3] See, for instance, Ryle (1949, chap. 8), Peacocke (1985), and Martin (2002).

[4] Although later my interest is in the difference between tactual and visual *experience*, I sometimes talk in terms of touch and vision. This is purely for ease and variety of expression.

positions do not generally even try to capture the phenomenology of sense experience. As for higher-order conceptions of the imagination, while they might still conflict with the strategy, it is perhaps clearer now that any conflict is to their detriment. The phenomenological differences between the various imaginings do correlate with those between the various sense experiences, and any account of the former that fails to capture these correlations is at least incomplete. Thus, either the higher-order conception is developed in such a way as to be consistent with the strategy, or it condemns our account of sensory imagining to incompleteness.

If the strategy appeals, one might wonder whether it can be broadened. Are there other phenomena that reflect the differences between the various modes of sense experience, so that we might learn about the latter by considering them? I think there are. Some symbols, that is, non-mental representations, are linked to the various kinds of sense experience in this way. The clearest example is provided by pictures. Pictures are visual in several ways. Most obviously, we have to use vision to interpret them.[5] However, I have argued, they are visual in a more intimate sense, too. The structure within which they represent what they do matches that within which visual experience represents what it does. Something similar might be true for auditory representations and auditory experience, as well as for tactual representations and the experience of touch—although in the tactual case the possibility of such representations is and may remain unrealized. However that may be, in what follows I largely ignore the possibility of broadening my strategy in this way.[6]

Elsewhere, I have pursued the strategy some way in its narrower form. I have offered an account of three forms of sense experience and the corresponding sensory imaginings: visual, tactual, and auditory (Hopkins 1998, chapter 7). Here I concentrate solely on vision and touch. Having briefly reviewed my earlier account of these two (section 2), I explore certain complexities in tactual experience that I earlier either left implicit or did not address at all (sections 3–5). That done, I consider various questions and problems produced by this new material (sections 6–8). Although I cannot answer all of the questions thus raised, I argue that the account says enough about tactual experience to capture, in an illuminating way, how it differs from visual and to capture the difference between tactual and visual imagining.

The Tactual and the Visual: The Basic Account

How, in terms of phenomenology, does visual experience differ from tactual? My answer appeals to the content of those experiences. However, it is content construed broadly. What matters is not the sorts of property or

---

[5] Or so one might think. In fact, there are such things as tactile pictures. See Lopes (1997).
[6] For the strategy in its generalized form, see Hopkins (2004).

the kinds of object the experiences represent but the structures within which those properties and things are represented.

A representation, be it mental or otherwise, is perspectival when it represents space from a point, or perhaps a set of points, within it. Tactual and visual experience are both, I claimed, perspectival. However, they are so in different ways. The central difference is that vision is the experience of spatial separation, touch the experience of co-location. In visual experience, things and places are presented as spatially separated in various ways from the point from which they are presented (the "point of view"). For instance, my current visual experience represents a cup as lying a short distance in front of me and slightly to the right, a framed photograph as rather farther away, in a direction both higher and to the left. In tactual experience, in contrast, things are represented as *in the same place as* a part of my body. If I reach toward the cup and touch it, I feel a part of its side as in the same place as (say) the tip of my finger.

I intend talk of co-location perfectly seriously. In particular, co-location must be distinguished from the weaker notion of adjacency. Tactual experience does not represent a part of my body as merely *next to* a part of some object; it also represents the two as in the same place. Why believe this? One reason (I offer a different argument in section 4) is the following. It seems a conceptual necessity that in tactual experience there be a one to one relation between those points on my body of which I am aware and those points on the object that I feel as in contact with the body points. Return to my fingertip touching the cup. I feel one point on the surface of my body and one point on the cup. I can come to feel more points on the cup perhaps by flattening my fingertip against the side. However, in doing so I become simultaneously aware of more points on my body. What I cannot do is to feel a single point on my body as in contact with two points on the surface of the object. The relation between points touched and points felt as touching is one to one, and necessarily so. If tactual experience were the experience of adjacency, this would be puzzling. After all, one point can be adjacent to two others. Not so if we appeal to co-location. Every point is co-located only with itself. So the best explanation for the one to one correlation is that tactile experience is the experience of co-location.

This argument directs us to a second, less central, difference between touch and vision. Since vision is the experience of separation, and since many points can be separated in different ways from a given point, we would not expect its structure to be one to one, and indeed it is not. In normal vision many points are simultaneously represented as spatially related to the one point of view. As I write, I see at one time many points in the space around me. Where touch is one to one, vision is one to many. That is, many points are seen at one time as spatially separated from the one point of view, whereas tactual experience exhibits a one to one relation between points presented as touched and points presented as touching. However, this second difference holds only of standard cases.

An extreme case of tunnel vision might involve just one point seen from the point of view (Martin 1992, 207/this volume chapter 10). Here the second difference between the two senses is effaced (the relation is one to one), but the key first difference remains. For even in such a case, the point seen is presented as *over there*, separated from the point of view.

These claims about differing perspectival structure allow us to distinguish tactual from visual experience. They also enable us to address the issue of sensory imagining. Visualizing is always perspectival. The visualized object is presented from a point within the visualized world, a point to which it is oriented and from which it is separated. If I visualize a castle, I might visualize it from above, from the side, even from more than one such point at once—but not from no point at all. So visualizing involves the representation of separation, from an analogue of the point of view. Tactual imagining always involves the representation of some part of an object as in the same place as some part of a body. If I tactually imagine velvet or a dead rabbit, I imagine the fabric or the still-warm corpse as in the same place as some part of some body. It may be highly indeterminate which part. It is certainly not necessary that I imagine the body as *mine* (compare: In visualizing, one need not imagine that the point of view is one that one occupies). However, if no such body is imagined, it is hard to see what renders the imagining tactual at all.

Or so I argued. I stand by these claims. However, there is rather more to tactual experience than has so far been allowed. The next section begins to say what by drawing out some of what is implicit earlier.[7]

TOUCH AND ONE FORM OF BODILY AWARENESS

We can begin our further investigation of touch by returning to vision. It is often remarked that a distinctive feature of visual perspective is that the point of view is not itself seen. Further, the point is necessarily invisible: It cannot be seen. The preceding account allows us to explain why this is so. Every seen point is represented from the point of view. Moreover, each seen point is represented as *separated* from that point. However, spatial separation just is distinctness of location, so no point

---

[7] By emphasizing that touch is experience of objects as related to parts of the body, my account is of the same general kind as that offered by Michael Martin (1992/this volume). However, I differ from Martin in placing the contrast between co-location and separation at the heart of the distinction between the tactual and the visual. Moreover, while I use that contrast in an attempt to characterize a difference in the way in which the two senses present space, Martin focuses on capturing a sense in which, while visual experience presents a space, tactual does not (section 1). Touch presents spatial objects, but not as located within a sense field; vision, in contrast, "is not only spatial experience but experience of space" (Martin 1993, 214). Thus, while I have learned a great deal from Martin's work, our views are distinct.

can be represented as separated from itself. So the point of view cannot be seen.[8]

What of the tactual case? There we would expect no parallel obstacle to the tactual presentation of the point of touch, the point on the body experienced as in the same place as a part of the object. Since points touched are represented as in the same place as the point of touch, and since a location can be represented as in the same place as itself, the point of touch can be felt. A little more perspicuously, the point of touch can be represented in tactual experience as explicitly as the point touched.

What is interesting about these last thoughts is that they present a puzzle. If experience represents the point of touch as the same place as the point touched, what differentiates the two? How does tactual experience succeed in rendering the two distinct, so that we are aware of more than simply a single location? The answer must lie in something other than spatial content. It lies in the tactual representation of *objects*. Tactual experience represents two things in one place. A part of my body is represented as in the same place as a part of the object touched. Thus, objects play a different role in tactual experience from the one they play in vision. It is not clear that visual experience necessarily involves the representation of objects at all. Whether it does turns on two things: on how rich a conception of *object* we are working with and on the need for places to be made visible. Unoccupied places can be seen, as when I see the empty spot where the snowman's now melted head used to stand, but they can be seen only against a background of occupied places (Martin 1992, 199/this volume, chapter 10). However, there is no requirement that the occupants be objects in any interesting sense. Mere instances of color properties would, for example, suffice. I might see nothing but a colored mist lying before me, with a differently colored patch at a distinct location directly ahead. Thus, the most basic contents of vision are purely spatial. The contents of touch, in contrast, are both spatial and objectual. There can be no tactual experience without the representation of two objects, one that is touching and one that is touched. The items are represented as spatially located and as numerically distinct. This suffices for tactual experience to involve objects in a richer sense than need be involved in vision.

It might seem paradoxical to represent two objects in this sense as in the same place. Isn't the state of affairs thus represented an impossibility? Even if so, this would hardly show my claims about tactual experience

---

[8] In one sense, a point can be represented as separated from itself. A point can be represented as *over there* and yet in fact be identical with the point from which it is represented. Consider, for instance, a picture depicting a mirror on a wall. The point from which the scene is represented might itself be depicted as reflected in the mirror. What cannot occur is that the point be represented as over there while being represented *as itself* (i.e., as the point from which things are represented). This fits the explanandum perfectly. For at least in principle, the point of view could be seen—perhaps in a mirror. What is not possible is that it be seen *as* the point of view.

to be wrong. Perhaps the phenomenology is indeed as I have argued, and every touch experience is, in part, illusory. However, there is nothing paradoxical about representing distinct objects as in the same place. If places are represented with sufficient imprecision, the represented state of affairs is not impossible. (Consider the claim that my hat and coat are both in the closet.) The oddity of tactual experience is just that it combines necessarily representing two objects with necessarily representing their location with sufficient imprecision to avoid the impossibility. In doing so it is distinctive but hardly paradoxical.[9]

Does it suffice for tactual experience that two distinct objects be represented as in the same place? Or perhaps that two objects be so represented and that one of them be represented, no matter how, as *my body*? Perhaps the representation of co-location is sufficiently distinctive that it forms the content of no other sensory state. If so, the formulations just given suffice to pick out the extension of tactual experience. However, whether that is so or not, there must be more to tactual experience than they allow. Neither formulation captures a key feature of that experience (i.e., that in it the two objects are not presented as on a par). Rather, one object is that *from which* the other is presented. One of the two objects must thus be presented in some privileged way, a way quite different from that in which the other is presented. Thus, it is not sufficient that two objects be represented, nor even that one is presented as my body—at least, not if that last condition can be met in just any way. Rather, in touch one of the two objects is presented *from the inside*, as we naturally say. Only my body can be so presented, but not every way of presenting my body presents it in this way. (Consider *seeing* some body part as mine.)

What is it for my body to be presented in this special way? This is a further question, but, if pressed, I would adopt the answer offered by Michael Martin (1995). According to Martin, for an object to be presented from the inside is for it to be presented as a locus of possible sensation. Tactual experience, at least in the form considered thus far, meets this condition in the most straightforward way by presenting one of the two objects as the locus of *actual* sensation, for that experience involves tactual sensation. I am made aware that a part of my body is in contact with another object via a feeling, the sensation of contact.[10]

---

[9] It would be paradoxical if the only way in which it could represent distinct objects were by representing them as differently located. For then it would represent the two as both in the same place and in different places. But why think this is the only way in which touch might represent distinctness? In effect, I go on to outline another way in which it can do so: by representing only one of the two objects *from the inside*.

[10] I take tactual sensation to be contentful. It represents some part of my body as in the same place as some part of some object. It is another question whether that sensation involves anything besides this content and whether that extra is itself further content. Part of the issue here is whether experience can represent co-location without involving tactual sensation (see section 5). However, part is also what to say about sensation in general so as to make sense of the thought that it presents the body "from the inside."

Awareness of one's body from the inside, however we cash this out, is one—in fact the most basic—form of bodily awareness. So even the simplest forms of tactual experience involve bodily awareness in this sense. Acknowledging this link between tactual experience and bodily awareness is the first significant expansion on the claims of the basic account.

TOUCH AND A SECOND FORM OF BODILY AWARENESS

However, there are other links between tactual experience and bodily awareness. Thus far we have considered only the simplest cases of the former. As we consider more complex cases, we quickly uncover the involvement of another form of bodily awareness.

The range of cases in which we tactually experience the world is broad. Here are some examples:

> *Simple touch*: I experience a single point on the body as in contact with a single point on some other object. For example, I touch a cup with the tip of my finger.
>
> *Multiple contact*: I experience more than one point on the body as simultaneously in contact with a corresponding number of points on some other object. For example, I touch a cup with the tips of two fingers.
>
> *Template*: I experience every point on some object's surface as simultaneously in contact with some point on my body. For example, I completely enclose a large marble in my hand.
>
> *Incomplete template*: I experience several points on my body as in contact with several points on an object that is presented to me as determinately thus and so in ways going beyond what those experiences of contact alone secure. For example, I touch a part of the cup with my five fingers and feel them to be touching *the circular rim of a cup*.[11]
>
> *Serial exploration*: Over some period I explore an object by moving parts of my body across its surface. At the end of the process I continue to touch the object. It is presented to me as determinately thus and so in ways going beyond what my current experience of contact alone secures. For example, I explore an object with the tip of one finger. At the close, the fingertip is touching just one point on the object. My tactual experience presents this point as *the corner of a cube*.

The preceding discussion is, in effect, limited to the first two kinds of example. No account of tactual experience that is restricted in this way can be satisfying. The list of cases is roughly arranged from the more basic to the more sophisticated. The earlier cases are more basic in two

---

[11] The case is Martin's (1992, 199/this volume, chapter 10).

ways. First, they are ones in which the experience presents us merely with *some* thing and perhaps with certain limited properties, such as solidity. The later cases introduce the tactual representation of other properties, such as shape, and of recognizable kinds (e.g., a cup). Second, the later cases involve content that goes beyond what the available sensations of contact could alone provide. I need to show how the account can be extended to include such cases. For, while some might be skeptical about whether the contents of tactual experience can be rich in these various ways, I am not.

The task of addressing the various issues raised by these cases will, in one way or another, occupy much of the rest of this essay. Let me begin with the second sort of case, that of multiple contact. I have already accepted the possibility of such a case in discussing the one to one relation between points touching and points touched. Nonetheless, even there the preceding discussion was incomplete. An important aspect of this sort of case has yet to be described.

Suppose I do feel two points on the object I am touching and thus two points on my body as in contact with them. This immediately raises the question of how those two body points are related. Both are experienced as points on my body and as located in space (since they are experienced as in the same place as parts of some other object). Thus, the question must make sense: What spatial relation obtains between them? It need not be that I can answer. Some strange disorder of the body might perhaps leave me unable to relate the two, but the question's coherence is guaranteed. There is thus, in any such case, at least the possibility that a subject is aware of how the various points of touch the subject experiences are related.

What is in question here is a second form of bodily awareness. Basic bodily awareness, remember, is awareness of some object from the inside. Here we are dealing with an awareness of how the various elements of one's body are, at a given time or across a range of such times, disposed. Not that the two notions are independent. As I intend the notion, bodily awareness in the second sense is restricted to those bodily elements one is aware of in the first sense. The body is the collection of those elements one is aware of from the inside. Bodily awareness in the richer sense is an awareness of the arrangement of those elements presented in that way. However, even if the two are not independent, they are clearly distinct: The second provides knowledge that the first does not, and a creature could presumably possess the first without having the second, even if not vice versa. We should also distinguish this second form of bodily awareness from the long-term body image, that conception one has across periods of time of the various *possible* arrangements of one's body, and in consequence the range of sizes and shapes it might, at a given moment, adopt. If you are invited to be a human cannonball, it is the long-term body image that governs your sense of whether or not you could fit into the mouth of a cannon. In contrast, if you are acting as the knife-thrower's assistant, it is the second form of bodily awareness that governs your sense of whether the blade the knife thrower is currently aiming will miss you.

The multiple contact case is not the only one to involve bodily awareness in this new sense. Consider the template example. In such a case, I might become aware that what I am holding is, say, spherical. However, I can do so only by being aware that the parts of my palm touching the marble themselves form a sphere. Awareness of how those parts are arranged is thus essential to my experiencing the shape of the marble, and it is not so merely as a causal condition for such experience. The experience is at once of a spherical object and of my palm as disposed spherically. Bodily awareness, in this sense, is thus part of the content of my tactual experience of the sphere. Similar points apply to the case in which the template I form is incomplete, as when my five fingers touch points on the rim of a cup.

What of the case of serial exploration? Although bodily awareness in the second sense is involved here, it is so in a more peripheral way. I could form no awareness of the shape of a cube explored with my finger if I were unaware of the movement of my finger through space and over time. For if I did not know how my finger had moved in limning the contours of a cube, how could I learn that it is cubic? This ability to track the progress of my finger is just the awareness we have been discussing. The only difference is that, instead of being awareness of the disposition of various body parts at a given time, it is awareness of the relations between the positions of a single body part across a series of times. However, this awareness is no more than a causally necessary condition for the resulting tactual experience. It does not form part of the content of that experience. When I finish exploring the cube and touch its corner, my experience represents a cube as stretching out beyond the point I am touching. It does not represent that cube *as* one I have recently wandered over. Someone could have an experience just like mine by taking a pill. Provided he were touching an appropriate cube with his finger, his experience would be wholly veridical. The fact that it was generated pharmaceutically rather than via tactile exploration might make it unusual and could certainly prevent it from counting as perceptual, but it would not render it inaccurate.

So not every case of tactual experience involves bodily awareness in this richer sense. The simplest cases need not involve it at all, and certain of the more complex ones do not involve it as part of their content. Nevertheless, it is integral to many tactual experiences.[12] Acknowledging

---

[12] Martin also stresses the role of bodily awareness in touch. However, I approach his conclusion via a different route. The earlier arguments begin, as Martin does not, with co-location and the one to one claim, and they end by distinguishing, as he does not, two senses of bodily awareness. Moreover, while I conclude that touch is dependent on bodily awareness, Martin adds that bodily awareness is likewise dependent on touch. He does so in order to accommodate what is, for him, the central feature of bodily awareness: that although bodily awareness necessarily only makes one aware of one's body, it presents

this raises as many questions as it answers, as the following sections show. I close this section, however, on a more positive note. Recognizing the role of bodily awareness in the second sense allows me to offer a fresh argument for the claim that touch is the experience of co-location.

Bring two of your fingertips together. According to the view on which tactile experience is that of adjacency, you should be aware of two objects lying in two, adjacent places. However, this is not how things are. You are aware of two objects, the tip of one finger and that of another. Given that these are parts of the body and that you are aware of them from the inside, there is a sense in which you are aware of two places. For the two objects form distinct locations in body space, the space given by the long-term body image. It is part of that image, for instance, that one fingertip lies at the end of a route from the torso through one arm, wrist, and hand and that the other lies at the end of a parallel route through the other limb. This way of differentiating the two objects by location infects one's bodily awareness in the second of the two senses distinguished earlier. For even when you are aware of the two fingertips as touching, you are aware of them as objects that might be located otherwise, without changing their location in body space—for instance, as they would be if you opened your arms. In this sense, you are aware of two places: two locations within body space (long-term body image) that happen, at the moment, to coincide (bodily awareness). However, this is the only sense in which you are aware of two places. In all other respects, the two objects are represented in the tactual experience you have when they touch as in the same place. Once we set aside location in body space, that experience makes us aware of just one place. Concentrate on your experience. In what sense, other than that given by location within body space, does it represent more than one place? As one prolongs the experience, the awareness of the distinct body parts can fade. If it does, one is left with an experience that seems wholly unitary. It does not divide in any way and in particular not into an awareness of two adjacent places.[13]

INTERIM SUMMARY

Let me sum up and elaborate a little my conclusions thus far. I have suggested that a full account of tactual experience will need to make use of at least four ideas. There is the experience of two objects as co-located. There is the idea of tactual sensation, the feeling that at least standardly

it as occupying a space that extends beyond it (1993, 213. See also 1992/this volume, chapter 10).

[13] Of course, in such experiences I *can* be aware of adjacent places. However, if I am, they are adjacent places on a single finger. Given the one to one correlation, they will also and equally be presented as adjacent places on the other finger. What, crucially, they are not presented as is adjacent places on distinct fingers: one on one finger, the other on the other.

embodies the experiential content just described. There is bodily awareness in the basic sense, the experience of an object from the inside. And
there is bodily awareness in the richer sense, an awareness of how the
parts of the body one experiences from the inside are arranged at a given
time, or times. How are these four elements related, and how do they
relate to the idea of tactual experience itself?

(i)   My most basic claim is that tactual experience is the experience
      of two objects as co-located. Nothing counts as the experience
      of touch unless it has this content.
(ii) Since it is essential to this experience that one of the objects be
      presented from the inside, tactual experience also essentially
      involves bodily awareness in the basic sense.
(iii) Does it follow that tactual experience essentially involves
      tactual sensation? Here I would like to be more circumspect.
      Given (ii), that experience essentially involves awareness of
      an object from the inside. If we accept Martin's understand-
      ing of that, then in touch the body is necessarily presented as
      a possible locus of sensation. Since tactual sensation is actual
      sensation, it provides one way to meet this requirement, but it
      is not clear that it is the only way. Perhaps the control we have
      over our limbs provides a way for them to be presented from
      the inside, that is, as possible loci of sensation, without any
      sensation having actually to occur. If so, and if that possibility
      can be deployed to generate an experience of co-location, then
      there could be tactual experience without tactual sensation.
      Brian O'Shaughnessy has described a case in which the subject
      manipulates a numbed limb to explore spatial features of her
      surroundings (1989, 41). He asks whether such a case would
      count as touch. My interest is in a slightly different question:
      whether it involves tactual experience. To force a positive
      answer, the case would need elaborating along the lines just
      sketched. I am not sure whether such elaboration is possible.
      However, until I know, it seems I should not commit myself on
      whether tactual sensation is necessary for tactual experience.
(iv) There cannot be tactual experience without bodily aware-
      ness in the basic sense. However, there can be such awareness
      without tactual experience and without tactual sensation. For
      instance, I might feel a pain in my foot without feeling any
      part of me to be touching anything.
(v)   Bodily awareness in the richer sense is two-way independent of
      tactual experience. The latter can occur without the former, as
      in the simplest conceivable cases. In addition, the former can
      occur without the latter, as when I am aware of the arrange-
      ment of my limbs even though, floating in a weightless environ-
      ment, I am not having a tactual experience of anything.

(vi) Bodily awareness in the richer sense involves basic bodily awareness. The latter, however, can occur without the former.

(vii) These complications in the account of tactual experience in no way blunt the edge of the view when we turn to tactual imagining. Tactual imagining is essentially the imagining of something presented as in the same place as some part of a body, a body imagined from the inside. So tactual imagining necessarily involves imagined bodily awareness in the basic sense. If one tactually imagines something of a certain shape, in many cases at least, one thereby tactually imagines parts of the imagined body as so arrayed as to be in contact with parts of the item of that shape. So tactual imagining can involve imagined bodily awareness in the richer sense.

However, these claims leave questions unanswered and problems looming. The rest of the essay describes some of these and makes at least the beginnings of an attempt to deal with them.

BEYOND CONTACT IN TACTUAL EXPERIENCE

All tactual experience involves represented co-location. Some parts of my body are represented as in the same place as parts of some other object. However, some tactual experience represents parts of the object other than those experienced as in contact with parts of me. This is true, for instance, in the incomplete template case. Only some parts of the rim of the cup are touched by my fingers. Yet my experience represents the rim as round, as a complete circle—and not, say, as fragmentary, my fingers resting where the only parts of the rim happen to be. It is also true of the serial exploration case. At the end of my investigation, my experience represents only one corner as in contact with my fingertip, and yet the object is represented as cubic, as extending beyond that point of contact in determinate ways. However, if tactual experience can represent untouched points, as well as touched ones, this raises a question. What is the structure within which these untouched points are represented? It seems that nothing said so far gives the answer. My claims about the one to one correlation between points touching and points touched precisely fail to apply to points that tactual experience represents, though not as touched. What is more, it is not clear that anything else mentioned earlier fills the gap.

This is not the only issue on which my account is silent. Consider any set of experienced points of contact, whether or not untouched points are also represented. These points of contact may be represented as disposed in a certain way, as forming a certain configuration, but in what way will that configuration be presented? What is the structure within which the various points of contact are given? Again, I have yet to say.

What I have said is that each point of contact is experienced as a place in which both a part of the body and a part of the object lie. I have said that these are necessarily related one to one, and I have said that an awareness of how the points touched are configured includes an awareness of how the points touching lie, that it includes bodily awareness in the richer sense. What I have not done is to say how, when the relation between two such body-point/object-point pairs is represented, it is so. Again, then, there is a gap in my view.

There are two things to say about these two lacunae. The first is that they are really one. The same materials will serve to fill both.

It is obvious what to say in answer to the question about the structure within which relations between points of contact are given. They are given in whatever way in general bodily awareness gives the spatial arrangement of the elements of the body. I can be aware of my fingertips forming a circular pattern regardless of whether I experience them as touching something else. The way in which that configuration is presented is the same whether they are hanging in the air or felt as resting on the rim of a cup. Earlier I claimed that feeling the shape formed by points touched involves an awareness of the shape formed by the body points touching them. I would go further: The way in which these two configurations are presented is the same. So the arrangement of the parts of the rim is presented in the same way as the arrangement of the parts of me felt as touching them. Furthermore, that last is presented in whatever way, in general, the arrangement of elements of the body is presented in bodily awareness. Bodily awareness thus holds the key to filling the second gap.

The other gap requires the same treatment. True, it concerns the representation of untouched points, whereas what I have just said applies to touched ones. However, in tactual experience, arrangements of untouched points are presented in fundamentally the same way as arrangements of touched ones. Of course, there is a key difference: Individual untouched points are not presented as in the same place as some part of me. However, the relations between such points and, for that matter, between them and points of contact are given in the same way as the arrangement of points touching. To see this, consider the incomplete template case, in which I touch only some of the rim but feel it to form a complete circle. Suppose that four of my fingers are touching the rim. I might add a fifth, directing it to a particular spot on the rim of which I am aware but which I do not yet touch. Before touching that spot, I am already aware of it in tactual experience. Once it is touched, I am aware of it as in the same place as one of my fingertips. However, this shift is the only one in the way that spot is represented. In particular, bringing my fingertip down onto it does not somehow transform the structure within which it is represented. The "before" and "after" experiences are continuous in every way, apart from the representation of contact. Since after contact that point on the rim is presented within whatever structure elements of the body are presented in bodily awareness, the same is true before contact.[14] Hence, the two gaps are one: Bodily awareness holds the key to both.

It is important to be clear about the way I propose to fill both gaps. The suggestion is not that in either case tactual experience *is* bodily awareness in the richer sense. I defined that awareness as restricted to parts of the body experienced from the inside. It is clear that tactual awareness of untouched points cannot fit this bill, nor for the same reason, can tactual experience of the configuration of points touched, as opposed to that of points touching. Rather, in both cases the suggestion is that tactual awareness of these features involves the same structure as bodily awareness. The way space is presented in the former matches the way it is presented in the latter.

The second thing to say, however, is to acknowledge that this is not so much to fill the gap as to suggest where an appropriate filling should be found. What is the structure within which bodily awareness (in the second sense) presents space? I have not said and do not know what should be said. I can do no more than mark this for further investigation. What I need is an account of the structure within which bodily awareness represents space (spatial relations). In addition, I need that account to be such that the same structure is plausibly found in some tactual experience in those cases in which bodily awareness is involved in the presentation of points of contact and in those in which the experience represents untouched points.

Thus, at least for the moment, for a good range of the spatial contents of tactual experience, my attitude is agnosticism. For the tactual presentation of untouched points or of the configuration of points of contact, I do not know how to describe the structures within which those contents are given. The remaining two sections of this essay ask whether I can afford this ignorance. For one might worry that it undermines two aspects of my position.

IS TOUCH PERSPECTIVAL?

The first part of my view threatened by the agnosticism described in the last section is my claim that tactual experience is perspectival. Throughout this essay I have assumed that the structure distinctive of tactual experience is a matter of a distinctive perspective on the space it presents. As I put it, touch and vision are both perspectival but in

---

[14] A parallel argument applies to the serial exploration example. There the resulting experience represents untouched points, but bodily awareness (in the second sense) is not involved as part of the content of that experience. Instead, it plays at most a causal role (section 4). Despite this, the presentation of the arrangement of untouched points is akin to the presentation of space in bodily awareness. For, as in the cup case, adding new points of contact (e.g., putting more of one's fingers or another hand on the cube) would not transform the structure within which points are presented. It would merely take them from being experienced as untouched to being experienced as touched.

different ways. However, if I am agnostic about the structure within which some tactual contents are given, can I even be sure that the structure in question is perspectival?

Agnosticism does not leave me speechless on this matter. It is possible to make an initial case both for and against the claim that touch is perspectival. The case for is familiar. I am agnostic only about some aspects of tactual experience; about others, I have said a good deal (sections 2–5). Among my central claims is the idea that touch is the experience both of an object and of the body, points on the former being presented from points on the latter. Since the intuitive notion of perspective is that of representing a space from a point or points within it, the core of my account gives touch good claim to be perspectival.

On the other hand, for those aspects of tactual experience about which I am agnostic, there seem to be grounds actively to doubt that the experience is perspectival. Consider again the case in which I touch four points on the rim of the cup, to which I then add a fifth. There is now a new point on the body from which some point on the cup is presented. However, this point can be added or subtracted again without putting any pressure on the structure within which the rim is represented. It is not, for instance, like a visual case in which, perhaps through some clever trick with mirrors, a second point of view is added to my existing perspective on a scene, one presenting the same objects from a different angle. In such a case, it is hard to see how the two points of view could be integrated. I might become expert at extracting information from such a setup, but my experience would remain fractured, an awkward combination of two visual units, each whole in itself. The tactual case is nothing like this. The fifth point of contact is integrated smoothly into the preceding experience. A new "point of touch" can be included without there being any tendency for the experience to decompose into separate presentations of the world, each from a distinct point. In addition, this does not simply mark the fact, which we have all along acknowledged, that tactual perspective differs from visual. It seems to challenge the claims of touch to be perspectival at all. For whatever else is true of the structure within which the various points of contact are presented, it seems to represent them so as to privilege none. Space is given in tactual experience in such a way that every point is represented in the same way as the others. Furthermore, that is the intuitive notion of a nonperspectival representation, the complement of the intuitive notion of perspective appealed to earlier.[15]

A natural objection is that this argument slides unfairly from the claim that every point of contact is represented in the same way to the claim that every point *tout court* is so represented. After all, at least some tactual experiences, including the case here discussed, represent untouched points. Since untouched points and points of contact are represented in

---

[15] As before, parallel points apply to the tactual representation of untouched points.

different ways, there are two classes of represented points, just as perspective requires. However, this line would redeem only some tactual experiences since not all exhibit the distinction. (For an example that does not, consider the template case.) It might be that only some tactual experience is perspectival, but that conclusion is sufficiently surprising to give us pause. Worse, even in the cases to which the line does apply (*incomplete template* and *serial exploration*), the skeptic can say more. True, in such cases some points are experienced as points of contact, whereas others are not. The arguments of section 6 precisely sought to show that these two sorts of point are nonetheless represented in fundamentally the same way (that is, within whatever structure governs the representation of location in bodily awareness). If so, even the distinction between these two looks insufficient to save the claim that these experiences are perspectival. All the points they represent are represented in fundamentally the same way. Perspective is precisely a privileging, at the fundamental level, of some represented points over others. How, then, can these experiences be perspectival?

Now, the two lines of thought I have sketched, for and against perspective, are not actually inconsistent. Tactual experience could be perspectival qua the representation of points on the object as in the same place as points on my body, while being nonperspectival qua the representation of the relations between those points of contact. However, it is hard to be entirely happy with this optimistic resolution. First, I have insisted that there is only one location at which each element of the body and each element of the object are represented since they are given as co-located. That seems to undermine the idea that *points* on one are represented from *points* on the other. Rather, *parts* of one are represented from *parts* of the other, and that seems to take this aspect of touch a step farther from perspective as intuitively conceived. The intuitive characterization speaks of representing space from a point within it. In touch, there isn't really the representation of a space, an interconnected realm of locations, until we introduce aspects of tactual content other than the representation of individual points of contact. Furthermore, these new aspects are precisely those that seem *not* to be perspectival. Second, these two aspects of touch are integrated, when both are present, into a single experience. It is the points of contact themselves that are represented as in certain configurations. How can the former be presented perspectivally while the relations between them are presented nonperspectivally? True, there is no difficulty in general with such combinations. Consider, for instance, those old maps in which cities are represented by little pictures of them (and thus perspectivally) but the relations between them are represented as they usually are on maps (and thus nonperspectivally). However, there is a certain fracture within such representations, precisely between the perspectival and the nonperspectival forms of representation. Is tactual experience no more integrated than this? Perhaps it is not, but one would like to be persuaded.

To the extent that the optimistic resolution is unsatisfactory, there is reason to try to settle the issue more conclusively. To do this, two things would be needed. I would need to form a view about the structure within which configurations of points of contact and untouched parts of the object felt are presented. That is, I would need to replace the mentioned expressed earlier with a positive view. I would also need a less intuitive grasp of the notion of perspective. Unfortunately, neither is available. I have already said that I do not know how to characterize the structure governing these tactual contents. I am no better off in knowing how to offer a more developed account of what perspective is. I can think of plenty of candidate analyses of the notion. The difficulty is that all of them either misclassify as perspectival items that are not (or vice versa) or simply fail to apply to types of representation that clearly divide into perspectival and nonperspectival subspecies. We also run into the first sort of problem if we appeal to formal features of the representation, such as whether the representation of some points depends in some way on the representation of others (and not vice versa). We also run into the second sort of problem if we appeal to the role of perspectival representations in our wider psychological economy (e.g., by identifying them as those that control action in some particularly direct way or as those representing things in relation to where I am).[16] Such characterizations might fit perspectival sensory states, but they are hard pushed to apply to states of imagining, let alone to external representations, such as pictures and maps. Yet if we have any purchase on the notion of perspective at all, I suggest it comes through thoughts such as that pictures are paradigmatically perspectival representations and maps are paradigmatically nonperspectival ones.[17]

Thus, I am not, in the end, able to answer the question about whether touch is perspectival. This is regrettable, but does it constitute a difficulty for my overall project? It does not. It is elegant to present the differences between tactual and visual as differences in perspective, but it is not essential. Whether or not the structure within which touch represents space is perspectival, it is distinct from that within which vision does. The differences described earlier hold whether they are the differences between two forms of perspective or between a perspectival system and a nonperspectival one.

---

[16] These ideas are common in the literature on egocentric frames of reference on space. For useful discussions, see Campbell (1995, chap. 1) and Brewer and Pears (1993).

[17] The notion of perspective here is just the intuitive one with which we have been working all along: that of representing a space from a point (or points) within it. It is, of course, to be distinguished from the notion of perspective as a drawing system. All representational pictures are perspectival, but only some conform to the rules for drawing in perspective.

It is possible to wonder whether some maps are perspectival: Perhaps they represent the terrain from a point high above. (See Wollheim 1987, 60–2.) However, with other maplike symbols such doubts have no purchase. Consider topological representations such as circuit diagrams and maps of the underground train system.

HAVE I INDIVIDUATED THE TACTUAL AND THE VISUAL?

The agnosticism of section 6 threatens another aspect of my view. This time it is one I can hardly afford to abandon. My central ambition has been to say enough about tactual and visual experience to individuate the two. I have attempted to do so by describing the structures within which they represent space, but my agnosticism precisely amounts to a limit to those claims. For some of the contents of some tactual experiences, I do not know how to describe the structure within which they are given. These contents are the representation of untouched points and the representation of the configuration of points of contact. However, if I do not know which structures govern these contents, how can I be confident that they differ from those that characterize vision? Once I concede agnosticism on that score, it is no longer clear that I have succeeded in my central individuative project.

In one respect, this worry is misplaced. The contents to which my agnosticism applies can never alone exhaust tactual experience. Neither untouched points nor the relations between points of contact can be tactually represented without points of contact being so. So any experience that has the former among its contents will also have contents sufficient to mark it as tactual. For all along my central claim has been that every tactual experience—and no visual one—represents the co-location of some part of an object with some part of my body. Thus, as far as the individuation of *experiences* goes, my agnosticism poses no threat.

However, it would be glib to claim that that is the end of the matter. To see what issue might be left unresolved, we need to distinguish at least two different projects of individuation. It helps to approach the two via a third.

(A) Suppose that we can take for granted the grouping of sensory experiences into different modes. We are presented with, say, five groupings. All of the tactual experiences are in one, and all of the visual experiences are in the other, and so on for the other modalities. Our task is to find a feature that tells us which grouping is which.

(B) Suppose that we can take for granted the bundling of sensory contents into (token) sensory experiences. We are presented with myriad such sense experiences. Our task is to find a feature that individuates (picks out) all of the tactual experiences, one that does the same for all of the visual experiences, and so on for the other modalities.

(C) We are presented with all of the possible sensory contents. Our task is to find a feature that individuates all of those that are (among) the contents of tactual experiences, one that does the same for all of those that are (among) the contents of visual experiences, and so on for the other modalities.

I hope it is clear that each of these tasks is more demanding than its predecessor. In other words, (A) takes for granted the work done by (B), just as (B) takes for granted that done by (C). To complete a later task is thus to complete any tasks that come earlier. My response, just given, to the worry that agnosticism about certain tactual contents hinders individuation in effect was that it does not prevent my view from completing task (B), at least for touch. Since only tactual experiences represent co-location, any experience representing that must be tactual, and any experience not doing so cannot be (and so, given our current restriction to visual and tactual, it must be visual). However, that assumes that the task is to allocate token experiences to the right category. It does not tell us how to combine sensory contents into such experiences—task (C). The residual worry is that my agnosticism prevents us from doing that. For points on the object represented as in contact with me, I have said enough to distinguish the tactual representation of such points from the visual. For untouched points and for the representation of the configuration of touched ones, I have not. Since I have said nothing about the structure within which these contents are given, I have said nothing to explain their claim to be tactual rather than visual.[18]

How are we to tackle (C)? One way is to adopt what I call the *direct strategy*. This is to find, for each sensory content, some feature that renders it tactual, visual, or . . . (for the other modalities). However, this assumes that each sensory content is, in itself, tactual, visual, or whatever. Why should we think this? Might some sensory contents not be mode neutral, that is, of a nature that allows them to figure in experiences in more than one modality? The possibility seems at least coherent. It might, indeed, be actual.[19] Of course, no tokening of a given content is mode neutral. On any given occasion in which an experience represents some property or object, that content will be tactual, visual, or whatever. However, it may be so simply by virtue of being part of the content of a tactual or visual (or whatever) experience. Something must render the experience as in that mode rather than another, but that work need be done only by some of the contents of which it is composed. The possibility remains that the rest bear no

---

[18] Matthew Nudds presents a version of this difficulty for my account:
   Suppose, though, that you see, but don't feel, the shape of an object that you both see and feel. How might we explain, on Hopkins' account, in virtue of what your awareness of the object's shape is . . . visual . . . [?] Appealing to the content of your experience does not seem sufficient: you have an experience which represents the shape of an object which is represented as spatially separate from your point of view and part of which is represented as in contact with a part of your body. From this description of the content we can conclude that you are both seeing and touching the object, but there is nothing in the description to tell us whether you see the shape of the object or feel it. (2000, 145)
[19] Whether it is so provides one strand in the tangle of issues underpinning Molyneux's question. See Hopkins (2005).

modal character of their own. This suggests a different way to handle (C). The *indirect strategy* is to find, for any tokened sensory content, something uniting it with other sensory contents. We first explain what makes various contents all elements in a single (token) experience, and only then can we explain what makes that experience belong to one mode rather than another.

The availability of this second strategy transforms the dialectical situation. As just noted, the strategy proceeds in two steps. We first explain what unites contents in a single experience, then explain what makes that experience tactual, visual, and so on. This second step is one we have already taken. For the task of sorting whole experiences into modalities is just task (B). We have no grounds on which to doubt that my account performs that task perfectly well. That leaves the first step. It is a serious question how to proceed with that. Certainly nothing already said offers much help, but that is at least in part because the remaining problem is not specifically one of individuating the senses. One can ask what unites various sensory elements in a single sense experience without having any interest in individuating the various forms of sense experience. In addition, one would expect a good answer to apply equally to all experiences irrespective of their mode. Thus, while we are driven to ask this question as part of an inquiry into what individuates the senses and in particular via the need to confront task (C), it seems that at this point the fate of the inquiry turns on issues of a more general nature. At least, that is the situation if we adopt the indirect strategy, which has the virtue of eschewing the dubious assumption its rival must make, that no sensory contents are mode neutral. None of this is to answer the question confronting my account. What it does suggest is that its current failure to fulfill task (C) is not due to inadequacy in what it has said and that we might reasonably wait on a resolution of these more general difficulties before judging its prospects with respect to (C).

Perhaps the choice between the direct and indirect strategies seems too stark. They differ over whether to assume that every sensory content has, in itself, a mode-specific character. Couldn't one agree that this assumption is dubious without thinking that my account has done all of the work of an individuative nature that it should? I think one could. My account captures the tactual and visual nature of certain sensory contents. It is not obliged to do that for all since, we suppose, some sensory contents are mode neutral. Nonetheless, it does not follow that it has captured all of the mode-specific contents there are. I agree that there may be more work to do here. I would go further and note that doing it may require me to abandon my agnosticism about the tactual representation of untouched points and of the configuration of touched ones. For perhaps these are among the mode-specific contents. Still, one can acknowledge that there may be work to do without being persuaded that there actually is. Beyond those I have identified and attempted to describe, are there other mode-specific contents for touch and vision? I am not, at present, sure.[20]

CONCLUSION

The thrust of my argument has been to concede that there is more to tactual experience than the basic account allows. Touch involves more than mere represented co-location of the body and some other object. Even that content involves bodily awareness in its basic form. More sophisticated contents also involve bodily awareness in a richer form. The way in which that awareness presents space dictates how tactual experience represents the relations between points of contact and how it represents untouched points on the object (when it represents either). In addition, there are serious questions about the structures thus imposed, questions to which I have at present no answers. In consequence, I am less confident than I was that tactual experience is perspectival, and I accept that there are individuative tasks I have yet to complete.

Despite all of this, I remain confident about my basic claims. They enable us to pick out the class of tactual and of visual experiences. They explain various aspects of those experiences, such as the invisibility of the point of view. They point beyond themselves in a structured and useful way, directing us to the aspects of tactual experience that must involve something more. Above all, they illuminate that experience by capturing something profound about its phenomenology. They thereby enable us simultaneously to make progress in individuating the sensory imaginings. It is perhaps unclear quite what it would be to understand a form of experience, but, if the basic account does not advance such

---

[20] It might seem obvious how to expand my characterization of the tactual so as to cover a wider range of sensory contents. I claim that many tactual experiences involve bodily awareness in the richer sense (section 4) and that the location of untouched points and the relations between touched ones are presented within the same structure as governs that awareness (section 6). Then why not say that untouched points are presented as lying within a space that includes the various parts of the body but as lying within that part of the space that extends beyond the limits of the body? This, like vision, is an experience of separation; however, rather than separation from a point, it is separation from (i.e., lying outside the limits of) a volume. Moreover, the volume in question is that experienced as occupied by the body (i.e., as that occupied by the object one is aware of from the inside). The point of view, in contrast, is a location, not an object, and is not presented as a possible locus of sensation.

This proposal might seem to fit well with Martin's approach to these issues. He, too, emphasizes that bodily awareness involves a sense of the space extending beyond the body's limits (see note 12). However, it is far from clear that the proposal can be squared with another Martin theme, that bodily awareness and touch do not present us with a space (see note 7). However that may be, as it stands the proposal does not appeal to me. The difficulty is that all that it says about the tactual experience of untouched points is, in my view, also true of our experience of sounds (Hopkins 1998, chap. 7, section 6). There is no point in distinguishing these tactual contents from visual ones if the price is that they cannot be distinguished from contents that are clearly auditory.

understanding in the case of vision and touch, then I do not know what would count as doing so.

References

Brewer, B., and J. Pears. 1993. Introduction: Frames of Reference. In *Spatial Representation*, ed. N. Eilan, R. McCarthy, and B. Brewer, pp.25–30. Oxford: Clarendon.

Campbell, J. 1995. *Past, Space, and Self*. Boston: MIT Press.

Denis, M., E. Mellet, and S. Kosslyn, eds. 2004. *Neuroimaging of Mental Imagery*. Hove: Psychology Press.

Hopkins, R. 1998. *Picture, Image, and Experience*. New York: Cambridge University Press.

———. 2004. Painting, Sculpture, Sight, and Touch. *British Journal of Aesthetics* 44: 149–66.

———. 2005. Molyneux's Question. *Canadian Journal of Philosophy* 35: 441–64.

Lopes, D. 1997. Art and the Sense Modalities. *Philosophical Quarterly* 47: 225–40.

Martin, M. G. F. 1992/present volume. Sight and Touch. In *The Contents of Experience*, ed. T. Crane, pp.196–215. New York: Cambridge University Press.

———. 1993. Sense Modalities and Spatial Properties. In *Spatial Representation: Problems in Philosophy and Psychology*, ed. N. Eilan, R. McCarthy, and B. Brewer, pp.206–218. Oxford: Clarendon.

———. 1995. Bodily Awareness: A Sense of Ownership. In *The Body and the Self*, ed. J. Bermudez, A. Marcel, and N. Eilan, pp.267–289. Boston: MIT Press.

———. 2002. The Transparency of Experience. *Mind and Language* 17: 376–425.

Nudds, M. 2000. Modes of Perceiving and Imagining. *Acta Analytica* 15: 139–50.

O'Shaughnessy, B. 1989. The Sense of Touch. *Australasian Journal of Philosophy* 67: 37–58.

Peacocke, C. 1985. Imagination, Experience, and Possibility: A Berkeleian View Defended. In *Essays on Berkeley*, ed. J. Foster and H. Robinson, pp.19–35. Oxford: Clarendon.

Ryle, G. 1949. *The Concept of Mind*. London: Hutchison.

Wollheim, R. 1987. *Painting as an Art*. London: Thames and Hudson.

14

The Senses

John Heil

THE PHILOSOPHICAL QUESTION

Human beings evidently experience the world in different ways. You hear, feel, see, touch, taste, and smell your surroundings. You sense the disposition and orientation of your body and, off and on, its internal state. Perception, it seems, is grounded in multifaceted sensory experiences: You perceive the world *by* sensing the world in various ways.

This relatively uncontroversial idea is often embellished in apparently innocent ways that can, on reflection, turn out to be less than innocent. One such emendation involves the idea that sensory experiences come by way of distinct "channels" or "avenues" (see Keeley [2002]/this volume, chapter 11). These channels, usually identified with the "sensory modalities," serve as vehicles for our awareness of external objects and goings-on.

This seemingly innocuous conception of the nature of perception has the potential to lead us down unproductive paths, or so I contend. Before jumping in over my head, however, let me pause briefly to reflect on the status of philosophical theorizing about the senses.

I admit to being less than confident that philosophers have much to contribute on the topic. You can understand my hesitation, perhaps, by thinking of philosophical work on color and color perception. Philosophers divide sharply into seemingly irreconcilable camps over the nature of color. Some regard color as a feature of the surfaces of material objects; others take color to be a characteristic of light reflected from objects' surfaces; still others, the color antirealists, hold that colors are at best "projections" of features of our own sensory states onto the world.

These differences look like deep substantive differences, but consider: All these philosophers accept as given empirical findings in "color science." Each of these differing philosophical views is presumably consistent with

Paper presented at a conference on "Individuating the Senses," University of Glasgow, 4 December 2004. A preliminary version was presented as a work in progress at Washington University in St Louis. On both occasions I benefited from comments and suggestions on the part of the audience.

our best assessment of the physical, physiological, and psychophysical nature of color and color perception. When they differ, then, what are philosophers who theorize about the nature of color differing *over*? What difference do the *philosophical* differences make? The same questions could be asked about philosophical accounts of the senses.

Perhaps the most that can be said is that we philosophers muddle through, finding perspicuous ways of describing a world revealed by empirical science. In so doing we endeavor to reconcile the scientific image and ordinary experience. We are not "underlaborers" exactly, but our contribution is elusive. This, at any rate, gives you a sense of my own lack of confidence in the deep significance of what I have to say here.

GRICE ON THE SENSES

At the risk of prematurely restricting the space of possibilities within which we might locate an account of the senses, I begin where H. P. Grice began in an influential paper published more than forty years ago. Grice (1962, 135/this volume, p. 85) looks at four ways you might go about distinguishing the senses:

(1) "by the differing features that we become aware of by means of them." Seeing, for instance, "might be characterized as perceiving . . . things as having certain colours, shapes and sizes; hearing as perceiving things . . . as having certain degrees of loudness, certain determinates of pitch, certain tone-qualities."

(2) "by [their] special introspectable character . . . disregarding differences between the characteristics we learn about by sight and smell, we are entitled to say that seeing itself is different in character from smelling."

(3) by reference to "differing general features of the external physical conditions on which the various modes of perceiving depend . . . differences in the 'stimuli' connected with different senses: the sense of touch is activated by contact, sight by light rays, hearing by sound waves."

(4) by differences in "the internal mechanisms associated with the various senses—the character of the sense organs and their mode of connection with the brain."

Grice's paper encompasses a nuanced discussion of these possibilities. Grice has little to say about the third criterion, "differences in the 'stimuli' connected with different senses," and even less to say about the fourth, which concerns the nature of sense "organs" and their neurological trappings. He focuses, instead, on criteria (1) and (2), which he clearly regards as most promising, concluding, albeit tentatively, that, despite appearances, these criteria are not "independent."

Think of Grice's first criterion as encompassing something like a tra-ditional Aristotelian conception of the senses. Different modalities func-tion to reveal different features of the world: each sense has its proper objects. A difficulty for such an account is that many features of the world are apparently detectable by more than one sense. You can both see and feel—and, perhaps, if you are a bat, hear—the shapes or sizes of objects. Indeed, it is a mark of the "primary qualities" that they are perceivable by more than one sense.

What of the second criterion: The senses are to be distinguished by reference to the character of experiences they afford? The thought here is that each modality has a distinctive phenomenology. Seeing evidently differs *qualitatively* from hearing, tasting, smelling, or feeling. Might the senses be distinguished by reference to the character of experiences aris-ing from their deployment?

One worry, Grice's worry, is that this criterion of demarcation threat-ens to collapse into the first criterion, that according to which the senses are to be distinguished by reference to their characteristic *objects*. The worry arises when we endeavor to explicate the character of sensory experiences independently of the character of objects experienced. Grice, echoing Moore, puts it this way:

> Such experiences (if experiences they be) as seeing and feeling seem to be, as it were, diaphanous: if we were asked to pay close attention, on a given occasion to our seeing or feeling as distinct from what was being seen or felt, we should not know how to proceed; and the attempt to describe the differences between seeing and feeling seems to dissolve into a description of what we see and what we feel. (Grice 1962, 144/this volume, p. 93)

If you are attracted to the currently fashionable idea that qualities of conscious experiences are at bottom qualities agents represent objects as having, this might be a natural line for you to take.

An appeal to the familiar distinction between primary and secondary qualities might be thought to support Grice's contention that the first two criteria are not in fact independent. Primary qualities (shape, size, motion, number, and the like) are standardly taken to be detectable by more than one sense. Secondary qualities, in contrast (colors, sounds, smells, tastes, feels) are, or seem to be, available only to a single sense. Perhaps by focus-ing on the secondary qualities we could locate a one-one mapping between features of perceived objects and features of sensory experiences.[1]

Suppose you are inclined to think that colors, for instance, are uniquely detectable by sight. Color experiences are necessarily visual, not perhaps because of their own special intrinsic qualities but because colors are detectable only visually. Imagine encountering a species of alien creature who evidently sense the world. Were we to discover that

---

[1] For an account along these lines, see Roxbee Cox (1970/this volume, chapter 5).

certain of these creatures' organs were dedicated to color detection, we would unhesitatingly associate the organs with sight—quite independently of ascertaining the intrinsic character of experiences produced by the operation of the organs. Indeed, had we evidence that the creatures' color experiences differed dramatically from ours, we might regard that as irrelevant to our decision to describe the creatures as exercising a sense of sight.

This suggests not simply that Grice's second criterion collapses into the first but also that the second criterion on its own is flatly incorrect. Does this vindicate the first criterion? Can we say with confidence that a sense is identifiable by reference to characteristics of sensed objects that it reveals?

Before venturing an answer to this question, it might be useful to look more closely at the status of secondary qualities. Here is one way to think about secondary qualities, what I take to be Locke's way. Primary qualities are qualities possessed by every object, including the fundamental objects—the corpuscles. Secondary qualities are arrangements of the primaries. If you put corpuscles together in the right way, you get something red. Its being red is a matter of corpuscles with such-and-such primary qualities being placed in such-and-such relations. We pick out these arrangements by reference to certain of their effects on us, but the arrangements themselves exist quite independently of perceivers. Secondary qualities, so conceived, are no addition of being, nothing "over and above" arrangements of objects possessing primary qualities. It is no wonder that such qualities would be of scant interest to physics.

Return to the idea that vision, whatever else it might be, involves the detection of objects' colors. Suppose you agree with Locke that colors are secondary qualities. If colors—or surface colors—are just arrangements of particles on the surfaces of objects, it would seem to be at most a contingent fact about us that colors are detectable only by means of sight. Were our sense of touch suitably refined, for instance, we might be able to discriminate the colors of objects by feeling them. More generally, if you rely on secondary qualities to distinguish the senses, and if secondaries are just arrangements of the primaries, you are unlikely to achieve a well-behaved taxonomy of the senses.

You might be tempted at this point to move back in the direction of Grice's second—experiential—criterion. The experiential criterion implies that it is not merely a contingent matter that the senses have their respective experiential "feels." This suggestion, however, apparently runs afoul of another currently popular thesis defended by philosophers who like to emphasize an "explanatory gap" between conscious qualities and material states of affairs.

If you are attracted to a strong contingency thesis, you are unlikely to find attractive the idea that the senses are to be identified by reference to distinctive qualitative characteristics of experiences they yield.[2] There need be no reason in the nature of things why the kinds of experience you have in looking at a ripe tomato could not be auditory or tactile in another creature. Given the contingency thesis, it seems possible that experiences we associate with one modality could be swapped with those of some other modality. Rather than an "inverted spectrum," this would involve a more striking qualitative inversion.

You might be skeptical about the possibility of sweeping qualitative inversions of this kind. If you accept a representational view of mental qualities, then you will regard such inversions as conceptually impossible. There are, however, plausible real-world cases of something that looks very much like a qualitative inversion.

PROSTHETIC VISION

One such real-world example of something that looks like a qualitative swap is provided by the tactile visual stimulation system, or TVSS.[3] One version of the TVSS consists of a television camera (its "eye") affixed to a pair of glasses and coupled to a mechanism that converts the visual image produced by the camera into an "isomorphic cutaneous display" in the form of a pattern of vibrations produced by vibrating pins arranged in a 40 × 40 grid. The grid is placed in contact with the skin (usually on the back or stomach or, in more recent implementations, on the *tongue*) of an experimental subject. Practice in the use of the TVSS enables blind persons to detect reasonably fine distinctions among objects scanned by the camera.

One experimental subject, G. Guarniero, provides an interesting account of his use of the device. "Only when I first used the system did the sensations seem as if they were on my back" (1974, 101). As he became more skilled in the use of the device, Guarniero became aware not of patterns of vibrations on his skin but of scanned objects:

> Very soon after I had learned to scan, the sensations no longer felt as if they were located on my back, and I became less and less aware that vibrating pins were making contact with my skin. By this time objects had come to have a top and a bottom; a right side and a left. (1974, 104)

Subjects like Guarniero, trained in the use of a TVSS, describe the experience—aptly, in my judgment—as "seeing with the skin."

Imagine an agent equipped with an augmented TVSS, one capable of representing all that can be visually represented. (If you doubt that such a device is possible, then imagine one capable of representing scenes

---

[2] If you think "zombies"—creatures resembling us in every physical respect but lacking a capacity for conscious experiences (Kirk 1974, 1994; Chalmers 1996)—are possible, Grice's second criterion is a nonstarter.
[3] White et al. (1970); Guarniero (1974). The account here borrows from Heil (1983, 13–18/this volume, chapter 7).

monochromatically in the way they might be represented visually by a monochromatic agent with poor eyesight.) Despite representational parity, the experience of "seeing" with a TVSS apparently differs qualitatively from the experience of seeing with the eyes. In both cases, the sensory medium is effectively "diaphanous" and perhaps difficult, even impossible, to describe independently of the features of objects it is used to represent. Indeed, there might be no functional difference between an agent equipped with a TVSS and a sighted agent. Both would describe their experiences in exactly the same way; both would be unable to detect the presence of objects if the lights were switched off or if an opaque screen were placed in front of the objects scanned. Even so, it is hard not to think that the agents' experiences differ qualitatively. Were a normally sighted agent suddenly forced to use a TVSS while the TVSS-using agent's eyesight were restored, both would find their experiences very different.

I do not know how to prove this. Trials with an actual TVSS would not obviously settle the matter.[4] Representationalists would be quick to emphasize the importance of representational richness, and the representational capacity of an actual TVSS differs dramatically from the representational capacity of the human visual system.[5] Nevertheless, it is hard to understand how merely increasing the representational acuity of a TVSS could result in its producing experiences qualitatively close to ordinary visual experiences.

GRICE'S SECOND TWO CRITERIA

Suppose I am right in thinking that Grice's first two criteria for distinguishing the senses—the properties-of-objects criterion and the qualities-of-experience criterion—are in fact independent. Does either criterion provide a satisfactory account of distinctions among the senses? I have said enough to suggest that it would be a mistake to appeal to differences in objects of perception to delineate the senses. The fact, if it is a fact, that we associate the perception of particular features of our environment with particular senses is apparently a contingent matter. If you know that a creature has a capacity to detect colors or sounds, do you thereby know that the creature does so via vision and audition, respectively? It is not obvious that you do.

---

[4] Note, however, that Guarniero describes his initial experience in using a TVSS as an experience of sensations on his back. Later, he says, these came to be felt as sensations of distal objects. It is natural to understand these remarks as supporting the idea that there is more to perceptual experience than is included in what qualities experience represents experienced objects as possessing. One representationalist response involves taking cases in which agents are putatively aware of qualities of experiences as just more representation. The qualities of Guarniero's sensations are just qualities he represents those sensations as having: representations of representations.

[5] Frank Jackson made this point in conversation.

What of Grice's third and fourth criteria: Might we distinguish the senses by reference to the kind of "stimulation" that affects them or by the nature of sensory "organs"?

Consider the fourth criterion. Might we determine that a creature is exercising a visual sense if we discovered that it possessed eyes or that it deployed an auditory sense if it had ears? One difficulty here is that it is hard to see how we could be in a position to identify an "organ" as an eye independently of recognizing it as an instrument of vision. In the case of terrestrial creatures, we can rely on anatomical similarities across species in identifying sensory organs, but this is a shortcut. It is no help at all if our aim is to spell out what is required for something to *count* as an organ of vision or audition. For these purposes we need to consider not merely actual creatures but possible creatures as well.

This point applies across the board. We could discover interesting similarities in modalities across species, but this in itself would not entitle us to appeal to these similarities in an account of what distinguishes the senses. The *philosophical* question is not whether we can identify sensory similarities across terrestrial species but whether we can provide a perfectly general accounting of what distinguishes one sense from another. Such an account must cover *possible*, as well as actual, creatures. This is why it can be useful to toss fanciful creatures into the mix when testing competing theories. Nonphilosophers find this time-honored philosophical practice endlessly frustrating, but giving it up would be tantamount to giving up philosophy.

Before turning to Grice's third criterion, let me mention one variant of the fourth criterion, a variant recently proposed by Kevin O'Regan and Alva Noë. According to O'Regan and Noë, who are interested in "visual consciousness," "vision is a mode of exploration of the world . . . mediated by knowledge of . . . sensorimotor contingencies" (O'Regan and Noë 2001, 940). The human visual system has a distinctive makeup that facilitates the pickup of information about the world. This system differs in a dramatic way from both the auditory and the proprioceptive systems. Differences among visual, auditory, and proprioceptive "sensorimotor contingencies" give us differences among the senses.

O'Regan and Noë could well be right, but they do not give us quite what we want. Reflect for a moment on the Molyneux question: could a person born blind who suddenly had his sight restored distinguish, by sight alone, a sphere from a cube? A Molyneux subject might be able to tell that the sphere was not the cube, the cube not the sphere without being able to say *which was which*. Similarly, O'Regan and Noë tell us how to recognize sensory modalities as distinct, without thereby providing a way of identifying the modalities thus distinguished.

It is hard to see how appeals to differences in sensory paraphernalia alone could provide us with an accounting of the senses. Such appeals presuppose an answer to the very question we are asking. This brings us back to Grice's third criterion. Might we identify the senses by reference to differences in the kinds of proximal stimulation from which they extract information? Might sight, for instance, be regarded as a process of extracting information from structured, ambient light, what Gibson (1966) called the "ambient optic array"? Hearing might be a process of extracting information from pressure waves in the medium (air or water, depending on a creature's "ecological niche"). Touch, on this view would involve obtaining information about objects via mechanical contact. Smell and taste might both be characterized by reference to chemical information borne by volatile and ingested sources, respectively.

Note that this strategy would explain why it might seem natural, in classifying "organs" of sense, to count as eyes "organs" devoted to the extraction of information from light, ears, those evolved to pick up information from impact waves in the medium, and so on. It would also explain how it could make sense to speak of a TVSS-wielding agent as "seeing with the skin."

Need we add other senses to this traditional list? The proprioceptive awareness we have of the disposition and orientation of our bodies might be included in a more exhaustive inventory. What of the abilities of other creatures—bats, for instance, or dolphins—to deploy "sonar" to locate objects in their environments? If the senses are distinguished by reference to kinds of "proximal stimulation," the exercise of such abilities need not be counted as the exercise of a genuinely different sense but rather as the extension or refinement of the sense of hearing. Honeybees and other creatures are sensitive to portions of the electromagnetic spectrum to which we are blind. Does this mean that honeybees have a sense that we lack? Maybe not. Again, it seems natural to describe honeybees as seeing what, owing to contingent limitations on our part, we cannot see. Honeybees are visually sensitive to regions of the electromagnetic spectrum continuous with those to which we are sensitive.

If this is on the right track, we have the ingredients for a serviceable taxonomy of the senses. To the extent that we regard a creature as extracting environmental information more or less continuous with a source implicated in the deployment of a particular modality, we would be entitled to describe the creature as exercising "the same" modality. To the extent that a creature has a capacity for the extraction of environmental information from a stimulatory source discontinuous with a source tapped by a given modality, we would be entitled to describe the creature as exercising a distinct sense.

Accepting my suggestion all but guarantees the possibility of borderline cases. It would be surprising, however, if a taxonomy initially devised to mark off distinctions useful in everyday affairs fitted neatly with subsequent scientific inquiry. The idea here is that, by appealing to a feature of our perceptual circumstances that involves a modest expansion of the ordinary conception of perceptual "inputs," we can arrive at a taxonomy that fits reasonably well with both everyday and scientific interests.

Before moving on, let me head off one potential source of misunderstanding.[6] Suppose vision, for instance, is tied to the extraction of information about the world from ambient light radiation. This need not be taken to imply that we see *light radiation*, whatever that might mean. Such a construal would confuse a vehicle of perception with perceptual objects, thereby conflating Grice's second and third criteria. In perceiving distal objects—tables, trees, environmental layout, or maybe Gibsonian "affordances"—the visual system makes use of stimulatory information in structured light. Information about the objects, not information about the light, is subsequently made available to what once was called the *understanding* and is nowadays called the "cognitive system."[7]

CHANNELING THE SENSES

Suppose something like this is right. A worry remains. Consider a familiar way of thinking about the nature of perception. Our contact with the world is by way of sensory "channels"; these are the sensory modalities. "Sensory surfaces" are stimulated and send messages to the mind (or brain or mind/brain) in the form of distinctive kinds of sensory representation. The brain integrates these representations and, "triangulating," produces a unified picture of the world.

On this model, sensory channels provide coded *descriptions* of the world but, as it were, in distinct *languages*. Sensory integration involves *translation* across languages. The sensory system so conceived is Quinean: Grasping the significance of a sensory language is a matter of being in a position to translate expressions in that language into expressions in a language in which the agent is fluent. In the normal case, we acquire a facility with sensory languages more or less simultaneously: In this regard we are, when it comes to sensory experiences, naturally *multilingual*.

To someone fluent in a language, it can seem obvious that words in that language have the significance they have. This, however, is the effect of "custom." The same holds for sensory languages. Locke, speaking I suspect for many, puts it this way:

> When we set before our eyes a round globe, of any uniform colour, v.g. gold, alabaster, or jet, 'tis certain, that the idea thereby imprinted on our mind, is of a flat circle variously shadow'd, with several degrees of light

---

[6] Keeley (2002, 12, 18–19/this volume, p. 231–33) could be cited here.
[7] Human and nonhuman creatures are sensitive to endless information-bearing stimuli. Only when this sensitivity is put to work by the creature is it appropriate to describe the pertinent sensitivities as "detectors." Might we identify sensory modalities with systems of detectors? Perhaps not. The thermoregulatory system makes intelligent use of elaborate systems of detectors, but you might resist regarding the thermoregulatory system as encompassing a sense. One possibility suggested earlier is that a sense makes information available to the cognitive system or understanding. For a different line, see Keeley (2002).

and brightness coming to our eyes. But we having by use been accustomed to perceive, what kind of appearance convex bodies are wont to make in us; what alterations are made in the reflections of light, by the difference of the sensible figures of bodies, the judgment presently, by an habitual custom, alters the appearances into their causes: so that from that, which truly is a variety of shadow or colour, collecting the figure, it makes it pass for a mark of figure, and frames to it self the perception of a convex figure, and an uniform colour; when the idea we receive from thence, is only a plain variously colour'd, as it is evident in painting.[8]

It is natural to think that spheres and cubes must look the way they do to us. But this impression, according to Locke, is illusory. The ties between qualities of sensory experiences and qualities of objects perceived are tenuous at best. It is, Locke contends, a brute, inexplicable fact that our experiences have the qualities they have:

> Let us suppose at present, that the different motions and figures, bulk, and number of such particles, affecting the several organs of our senses, produce in us those different sensations, which we have from the colours and smells of bodies; v.g. that a violet, by the impulse of such insensible particles of matter of peculiar figures, and bulks, and in different degrees and modifications of their motions, causes the ideas of the blue colour, and sweet scent of that flower to be produced in our minds. It being no more impossible, to conceive, that God should annex such ideas to such motions, with which they have no similitude; than that he should annex the idea of pain to the motion of a piece of steel dividing our flesh, with which that idea hath no resemblance. (Locke 1690/1978, vol. 2, viii, 13)

It is not obvious how strongly Locke himself intended this thesis to be taken. At times Locke hints that our inability to see why sensory experiences of a particular sort accompany material events of a particular kind is simply an unfortunate byproduct of our finite natures. Had we access to the "finer interstices" of nature, the connections might be evident. At other times, however, Locke seems to be articulating a theme popular among those who regard conscious experiences as brute accompaniments of neurological goings-on, accompaniments flatly incapable of further explanation.

In any case, for Locke, it appears there is no reason in the nature of things for experiences in particular modalities to be as they are. A rose looks and smells a particular way. This appears to be an irreducible fact about us, not something capable of further explanation. Locke's official view is that experiences of objects' primary qualities "resemble" those qualities, while experiences of secondary qualities need be nothing at all like their causes. However, the "resemblance" here is scarcely obvious. This becomes evident in Locke's discussion of the Molyneux

---

[8] Locke (1690/1978, vol. 2, 9, viii) is anticipating something like the "McGurk effect" (McGurk and MacDonald [1976]).

question:

> Suppose a man born blind, and now an adult, and taught by his touch
> to distinguish a cube and a sphere of the same metal, and nighly of the
> same bigness, so as to tell, when he felt one and t'other, which is the cube,
> which is the sphere. Suppose the cube and sphere placed on a table, and
> the blind man to be made to see. Quære, whether by his sight before
> he touch'd them, he could now distinguish, and tell, which is the globe,
> which the cube. (Locke 1690/1978, vol. 2, 9, viii)

Now you might think that, if experiences of objects' primary qualities *resembled* those qualities, a Molyneux subject would be able immediately to discern spheres and cubes by sight alone. If both tactual and
visual experiences of cubes and spheres *resembled* cubicity and sphericity, it would seem a relatively straightforward matter to recognize a
visual experience of cubicity and sphericity on the basis of prior tactual
acquaintance with these qualities.

Locke, however, siding with Molyneux, thinks not. True, it would
seem natural to an ordinary sighted agent to regard spheres as looking
just as they feel: *spherical*. In the same way, however, it might seem
natural to a child that "chair" means chair. A child is apt to forget that
the significance of words lies outside the words themselves. We are apt
to forget, Locke might say, that the significance of visual experiences
lies outside the intrinsic features of those experiences. Assuming that a
blind person who has had his sight restored is in a position to understand
what he is seeing is like assuming that someone encountering a language,
Urdu, say, for the first time would be in a position to grasp the significance of utterances in Urdu.

BEYOND SENSORY CHANNELS

You can get a feel for the emerging conception of the modalities by imagining a controller, Lilian, who sits secluded in a dark room in front of several—five or six—television monitors. Each monitor is attached to a bank
of sensors, and each displays a running description of goings-on outside
the room. One monitor describes objects' colors and visual shapes; another
describes their smells; still another provides a description of sounds they
make. We might suppose that descriptions produced on each monitor are
in different languages. By scanning these monitors, Lilian, fluent in the
pertinent languages, obtains a fix on the external environment. Eventually
Lilian could lose the sense that she is scanning text and come to think of
herself as in direct contact with the world the text describes.

Each television monitor (together with its associated input devices)
serves Lilian as a channel of information concerning the outside world,
each goes proxy for a sensory modality. Now imagine we are moved to
ask what distinguishes these channels and, more generally, what "individuates" distinct channels. Here are four possibilities:

(1′) Channels are distinguished by features of the world they describe.

(2′) Channels are distinguished by orthographical differences in the languages in which these descriptions are couched.

(3′) Channels are distinguished by the nature of the stimuli affecting their respective sensors.

(4′) Channels are distinguished by reference to the makeup of the sensors themselves.

You will recognize these as counterparts of Grice's four criteria. It should be clear that the pros and cons of those criteria are reflected in our imagined case. The first option looks unsatisfactory because features of the world seem describable in more than one "language." The second option fails once you recognize that languages could be "inverted." The fourth option apparently smuggles in considerations grounded in options (1)–(3).

This leaves the third option, the option I have suggested comes closest to providing a plausible taxonomy of the senses. Is this the end of the story? I doubt it. Although it seems possible to provide a taxonomy of sensory modalities that conforms fairly well to traditional conceptions of such things, efforts to distinguish the senses could obscure more than they reveal. I have in mind a number of salient features of perception, including the following:

(1) The very same features of the world can be "accessed" by means of different modalities.

(2) Often, or *typically*, perceiving is a cooperative, temporally extended affair involving active exploration incorporating more than one sense. We move among, manipulate, stroke, ingest, sniff, and listen to objects in the course of investigating our environment. In so doing we unselfconsciously take ourselves to be moving among, manipulating, stroking, ingesting, sniffing, and listening to the *same* objects.

(3) Talk of channels suggests what is probably false, that the senses are "impenetrable" to one another. On the contrary, exploration in one modality can be dependent on and guided by feedback from another modality.

(4) Perceptual systems—or the modalities—are geared to work in concert toward a common end, that of enlightening us as to the environment we inhabit. I am enough of a Gibsonian to think that this involves the detection of "invariancies" multiply "encoded," hence available to more than one sense.

(5) The idea that we construct a unified picture of the world by assembling and manipulating discrete sensory clues is arguably a relic of the kind of atomistic psychology associated with eighteenth-century empiricism.

The list could doubtless be expanded, but it is sufficient to express my ambivalence over modalities conceived of as sensory "channels."[9] Perceiving is an activity undertaken by agents by means of the several senses. Gibson's contention that we should replace talk of sensory modalities with talk of sensory *systems* is a move in the right direction. Sensory systems overlap, cooperate, and share resources. In deploying our senses we gain access to a unified world. The world emerges, not piecemeal by the assembling of discrete pictorial elements, but, in Wittgenstein's memorable phrase, as light dawns gradually over the whole (1969, §141).

References

Butler, R. J., ed. 1962. *Analytical Philosophy*, 1st ser. Oxford: Blackwell.

Chalmers, D. C. 1996. *The Conscious Mind: In Search of a Fundamental Theory.* New York: Oxford University Press.

Descartes, R. 1641/1986. *Meditations on First Philosophy: With Selections from the Objections and Replies*, trans. John Cottingham. Cambridge: Cambridge University Press.

Gibson, J. J. 1966. *The Senses Considered as Perceptual Systems.* Boston: Houghton Mifflin.

Grice, H. P. 1962. Some Remarks about the Senses. In Butler, 133–53.

Guarniero, G. 1974. Experience of Tactile Vision. *Perception* 3: 101–104.

Heil, J. 1983. *Perception and Cognition.* Berkeley: University of California Press.

Keeley, B. L. 2002. Making Sense of the Senses. *Journal of Philosophy* 99: 5–28.

Kirk, R. 1974. Zombies versus Materialists. *Aristotelian Society Proceedings*, suppl. vol. 48: 135–52.

———. 1994. *Raw Feeling: A Philosophical Account of the Essence of Consciousness.* Oxford: Clarendon.

Locke, J. 1690/1978. *An Essay concerning Human Understanding*, ed. P. H. Nidditch. Oxford: Clarendon.

McGurk, H., and J. MacDonald. 1976. Hearing Lips and Seeing Voices. *Nature* 264: 746–48.

O'Regan, J. K., and A. Noë. 2001. A Sensorimotor Account of Vision and Visual Consciousness. *Behavioral and Brain Sciences* 24: 939–1031.

Roxbee Cox, J. W. 1970. Distinguishing the Senses. *Mind* 77: 530–50.

Stoffregen, T. A., and B. G. Bardy. 2001. On Specification and the Senses. *Behavioral and Brain Sciences* 24: 195–261.

White, B. W., F. A. Saunders, L. Scadden, P. Bach-y-Rita, and C. C. Collins. 1970. Seeing with the Skin. *Perception and Psychophysics* 7: 23–27.

Wittgenstein, L. 1969. *On Certainty*, ed. G. E. M. Anscombe and G. H. von Wright, and trans. D. Paul and G. E. M. Anscombe. Oxford: Blackwell.

---

[9] See Stoffregen and Bardy (2001) for a very different argument to a similar conclusion.

15

A Proprioceptive Account of the Sense Modalities

John O'Dea

INTRODUCTION

On what do we base our judgments about the sense modality of occurrent perceptual experiences? Part of the interest in this question arises not intrinsically but in virtue of its connection with another issue, namely the truth or otherwise of the representational theory of experience (RTE). That connection motivates this essay. According to the RTE, the *contents* of a perceptual experience are all that we are aware of in having it and therefore all that a theory of experience needs to explain.[1] Those opposed to RTE tend to hold that, in addition to what a perceptual experience is *of*, we are also aware of what the experience *feels like* and that therefore any theory of experience needs to account for *both* elements. A major source of disagreement between representationalists and their opponents is therefore not so much the extent to which experiences can be explained in terms of their content as the sorts of properties of experiences that *need* to be explained.

One reason to think that antirepresentationalists are right to insist that experiences have a "feel" in addition to their content comes from an argument given by Grice (1962) that unless we acknowledge that we can be aware of the "introspectible character" of perceptual experience in addition to its content, there is no way to properly account for the division of the senses into different modalities. Grice argued that it is a conceptual truth that what makes a perceptual experience *visual, auditory, tactile, olfactory,* or *gustatory* is its distinct introspectible character. If Grice is right, the representational theory of experience is in trouble.[2] This makes it an interesting question: What is it about a visual perception—if anything—such

---

[1] See Dretske (1995), Lycan (1996), and Tye (1995).
[2] Grice's argument has received recent attention by Ross (2001), Keeley (2002/this volume, chapter 11), and Nudds (2003).

that it is specifically visual? Here I discuss the standard answers to this question and the problems with each before offering a novel answer that is consistent with an appropriately broad construal of RTE and yet accepts the common intuition that drives Grice's conclusion. The account I offer draws, in a way to be explained, on a Gibsonian insight that perceptual experience is proprioceptive, as well as exteroceptive.

THE GRICEAN OPTIONS

Grice's work, as it were the *locus classicus* of this issue, is a fascinating early attempt to understand how transparency considerations (that we seem to see "through" an experience to its object) can be made consistent with the intuition that experiences have an introspectible "feel" some decades before the issue received anything like the attention it now enjoys. For reasons I do not explore here, I think it is a failed attempt but a far more interesting failure than recent attempts to do the same thing. Indeed, Grice was in effect trying to bridge what Block (1996, 16) has infamously labeled "the greatest chasm in philosophy of mind," something attempted as rarely as the label implies.

The discussion in "Some Remarks About the Senses" (Grice 1962/ this volume, chapter 4) is ostensibly confined to the issue of the distinction between the senses—of what it is about a visual experience, for example, such that it is specifically a visual experience. He concludes, in part, that all visual experiences and the like share a special introspective character (a "generic resemblance") that nonvisual experiences lack and that a difference in this respect makes for a difference in respect of sense modality. However, this sits uneasily with his acceptance that experiences are transparent, and so there follows a discussion, which I do not describe here, of how these could be made compatible.

Was Grice right that in order to distinguish between the senses we must impute a "special introspectible character" to sense experience? This is the question I explore in this essay. An obvious place to begin the exploration is with a clear sense of the alternatives. In this respect Grice's work is an ideal starting point; he presents us with a list that has survived discussion of the issue for about a half century. These are the possible alternatives, according to Grice (1962, 135/this volume, 85) (I am paraphrasing):

1. the properties we are made aware of by the experience (colors, sounds, etc.)—the kinds of *intentional content*, as we would now put it
2. the "special introspectible character" of the perceptual experience itself, which we might reasonably translate as the "qualia" of the experience

3. the external conditions, or stimuli, connected with the perception
4. the internal processes—the sense organs and so forth—connected with the perception

Let me call these respectively the *content* criterion, the *qualia* criterion, the *stimulus* criterion, and the *sense organ* criterion. Before we go further, it is worth mentioning a modern response to Grice's quest for the *criteria* for distinguishing the senses, namely that "sense modality" may be a "cluster" concept, such that several criteria are relevant to the concept, but none necessary, and in different contexts, different criteria may be weighted differently. This response would be a misreading of what is at stake. Even if "sense modality" or "vision" *is* a cluster concept in this sense, the question of *which* cluster remains relevant to contemporary discussions since one of the main foci of debate on the distinction between the senses is, in effect, whether there are *any* circumstances in which qualitative character as distinct from content is relevant to the distinction—or, in other words, whether the cluster *includes* qualitative character. Grice succeeds in showing that it is if he can show that there are *some* contexts in which qualitative character plays a deciding role. Moreover, of course, to show that qualitative character sometimes plays such a role is enough to show, among other things, that at least some sense experiences really do have it.

For the next four sections I discuss each possibility in turn in the light of recent debates. I begin with the least defended, the stimulus criterion.

THE STIMULUS CRITERION

So-called sensory substitution systems create an interesting problem for the stimulus criterion. These are apparati that transform one sort of stimulus into another. The best-known of these is Bach-y-Rita's TVSS (tactile vision substitution system), which detects light waves and produces pressure signals on a grid placed on the skin. Other mechanisms detect light and produce sounds or mild electric shocks. In these cases it seems an open question what the stimulus really is—whether, in the case of TVSS, the stimulus is light waves or pressure. It depends on whether we are inclined to include the mechanism itself as part of the perceiver. If the nature of the stimulus is the crucial criterion for deciding the sense modality, then it should be an equally open question whether the wearers of these devices *see* the obstacles in their environment or hear or feel them. It is, however, clear that visual sensory substitution systems are not literally a *cure* for blindness. They are merely *aids* for people who are blind, and this is not merely a question of detail. Although it is true that sensory substitution systems provide poorer information than is typically available through the eyes, it would be no less absurd to say that these systems are restoring *partial* sight to people who are blind, though clearly they are restoring certain *abilities.*

A second, but it seems to me equally decisive, problem is there is actually a far from perfect correlation between types of stimuli and the sense modalities. The light waves responsible for seeing can also be responsible for the tactile feeling of heat—give or take a few nanometers of wavelength; sound waves can be felt tactilely; and so on.

THE CONTENT CRITERION

There are a number of ways we might, as per the *intentional content* criterion, try to draw a distinction between the senses using the contents of perception. For a first attempt we might go through the list of properties we perceive and divide them into five groups according to the modality that perceives them. This will not work, however, because a lot of properties—they even have a collective name, the *common sensibles*—are common to different senses. These are mostly spatial properties—size, shape, location, and so on—but we might also include sweetness here since arguably it is perceived by smell and by taste.

Another way is to distinguish each sense by a single property that is unique to that sense. So, for example, what makes sight *sight* is that it is a perception of—among other things—color; hearing is a perception of, among other things, *sound.* The problem with *this* is that some senses perceive more than one property uniquely. Touch, for example, includes the perception of both pressure *and* temperature, uniquely in each case. The "unique property" criterion would make it mysterious why pressure and temperature are not considered unique senses. One might respond here that they *ought* to be, but even sight, a single sense if there is such a thing, perceives more than one property uniquely—*hue* and *brightness*, to name two. This way is not going to work, either.

A third way to try to use the content criterion is in terms of a *range* of properties. This is actually Fred Dretske's proposal. According to this, we identify a sense modality with a unique *range* of properties perceived. So, for example, we characterize sight by the fact that, when we see, we are aware of size, shape, location, movement, hue, brightness, saturation, and perhaps a few more qualities. The different lists for the different sense modalities will overlap, particularly in respect of the common sensibles, but there will be a unique list for each modality.

But this way also fails. Although each sense might be said to involve the perception of a unique list of properties, without some principle tying the members of the list to each another, there seems no reason for favoring the lists we all agree on for random alternatives. Grice saw this problem, and he considered the following answer. Under certain conditions each member of a "modality list" will share what he called a *detection link* with the other members of the list. So, for example, we are always perceptually aware of either *both* hue and brightness or of *neither*. The perception of them goes together. When our only contact with an object is visual, it will likewise be the case that we are either aware of the color, shape, *and* size of the object, or we will be aware of neither; all three properties will thereby share a detection link. Grice's reply to this idea—the right one, it seems to me—is that the detection link is not always there. When we are seeing *and* touching a coin, for example, the perception of shape remains even when one closes one's eyes, so the detection link between the members of the visual list is lost. In these cases, however, there is not all of a sudden any confusion about whether we are seeing the shape of the coin. To put the point another way—in the way Grice put it—the detection link idea implies that in some cases we have to follow a certain procedure to figure out whether we are seeing or touching a certain property. However, he wrote, "It seems certain that we never do use any such method"—that the question "never seems in the slightest doubt" (Grice 1962, 140/this volume, p. 89).

Of course, when you are seeing and touching an object, and you close your eyes, even if you are still perceptually aware of the object's shape by touch, clearly you no longer *see* its shape. So there is still a detection link between the object's color and its *visible* shape. However, there does not seem to be any way of characterizing visible shape without presupposing the idea of a sense modality—at least if the only resources at one's disposal are the properties perceived. Whatever it is to be *visibly* square, presumably it is to be *square* in exactly the same way that tactile squares are square. That is to say, there is only one relevant way in which the object itself can have the property of squareness. There is no such *property* as visible squareness as distinct from tactile squareness.

In the absence of further ideas that lack one or another of these problems, we have to conclude that the content approach fails.

THE QUALIA CRITERION

According to the *qualia criterion*, experiences within a sense modality share, or at least resemble, qualitative character, and it is by that character that we can recognize an experience as belonging to one sense modality or another.

This is in fact Grice's proposal, though he saw a significant problem with it. If the perception of some property is an instance of seeing just in case it has a particular feel—which is different from the property perceived—then it ought to make sense to say that the perception of exactly those properties we hear could have the feel that sight actually has, and we would in that case *see* sounds. Grice had the strong intuition—one I think most share—that whatever is the relationship between content and character, it cannot be *that* easy to change the modality of a perceptual experience.

Grice did, however, argue that, despite this difficulty, a difference in phenomenal character, irrespective of the content of a perception, *could* mean a difference in modality. The basis of his argument is a thought experiment. In this thought experiment, we are asked to imagine meeting a Martian who looks very like a typical human, with the single exception that it possesses four eyes—one pair in the normal place and another immediately above on the forehead. The pairs of eyes are physiologically the same and mediate the perception of the very same properties: colors, shapes, and so on. However, it happens that the Martian uses different verbs to describe seeing through the bottom pair and seeing through the top pair—say, x-ing and y-ing. Moreover, and crucially, when asked whether x-ing and y-ing feel any different, the Martian responds, "Oh yes, there is all the difference in the world!"

In this case, Grice claims, we should surely say that x-ing and y-ing are different senses and therefore that the question of whether there is an introspectible difference between two perceptual states is indispensable to the question of whether they are in different modalities and consequently that introspectible character is in general relevant to the distinction between the senses.

What Grice is attempting to do is to get around the question of our actual experiences and in particular the vexed question of the relationship between content and character. So he describes a creature for whom content and character *are* distinct, putting aside the question of whether that creature is *us*. Since in this case a difference in qualitative character, keeping the content constant, *does* seem to mean a difference in sense modality, our *concept* of a sense modality must be sensitive to qualitative character as distinct from content. Moreover, since our concept of a sense modality is based, by hypothesis, on experience, it must be the case that we *experience* qualitative character as distinct from content.

There are a number of problems with this argument, not the least of which is the idea that phenomenal character and intentional content *might* be distinct if they are *actually* the same thing. However, the main problem is best brought out by a variation on the thought experiment. Here is the variation: Rather than possessing two sets of eyes, the Martians we imagine are from all appearances exactly like us. So there is no x-ing *and* y-ing; there is just x-ing. Now instead of proclaiming "all the difference in the world" between using one set of eyes and the other, however, these Martians proclaim all the difference in the world between using their eyes in the *morning* and using them in the *afternoon*. In this case, despite the qualitative difference, there is no temptation to suggest that in the morning they are using one sense modality and in the afternoon they are using another. So whatever is going on in Grice's thought experiment, we cannot draw from it the simple conclusion that a difference in qualitative character makes for a difference in sense modality.

THE SENSE ORGAN CRITERION

Finally, the *sense organ criterion* has been defended by a number of people on a number of grounds. Here I focus on an argument by Brian Keeley, its main proponent. Though I argue that Keeley's argument fails, I go on to propose an alternative type of sense organ account.

Keeley (2002/this volume, chapter 11) arrives at the sense organ criterion via a process of elimination. He writes that the problem of distinguishing the senses is not merely an abstract philosophical problem; it is also a *biological* one, discussed at length by biologists in relation to the star-nosed mole. It is controversial whether this mole's nose—or what looks like a nose—is part of a sense of smell or a novel sense, such as an electrical one. This problem looks very much like Grice's original problem, namely, how to assess a claim that a creature possesses a novel sense, so it is very interesting to see how biologists actually try to solve it.

For our purposes the most significant thing they do is to dismiss psychology entirely. The move is not defended by the biologists who are party to the debate, but Keeley defends it for them in the following way. In order to use the contents of experiences to differentiate the senses, we need to distinguish direct from indirect content. For example, although the perception of temperature is, in us, a kind of tactile sense, when we see a glowing red hot plate, we often say that it *looks* hot; alternatively, we might say of a rose that it *looks* fragrant. We need to be able to ignore these indirect contents if we are to be able to use the content criterion. Grice also saw this problem for the content view, and Keeley endorses Grice's solution, which is to make the distinction in terms of qualitative character; so, to directly perceive redness is for redness to be part of the qualitative character of the experience. In cases of indirect perception there is no associated qualitative character. So, in order to distinguish the senses in virtue of the *contents*, we need to be able to refer to the phenomenal character of the experiences (Dretske [1999], at least, has since addressed this problem, successfully I take it, by introducing a distinction between property awareness and fact awareness, but I grant the point here for the sake of the argument).

The problem, then is this: In the case of the star-nosed mole, for familiar reasons it is impossible to say what the character of its experiences is or, crucially, whether the mole even *has* experiences with phenomenal character. However, even if we suppose that the mole in fact has no phenomenal experiences, that does not seem to dissolve the problem. It *still* makes sense to ask whether the mole's nose is part of a sense of smell or of electricity. Therefore, neither psychological criteria will work, leaving the sense organ criterion as the only one standing. This does not mean that the problem is solved since it remains to discover what distinguishes *sense organs* from each another. Keeley gives an interesting and detailed account of what that distinction amounts to, but I do not follow that up here. Instead I focus on Keeley's argument that psychology does not really matter to the distinction.

It seems unarguable that our actual basis for judging of ourselves that we are using one modality rather than another is *experiential*. Compare, for example, the difference between being touched on the tongue and being touched on the nose with the difference between a sweet taste and a sweet smell. In the former case the difference is simply a matter of location, but the latter difference is clearly more than that. Or take the difference between feeling a vibration with one's skin and *hearing* it. Again, the fact that one is an instance of touch perception and the other is an instance of auditory perception is just obvious—the nature of the respective experiences makes it plain.

To say this is not to go out on a limb—the idea is extremely common in the literature. Nudds (2003, 31) takes as given "the obviousness of the fact that we have five senses"); Grice (1962, 140/this volume, p. 89), on the question of whether any given perception of a spatial property is visual or tactile, writes that "the answer to such a question asked about ourselves never seems in the slightest doubt"; most revealing of all, even Keeley himself (2002, 5/this volume, p. 220), in the very beginning of his article, claims that "one of the most striking phenomenological facts about the human perceptual experience of the world is that it is divided into *modes*." So even for Keeley one can *make sense* of the division into sense modalities in terms of the phenomenology of perceptual states.

Some further evidence for this comes from cross-cultural research. If the division into five senses is a constant across cultures, this would *suggest* that it is based more or less directly on experience. This is what we find. According to Jütte (2005), the list of five senses that we are familiar with is the same list we find being taken for granted in records from ancient Greece, India, and China. One would expect cross-cultural variation if the list we have of the five senses is compiled through even a small amount of theorizing (or even, for that matter, a small amount of arbitrariness). Since this seems to be lacking, we can take this lack as support for the idea that the list is based more or less directly on experience.

Now it does happen to be the case, of course, that a difference in sense modality comes with *some* physiological difference or other at the periphery. So there is perhaps some room for arguing that while, as it were, our "surface judgments" about sense modality are phenomenologically based, what those judgments actually pick out are the physiological differences—on analogy with the distinction between surface judgment about the presence of water and the chemical kind that those judgments actually pick out. The big problem with this is that while the surface properties of water are also those of H_2O, it is very implausible that the surface properties of a sense modality—by hypothesis its phenomenology—are the surface properties of sense organs. Sense organs may cause experiences, but it would be a very odd view according to which sense organs themselves had experiential properties.

To this problem we can also add the implausible consequence of Keeley's view that prosthetic devices cannot restore perception in a sense modality; at most they can add a new modality. By all accounts, however, hearing implants really can enable a deaf person *literally* to hear.

So what about the star-nosed mole problem? Without access to its psychology, does this mean that the sense modality associated with its nose is inaccessible? I think the answer is yes. However, there is an analogous problem that is not inaccessible. Let me call this the "physiological problem of the senses." This is more or less the question that occurs to us when we see the star nose on the mole, namely, "What on Earth does that thing *do?*" Is it a limb or a sense organ, and if the latter, what information is it collecting and how? These are all interesting questions to ask, and indeed they *are* the focus of the star-nosed mole problem as it is discussed in biological circles. However, because none of them are straightforwardly linked to *how*, if at all, the mole becomes aware of whatever information it is detecting, they are at most analogous to the traditional question of whether the nose indicates some novel sense modality—which is not, obviously, to say that the biologists' questions are not fascinating questions in their own right; they are simply different questions.

Although the problem of the star-nosed mole is insoluble for what we can now recognize as the traditional sense of sense modality, this was only so on the assumption that we lack access to the mole's psychology. However, we do not—or will not always—*completely* lack access to the mole's psychology, so we can still ask what we would *have* to know about it in order to know which senses to attribute to it. And this is in effect to ask what it is about *our* psychology—about, in particular, our perceptual experiences—upon which we make judgments about sense modality. In the next section I draw on suggestions made independently by D. M. Armstrong and J. J. Gibson.

PERCEPTUAL EXPERIENCE AND THE SENSE ORGANS

It is usual to treat the sense organ criterion as physiological. One fairly obvious reason for this is that sense organs themselves are generally thought of in physiological terms as eyes, ears, and so forth. Keeley (2002/this volume, chapter 11) has shown that the notion of a sense organ is poorly understood, and although he nevertheless assumes a biological notion as well, there is room for a partly *psychological* notion of a sense organ. Take, for example, Armstrong's (1968, 211–13) characterization of a sense organ (noted by Keeley) as "a portion of the body which we . . . move at will with the object of perceiving what is going on in . . . our environment."[3] This seems to me a perfectly plausible

---

[3] Keeley (2002/this volume, chapter 11) points out Armstrong's characterization.

characterization of a sense organ in the ordinary sense of the phrase. Now although sense organs so characterized are *portions of the body* and thus physiological, they are portions picked out psychologically by reference to a "will." This is exactly right: The eyes are what we *use* to see, the ears are what we *use* to hear, and so on, where "use" must be treated intentionally. I use my eyes to see, but I do not use—not in the same sense—my orbital muscles to see, even though it is *in fact* my orbital muscles that I am using when I swivel my eyes in their sockets. Armstrong's characterization of a sense organ is really a sort of subjective characterization, that is to say, an account of the psychological significance of sense organs. Though Armstrong does not say so, it is plausible that this significance arises early in the cognitive chain—indeed, it seems to me, at the level of the perceptual experience itself. The eyes are characterized *in perceptual experience* not as biological entities but rather, as it were, as tools. Or so I argue.

What is the significance of this? Note again that the main difference between Grice's Martian thought experiment and my variation is that in the former the Martian has two sets of eyes and in the latter only one. This is the key difference between the two scenarios, and it makes all the difference to our intuitions. *Given* that there are different sense organs involved, qualitative character really does make a difference to our intuitions about sense modality. There is a reason that our intuitions are sensitive to this combination in particular and that a specific aspect of our experience captures the combination—what I call, for want of a better name, the *feeling of using a sense organ*.

Writing of the "feeling" of using a sense organ will be provocative to some. I might equally have used the term "awareness" rather than "feeling." Part of a perceptual experience is an *awareness* of the sense organ being used. I use the term "feeling" to express some agreement with antirepresentationalists who claim that a perceptual experience involves more than just awareness of the object of the perception. Plainly, being aware when you are seeing *that you are using your eyes* is to be aware of more than what you are seeing. The idea, to borrow a phrase of Gibson's, is that perceiving is *proprioceptive*, as well as *exteroceptive*, and that the senses themselves are distinguishable proprioceptively.

Indeed, the idea that the phenomenology of an experience is directly informative of the sense organ involved has similarities with a position put forward by J. J. Gibson (1966). Gibson is best known for a thesis about the content of perceptual experience—that it is not directly of objects and properties but rather of possibilities for action, or "affordances," as he put it. This is *not* the idea of Gibson's that I have in mind. One of his less radical proposals was that it is wrong to think of the psychology of perception in purely passive terms. Some of our behaviors—some of the actions we perform—are distinctly perceptual. An obvious example is moving one's eyes—that is to say, *looking around*. Gibson called these sorts of behaviors "exploratory behaviors" and called attention to a history within psychology of noting this special class of perceptual actions, going back at least to Pavlov (1927), who termed them "investigatory responses." He argued that each of the five senses involves a distinct set of exploratory behaviors and that, moreover, for any perceptual experience, implicit in the experience itself is an awareness of the corresponding set of behaviors.

Now these different sets of exploratory behaviors have what we might call different *foci*. In the case of vision, the focus of behavior is the eyes. The head is involved, of course, but clearly it is no accident that in the vernacular "to look" is "to use your eyes." We can roughly identify this focus of action with *sense organs*—not in the sense simply of the parts of the body that sense things but rather as the parts of the body that we *use* to sense things.

So how do we get from an awareness of the appropriate set of exploratory behaviors, as I had originally put it, to awareness of *using our eyes*. There seems to me to be a natural translation between the two. To see is not simply to be having an experience that represents that things are thus and so in the world in front of one—though, of course, it is partly that. It is also to know what to *do* to see what the world is like to one's right or left. And this involves being aware that I am doing something in order to see exactly what I am seeing and that my awareness that the world is thus and so in front of me is made possible by what I am doing with my eyes. In seeing, I am aware that the world is thus and so *and* that my eyes are responsible for my being so aware. As Gibson put it:

> The perceptual systems, as it turns out, correspond to the organs of active attention with which the organism is equipped. They bear some resemblance to the commonly recognized sense organs, but they differ in not being anatomical units capable of being dissected out of the body. Each perceptual system orients itself in appropriate ways for the pickup of environmental information. . . . Head movements, ear movements, hand movements, nose and mouth movements, and eye movements are part and parcel of the perceptual systems they serve. These adjustments constitute modes of attention . . . and *they are the senses only as the man in the street uses the terms*, not as the psychologist does. (my emphasis; Gibson 1966; 58)

There are a number of further reasons for thinking that perceptual experiences really do include an awareness of sense organs as part of their phenomenology and that this grounds our intuitions about sense modality, which in turn explains why there are traditionally only five senses.

First, although the idea that perceptual experiences include an awareness of using a sense organ is not explicitly raised in the philosophical literature, it is suggested by various remarks. Norton Nelkin (1990/this volume, chapter 9), for example, argues that we might historically have distinguished the senses according to a noticed correlation between the phenomenal character of a perception and the sense organ responsible; Peter Ross (2001, 504), getting a bit closer, holds that "it is obvious to us which sensory organ we use to perceive a particular property," meaning in the context that it is obvious in *experience*. Dominic Lopes (2000, 45), closer still, asserts that "it seems that the phenomenal character of each sense includes or makes possible an awareness of the organs by which the sense operates. What it is like to touch things tells us that we touch with the skin, as what it is like to see makes us aware that we see with the eyes." Indeed Lopes's assertion is exactly my position *sans* the "or makes possible" clause.

Second, if we accept that some of our actions are "exploratory" in Gibson's sense, it is necessary to posit some kind of proprioceptive awareness of the source of sensory information. Actual exploration of the world tends to require at least an implicit knowledge of the link between the information that is coming in and the means to control the appendage responsible for its coming in. This is, of course, Gibson's point, and it is this that in our case constitutes, I claim, the "feeling" of using a sense organ that is part of perceptual experience.

Third, as mentioned earlier, it is an odd fact that some rather obvious senses were never included in the traditional five. The account I am proposing can explain this: In these cases there is no *feeling* of using any sense organ at all. The clearest examples of this are proprioception and the senses of balance. Proprioception, which used to be called "the muscular sense" in the nineteenth century, is the sense of where one's limbs are positioned. It is how you know, when you close your eyes, where your arms and legs are. However, whereas to look is to *use* your eyes, to propriocept is not to *use* anything, at least—and this is the crucial part—not consciously. You are simply *aware* of the position of your limbs (indeed people tend not to be aware that they *do* know the position of their limbs other than through sight or touch; try asking). Similarly with the sense of balance; you do not need visual, tactile, or any other cues to know which way the ground is. However, there is no part of the body that we are aware of *using* to find that information out. If my account is correct, it makes sense that these were never counted as sixth or seventh senses.

Finally, and most important with regard to the debate about representationalism, this account is compatible with RTE since we can construe the feeling of using a sense organ as a *representation* of which sense organ is being used. To be aware that one's eyes are responsible for an experience as of an apple is to represent that one's eyes are so responsible. To be sure, this does not to conform to the letter of RTE as some represesentationalists understand it,[4] but it is certainly in keeping with its spirit, which I take to be that what we are aware of in having a perceptual experience is exhausted by the representational contents of that experience.

An important test for a representationalist theory—of anything—is how it deals with the possibility of *mis*representation. The

---

[4] See Tye (1995).

representationalist story I having been telling mandates the possibility that I might be aware of using one sense organ in the perception of some state of affairs, while in actual fact another sense organ is really being used. Such a possibility might even be thought *likely* to come about on occasion, given the account I have proposed. Conversely, it is important evidence in favor of the theory if there are such cases describable as misrepresentation of this sort. Fortunately for my account, there are. These are phenomena known as "facial vision."[5]

"Facial vision" is a phenomenon whereby some people—particularly blind people—are able to perceive the rough size, shape, and location of objects around them through a sensation that is described as one of "pressure" on the face. It turns out that the auditory system is responsible for these perceptions by gathering echolocatory information about the space around the perceiver.

Those who experience facial vision reportedly think of it as a tactile experience. Indeed, we can believe that *is* a tactile experience insofar as it is the skin on the face that it seems to them that they are using—and which, no doubt, the people in question move about in order to facially perceive better. But it is an *illusory* experience. The ears, not the facial skin, are the organs actually used in facial vision. In this case the behavioral consequences of the mistake are minimal since the sort of movement one would perform knowing that the ears are the responsible organ are more or less the sort of movements actually performed in any case (the ears and the skin of the face not being capable of independent movement and in proximity). No doubt this is the reason the illusion is never discovered as such except through careful tests.

CONCLUSION

The account I am giving here allows us to *count* senses, but it does not yet allow us to answer Grice's question or solve the star-nosed mole problem. If it feels to the mole as though it is using its nose to perceive, then that ought probably to count as a distinct sense, in my view. But is it a sense of smell? The question is moot. What I am proposing is *not* primarily a claim about the best analysis of the *concept* of a sense modality. Rather, it is a claim about the phenomenology of experience and in particular about that aspect of sense experience that is responsible for our judgments about sense modality. It is a claim about what it is about visual experiences such that we judge them as a group to be distinct from other experiences, and so on for auditory, tactile, olfactory, and gustatory experiences.

---

[5] See Lopes (2000) for a discussion of facial blindness in a philosophical context and Grantham (1995) for an introduction to the science.

If I am right that perceptual experience includes a proprioceptive element in the sense explained earlier, then we can account for Grice's intuition that we need more than simply the (exteroceptive) content of perception to account for judgments about sense modality without having to deny that in having a perceptual experience we are only aware of its content. Proprioceptive contents are still, after all, contents. The representational theory of experience has its problems, but the difference between the sense modalities is not one of them.[6]

References

Armstrong, D. M. 1968. *A Materialist Theory of Mind*. London: Routledge and Kegan Paul.

Block, N. (1996). Mental Paint and Mental Latex. *Philosophical Issues* 7; 19–49.

Dretske, F. 1995. *Naturalizing the Mind*. Cambridge, Mass.: MIT Press.

———. 1999. The Mind's Awareness of Itself. *Philosophical Studies* 95: 103–24.

———. 2000. Reply to Lopes. *Philosophy and Phenomenological Research* 60: 455–59.

Gibson J. J. 1966. *The Senses Considered as Perceptual Systems*. Boston: Houghton Mifflin.

Grantham, W. 1995. Spatial Hearing and Related Phenomena. In *Hearing*, ed. B. C. J. Moore. San Diego: Academic Press: 297–345.

Grice, H. P. 1962. Some Remarks about the Senses. In *Analytical Philosophy*, 1st ser., ed. R. J. Butler. Oxford: Blackwell: 133–153.

Jütte, Robert. 2005. *A History of the Senses: From Antiquity to Cyberspace*. Malden, Mass.: Polity.

Keeley, B. L. 2002. Making Sense of the Senses: Individuating Modalities in Humans and Other Animals. *Journal of Philosophy* 99: 5–28.

Lopes, D. M. M. 2000. What Is It Like to See with Your Ears? The Representational Theory of Mind. *Philosophy and Phenomenological Research* 60: 439–53.

Lycan, W. G. 1996. *Consciousness and Experience*. Cambridge, Mass.: MIT Press.

Nelkin, N. 1990. Categorising the Senses. *Mind and Language* 5: 149–64.

Nudds, M. 2003. The Significance of the Senses. *Proceedings of the Aristotelian Society* 104(1) (September): 32–51.

Pavlov, I. 1927. *Conditional Reflexes*, trans. G. V. Anrep. Oxford: Oxford University Press.

Ross, Peter. 2001. *Qualia* and the Senses. *Philosophical Quarterly* 51: 495–511.

Tye, Michael. 1995. *Ten Problems of Consciousness: A Representational Theory of the Phenomenal Mind*. Cambridge, Mass.: MIT Press.

---

[6] Versions of this essay were presented at universities in Sydney, Canberra, Melbourne, and Hong Kong. I am very grateful for all of the very useful comments and suggestions offered by those present.

16

The Senses as Psychological Kinds

Matthew Nudds

The distinction we make between five different senses is a universal one.[1] Rather than speaking of generically perceiving something, we talk of perceiving in one of five determinate ways: We see, hear, touch, smell, and taste things. In distinguishing determinate ways of perceiving things, what are we distinguishing between? What, in other words, is a sense modality?[2] An answer to this question must tell us what constitutes a sense modality and so needs to do more than simply describe differences in virtue of which we can distinguish the perceptions of different senses. There are many such differences—the different perceptions involve different sense organs, sensitivity to different kinds of stimuli, and the perception of different properties, and they involve different kinds of experiences—but which, if any, of these differences are those that really matter?

I

To say what is constitutive of a sense modality, we need to say what all instances of perceiving something with a particular sense have in common in virtue of which they are instances of perceiving with that

---

[1] Or almost universal: It is possible that some cultures distinguish fewer than five senses (by grouping together two senses we distinguish), but I have not been able to find a description of any culture that distinguishes more than five senses (for the anthropology of the senses, see Howes 1991). In talking of the distinction we make between senses, I am talking about the distinction we *actually* make (and have made for at least two thousand years) between five senses. There may be other distinctions that we could make or even ought to make; I am not talking about them.

[2] Throughout this chapter I use "sense modality" to mean "sense modality as we commonly understand it" and am agnostic about the nature of its referent. In other contexts "sense modality" may be taken to refer to something specific—in physiology, to anatomically individuated sensory transducers, for example. It does not follow from the fact that common sense and physiology use the same term that they are talking about the same kind of thing. Moreover, it does not follow from the fact that science distinguishes more than five senses that common sense is mistaken: That depends on whether common sense and science are talking about the same kind of thing.

sense.[3] Many philosophers suppose that there is an obvious answer to this question. In order to perceive something one must have an experience of it.[4] Seeing something requires having a *visual* experience of it, hearing something requires having an *auditory* experience of it, and so on. The different kinds of experiences involved in perceiving are what constitute perceiving with different senses. We *see* something just in case we perceive it in virtue of having a visual experience of it; *hear* something just in case we perceive it in virtue of having an auditory experience of it, and so on. To answer the question in this way is to give an *experiential account* of the senses.

Of course, such an account would be circular if the only explanation we could give of what makes an experience a visual experience is that it is the kind of experience involved in seeing things. A defender of the experiential account must suppose, therefore, that we can distinguish experiences into kinds corresponding to each of the senses simply in virtue of their character *as* experiences. That is, they must suppose that there is some property that is intrinsic to experiences that can explain the distinction, a property that is independent of how experiences are produced. *Nonexperiential accounts*, by contrast, explain the distinction by appeal to the nonintrinsic properties of experiences.[5]

Although much of what we perceive about the things around us we perceive with more than one sense, we experience the world as unified. When we see and hear a car passing in the street, we are aware of the car and its properties—its color, how it sounds, where it is, how big it is, and so on; when we look at something that we hold in our hand, we are aware of the object and its properties—its weight, shape, and color. In both cases, we are aware of properties that are in fact perceived with different senses as properties of a single object. Our perceptual system integrates information about the object that is picked-up using different senses to produce a unified experience of the object as having those properties. To say that we experience the world as unified is just to say that when we perceive properties that are properties of a single object, they are normally experienced as such even when they are perceived with different senses.[6]

It is often remarked that perceptual experience is transparent. When we reflect introspectively on our experience, the only objects and properties

---

[3] An account that failed to explain what all of the perceptions of a single sense have in common would not explain why we make a distinction between *five* senses.

[4] This used to be accepted as an a priori truth; some philosophers now think (wrongly in my view) that phenomena such as blindsight show that it is false.

[5] My labeling here is stipulative. Some strongly externalist accounts of experience end up in the nonexperiential category because they take aspects of experiences to be constituted by mind-independent objects.

[6] Since a perceptual system that integrates information about an object picked up with different senses is less likely to get things wrong about that object, it is evolutionarily advantageous that our senses do this (see Lewkowicz and Kraebel [2004] and Bertelson and de Gelder [2004]).

to which we can attend are those objects and properties of which we are apparently aware in having the experience. As a consequence, just as the *world* seems unified in experience, so our *experience* of the world seems unified to introspection. In shifting our attention between aspects of an experience that is produced by different senses, we are simply shifting attention between different properties of the objects of which we are apparently aware in having that experience. We cannot attend to a visual or an auditory experience as such, only to the objects and properties that we visually and auditorily perceive (or apparently perceive).[7] If that is right, then there is nothing of which we are aware solely on the basis of introspecting our experience that is sufficient to explain the distinction we make between different senses.[8] That makes it doubtful that we can distinguish experiences into kinds that correspond to the senses on the basis of their character *as* experiences and doubtful, too, that we can give an experiential account of the senses. It seems more plausible to suppose that in distinguishing experiences into kinds we are distinguishing between them on the basis of how they are produced.

Although our (unified) experience of objects and their properties is produced by the operation of different sensory mechanisms,[9] this is not apparent to us in introspection.[10] It is a fact that we can discover only by reflecting on what is involved in coming to be aware of objects and properties (that is, by reflecting on the different ways in which we come to perceive things).[11] In virtue of the fact that perception involves different perceptual mechanisms, there are various, different causal conditions that have to be satisfied in order to perceive, and these vary for different properties. Some properties we perceive by, for example, looking at objects, others by touching objects, and so on. We can explain why we distinguish perceptions into perceptions of different senses by appeal to our understanding of the connection between what we can perceive and the satisfaction of these different causal conditions associated with different perceptual mechanisms. The best explanation, therefore, of the

---

[7] Here I am expressing a fundamental disagreement with Keeley, who claims that "One of the perhaps most striking phenomenological facts about human perceptual experience of the world is that it seems to be divided into modes. . . . The existence of separate sensory modalities would seem to be a brute fact about perception, if ever there was one" (2002, 5/this volume, p. 220). He does not say what features of experience he takes to support his claim.

[8] I am assuming that we cannot explain the distinction in terms of the objects of experience for the simple reason that the very same objects and properties can be perceived with more than one sense. For the senses to be individuated in terms of their objects there would need to be one kind of object "proper" to each sense. I discuss this in Nudds (2003, sec. 3).

[9] I use the terms "mechanism" and "process" interchangeably.

[10] For a discussion of the limits of introspection, see Martin (1997).

[11] This means that prior to having such a reflective understanding we can make no distinction between senses. The developmental evidence supports this claim (Yaniv and Shatz [1988]; O'Neill, Astington, and Flavell [1992]). For a discussion of whether chimpanzees have a reflective understanding of seeing, see Povinelli and Eddy (1996) and the debate between Tomasello et al. and Povinelli and Vonk in Hurley and Nudds (2006).

distinction we make between different kinds of experience—between visual experience and tactile experience and so on—is in terms of a reflective understanding of the connection between experiences involved in the perception of certain kinds of objects and properties and the different ways we perceive those objects and properties—that is, in terms of the different ways those experiences were produced.

My suggestion, then, is that the most plausible explanation of the distinction we make between senses is that we distinguish perceptions into perceptions of different senses on the basis of a reflective understanding of how those perceptions were produced. In doing so, we are distinguishing between perceptions produced by different kinds of sensory mechanism, and so our concepts of the senses must be concepts of different kinds of sensory mechanism. This provides an answer to the question of what constitutes a sense modality. A sense modality just is a kind of sensory mechanism, and all instances of, say, *seeing* something are instances of seeing that thing in virtue of their having been produced by a single kind of sensory mechanism—the sensory mechanism of vision.

One might object that the distinction we make between different senses is a universal and common-sense one; it is a distinction made with only a vague and superficial understanding of the nature of our sensory mechanisms by people who perhaps know little more than that seeing involves looking, touching involves contact, and so on. It is just not plausible, therefore, to think that in distinguishing different senses we are distinguishing between perceptions on the basis of the way that they were produced, nor that our concepts of the senses are concepts of these different kinds of sensory mechanism.

I agree that it is implausible to think that in making the distinction between five senses we deploy detailed knowledge of, or a theory of, the mechanisms of perception, but distinguishing between perceptions on the basis of the kind of sensory mechanism that produces them does not require such knowledge, any more than making common-sense distinctions between animal species requires knowledge of evolutionary theory or distinguishing between different kinds of metals requires knowledge of atomic theory. In all of these cases we can use concepts that refer to different natural kinds without knowing what makes something an instance of the kind in question. This is because it is possible to give an account of what determines the reference of the concept independently of an account of what determines the concept's extension and so give an account of the nature of the concept that does not require knowledge of what makes something a member of the kind.[12]

In claiming that the senses are different kinds of sensory mechanism and that our concepts are concepts of kinds of sensory mechanism we

---

[12] I have in mind the kind of account suggested by Putnam (1975) and the view of kinds described by Millikan (2005).

need be committed to no more than that a similar explanation can be given of our concepts of different senses. There are two requirements that such an explanation must satisfy. First, it must explain how the reference of our concepts of different senses is fixed independently of an account of what determines their extension; second, it must show that the relevant sensory mechanisms exist and so determine the extension of the concepts. If either of these requirements is not met, then our common-sense distinction between five senses cannot be a distinction between kinds of sensory mechanism.[13]

Reference fixing requires an understanding of the casual dependence of perceptions on different ways of perceiving; that understanding may simply consist in the capacity to think of our perception of one kind of property as being produced differently from our perception of some other kind of property. Someone who understands the connection between perceiving different properties of things and looking at them, touching them, putting them in their mouth, and so on has such a capacity. So, for example, we might think that the perception of an object is an instance of seeing it just in case it is produced as a result of the operation of the sensory mechanism that involves looking at the object; it is an instance of touching an object just in case it is produced as a result of the operation of the sensory mechanism that involves contacting the object with a part of our body, and so on. By grasping such principles we can refer to the different kinds of mechanism that enable us to perceive—the mechanism that involves looking, the mechanism that involves contact, and so on—without having detailed knowledge of the operations of those mechanisms and without knowledge of what determines the extension of concepts of perceptions produced by these different mechanisms. The first requirement, then, can be met.

What about the second requirement? Here the question is, in large part, an empirical one: Does our perceptual system consist (in part) of five kinds of sensory mechanisms? If our concepts refer to kinds of perceptual mechanisms, then the mechanisms must actually exist to be referred to by our concepts. What does that require? It requires that there exist a sensory mechanism corresponding to each of the ways we commonly distinguish perceptions: a mechanism that enables us to see, a mechanism that enables us to hear, and so on, and it requires that there exist a single kind of mechanism that produces all (or most) of the perceptions that we commonly classify as being of a single sense: All (or most) of the perceptions we commonly classify as instances of seeing must be produced by a single kind of mechanism, all (or most) of those of hearing

---

[13] Failure of reference does not itself show that our concepts are not natural-kind concepts but does show that judgments involving those concepts are never true. If we have reasons to think the judgments can be true, then we have a reason to think the concepts are not natural-kind concepts. I argue later that we do have reasons to think the judgments can be true.

must be produced by a single kind of mechanism, and so on. Since we actually make a distinction between and have concepts of five senses, it must be possible to identify five perceptual mechanisms for these concepts to refer to:[14] If there are five such mechanisms, our concepts may refer to them; conversely, if there are not five such mechanisms, our concepts of the five senses cannot be concepts of kinds of perceptual mechanisms. Although appealing to kinds of perceptual mechanism in order to explain what the distinction between senses consists of does not require that we know a theory of the mechanisms of perception, it does require that such a theory would make a distinction between five kinds of perceptual mechanism.[15] So the question we need to answer is this: Does a theory of the mechanisms of perception distinguish five kinds of sensory mechanisms? A theory of the mechanisms of perception must explain the mechanisms that enable us to perceive things; such explanations are psychological; therefore, a theory of the mechanisms of perception is a psychological theory of perception.[16] The question we need to answer is therefore this: Does a psychological theory of perception distinguish five kinds of perceptual mechanisms or processes? This is the question that I address in the remainder of this chapter.

I have argued that the best explanation of our everyday classification of perceptions into perceptions of five different senses is that it reflects the underlying psychological organization of our perceptual system. Such a suggestion is plausible only if our perceptual system has the appropriate organization. One way to determine whether it does would be to simply consult a psychological theory of perception. Unfortunately, there is as yet no such theory to consult. There are theories, or parts of theories, of some aspects of our perceptual system, but nothing like a complete theory.

How, then, should we proceed? In what follows I argue that even if we do not have a complete psychological theory of perception, we do know what form a theory that distinguishes five kinds of perceptual mechanisms would have. We know, too, what the empirical commitments of a theory of that form are. In advance of knowing a complete psychological theory of perception, therefore, we can attempt to determine whether the empirical commitments of a theory of the right form are met. Although we might never be in a position, prior to having a

---

[14] I am assuming that our common-sense distinction is correct; I discuss the possibility that it is mistaken—that there are not five senses *as we conceive them*—later.

[15] Whenever I talk of perceptual mechanisms, I mean mechanisms that produce perceptions of the kind we commonly classify as perceptions of the five senses. Of course, there may be other mechanisms that, on some understanding of what it is to perceive, count as perceptual—there may be a mechanism involved in proprioception, for example. They are irrelevant to the question I am discussing.

[16] I am making the (relatively uncontroversial) assumption that our capacity to perceive is appropriately explained at the psychological level rather than at any lower level—that generalizations in a theory that explains how we perceive will quantify over psychological states and processes.

complete theory, to show that the commitments are met, we might find evidence that shows that they are not met; that is, we might find evidence that rules out the possibility of there being five kinds of sensory mechanism.

What form would a psychological theory of perception have? We postulate psychological mechanisms in order to explain the psychological capacities of an organism, like the capacity of an organism to perceive its environment. What form should the explanation of a psychological capacity have, and how in general can we explain such a capacity? It is commonly supposed that we can explain psychological capacities *functionally*. The most detailed philosophical account of functional explanation is Robert Cummins's and Jerry Fodor's (see especially Cummins [1983] and Fodor [1968, 1983]). In what follows I begin by giving a brief account of functional explanation and then describe its empirical commitments.

According to Cummins, we can explain a complex *psychological* capacity in the same way that we explain any other *complex* capacity: by analyzing it into simpler elements. There are two ways in which this can be done. We can give what he calls a *functional analysis* of the capacity itself, and we can give a *compositional analysis* of the system that has the capacity. Since what makes an explanation the explanation of the capacity of a particular system is that the system actually realizes that capacity, an adequate explanation often requires both kinds of analysis. This sets an empirical constraint on the analysis of any capacity of a system: The analyzing capacities must be shown to be capacities of the system that has the capacity. This point should be noted; we will see that it has some important consequences.

Compositional analysis explains a system's possession of a capacity by decomposing the system into parts. The system's possession of the capacity is then explained "by appeal to the properties of [the system's] components and their mode of organization" (Cummins 1983, 15). Analyzing a system in this way has an explanatory value "when we come to see that something having the kinds of components specified, organised in the way specified, is bound to have the target property," namely, the capacity that we want to explain (ibid., 17). Since the components we use to analyze a complex capacity often themselves have capacities or properties that we want to explain, this process of analysis is recursive.

The functional analysis of a capacity consists in analyzing it into a number of simpler or less problematic capacities in such a way that the organized activity of the analyzing capacities amounts to the activity of the analyzed capacity. This has explanatory value because we can come to see how a series of relatively simple capacities operating together in a certain way can together constitute very complicated capacities.

The functional analysis of a capacity is often a preliminary step to explaining how a system possesses that capacity. We begin by analyzing the capacity into a number of simpler capacities and then explain how some system realizes or possesses the complex capacity by showing that various component parts of the system themselves realize or possess the simple capacities described by our analysis. Thus, functional analysis goes together with compositional analysis when we show that the analyzing capacities are capacities of components of the system.

Fodor suggests that psychological explanations employ just this methodology; such explanations, he says,

> have characteristically exhibited two phases that, although they may be simultaneous in point of history, are nevertheless distinguishable in point of logic . . . in the first phase of psychological explanation, the primary concern is with determining the functional character of the states and processes involved in the etiology of behaviour. . . . The second phase . . . has to do with the specification of those biochemical systems that do, in fact, exhibit the functional characteristics enumerated by the phase-one theories. (Fodor 1968, 107–109)

Although functional analysis often goes together with compositional analysis, it does not always do so. Sometimes we can analyze the capacity of a system into other capacities that are capacities of the system as a whole and not capacities of any of its components. Consider, for example, the capacity of a cook to bake a cake. Such a capacity can be analyzed into a (sequence of) simpler capacities—to break eggs, to follow instructions, to mix ingredients together, and so on—which are not capacities of some part of the cook; they are just capacities that the cook has (capacities, we might say, of the whole cook). We could provide an explanation of the cook's capacity to bake a cake by providing a functional analysis of the capacity, but not a compositional analysis of the cook.

In practice, when we attempt to explain the capacity of a system, we often need to analyze the complex capacity of the system into simpler capacities of the system as a whole before attempting any compositional analysis of these capacities. It is often possible to analyze the complex capacity of a system in different ways, and, since the different analyses will have different implications for the structure of the system that instantiates them, it will be important to distinguish these analyses when we come to explain the instantiation of a capacity by a particular system. The same capacity might, for example, be the product of two distinct and simpler capacities of the system as a whole, or it might be a single complex capacity of the system—we need to know which before attempting to provide any further compositional analysis.

A concrete example is provided by a class of distributed networks that are commonly used for simulations of cognition. Such networks are set up so as to have a particular steady-state function—to produce a certain kind of output given a certain input—but the network can also "learn" to produce a particular output given a particular input. We can analyze the complex capacity of this system into two simpler capacities—to produce a steady output and to learn—which are both capacities of the whole system or network, not of components of it. Yet the same complex capacity could be implemented by a system having two distinct components, each possessing a simpler capacity (see Shallice 1988, 252).

If it is to be explanatory of a system's possession of a capacity, the functional analysis of the capacity must terminate in capacities that we can show are instantiated by the system. Since there will usually be more than one way in which a capacity can be analyzed, what makes an analysis an explanation of the capacity of a particular system is that the system instantiates the analyzing capacities. If the system does not instantiate the capacities described by our analysis, then we will not have explained how this particular system has the capacity. In order to substantiate the claim that we have provided an analysis of some capacity of, say, the human brain, we need to show that our analysis is in fact instantiated by the brain. This requirement is what sets an empirical constraint on correct analysis. If, for example, we analyzed some complex capacity into two simpler and distinct capacities of the whole system, we would look for evidence that these capacities are in fact independently instantiated by the system, and our claim to have provided an analysis will be undermined if we cannot show the analyzing capacities to be independently instantiated.

This method of explanation can be used to explain both the operation of a complex capacity and the possession of that capacity by a system. We can think of the psychological capacities of an organism as complex capacities instantiated by them and so can use this combination of functional and componential analysis to explain the operation and instantiation of the psychological capacities of an organism.

A complete functional explanation of some capacity of a system has the form of a hierarchy of levels. The top level is simply a description of the capacity to be explained; an analysis of this capacity constitutes the next level down, and each of the lower levels in turn provides an analysis of the level above. Each analysis of a higher-level capacity is constrained by the requirement that the components of the analysis actually be instantiated by the system. If we cannot show that the lower-level description is a description of capacities of components of the system, then we have a reason to reject it as an explanation.

Suppose that psychological capacities can be given functional explanations. Then a necessary condition for there being five kinds of sensory mechanism is that a functional explanation of our capacity to perceive distinguishes independently identifiable subfunctions, each of which functions in such a way that it can be plausibly identified with the operation of one of the senses.

Even in the absence of a functional explanation of our capacity to perceive, we know what form such an explanation would take were it to analyze the capacity to perceive into five distinct sensory capacities. Given that the capacities of an empirically adequate analysis must be instantiated, we know, too, what structures or mechanisms the brain must instantiate for such an analysis to be correct.

That means that, in advance of having a complete functional explanation of our capacity to perceive, we can look for evidence either that the brain does or does not have the relevant structures or mechanisms. Such evidence would constitute evidence for or against the existence of five kinds of sensory mechanism independently of having a complete functional explanation. Evidence of this kind might never be such that we could confidently say, in advance of a complete explanation, that there were five kinds of sensory mechanism, but it might convince us that there were not five such capacities.

Isn't it just obvious that there are five such capacities? After all, we can use each of our five senses independently of the others—we can perceive something by seeing or by hearing alone without perceiving it with any other sense. Does that not suggest that, prior to any componential analysis, an initial *functional* analysis of our capacity to perceive should distinguish five independent subcapacities, one corresponding to each sense, and therefore that all we should expect from further analysis of these capacities is an explanation of *how* each of them is actually instantiated by mechanisms in the brain?

However intuitively obvious it might seem, it does not follow from the fact that we can use each of our senses independently of the others that a functional explanation will produce an analysis into five subcapacities. Distinct capacities that normally operate together may realize distinct functions; whether or not they do so depends on their overall functional organization. Therefore, each independently usable sense may not be a single capacity but instead be instantiated by a number of distinct capacities operating together. Moreover, there may be functionally significant interdependencies between the capacities that instantiate what we normally regard as distinct senses, interdependencies that in normal circumstances we do not notice.

To see this, consider the example of vision. A capacity is individuated by its functional role, its function being to map types of input onto types of output in a certain way.[17] If a capacity is an input-output mapping, then to claim that a sensory modality is instantiated by a single capacity is to claim that there is some mapping of input states onto output states of the brain, which instantiates it. We will have identified such a capacity when we have identified its inputs and its outputs and the relation between them; two capacities will be identical only if they map the same kind of inputs onto the same kind of outputs in the same way. If vision is a single capacity, then it must consist of some single mapping of inputs onto outputs. If there exists no one kind of input or no unique kind

---

[17] Cummins says that "to ascribe a function to something is to ascribe a capacity to it that is singled out by its role in an analysis of some capacity of a containing system" and that "X has a disposition to d if X would manifest d were a certain range of events to occur. To explain a disposition is to explain why d comes about when precipitating conditions occur." A disposition is the same as a capacity for Cummins (1983, 195n1).

of output, then vision would not be a single kind of capacity. Evidence against such uniqueness would be evidence against the claim that vision is a single capacity.

Marr, in his discussion of the function of vision (a function whose hypothetical workings he goes on to describe in detail) takes the *input* to the visual capacity to be fairly obvious:

> A process may be thought of as a mapping of one representation onto another, and in the case of human vision, the initial representation is in no doubt—it consists of arrays of image intensity values as detected by the photoreceptors of the retina. (1982, 32)[18]

Whatever the output of vision may be, the input must be the light that is detected by the retina. We might think that something similar is true of the other senses; it is fairly easy to distinguish anatomically different sensory "transducers"—those parts of the body (the sense organs)—that are sensitive to various different kinds of stimuli and hence detect different kinds of information about the physical world. All of the information we have about the world comes to us thanks to the operation of these transducers, so we know that the input to whatever perceptual capacities we have can be no more than what is detected by them, and each of them can be used independently of the others. It might seem safe, then, to infer from this that the input of each of the different sensory capacities is just what is detected by each sense organ—in the case of vision, arrays of light intensity values. However, we want to know whether there is a *single* capacity corresponding to each transducer, and that depends in part on how the transducer itself functions.

The retina contains neurons that are sensitive to different features of the visual array, and—a fact "that is often not appreciated"[19]—projections from the neurons in the retina travel to a number of different targets in the brain. So, that the retinal image is the input to a single capacity rather than that different properties of the image are inputs to distinct capacities is an assumption that may turn out to be false. It is possible that we could find evidence that there are several kinds of visual output, which would be evidence that there is not a single input-output mapping for vision. That would suggest that vision is not a single capacity. The same may be true of the other sense organs: Empirical investigation of their function is required to determine whether or not it is.

---

[18] Marr talks of processes where I talk of capacities; the difference is not important from the point of view of my argument.

[19] Milner and Goodale (1995, 3). Physiological and anatomical studies have distinguished several distinct classes of retinal ganglion cells, each of which appears to be involved in the analysis of a different aspect of the visual scene. The cells form two channels of information that remain partially segregated through higher cortical regions (see Cowey 1979). Recently a similar neuronal specialization has been found in the auditory cortex of nonhuman primates (Romanski et al. 1999a, 1999b); I discuss this later.

If it does not follow from the fact that we can use each sense independently of the others that there are five kinds of sensory capacity, then what would be evidence for the existence of five such capacities? If the correct analysis of our capacity to perceive analyzes it into five distinct capacities, one of which is a single visual capacity, then we should expect to find a visual capacity instantiated in the brain as a single kind of mapping of inputs onto outputs. If, on the other hand, our visual capacity is analyzed into two distinct parallel capacities, then we should expect to find it instantiated as two distinct input-output mappings in the brain. The existence of two such visual capacities would undermine the identification of our everyday concepts of the senses—in particular that of vision—with concepts of kinds of psychological capacity.

Even before we have a complete psychological theory of perception we can look for evidence that there is a single visual capacity instantiated by the brain, so here we have a clear example of how we might actually go about deciding whether our concepts of the senses are natural kind concepts. Evidence for or against the claim that the senses are natural kinds will therefore take the form of evidence that the brain does or does not instantiate distinct sensory capacities or distinct kinds of input-output mappings.

Suppose that we find evidence that there is not a single input-output mapping for vision. That would seem to be enough to undermine the claim that there is a single visual capacity and so undermine any identification of our concept of vision with the concept of a natural kind. The question is not, however, quite so clear cut. I have been supposing that psychological capacities can be explained functionally and have described what kind of evidence would show that a functional explanation of perception would undermine an identification of our concepts of the five senses with psychological capacities.

However, the question of whether we can explain the capacity of some system functionally is not itself trivial: It depends in part on the kind of structure the system has. An adequate functional explanation is one whose analyzing capacities can be shown to be instantiated by components of the system. If the organization of the system whose capacities we are attempting to explain does not have a componential structure, it will not be possible to show that a functional analysis is instantiated by the system—there would be no components of the system to instantiate the relevant capacities. Given that this structural organization is a necessary condition for functional explanation, evidence that some system does not instantiate a particular capacity is not necessarily evidence that the system lacks that capacity: It may show instead that the system lacks the kind of structure that makes functional explanation appropriate.

According to the model of functional explanation that I have described, we can explain a psychological capacity by analyzing it into subcapacities, and we can show that the analysis is the correct analysis of the capacity of a particular thing or system by showing that the analyzing capacities are capacities of parts or components of the system and that they are instantiated by components of the system. Suppose, for example, that we analyze the complex capacity of some system into two parallel capacities, each of which is a capacity of the system as a whole. To show that this analysis is correct, we would need to show that both capacities are in fact instantiated by the system in the way our analysis describes. That means the system must be shown to instantiate two independent capacities (together with any component capacities we postulate in further analyzing these capacities). If two capacities of the system are independent of one another, then, since component capacities are, in turn, individuated in terms of their role in the analysis, each set of their component capacities must itself be independent of the other. So, in order to show that such an analysis is the correct analysis of the capacity of the particular system that we are attempting to explain, we need to show that the system has components that instantiate those capacities in the way the analysis describes. If the analyzing capacities are not instantiated, then we cannot claim to have provided an analysis of the capacity of this particular system: Although we might have provided an analysis of the capacity and so given an explanation of how some arbitrary system could have this capacity, we would not have explained how this particular system actually has the capacity. If we cannot show that the system really instantiates two independent capacities, then our analysis will not be the correct explanation of the capacity of this system. Fodor describes this kind of procedure:

> [H]aving arrived at a . . . theory of the kinds of operations performed by the mechanisms that are causally responsible for behaviour, one then "looks inside" to see whether or not the nervous system does in fact contain parts capable of performing the alleged functions. . . . The physiological psychologist's task of determining what, if any, organization into subsystems the nervous system of an organism exhibits is precisely the problem of determining whether the nervous system has subsystems whose functional characteristics correspond with those required by antecedently plausible psychological theories . . . it is clear that a psychological theory that attributes to an organism a state of process that the organism has no physiological process capable of realising is ipso facto incorrect. . . . If no such mechanisms exist, then the [analysis of that capacity] is the wrong model for the functional organization [of that capacity]. (1968, 109–10)

If the nervous system does not have subsystems that correspond to our theory, then the theory does not provide an explanation of the psychological capacity or associated behavior. Therefore, if the model of functional explanation is to be applicable to the various psychological capacities—capacities like vision and memory—that we ordinarily attribute to people, then the system that instantiates these capacities (the human nervous system and brain) must have a certain kind of structure, and it must have what Fodor calls a "modular" structure: That is, its various distinct capacities must be implemented by collections of subcomponents (parts of the nervous system and brain) that are themselves independent of one another.[20] Were the brain to lack this kind of modular structure, then we could not explain its capacities functionally because there would be no way to determine empirically which of two alternative analyses of the same psychological capacity was correct.

Given the empirical commitments of this form of psychological explanation and in advance of a complete explanation of perception, evidence against the existence of five sensory capacities corresponding to the five senses will be equivocal. On the one hand, we could take it to be evidence that the correct functional explanation of the senses will not in fact distinguish five sensory capacities; on the other hand, we could take it as evidence that the human nervous system and the brain lack the kind of modular structure required for this model of psychological explanation to apply to it.

Functional explanation of the form I have described sets a very strong constraint on explanation. Psychologists can and do construct explanations of people's psychological capacities, and they do so by constructing models of how those capacities are realized in the brain. Such explanations often distinguish capacities at one level even when they are produced by the operations of subcapacities that are not entirely distinct at a lower level. If that is so, then, in practice at least, psychologists do not necessarily individuate analyzing capacities by their role in the analysis of higher-level capacities since they may also play a role in the analysis of other capacities that we distinguish at the higher level. In effect we can see functional explanation as placing too strong a constraint on adequate explanation—a constraint that has the effect of making it too easy to find evidence against a proposed explanation of a capacity. Could there not be other, less demanding ways of empirically determining which of two (or more) alternative analyses of a psychological capacity is a correct analysis of the brain's capacity? If our model of psychological explanation is to be consistent with psychological practice, then we need to weaken the instantiation requirement on adequate explanation and hence raise the level of evidence required to show that a particular analysis is not instantiated by a system. What form should this model of explanation take, and what kind of evidence do psychologists in practice appeal to in providing an analysis of a particular psychological capacity? The best way to answer

---

[20] For Fodor (who introduced the term in Fodor [1983]), a module is actually a subcomponent with a special set of properties: "A module is, inter alia, an informationally encapsulated computational system—an inference making mechanism whose access to background information is constrained by general features of cognitive architecture, hence relatively rigidly and relatively permanently constrained" (1990, 200–201). The term "modular" is now often used to describe functionally specialized subcomponent structures that lack these properties; such structures are modular in a weaker sense than Fodor's.

these questions is to consider a concrete example: the explanation of memory. I have simplified it somewhat to make the point more clearly.

We know that memory is the capacity to store certain kinds of information; we do not know what kind of information is stored in what way, nor do we know how it is stored. If we want an explanation of our memory capacity, then we must begin by attempting to characterize the capacity to remember in detail. On the face of it there is more than one way to characterize a person's capacity to remember things. We might characterize it as a single, general-purpose capacity that we can use to remember any kind of information or as consisting of several distinct capacities to remember different kinds of information: the capacity to remember the way to get into the center of town may be different from the capacity to remember how to perform a mathematical calculation or to remember the date of one's birthday or the smell of a flower. An explanation of memory must begin, therefore, with the most detailed description that we can give of a normal person's capacity to remember. The content of such a description may be far from obvious; as Churchland comments, what the mind is doing "even described at the level of input-output functions of the system—is not an observational matter, to be read off simply by looking at the behaving organism. Rather, it is a deeply theoretical matter. Some initial theory is essential to get the whole enterprise going."[21] The theory here will take the form of hypotheses about the role of memory in various kinds of behavior. That is, we hypothesize psychological capacities that are responsible for people's behavior. The capacities we hypothesize must be sufficiently complex to account for whatever behavioral abilities people are shown to possess. Producing this kind of description is likely to involve a certain amount of empirical investigation: We need to experiment, to test people, and so on in order to determine what they can do. Once we have discovered what people can do—what they can remember and in what circumstances—and produced an analysis of their capacity, we can attempt to locate the mechanisms that instantiate the capacities that our analysis postulates.

I have suggested that failing to find such mechanisms does not show that the analysis of the particular capacity we are attempting to explain is incorrect; it may simply be that the capacity is instantiated by a system that lacks the required kind of structure. How, then, do psychologists determine whether an analysis—a theory of memory—is correct?

When constructing an account of people's capacity to remember—a psychological theory or model of memory—psychologists do not just use evidence of what people can do; rather, they use evidence of what they cannot do: Their theories are often based on studies of the abilities of people with brain damage. By studying what capacities remain intact

---

[21] Churchland (1989, 374); also see Fodor (1968, chap. 3).

in the absence of others—by looking at how capacities dissociate when the brain is damaged—it is possible to learn about the structure of the intact capacity. Shallice provides a succinct explanation of the kind of methodology they employ:

> The importance of dissociations stems from an inferential asymmetry between associations and dissociations, if observed impairments faithfully reflect damage to an underlying modular system. If one patient shows an association between two types of deficit and a second shows a dissociation, with one of the abilities being preserved, then a simple explanation of the overall pattern exists. The observed dissociation can be presumed to arise from a lesion that has affected only one side of a functional line of cleavage in the modular system; the association is presumed to result from a lesion that has crossed this line.[22]

In fact, it is more important to look for double, rather than single, dissociations between two abilities. Two abilities are doubly dissociated if each one can be impaired without the other being so. This suggests that different underlying psychological capacities or mechanisms are required for the two abilities. A double dissociation is more significant than a single one because a single dissociation is compatible with the possibility that the same capacities underlie the two abilities but that the impaired ability simply taxes those capacities more heavily (and so stops working first, or works much less well, when they are damaged).

This approach has proved useful for understanding the mechanisms of memory.[23] In some people with damaged brains, memory impairment— amnesia—occurs as a circumscribed disorder without any cognitive impairment. Although we tend to think of memory as a single capacity to remember things, the study of people with amnesia has provided evidence for distinguishing two kinds of memory: short- and long-term memory. People with amnesia can remember things for short periods of time but not for longer periods. One psychologist of memory concludes that such results "suggest a distinction between at least two kinds of memory" (Squire 1989, 504)—or two kinds of capacity: the capacity to remember things for short periods of time and the capacity to remember things for longer periods of time. People with amnesia are in fact often able to learn things—they are often able to learn how to perform certain motor, perceptual, and cognitive tasks. They can, in other words, still remember some kinds of things for longer periods of time, which suggests that we should distinguish different kinds of long-term memory. It is this kind of evidence psychologists appeal to in attempting to characterize a particular psychological capacity that they want to explain; it

---

[22] Shallice (1988, 5). This methodological approach is relatively recent, and interest in it has greatly increased over the past quarter century or so. Shallice's book is an excellent discussion of its theoretical underpinnings. Note that Shallice is using "modular" in a weaker sense than Fodor.

[23] Some of the relevant evidence is summarized in Squire (1989).

is evidence that, in the case of memory, appears to show that what we thought of as a unitary capacity is in fact the joint operation of distinct capacities.

Although this evidence suggests that we need to distinguish different kinds of memory, it is possible that the kind of fragmentation of capacities revealed by amnesia has no functional significance and does not reflect the underlying structure of the mechanisms of memory. In order to show that the analysis is correct, we need to show that these different capacities are in fact instantiated by the brain; if we are not able to do so, we will have to go back and revise our initial characterization. But do they need to be instantiated in the way required by functional analysis, by a strongly modular structure? No, because there are other kinds of brain structure that would produce the patterns of dissociation that count as evidence of distinct capacities of the system.[24] Suppose, for example, that each of two subcapacities can function effectively without the other but that there is some interaction between them. The interaction might be such that, for example, the two capacities are not able to produce conflicting outputs. According to the model of functional explanation, such interactions would rule out viewing these subcapacities as components of distinct, higher-level capacities, and yet in the situation in which one of these subcapacities is damaged, the other may continue to function more or less normally. In that case it may be appropriate to treat each subcapacity as a component of two different, higher-level capacities. Our decision to treat these subcapacities as distinct from one another may depend on whether we can specify the functions of each of the capacities of which they are part independently of one another. Evidence from a higher level—relating damage to a particular structure to changes in a subject's behavior, for example—may lead us to treat components that interact at a lower level as distinct. Alternatively, suppose that two capacities are realized in overlapping areas of the brain. One capacity A might require regions X and Z of the cortex, and another capacity B might require regions Y and Z. Higher-level evidence might lead us to count X and Y as contributing to the function of two independent capacities even though they are not realized independently of one another. Despite interactions, we would still regard A and B as distinct.[25]

We should view the relation between a single subcapacity and the rest of the system in which it is embedded as on a continuum. Our decision

---

[24] For further discussion, see Shallice (1988, chap.11). Farah (1994) discusses several dissociations that she argues could be explained in terms of damage to a nonmodular system. The interpretation of the sensory dissociations that I describe later in terms of damage to a modular or functionally specialized system is supported by anatomical evidence that is absent in the cases Farah describes.

[25] Overlapping or shared cortical areas do not entail the existence of a single function. Two distinct processes can overlap and may do so when areas of the cortex contain differently sensitive neurons. So what may seem like an "obvious" shared input to vision or audition, for example, can in fact be an input to more than one process or function.

as to whether to treat two capacities as genuinely distinct or not will be determined by the extent to which the operation of a subcapacity depends on outputs of other subcapacities of the system of which it is a part and by how they relate to the state of the rest of the system. There may be certain relations between subcapacities that are of far greater importance to the operation of the capacity than others; we can group together and distinguish components on the basis of the strength or importance of the connections between them. For as long as all of the components of a capacity have strong connections to one another and weak connections to the components of other capacities, we can view the components as genuinely instantiating that capacity and the capacity as genuinely distinct from others.

It is possible, then, to say when some proposed analysis of a capacity has a genuine functional significance even when the system whose capacity we are attempting to explain lacks a strongly modular structure. The difference between this approach—explanation in terms of functional specialization—and functional explanation is that it allows that there is explanatory value to an analysis that shows how complex capacities can emerge from the interaction of functionally specialized components even when we cannot precisely characterize the function of those components and the contribution they make to the system as a whole and even when they do not stand in the very tight relationships to the analyzed capacity required by functional analysis. This approach still makes an empirical assumption, namely, that the brain has functionally specialized regions rather than a generally homogenous form, but there is ample evidence—from anatomical and functional-imaging studies, for example—to support this assumption.

I have been describing what would be evidence for and against the claim that the human perceptual system consists of five kinds of psychological mechanism and have suggested that philosophical accounts of psychological explanation—which view psychological explanation as a form of functional explanation—have an implausibly high standard of empirical adequacy. When we look at examples of actual explanations, we find that, in practice, psychologists treat as distinct capacities that are instantiated by components that are not entirely independent of one another, for as long as they have evidence that those capacities form part of functionally specialized subsystems. Given the structure of the brain and nervous system, this weaker model of functional explanation is an appropriate model for explaining human psychological capacities and the human perceptual system. The question of whether the human perceptual system consists of five kinds of psychological mechanism is, therefore, the question of whether the brain instantiates five functionally specialized perceptual capacities corresponding to each of the senses.

If our everyday concept of seeing is the concept of a kind of perceptual mechanism, then our capacity to see must be instantiated by a single kind of psychological process. Evidence that vision is instantiated by a single process is evidence that there is a single, functionally significant process whose operation enables us to see. In fact, there is evidence that suggests this is not the case.

The primate visual system comprises a large number of anatomically distinct visual areas, each of which appears to process information about different aspects of the visual scene. Different areas are specialized for processing information about color, motion, pattern, form, depth, and various other attributes (evidence for their function comes from a number of sources, including, for example, deficits following brain damage, evidence of selective responsiveness of neurons in the area, and functional brain imaging (Zeki 1993). There are many interconnections between these areas, among which two significant pathways—a dorsal pathway and a ventral pathway—have been indentified.[26] The primary visual cortex (to which the majority of neurons from the retina ultimately project) makes a different contribution to each pathway so that, although its destruction completely deprives "ventral" neurons of visual input, "dorsal" neurons remain responsive. They do so in virtue of the role played by subcortical visual areas in the dorsal, but not the ventral, pathway. The different cortical and subcortical areas involved in the two pathways suggest the *dual-stream hypothesis*: the hypothesis that these two anatomically distinct pathways implement distinct and relatively functionally independent psychological processes. The strongest support for this hypothesis comes from neuropsychological studies of subjects with brain damage. The cases are relatively well known, and I describe them only briefly.[27]

Cortical blindness is the result of bilateral lesions in the occipital lobe of the brain involving the primary visual cortex. These lesions mean that although the eyes and optic nerve could function normally, subjects cannot see objects in their blind field. We might expect damage to the primary visual cortex to produce complete deafferentation from the retina, but some cortically blind subjects are able to respond to visual stimuli. This phenomenon has become known as blindsight. Subjects with blindsight are unable to report the presence or nature of objects presented in their blind field and so are often said to be visually unaware of such objects. Their residual visual capacity can be detected only when they are placed in forced-choice situations, in which they are encouraged to

---

[26] The dorsal pathway links the primary visual cortex through the middle temporal area to the posterior parietal lobe, and the ventral pathway links the primary visual cortex, through area V4, to the inferotemporal region.

[27] That they function relatively independently of one another was first suggested by studies of brain-lesioned monkeys. This led to a distinction between a "what" and a "where" function—one stream functions to compute information about the size and shape of objects; the other (the dorsal stream) to compute information about its spatial location. The neuropsychological studies I describe later have been taken to show that the distinction should not be understood in terms of the different kinds of information computed by each stream but the use to which the information is put—not a "what" stream and a "where" stream but "vision for judgment" and "vision for action."

make a response either by moving their eyes or by reaching or pointing to a target object that they deny they can see. They are able to discriminate and localize such objects at levels well above chance.

A similar dissociation between awareness and action is found in some subjects with visual agnosia. Subjects with apperceptive agnosia are not blind but are unable to perceive or recognize objects; they can detect visual features and have good acuity but do not experience features as surfaces or as grouped into objects and so cannot perceive shapes or recognize objects.[28] One such subject, DF, suffered damage to her visual cortex following carbon monoxide poisoning. As a result she was unable to recognize everyday objects and faces or identify simple shapes and also had subnormal color perception. She was unable to judge or use her fingers to show how big objects were or in which orientations. Despite these substantial visual impairments, she was normally accurate when object orientation and size were used to guide an action. Although she could not judge when objects were the same or different in shape, when she had to pick up an object, she adjusted her fingers to grip it optimally, and when she had to post a card through a slot, her movements were fluid and accurate even though she could not match the orientation of the slot with another.[29] As with blindsighted subjects, although she lacks visual awareness of properties of objects, DF is able to use visual information about those properties to guide her actions.

Subjects with optic ataxia—typically following damage to the posterior parietal cortex—have visuomotor deficits and are unable to reach accurately for visually presented objects or to accurately grasp an object between finger and thumb or orient a card correctly in order to post it through a slot. They are nonetheless able to make accurate perceptual reports of the location and orientation of visually presented objects, and they can accurately indicate the size of an object with their fingers or rotate a slot to match the orientation of one presented to them. Their difficulty in reaching toward and grasping objects cannot, therefore, be explained in terms of their lacking perceptual awareness of the relevant properties of objects. Nor do they simply have a motor deficit since they can perform nonvisually guided actions normally; they can, for example, reach to places on their own body with normal accuracy. Although the exact form of deficit produced by optic ataxia varies from subject to subject, it is best explained in terms of an underlying deficit in a visuomotor system—that is, a system that functions to produce visually guided

---

[28] Associative agnosics, in contrast, can perceive objects normally but are unable to attach a name to them. For more details, see Farah (1994). The dissociation between vision and action is associated only with apperceptive agnosia.

[29] See Milner and Goodale (1995). Perenin and Rosetti (1996) describe a blindsight patient who was asked to post a card through a slot and grasp blocks in the blind field. Although the subject lacked awareness (could not report, denied seeing, etc.), their posting was accurate, and their grasping was appropriate for the object.

actions—that can be damaged at different points.[30] Subjects with optic ataxia have intact visual perception but an impaired ability to use visual information to guide their actions and therefore show a dissociation between perception and action that is the reverse of that found in subjects with blindsight or agnosia.

In these neuropsychological cases, selective damage to the visual system affecting only one of the two visual pathways produces a visual dissociation. Damage to the ventral pathway leaves subjects unable to perceive visually presented objects but able to use visual information about those objects in guiding their actions; damage to the dorsal stream leaves subjects able to perceive objects but apparently unable to use visual information to guide actions directed toward objects they can see. This pattern of dissociation supports the hypothesis that the two visual pathways implement functionally independent processes: one that enables subjects to use visual information to guide object-directed actions and another that enables the visual perception of objects required for subjects to make judgments about them, form intentions to act on them, and select and discriminate among them.

The problem this poses for the view that in distinguishing the senses we are distinguishing between kinds of sensory mechanism is that there is no *single* mechanism of vision corresponding to our concept of seeing. The evidence I have described suggests that there are at least two distinct mechanisms or processes involved in vision. If there are two mechanisms, then our common-sense concept of vision fails to refer to a single kind of mechanism; that is, it fails to refer.[31] Moreover, if there are two mechanisms, then appealing to perceptual mechanisms will not answer the constitutive question—it will not tell us what all instances of visual perceiving have in common in virtue of which they are instances of seeing.

It might be objected that although the evidence I have described shows that there is more than one visual process, it does not show that our common sense concept of vision fails to refer to a single process. The evidence shows a dissociation between the visual process implemented in the ventral stream, which produces conscious perceptions, and the visual process implemented in the dorsal stream, which controls action. If the reference of our concept of vision is fixed in the way I described earlier, in terms of the causal process that plays a role in producing our perceptions of certain kinds of features of objects, then our concept will refer to the process that plays a role in producing our conscious perceptions, that is, the process implemented in the ventral stream alone. That there is a distinct process that controls action does not show that in thinking

---

[30] Milner and Goodale (1995, 92ff).
[31] The situation is similar to the jadeite/nephrite case that Putnam describes (1975, 241). In effect a presupposition of our reference fixing—that the majority of the things we refer to belong to a single kind—fails.

about the process that produces perception we do not successfully refer to a single psychological process.

There are two replies that can be made to this objection.[32] First, the objection supposes that we think of vision simply as the process that produces conscious perceptions of things and not more generally as the process that produces conscious perceptions of things and enables us to act successfully on things that we can see. However, it is not clear that we do think of vision in that narrower way. Suppose that you pick up an object that you can see. If you were asked why you moved your hand to that place (the place where the object was), you are likely to say that it was because that is where you saw the object to be. It may not have been a conscious perception that guided your action to that place; nonetheless, you appeal to vision in explaining your action. If that is right, then we do not think of vision simply as the process that produces conscious perception, and so our reference-fixing procedures do not pick out only the visual process implemented in the ventral stream.

Second, the objection—even if successful—cannot provide a general method for defending a natural-kinds account of the senses since it applies only to the case of vision, and yet the psychological structure of the visual system, which undermines the claim that vision is not a single capacity, is not unique to vision; it reflects a general organizational principle of the human brain. The processes that instantiate the other senses are similarly modular and task dependent in organization, and we are likely to find that they are not instantiated by a single psychological mechanism. Just this is true for the only other sense that has been studied in any detail: auditory perception.

The functional organization of the auditory system is far less well understood than that of the visual system; however, just as the existence of a number of circumscribed and specific visual deficits provides evidence for modularity in vision, so a number of similarly circumscribed hearing deficits provide similar evidence for the modularity of the auditory system. These deficits include, for example, cortical deafness (deafness caused by damage to the brain rather than the ears); pure word deafness (an inability to understand spoken words despite intact hearing, speech production, and reading ability); auditory agnosia (the auditory analogue of visual apperceptive agnosia); and phonoagnosia (an impaired ability to recognize familiar voices). Since the modules could all be subcomponents of a single processing stream, a modular structure alone is not inconsistent with the existence a single auditory processing system, but three kinds of evidence suggest that these modules are organized into at least two functionally independent systems. The evidence is ana-

---

[32] A third kind of response challenges the idea that the experiential states involved in perception are distinct from those involved in the control of action. For an example of such a challenge, see Nudds (manuscript).

tomical (from nonhuman primates) and neuropsychological[33] and from functional imaging data.

Neurophysiological studies of nonhuman primates have described distinct projections from areas of the auditory cortex that respond to different auditory information, along the dorsal and ventral pathways (Romanski et al. 1999a, 1999b). One of the pathways responds to auditory spatial information, the other to nonspatial information; this suggests that they implement different processes. The suggestion is supported by functional imaging studies. A number of imaging studies, using fMRI and PET, have attempted to determine the extent to which sound identification and sound localization involve different neural pathways. In one such study (Alain et al. 2001) subjects had to say whether two sounds appeared to come from the same or different locations or whether they had the same pitch. Different brain areas, corresponding to the pathways identified anatomically, are activated for the two different tasks. The authors conclude that the neural systems involved in identifying and localizing auditory objects are functionally and neuroanatomically segregated.[34] These results have been reproduced in a number of similar studies.[35]

Subjects with normal hearing can effortlessly recognize a wide range of environmental sounds—such as those produced by dropped objects, poured liquids, and animals—and are often able to localize the source of such sounds on the basis of hearing them. Subjects with auditory agnosia have adequate hearing but are unable to recognize familiar sounds and so are unable, for example, to match a sound to a picture of the kind of object that makes the sound. Although it often occurs together with other auditory deficits, auditory agnosia can occur as a circumscribed disorder. Subjects with spatial hearing deficits may be unable to localize the source of a sound or perceive its motion and so are unable to indicate either the position on their head corresponding to the apparent location of a sound played over headphones or the direction—right to left or left to right—in which the source appears to move.[36] Several case studies have described subjects who are able to perceive the location and movement of the source of sounds but have severe auditory agnosia and so cannot recognize the sounds; other subjects are unable to localize sound

---

[33] The deficits may be double dissociated, which suggests that they should be explained in terms of damage to a functionally specialized or modular system (see Polster and Rose 1998).

[34] Maeder et al. (2001) describes an fMRI study to determine whether auditory information relevant to recognition and localization is processed by distinct neural populations. They found that differences in patterns of activation were apparent in passive listening tests, suggesting that the difference is not due to motor aspects of the task but rather corresponds to an organizational principle of the human auditory cortex.

[35] A recent survey of thirty-six imaging studies (Arnott et al. [2004]) has found that the results were consistent with the two-system model of auditory organization in humans.

[36] The apparent location and movement of sound sources in the azimuthal plane can be varied by changing the interaural time difference of the sound when played over headphones.

sources or perceive movement but have a normal ability to recognize sounds.[37] The deficits are the result of lesions localized in the parts of the brain corresponding to the two anatomically identified pathways. The double dissociation is consistent with the evidence from functional imaging and suggests that the processes that subserve auditory recognition and auditory spatial perception can function independently of one another. This suggests that, as in the case of vision, the auditory system comprises at least two independent, functionally specialized capacities,[38] one of which is involved in sound recognition and the other in the localization of sound sources.[39]

This functional organization undermines the claim that auditory perception involves the operation of a single perceptual mechanism and so undermines the suggestion that in distinguishing the senses we are distinguishing between kinds of sensory mechanism. There is no single auditory mechanism corresponding to our everyday concept of hearing; there are at least two distinct mechanisms. Therefore, our common-sense concept fails to refer. Since both auditory processes contribute to the conscious perception of sounds and their sources (each process enables us to perceive different features of sound sources), the reply I considered to the visual case—that only one of the two processes enables us to perceive and so only one is the reference of our common-sense concept—cannot be made here.

Although I have only considered two senses, the general pattern that emerges suggests that the psychological organization of the perceptual system in general just does not correspond to the distinction we make between five senses. In both cases what we regard as a single sense is implemented in distinct psychological mechanisms. In addition to this fractioning or splitting of mechanisms *within* a sense, evidence is emerging of a great deal of interaction *between* the processes that implement distinct senses.[40] Such multi- or intersensory processes play a role in

---

[37] For example, Clarke et al. (2000) describe four patients with localized brain lesions, two of whom have normal auditory localization and motion detection but severe impairment of auditory sound recognition. Their visual perception was normal.

[38] There may be more than two. Ducommun et al. (2002) describe a patient with circumscribed cortical motion deafness but intact ability to localize sound sources, suggesting that the mechanisms underlying these capacities are distinct. Their data "support the existence of highly specialized and partially overlapping processing networks for both sound localization and sound motion perception" (86).

[39] The two systems in auditory perception are widely described as implementing "what" and "where" processes, which are distinct in virtue of computing different kinds of *information* about sound sources; although the initial characterizations of the two systems in vision was similarly in terms of "what" and "where" (as informationally distinct), they are better characterized as a vision-for-action system and a vision-for-perception system, where both systems may process the same kind of information (both, for example, process spatial information) but each has a different *function*. I know of no attempts to distinguish in audition the role of spatial information in guiding action from the role of spatial information in perception.

[40] Two recent collections presenting some of this evidence are Spence and Driver (2004), and Calvert, Spence, and Stein (2004).

explaining the unified nature of our experience that I described earlier and are responsible for illusions such as the McGurk effect (McGurk and MacDonald 1976). I hope to discuss the implications of these inter-actions—both for an account of the distinction between senses and for perception more generally—on another occasion, but it is worth point-ing out now that the existence of psychological mechanisms that play a role in producing our perceptions and are intersensory is further evi-dence against the suggestion that the senses are psychological kinds. It is not just that a psychological theory of perception distinguishes more sensory processes than we commonly distinguish senses; it distinguishes processes in a way that cross-cuts our common-sense distinction.

I have described evidence that two senses—vision and audition—are not realized by single processes but that perceptions that we commonly categorize as of a single sense may in fact be produced by the operation of two (or more) processes. That, I think, undermines the suggestion that the senses are natural kinds—it undermines the suggestion that the distinction we actually make between different senses tracks a natural distinction between kinds of psychological processes,[41] and it shows that we cannot appeal to the psychological processes involved in perception to answer the question with which I began: What do all instances of seeing have in common in virtue of which they are instances of seeing? Whatever it is they have in common—whatever it is that makes a *visual* perception a *visual* perception—it is not that they are produced by a single kind of sensory mechanism.

The senses are not sensory mechanisms, but does it follow that they are not natural kinds? Couldn't they be a different—nonpsychological—kind of kind? Might they not, for example, be kinds of sense organ or kinds of (neuro-)anatomical structure or mechanisms individuated in terms of their sensitivity to different kinds of energy or stimuli? The answer, I think, is no.

Kinds of anatomical structure are individuated relative to a theory of anatomy, and in general such a theory will make distinctions—in terms of structures of nerves and so on—that are more fine grained than those made by psychological theories. Anatomical structures may be grouped into larger structures in virtue of their functional organi-zation; these larger structures are then individuated in terms of the theory that describes their functional organization. It follows that if the senses are not psychological kinds, then they are not anatomical kinds, either. Psychological theories group together anatomical struc-tures in virtue of their functional organization. If two processes are

---

[41] Of course, psychologists describe the processes as *visual* and auditory processes, but that is just because they both play a role in producing perceptions which common sense labels as visual and auditory. Independently of the fact that we commonly distinguish five senses, the psychological organization of our perceptual system would not give us grounds for distinguishing five kinds of sense.

psychologically distinct, then they will be instantiated by distinct groupings of anatomical structures; conversely, evidence that two processes are not anatomically distinct would be evidence that the processes are not distinct at the psychological level. There are not five kinds of psychological mechanism; therefore, there are not five kinds of anatomical structure, either, and the argument that the senses are not kinds of psychological mechanism entails that the senses are not kinds of anatomical structure.

There are well-known and decisive objections to the idea that the senses might be kinds of sense organ. These objections point out that there can be no explanation of why we distinguish five kinds of sense organ, which is independent of the fact that we distinguish five kinds of sense modality[42] and hence that appealing to kinds of sense organ will not explain why we distinguish five senses. The very same objection can be made to the suggestion that in distinguishing senses we are distinguishing perceptions that are produced by different kinds of stimuli. Although the perceptions we distinguish are brought about by processes that involve sensitivity to different kinds of stimuli, there can be no explanation of why we distinguish five senses in terms of the stimuli that bring them about. Different kinds of stimuli produce perceptions we commonly think of as perceptions of a single sense, and the same kind of stimulus can produce perceptions that we commonly think of as of different senses. Light shades into heat, sound waves into felt vibrations, smell into taste, and so on.

There is a reason for thinking that if the senses are natural kinds, then they must be psychological kinds. If our concepts of the senses are natural-kind concepts, then their references will be fixed in terms of how our perceptions are brought about. An account of how our perceptions are brought about will be an account that explains those perceptions; an account that explains perceptions will be a psychological account.[43] If, therefore, we distinguish the perceptions of different senses in terms of the way they were brought about, then we are distinguishing them in terms of the kinds of psychological mechanisms or process that produced them. So if our concepts of the five senses are natural-kind concepts, then they are concepts of kinds of psychological mechanisms, and if the senses are not kinds of psychological mechanisms, then they are not natural kinds.

I have argued that, for the two senses that I have examined at least, a necessary condition for their being natural kinds is not met, and hence

---

[42] See, for example, Roxbee Cox (1970, 533/this volume, p. 103).
[43] Explanations must capture significant generalizations, and generalizations across perceptual states will be at the psychological level; a perceptual state is also a physical state, but a physical explanation of a perceptual state will be too specific to explain the occurrence of a kind of perceptual state: The perceptual state could occur even if the physical state did not.

our concepts of those senses do not refer to natural kinds. This conclusion follows because there are not five kinds of sensory mechanism
corresponding to our common-sense concepts of five senses. Whatever
those common-sense concepts are concepts of, they cannot be concepts
of kinds of sensory mechanism and so are not natural-kind concepts.

It might be objected that this conclusion follows only if our common-
sense distinction is correct and we really do have five senses. What reason is there to conclude from the fact that there are not five sensory
mechanisms that our concepts are not natural-kind concepts rather than
that our common-sense distinction is mistaken? Does the psychological
evidence not show that in fact we have more than five senses?

Our folk-scientific concepts are often wrong. The situation with
respect to our common-sense concepts of the senses would be the same
as that with respect to many other common-sense distinctions or classifications. In these other cases, if we discover that our concepts do not
correspond to natural kinds, we revise our concepts. When it was discovered that jade and nephrite, instances of which we treated as being
of the same kind, are in fact of different kinds, we did not conclude that
our concepts were not concepts of kinds of minerals but that we were
mistaken. If we thought that, then we would be adopting an error theory
of the senses. We make a distinction between five senses, but the distinction we make is wrong.

In the case of the five senses, it is more plausible to think that our
concepts are not concepts of natural kinds than that the distinction is
mistaken. This is for two reasons. First, the initial reason for claiming
that our concepts might be concepts of natural kinds is that, if true, it
explains the distinction we make between different senses. However,
if there are no natural kinds corresponding to our concepts, then the
claim does not explain the distinction, and that reason is undermined.
To maintain an error theory of the senses, we need some additional reason for thinking that our common-sense concepts are (failed) natural-
kind concepts.

The second, and more decisive, reason is that our concepts of the five
senses are common-sense folk psychological concepts, as central as any
to our understanding of ourselves and others. For most, if not all, folk
psychological states, being in a state of one kind rather than another
matters; it has some explanatory significance, often because being in
that kind of state has consequences for one's behavior—one's judgments
and actions. In giving an account of folk psychological states, in saying
what makes them different from one another, we aim to spell out these
consequences; in giving an account of what is characteristic of different
kinds of psychological states we must give an account of their explanatory significance. It is plausible to think that concepts of these different
states are part of our folk psychological repertoire of concepts *because* of
the explanatory significance that being in one rather than another such
state has.

Now the problem with an error theory of some common-sense folk-psychological concept or distinction is that it rules out the possibility of giving any account of the explanatory significance of the concept or distinction. This is because concepts that fail to refer cannot feature in true explanations; the concept of vision fails to refer, so that someone sees something cannot be explanatory of any of that person's subsequent behavior. If we think that the fact that someone sees something is explanatory, and if in general we think that the distinction we make between different senses has an explanatory significance, then we should reject an error theory of the senses.[44]

So where does that leave my attempt to say what a sense modality is? There are, I think, a number of options. First, my suggestion that, in distinguishing perceptions into the perceptions of different senses, we are distinguishing them on the basis of how they were produced could be rejected. That suggestion depended in part on the idea that experience is transparent to introspection. If that is wrong, then perhaps there are differences in the character of the experiences involved in the perceptions of different senses. Or one might suggest that two experiences can differ in their phenomenological character without differing in the objects and properties to which we can attend in introspecting them. Grice held such a view and suggested that the senses can be distinguished by appeal to the special character of our experience, which "resists both inspection and description" (Grice 1967, 259/this volume, 93).

Alternatively, we might hold on to the idea that the senses are psychological mechanisms and adopt a kind of moderate error theory. Common sense is right in distinguishing perceptions on the basis of how they were produced but wrong in making the distinctions as it does. This suggestion takes seriously the idea that common-sense psychology is a kind of protoscientific psychology, liable to revision in the light of empirical discoveries.

Alternatively, we could accept that in distinguishing different perceptions we are distinguishing them on the basis of how they were produced but give up on the idea that we can explain or give an account of the different ways that perceptions are produced that is independent of our practice of making the distinction. According to this approach, all visual perceptions are produced in the same way, and different ways of perceiving are individuated relative to a social practice of explaining and understanding behavior. On this view a sense modality is what might be called a *social* kind rather than a *natural* kind. Such an account may provide the best account of what a sense modality, as we commonly understand it, actually is.[45]

---

[44] In Nudds (2003) I argue from the need to give an account of the significance of our concepts of different senses to a more anthropocentric account of the nature of the senses.

[45] I outline and defend a view of this kind in Nudds (2003).

References

Alain, C., S. Arnott, S. Hevenor, S. Graham, and C. Grady. 2001. "What" and "Where" in the Human Auditory System. *Proceedings of the National Academy of Sciences* 98(21): 12301–306.

Arnott, S., M. Binns, C. Grady, and C. Alain. 2004. Assessing the Auditory Dual-Pathway Model in Humans. *Neuroimage* 22: 401–408.

Bertelson, Paul, and Beatrice de Gelder. 2004. The Psychology of Multimodal Perception. In *Crossmodal Space and Crossmodal Attention*, ed. C. Spence and J. Driver. pp.141–78 New York: Oxford University Press.

Calvert, Gemma, Charles Spence, and Barry E. Stein. 2004. *The Handbook of Multisensory Processes*. Cambridge, Mass.: MIT Press.

Churchland, Patricia. 1989. *Neurophilosophy: Toward a Unified Science of the Mind-Brain*. Cambridge, Mass.: MIT Press.

Clarke, S., A. Bellmann, R. A. Meuli, G. Assal, and A. Steck. 2000. Auditory Agnosia and Auditory Spatial Deficits following Left Hemispheric Lesions: Evidence for Distinct Processing Pathways. *Neuropsychologia* 38: 797–807.

Cowey, Alan. 1979. Cortical Maps and Visual Perception. Grindley Memorial Lecture. *Quarterly Journal of Experimental Psychology* 31(1) (February): 1–17.

Cummins, Robert. 1983. *The Nature of Psychological Explanation*. Cambridge, Mass.: MIT Press.

Ducommun, C. Y., M. M. Murray, G. Thut, A. Bellmann, I. Viaud-Delmon, S. Clarke, and C. M. Michel. 2002. Segregated Processing of Auditory Motion and Auditory Location: An ERP Mapping Study. *Neuroimage* 16(1): 76–88.

Farah, Martha J. 1994. Neuropsychological Inference with an Interactive Brain: A Critique of the "Locality" Assumption. *Behavioral and Brain Sciences* 17: 43–104.

———. 2004. *Visual Agnosia*, 2nd ed. Cambridge, Mass.: MIT Press.

Fodor, Jerry. 1968. *Psychological Explanation: An Introduction to the Philosophy of Psychology*. New York: Random House.

———. 1983. *Modularity of Mind*. Cambridge, Mass.: MIT Press.

———. 1990. Précis of Modularity of Mind. In *A Theory of Content and Other Essays*. pp.195.206 Cambridge, Mass.: MIT Press.

Grice, H. P. 1967. Some Remarks about the Senses. In *Studies in the Way of Words*, ed. H. P. pp. 248–67 Grice. Cambridge, Mass.: Harvard.

Howes, David. 1991. *The Varieties of Sensory Experience: A Sourcebook in the Anthropology of the Senses*. Vol. 1, *Anthropological Horizons*. London: University of Toronto Press.

Hurley, Susan, and Matthew Nudds, eds. 2006. *Rational Animals?* New York: Oxford University Press.

Keeley, Brian L. 2002. Making Sense of the Senses: Individuating Modalities in Humans and Other Animals. *Journal of Philosophy* 99: 5–28.

Lewkowicz, David J., and Kimberley S. Kraebel. 2004. The Value of Multisensory Redundancy in the Development of Intersensory Perception. In *The Handbook of Multisensory Processes*, ed. G. Calvert, C. Spence, and B. E. Stein. pp.655–80 Cambridge, Mass.: MIT Press.

Maeder, P. P., R. A. Meuli, M. Adriani, A. Bellmann, E. Fornari, J. P. Thiran, A. Pittet, and S. Clarke. 2001. Distinct Pathways Involved in Sound Recognition and Localization: A Human fMRI Study. *Neuroimage* 14(4): 802–16.

Marr, David. 1982. *Vision*. New York: Freeman.

Martin, M. G. F. 1997. The Shallows of the Mind. *Proceedings of the Aristotelian Society*, Suppl. 71(1): 75–91.

McGurk, H., and J. W. MacDonald. 1976. Hearing Lips and Seeing Voices. *Nature* 264: 746–48.

Millikan, Ruth. 2005. Why (Most) Kinds Are Not Classes. In *Language: A Biological Model*. pp. 106–20. New York: Oxford University Press.

Milner, A. David, and Melvyn A. Goodale. 1995. *The Visual Brain in Action*. New York: Oxford University Press.

Nudds, Matthew. 2003. The Significance of the Senses. *Proceedings of the Aristotelian Society* 104(1): 31–52.

———. 2007. Manuscript. Visually Guided Action and the Directive Content of Experience. http://homepages.ed.ac.uk/mnudds/papers/shtm.pdf.

O'Neill, Daniella K., Janet Astington, and John H. Flavell. 1992. Young Children's Understanding of the Role That Sensory Experiences Play in Knowledge Acquisition. *Child Development* 63: 474–90.

Perenin, M., and Y. Rossetti. 1996. Grasping in an Hemianopic Field: Another Instance of Dissociation between Perception and Action. *Neuroreport* 7(3): 793–97.

Polster, Michael, and Sally Rose. 1998. Disorders of Auditory Processing: Evidence for Modularity in Audition. *Cortex* 34: 47–65.

Povinelli, D. J., and T. J. Eddy. 1996. *What Young Chimpanzees Know about Seeing. Monographs of the Society for Research in Child Development*, serial no. 247, 61(2): 1–151. Malden, Mass.: Blackwell.

Putnam, Hilary. 1975. The Meaning of "Meaning." In *Mind Language and Reality: Philosophical Papers*, vol. 2. New York: Cambridge University Press.

Romanski, L. M., J. F. Bates, and P. S. Goldman-Rakic. 1999a. Auditory Belt and Parabelt Projections to the Prefrontal Cortex in the Rhesus Monkey. *Journal of Comparative Neurology* 403(2): 141–57.

Romanski, L. M., B. Tian, J. Fritz, M. Mishkin, P. S. Goldman-Rakic, and J. P. Rauschecker. 1999b. Dual Streams of Auditory Afferents Target Multiple Domains in the Primate Prefrontal Cortex. *Nature Neuroscience* 2(12): 1131–36.

Roxbee Cox, J. W. 1970. Distinguishing the Senses. *Mind* 79: 530–50.

Shallice, Tim. 1988. *From Neuropsychology to Mental Structure*. New York: Cambridge University Press.

Spence, Charles, and Jon Driver. 2004. *Crossmodal Space and Crossmodal Attention*. New York: Oxford University Press.

Squire, L. R. 1989. Mechanisms of Memory. In *Molecules to Models: Advances in Neuroscience*, ed. K. L. Kelner and D. E. Koshland. pp. 235–50. Washington, D.C.: American Association for the Advancement of Science.

Yaniv, Ilan, and Marilyn Shatz. 1988. Children's understanding of perceptibility. In *Developing Theories of Mind*, ed. J. W. Astington, P. L. Harris, and D. R. Olson. New York: Cambridge University Press.

Zeki, Semir. 1993. *A Vision of the Brain*. Oxford: Blackwell Scientific.

17

Tastes, Temperatures, and Pains

A. D. Smith

This essay does not directly address the core topic of the present volume: that of how we distinguish between the various senses. It does, however, address a problem that arises only because of certain ways in which the senses do differ from one another. More precisely, it arises because of the differences in the ways that our senses are able to function perceptually.

I have written just now of the *ability* of a sensory modality to function perceptually since I reject the common equation of what is sensory with what is perceptual. As I argue in my book on perception (Smith 2002, 125–32), any sense modality, where this is understood simply as a way of experiencing sensory qualities, or qualia, can function either perceptually or nonperceptually. In the latter case, what the sense gives rise to are mere sensations, not perceptions. In order for a sense to function perceptually it must be able to give us experiences that are as of objects distinct from the experiences themselves. When I hear a sound, I have an auditory experience. However, *what* I hear, the *object* of the experience, is presented as having characteristics that are quite different from any experience. A sound is usually heard as being at or coming from a location some distance away from me; its spatial relation to me can change, and it is presented to me as something whose existence does not depend on me. Only when an experience has an object ostensibly possessing such features of independence and distinctness from me is such an experience phenomenologically perceptual in character. No type of experience, qualitatively characterized in terms of the sensory qualities experienced, is necessarily perceptual in character in this way. A baby in the womb may have a ringing in its ears. This is an auditory experience, clearly akin to the perception of sounds. However, there would, phenomenologically, be no object distinct from the experience for the baby. What we have in such a case is a mere auditory sensation. Such a baby may also have visual experiences—of darkness or "brain gray," as psychologists call it, as we do when we close our eyes, and it may experience phosphenes. None of this would amount to more than mere visual sensation.

If, however, it is true that no type of experience, specified in terms of the sensory qualities (or qualia) of which it affords enjoyment, is necessarily perceptual in phenomenological character, we need some account of what it is, over and above the sheer qualitative character of an experience, that makes it perceptual in character. In Smith (2002), I suggest that there are, in fact, three grounds for perceptual consciousness, which may operate independently of one another. Because of this independence, the senses can differ over which ground it is that is being exploited so as to make them more than the mere generators of sensation. Since the problem that I propose to address here arose for me precisely because of the threefold source of perceptual consciousness that I accept, I briefly sketch this tripartite theory, if only so that the problem I have in mind can emerge clearly as a problem for the reader.

One source of perceptual consciousness is phenomenal three-dimensionality. Here an object is presented a distinct from one in virtue of being presented as at a spatial distance. Not all perceptual experiences are phenomenally three dimensional, however. Consider the case of the subjects of Molyneux's question *before* any operation to restore their sight. Before an operation such subjects, although unable to see anything as being at any distance from them, are not completely blind. They are able to see light and darkness—*physical* light and darkness. Vision, for them, though extremely rudimentary, is perceptual in character despite its lack of three-dimensionality because their visual experiences are what I term "kinetically structured." What I mean by this is that such experience features what psychologists call "position constancy." When such subjects see a light and move their head while looking at the light, the light will change location in the visual field, but it will not appear to move. No such thing is possible at the level of mere sensation, and it gives to the objects of experience a distinctness from the experience itself that suffices for perceptual consciousness. The third source of perceptual consciousness is what, after Fichte, I call the *Anstoss*. This is the sense of something resisting one's movement, as when one grasps or bumps into an object. In such cases one's active movement is *checked* by the solidity of the object. In my view, any sense, in order to be perceptual, must feature at least one of these basic perceptual phenomena.[1]

---

[1] At the conference from which this volume arose, John Heil suggested "whiteout" as a possible counter-example to this claim. We are to imagine a subject so completely surrounded by uniform whiteness that, visually, a *Ganzfeld* is produced. There would be no three-dimensional depth to such a visual experience; position constancy would not be in play, however much the subjects moved their eyes or head, because of the uniformity of the surroundings, and the *Anstoss* is irrelevant because we are dealing with the sense of sight. Yet surely this is or could be a genuine perception. The whiteness experienced might be that of, say, a blizzard. This kind of example is, in fact, implicitly covered by what I say in Smith (2002, 179–80) about preoperative Molyneux subjects, but the point needs to be made more explicitly. Consider subjects who are looking at a stationary light without themselves moving. Before these subjects move their head or eyes, position constancy is not actually in play. Nevertheless, it is *operative* for that sense—which is why,

The sense of taste, however, would seem not to be accounted for by the aforementioned theory. Experience of a flavor as such is not phenomenally three-dimensional in character, nor does it feature position constancy, nor does it involve the *Anstoss*. In Smith (2002) my response to this fact is to say that taste is a *derivatively* (or *dependently*) perceptual sense. We hold that we can taste *objects* in our mouths (and not merely "have a taste" in our mouths, as we say) only because we *feel* them there. Gustatory perception requires tactile perception in order to acquire an object distinct from itself; and tactile perception is intrinsically perceptual in virtue of featuring either position constancy or the *Anstoss*. In the absence of an object being felt in one's mouth, one's gustatory experience would be mere sensation. The distinctive flavors that we experience in this sense modality are attributed to objects only because they are experienced while feeling such objects.

It is not only the sense of taste that exhibits such touch-dependent perception, though it is the only sense where it is found across the board. It is also found, for example, in the perception of surface temperature. It, too, as reflection should indicate, is intrinsically bereft of any of three basic sources of perceptual consciousness. I believe that we are once again dealing with a case of derived perception. We can take ourselves to be perceiving a warm or cold object only because we are aware of that object through touch. It is the sense of touch that originally presents the object as a distinct object of perception, and it is on the basis of this perception that various qualities of heat and cold are attributed to that very object. In the absence of such tactile perception, any sensations of heat would be merely that. Such mere sensations would give us at most an awareness that a part of our body was warm or cold.[2]

I can now state the problem that I wish to address. In fact, in order to appreciate this problem, you do not have to endorse the tripartite perceptual theory I have just sketched. All that is required is that you accept something that that theory entails but that might be accepted independently: namely, that taste perception and the perception of surface temperature are cases of dependent perception. It is specifically this fact that gives rise to the problem in question. The problem is this: Why

---

when the subjects do move, such constancy actually comes into play. It formerly was not in play simply because of the contingencies of the situation: namely, the absence of relative movement between subject and perceived object. The same holds for the whiteout situation. It is the contingencies of the perceptual situation—in this case, the uniformity of the stimulus—that explain why position constancy is not actually in play. Nevertheless, such constancy is operative because if there were, say, a dark patch in the otherwise white surroundings, and the subject moved while seeing it, position constancy would actually come into play. It is (and was) my view that, in the absence of the other two grounds, it is necessary for perceptual consciousness that position constancy be *operative*—not necessarily in play. I thank Professor Heil for forcing me to clarify this point.

[2] And not necessarily even that. The body itself has to be "constituted," to use a Husserlian term, and mere sensation cannot achieve this. For more on this issue see Smith (2002, 155–58).

do we not attribute (some) *pains* to "external" physical objects? After all, the situation with some pains would seem to be very similar to that with our perception of flavors and surface temperature. If I put my hand on a very hot object so that it burns me, the pain I feel seems to occur in tandem with the tactile perception of the object in just the way that a milder experience of heat does. Indeed, pains sometimes have an even more precise correlation with the tactile perception of an object than do some derived perceptions. When a very tasty morsel is in the mouth, for example, its flavor can fill the whole mouth (and, indeed, extend beyond, into the nasal passages). When I touch a burning object, however, the burning pain is felt precisely in that part of the body that is touching the object. Some sorts of pain are not like this, of course. Headaches and stomachaches are not experienced in tandem with the tactile perception of any alien body. The question, however, is why those pains that *do* occur in tandem with tactile perception never acquire derivative perceptual status.[3]

Before addressing this question, however, I would like to say a little more about the claim that we do not attribute pains to physical objects.[4] For the very idea that we might do so may strike one as silly. A pain, after all, is a kind of experience. So, to attribute a pain to a mere physical object, such as a pin that is sticking in you, would be to credit it with an experience (i.e., to regard it as sentient), and that is silly. Now, this may be true (indeed, I think it is), but simply to assert it is not adequate since such mere assertion is open to the following rejoinder. It is not pain that is an experience, but our experience of pain. So the question can perhaps be reformulated as follows: When we experience pain, why do we not attribute—not the experience itself, but—*what* we experience to a physical object? Alternatively, when we experience a pain, what we are aware of has a certain character or quality: It is stinging in the case of nettles, burning in the case of fire, and so on. Why do we not attribute those *qualities* to physical objects? If we did, the idea goes, we should not be attributing any experiences to those objects but only qualities that we can and do experience. To this, in turn, one may object that with pains there is no distinction between act and object of

---

[3] In this essay I focus on pain, but the same issue may be thought to arise for any type of bodily sensation that can be felt on the surface of one's body. We can imagine, for example, a certain sort of tingling sensation occurring on the skin when and only when, by and large, a certain kind of object is touched. A full discussion of this issue is not possible here, but I would make one brief point. Such other sensations involve some degree of discomfort or unease. I think that my remarks about painfulness can be applied to such cases because of this. If, however, there are or could be bodily sensations that are not uncomfortable and can be experienced on the surface of the body, then I see no reason in principle why they should not attain derivative perceptual status.

[4] We attribute pains to our bodies, of course, or at least locate them there, and our bodies are "physical objects." The qualification that the physical objects to which we do not attribute pains are objects other than our own bodies should always be understood in what follows.

awareness. Pains are mere sensations or modes of feeling. This, however, merely begs the question. More precisely, it fails to address the question why, when a pain is felt in tandem with a tactile perception, a distinction between act and object is not introduced. It is, indeed, my own view that, in the absence of suitable tactile experience, experiences of taste and of heat and cold are mere sensations. Only when taste and temperature qualities are experienced in tandem with the tactile perception of an object are they taken to be qualities of an object that is distinct from our experience of it. However, when such a harnessing of two sensory modalities in this way does occur, a phenomenological distinction between experience and object structures the entire experience. The question is why this does not occur in the case of pains. Relatedly, it might be said that the reason we do not attribute pains to physical objects is that they are subjectively located in our own bodies. That is where they are felt to be. The question is, however, why this is so. For, independently of association with tactile perception, sensations of taste and of heat and cold would, I hold, be simply located in our bodies. When, however, they occur in tandem with feeling an object, flavors and temperatures are attributed to the object. The question is why this does not occur in the case of pains.

I have been assuming that we do not treat experiences of pain as perceptual: at least not as constituting perceptions of objects other than our own bodies. This has, however, been denied by at least one writer: "Pain can be accepted as a sense in the way in which smell is a sense. We can smell smells, and we can pain pains" (McKenzie 1967–1968, 189). I do not propose to discuss this bizarre suggestion. I mention it because of a response that it elicited from George Pitcher. His principal objection to the proposal was that it is incompatible with our concept of pain. One reason that Pitcher's response is unsatisfying is that he admits that "we might have the concept of pain that he [McKenzie] sketches in place of the one we actually do have" (Pitcher 1968–1969, 103). In fact, I do not think that is true. Nonetheless, if it were, we would need some account of why we do not have this alternative concept of pain, and that account would have to consider the character of our experience of pain. It is surely because of the nature of pain experience that our concept of pain is what it is. Examining this nature is what this essay is about. In any case, I am not really interested in our "concept" of pain. What concerns me is the nature of the *experience* of pain. Why is it, phenomenologically, not perceptual in character, that is, why does it not ostensibly present an object distinct from the experience itself?

I now consider a number of suggestions as to why, indeed, we do not attribute pains (or pain qualities) to external physical objects. We can be helped to home in on the correct answer to our question by seeing why all of these suggestions are inadequate. I begin with a well-known paper by Grice, in which he makes a number of such suggestions (Grice 1962, 134–35/this volume, pp. 84–85). One of his suggestions is that pains "are not greatly variegated, except in intensity and location." Heat perception, however, is even less variegated. There is a variety of different kinds of pains (stinging, aching, burning, gnawing, etc.), whereas in perceiving temperatures we experience qualities that differ, apart from location and duration, either solely in the degree to which a single quality is present or solely in the degree to which two qualities are present (depending on whether you think of hot and cold as varieties of a single determinable quality or as being two different qualities). Again, we can easily imagine taste being a much more rudimentary sense than it is, giving us a far more restricted range of tastes. That would hardly deprive it of perceptual status.

Another of Grice's suggestions is that almost any object can inflict pain on us, so that "our pains are on the whole very poor guides to the character of the things that hurt us." However, is looking blue, say, even in normal circumstances and for a normal observer, a good guide to the character of the thing that thus appears? It is a good guide to a thing's being blue, of course, but then inflicting pain is a good guide to a thing's being a source of pain. If, however, what is being required is that a genuinely perceptible quality be a good guide to some independently specifiable character of the thing, then being (or looking) blue is no such guide. What, after all, apart from being blue, do a bluebell and a blue sky have interestingly in common? Conversely, some pains are quite distinctive of the objects that give rise to them. Just think of a nettle sting.

The two previous suggestions, moreover, share an additional fault in that they both imply that it is an empirical matter—we need to wait and see—whether a certain experience is phenomenologically perceptual or a mere sensation. We would have to discover through experience that pains are not greatly variegated in nature and that they can be inflicted upon us by a wide range of objects. So, before we made such discoveries, pains should be perceptual for us. This is surely absurd. For this additional reason, therefore, Grice's first two suggestions are seriously wide of the mark. If we are to learn why pain experiences are not perceptual character, it can only be by discerning something about the character of pain experience itself as it occurs. In addition, this must be a matter either of the qualitative character of such experiences or of the way in which the experience of pain itself relates (or does not relate) to the experience of feeling an object. The next few suggestions focus on the latter possibility.

There is, suggests Grice, "no one standard procedure for getting a pain." He contrasts this with the case of smell, where the procedure in question is inhaling. There is, however, no "procedure" at all for perceiving radiant and ambient heat or for hearing sounds (just think of alarm clocks). Perhaps the suggestion is that with pains there *is* a "procedure," but no standard one. Consider this question: "Is a brick painful?" Insofar as we are inclined to answer such a question at all, the answer can only be that it depends. A brick is not painful if I pick it up; it is if I drop it on my foot. So, the suggestion would go, it is not objects per se that are painful but events involving objects. This explains why we do not attribute pain qualities to the objects themselves. The problem with this suggestion is that there *is* a standard procedure for coming by many pains: namely, touching a relevant object. This is why we talk about various kinds of object as being "painful to the touch."

In fact, Grice allows that, in some few cases where there is a standard procedure for acquiring a pain in relation to a certain kind of object, it is appropriate to describe that kind of object as "painful." The example he gives is a thumbscrew. Because there is a standard procedure here, we can describe this "as being a painful instrument." Our present concern, however, is not with the question of the appropriateness of describing things, with or without qualification, as "painful." Our present concern is with whether we attribute pains or pain qualities to objects. Even if we are perhaps happy to describe a thumbscrew as painful, we do not suppose that it possesses the quality we are so painfully aware of when it is applied to us. Since we do not do this even in relation to objects where there is a "standard procedure," the presence or absence of such a procedure is irrelevant to the issue we are concerned with.

Another suggestion, not from Grice, is that pains (of the sort we are concerned with) persist after we stop touching the relevant object. Pain experiences are not sensitive to the presence or absence of a relevant physical object—something that is the hallmark of perception. Unfortunately, precisely the same thing is found with taste. Sometimes we say that we just cannot get a certain taste "out of my mouth." In such cases, no doubt, particles of the physical object in question remain in the mouth. Experientially, however, we are not aware of this but only of the persisting taste. Perhaps a taste is less intense when a tasty object is not actually in contact with the tongue, but this is also true of some pains that result from contact with a physical object.

A final suggestion derives from Wittgenstein's brief discussion of "pain patches" (Wittgenstein 1978, §312). What seems to be crucial in this suggestion that we might attribute patches of pain to the surfaces of certain objects is that part, but only part, of a surface should cause pain when we touch it. I cannot see that this is of any real significance. Not every part of a nettle stings us, but only its leaves (and sometimes not all of them do). Indeed, not all parts of a suitable nettle-leaf sting, but only its top surface. Even if the part of a nettle leaf that can sting us were restricted to a small central area, I cannot think that this would lead us to attribute pain qualities to those areas. Some parts of the surface of an automobile engine are painfully hot (when it is running), and others not, but we do not (and would not easily be induced to) talk of pain patches here. Nor do we in the case of certain modern electric stoves in which the heating elements are located under a continuous surface. There might be "heat patches" when the stove is turned on perhaps, but not "pain patches." It is not clear, from Wittgenstein's very brief discussion, that the idea of pain patches is supposed to involve the attribution of *pain qualities* to physical objects. Only if it does, however, is it relevant to the present discussion. However, if it does, I find the suggestion wholly implausible.

I cannot think of any more relations between the experiences of pain and the objects that inflict them that might plausibly be cited as constituting a disanalogy to all perceptual situations, so I now turn to a consideration of the intrinsic, qualitative character of pain in the hope of finding the answer to our question.

What do all pains have in common in terms of felt quality? Only, as far as I can see, one thing: They are *painful*. I take this as a primitive experiential term.[5] It cannot, for example, be analyzed in terms of dislike, aversion, or "negative affect." Since there are plenty of things other than physical pain to which we are averse, there can certainly be no simple equation here. However, nor can there be, as far as I can see, a more complex analysis, such as one that brings in a reference to intensity, such as the following: Pain is that which, at greatest intensity, we are most averse to. The Christian martyrs were considerably more averse to renouncing their faith than they were to suffering the most extreme agonies. This objection cannot be deflected by suggesting that the aversion in question be instinctive or unacquired. One might have such an instinctive horror of, say, a spider or a horribly distorted face that one would much rather suffer extreme pain than be subjected to the presence of such a thing. Nevertheless, even if it is true that the only thing that pains have essentially in common is their painfulness, it may seem far from clear how this fact can help us to answer our question about why we do not attribute pain qualities to physical objects. In what remains of this essay I attempt to make out the case.

The pains that we are concerned with are those that occur in tandem with the tactile perception of objects. Let us consider the latter in a little more detail. When you touch an object and thereby feel it, two experiences of perceptual significance typically occur: the *Anstoss* (resistance to your activity) and pressure sensations. As I argue in Smith (2002), these two are independent of one another. Either can occur in the absence of the other, though typically they do not. In that book I somewhat downplay the significance of pressure sensations in favor of the *Anstoss*. The reason for this is that I primarily argue there that no type of sensation, qualitatively specified, not even a pressure sensation, is essentially perceptual in character.[6] Nevertheless,

---

[5] "Pain" and "hurt" are commonly applied to things other than "physical" pain. The death of a friend will pain one, and someone's "cutting" words can hurt one. I regard these as metaphorical extensions of the basic sense of these terms, which applies only to "physical" pain.

[6] The *Anstoss*, by contrast, is not to be accounted for in terms of sensations and is intrinsically perceptual in character. See Smith (2002, 159–60).

pressure sensations certainly can be and indeed typically are perceptual. How does this come about? The most obvious way in which pressure sensations can acquire perceptual value is through association with the *Anstoss*.[7] When you touch an object, the felt check to your movement commonly goes together with the resisting object's causing pressure sensations in the part of your body in contact with that object. Through association with the *Anstoss* pressure sensations acquire perceptual value, so that even when they are subsequently experienced in the absence of any resistance to any action of yours, it will immediately seem to you that an object is touching you. In such circumstances, as when a fly lands on your arm, pressure sensations have the status of *acquired perceptions*.[8] The notion of an acquired perception is different from that of a "dependent perception," which I have already introduced—and in two ways. First, an experience in a certain sensory modality has the status of a dependent (or derived) perception only if it is necessary that, whenever such perception occurs, perception of the same object in some other sense modality also occurs. There is no such necessity where acquired perception is concerned. Second, dependent perception is not based on past association, whereas acquired perception essentially is.[9]

Although in my book I somewhat downplay the role of pressure sensations in tactile perception, in the present context we need to focus on this role because, although the *Anstoss*, in the absence of any pressure sensations, can indeed give us perceptual awareness of a resistant physical object, it seems to me that it, even when accompanied by, for example, heat sensations in the part of the body in contact with the touched object, would not constitute perceptual awareness of that object as, say, warm. Imagine that a person's hand is selectively desensitized. This person experiences no pressure sensations in his hand, but he can feel heat sensations when a warm object is placed on it. Suppose that this person presses against a warm object. Through the *Anstoss* he perceives the resistant object, though without any pressure sensations. He also feels heat in his hand. It seems to me that this subject would not immediately take the heat to be that of the impinging object.[10] To feel the heat of a

---

[7] There is another way as well, which I mention in Smith (2002, 154–55). Pressure sensations can be felt while you move a part of your body across the surface of an object. This can feature position constancy, which is one of the three sources of perceptual consciousness.

[8] I mention acquired perception at three points in Smith (2002, 144, 158, 174).

[9] I am not suggesting that mere association is enough to generate acquired perception, but I cannot explore here what the fuller story might be.

[10] Since sensitivity to temperature can indeed be preserved in the absence of any sensitivity to touch, this claim is open to empirical refutation. Unfortunately, I have been unable to find any direct test of my hypothesis. The closest I have come to relevant findings are the following two cases, both inconclusive. "Since he has normal perception of warmth and touch in the face, but only of warmth in the hand, it is interesting that he cannot, or does not, use warmth of the hand alone to identify self from non-self" (Cole 1995, 85). This may seem direct confirmation of my contention. I should point out,

physical object is to be *sensitive* to the presence of that object in a particular part of your body—the part that is in contact with the object. To
feel a warm object against your skin is to feel a *warm surface* or, at a min-
imum, a *warm pressure*. If only the *Anstoss* were giving you perception
of the object through touch, you would not be sensitive to the object's
presence against your skin *at the point of contact*. When, in normal circumstances, you feel a warm object against your skin, your experience
of the pressure and of the heat meld into one, so that the heat seems to
be the heat of what you feel pressing against your skin. In the case of
heat sensations accompanied merely by the *Anstoss*, I cannot see that
any such melding would take place since your perceptual awareness of
an impinging object is not constituted by any sensitivity to that object at
the point of contact.[11] All of this applies *mutatis mutandis* to the perception of taste. Both sorts of perception are not just dependent on tactile
perception of an object but are also specifically dependent on pressure
sensations functioning perceptually. In order for temperature and taste
sensations to become derivatively perceptual we need a *dual sensitivity*
at a single place on our skin to an impinging object—something that the
Anstoss cannot afford.

If any pains were to have the status of touch-dependent perceptions,
they would have to involve just such a dual sensitivity at the point of
contact with an object. Furthermore, once again, for essentially the
same reasons as earlier, this would have to involve a melding of pain
sensations with, specifically, pressure sensations. The *Anstoss*, again, is
irrelevant. So, if pains indeed cannot attain such perceptual status, it
must be because they do not and cannot meld with pressure sensations
in the way required for a dual sensitivity to an object. The crucial question now is, Why not? Some pains do, after all, occur in tandem with
pressure sensations in a way that may seem very similar to the way that
heat sensations occur in tandem with pressure sensations when we feel
a warm object. Suppose, for example, that the point of a pencil is resting on your skin and you feel it. The pressure is increased, and it starts

---

however, that the subject in question here, Ian Waterman, was so severely impaired that
not only did he experience no touch sensations below the neck, but even the *Anstoss*
was all but absent as well. (On this last point, see further Cole and Sedgwick [1992].)
Another report mentions a deafferented subject who, surprisingly, had managed to tell,
with eyes closed, that her arm, which was resting on a tabletop, had been moved by
the experimenter. In response to the question how she had managed to do this, "she
explained very clearly that the table surface was cool and she thereby felt the shift of her
arm" (Paillard 1999, 203). This latter finding may seem to count against my suggestion.
Nothing, however, is said in the report to rule out the subject's knowledge that the table
was cold being inferential.

[11] Perhaps noting the coincidence of warm or cold sensations at a point of the body
where, through the *Anstoss*, resistance is perceived could give rise to *acquired* perception
of the warmth and coldness of impinging physical objects, but not, as far as I can see, to
the sort of *derived* perception that is at the heart of the problem I am addressing.

to hurt. At the point where it starts to hurt a new quality becomes present to consciousness: a sharp, stinging quality. It is *this* that is painful: something that simply was not present earlier. This quality does not feel like just a more intense form of the pressure sensations you were having before. Someone could experience such a painful sensation and not associate it with pressure or pressure sensations at all. After all, such a stinging pain is not much different from what a mild, short-lived wasp sting would be like, where there is no sense of pressure at all. This, however, is just as things should be if we are to have a case of dependent perception. For compare this case with one where we feel an object that is pressing against us begin to grow warm. Here, too, a new type of sensation enters the picture. This time, however, the new sensation melds with the pressure sensation so as to give us perceptual awareness of a warm object. Why does a dependent perception not ensue in the case of pain as it does here?

The answer, I suggest, is to be found in the simple fact that pains are painful. In the case of the pencil pushing into one's skin, the painful sensation does not meld with the pressure sensation because the painfulness of the former *distracts* one from the sensations of pressure. It is not only the case, as I stated earlier, that a painful sensation, even in the simple case where the pain is due solely to intense pressure, is not a way of being sensitive to that pressure; the onset of pain, rather, constitutes a *lack* of such sensitivity. As Brentano wrote, "When someone is cut he has no perception of touch . . . there is only the feeling of pain" (Brentano 1973, 82). By contrast, a sensation of warmth, because it is not painful, does not impede awareness of the pressure sensations that are felt when a warm object is touched. The same goes for taste sensations when they function perceptually. So it is not the fact that a pain sensation, even when it arises from pressure, is qualitatively quite different from any pressure sensation that is significant for the resolution of our problem. What is significant, rather, is the way in which feeling pain is *in tension* with feeling pressure.

Consider a more complex case, where pain occurs in a perceptual situation that itself involves dependent perception, for here we should be able to discern a different role played by the pain from that played by the sensation that is functioning in a dependently perceptual way. Suppose you have your hand on a warm surface that becomes painfully hot. Initially you feel a warm surface or a warm pressure. The sensation of warmth melds with the sensation of pressure to give a dependently perceptual awareness of a warm object. As soon as the experience starts becoming painful, however, a new quality emerges. This quality that you find painful—the "burning" quality, we might call it—is not just a more intense sensation of heat, for that would not account for what is new in the situation. Of course, when we feel an object getting warmer, we can say that at each stage there is something new: a greater degree of heat. Still, we can consider what is going on as an unchanging process of something getting hotter. However, as soon as the object gets painfully hot, something new is added even to this process. The "burning" quality is qualitatively different from anything possessed by the earlier sensations in the series. It does not differ merely in degree. If someone touches a warm object on one occasion and a warmer object on another, this person will, if he compares them, instinctively regard the two experienced qualities as being the same and as differing only in degree. If this person then suffers a burn, he will *not* instinctively regard this as yet again the same quality, with only a difference in intensity. The *quality* is different. Indeed, we talk of people being "burned" not only by hot things but also by intensely cold things, such as dry ice. The "burning" sensations will be more or less the same in the two cases and not related to heat rather than cold in either case. Indeed, I am suggesting, they will not intrinsically, qua experiences, be related to either (rather than being related to both). Such a burn is incompatible with even seeming to perceive heat or cold. Brentano also concurs with this point, for the passage from which I earlier quoted reads in full as follows: "When someone is cut he has no perception of touch, and someone who is burned has no feeling of warmth, but in both cases there is only the feeling of pain" (Brentano 1973, 82). Brentano does not state, but perhaps implies, what the crucial element is in this second kind of case. If, in the case of a burning pain, there is "only the feeling of pain," then such pain excludes *both* a perception of warmth *and* a perception of pressure. This is hardly surprising since, before the onset of the pain, these two were fused in the phenomenological unity of a derived perception. Since, to the extent that we are focused on the pain in this type of situation, we are distracted not only from temperature *but also from pressure*, we lack the melding of pain and pressure sensations that is necessary for dependent perception.

Note that I am not suggesting that, when one feels pain, in the sort of situation that is in question here, one is necessarily wholly unaware that something is pressing into one—and not just because the *Anstoss* may be in play. If someone rams a fairly hot object into the palm of your hand, you may well feel both pressure sensations and pain, but you will feel the pressure *despite* the pain. This becomes clear when we consider cases of the sort here in question that involve *intense* pain. Here, surely, an appreciation of pressure would indeed be wholly absent, so distracted would we be by the sheer pain involved. Such intense pain simply *obliterates* any sensitivity to the pressure through pressure sensations. I am not suggesting that intense pain totally obscures awareness of all other sensations. That would be true, at most, of excruciating pain. It is, rather, that intense pain obliterates any sensations that would otherwise be felt *where the pain is felt*. However, that, of course, is just where the pressure sensations would be felt that would have to meld with the pain so as to produce a dependent perception. So even intense pain may well not obliterate an experience of pressure through the *Anstoss*. Still, that, as we have seen, is unable to facilitate dependent perception. Even when pain is not so intense, we still find a distraction, to the extent that we focus on the pain, from any other sensations in that part of the body. This is precisely what we do not find in cases of dependent perception, where there is no conflict of any kind between experiencing pressure and experiencing sensory qualities such as temperatures and tastes.

What accounts for this antagonism between pain and other forms of sensation is, it seems to me, nothing but the sheer painfulness of pain. In virtue of this alone, pain has, phenomenologically, a certain self-announcing "opacity" to it that disallows it from melding with another type of sensation in the way required for derived perception. Only by being derivatively perceptual could pain be something other than a mere sensation. As it is, pain is just that. It has no object distinct from itself, and it is felt nowhere but in one's own body. These two features of pain would, if offered as an answer to our central question of why we do not attribute pain qualities to physical objects, have been inadequate, given the apparent analogy between the experience of some pains and indisputable cases of dependent perception—such as that of taste and temperature. Only by seeing why pain cannot be dependently perceptual do we properly understand why pain possesses these two features. Only by seeing how the very painfulness of pain puts it in tension with other modes of sensing located at the same place in our body can we understand why it is that in feeling pain one is, if I may echo Luther, *incurvatus in se*: curved or turned in upon oneself, intent upon a condition of oneself rather than the condition of any "external" object.

References

Brentano, Franz. 1973. *Psychology from an Empirical Standpoint*, trans. Antos C. Rancurello, D. B. Terrell, and Linda L. McAlister. London: Routledge.

Cole, Jonathan. 1995. *Pride and a Daily Marathon*. Cambridge, Mass.: MIT Press.

————— and E. M. Sedgwick. 1992. The Perception of Force and of Movement in a Man without Large Myelinated Sensory Afferents below the Neck. *Journal of Physiology* 449: 503–15.

Grice, H. P. 1962. Some Remarks about the Senses. In *Analytical Philosophy*, 1st ser., ed. R. J. Butler, 133–53. Oxford: Blackwell.

McKenzie, J. C. 1967–1968. The Externalization of Pains. *Analysis* 28: 189–93.

Paillard, J. 1999. Body Schema and Body Image: A Double Dissociation in Deafferented Patients. In *Motor Control Today and Tomorrow*, ed. G. N. Gantchev, S. Mori, and J. Massion, 197–214. Sofia: Academic Publishing House.

Pitcher, George. 1968–1969. McKenzie on Pains. *Analysis* 29: 103–105.

Smith, A. D. 2002. *The Problem of Perception*. Cambridge, Mass.: Harvard University Press.

Wittgenstein, Ludwig. 1978. *Logical Investigations*, trans. G. E. M. Anscombe. Oxford: Blackwell.

18

The Sense of Agency

Tim Bayne

The motion of our body follows upon the command of our will.
Of this we are at every moment conscious.

David Hume, *An Enquiry concerning
Human Understanding*, 1748

INTRODUCTION

Hume was perhaps guilty of a certain degree of hyperbole in claiming that we are continually aware of ourselves as agents, but it is certainly true that agentive self-awareness is a frequent component of the stream of consciousness. The question with which I am concerned in this chapter is where we ought to locate states of agentive self-awareness—"experiences of agency," as I also call them—in cognitive architecture.

To a first approximation, we can distinguish between three broad departments of the mind: perception, thought, and action. Perception processes information about the world (where this can include the state of the subject's own body) and makes it available for cognitive consumption. Perceptual systems include among their number not only the five traditional senses but also those systems responsible for the various kinds of bodily sensations, such as experiences of joint position, pain, nausea, hunger, thirst, and the need for oxygen. The department of thought is responsible for doing something with the information that it receives from perception—it is in the business of theoretical and practical reasoning. And the function of the department of agency is to implement the commands that it receives from thought. Its job is to plan and execute action in conjunction with the department of thought.

Where in this picture does agentive experience fall? I argue that agentive experiences are best thought of in perceptual terms—they are the products of a dedicated perceptual system (or perhaps systems). Just as we have sensory systems that function to inform us about the distribution of objects in our immediate environment, damage to our limbs, and our need for food, so, too, we have a sensory system (or systems), whose function it is to inform us about facets of our own agency.

The chapter unfolds as follows. The following section introduces the notion of agentive self-awareness and presents a sketch of the perceptual model; the remainder of the chapter provides an argument for the model, chiefly in the form of showing that its central rivals—the doxastic and telic models—are untenable. Section three examines the doxastic model of agentive self-awareness, according to which agentive self-awareness is solely a matter of judgment and is located within cognition. Section four examines the telic model of agentive self-awareness, according to which experiences of agency are located within the action system. Neither the doxastic nor the telic model provides us with a plausible analysis of agentive experience. Section five reinforces the intuitive case for the perceptual model of agentive experience by showing that a number of the most important objections to it can be met. My overall aim in this chapter is not to present a knockdown case for the perceptual model but rather to show that it ought to be regarded as a viable option. On this view, talk of "the sense of agency" is no mere *façon de parler* but picks out a genuine sensory modality, at least in a fairly broad sense of the term.[1] Our conception of the senses ought to be wide enough to include room for the idea that there might be at least one system that is in the business of representing one's own agency.

THE PERCEPTUAL MODEL OF AGENTIVE EXPERIENCE

Consider the following vignette:

It's your first day as a waitperson, and you are pouring water into a glass from a jug. As you pour the water, you experience yourself as an agent. You experience yourself as someone who is doing something rather than someone to whom things are merely happening. The experience of yourself as an agent is modulated in various ways. In pouring the water, you experience yourself as trying to avoid being distracted by the commotion in the kitchen. This attempt to control your attention is experienced as effortful—as difficult. You also experience yourself as having some degree of autonomy in controlling your attention. Having poured the water, you deliberate as to whether or not you should ask your customers whether they are ready to have their order taken. This act of deliberation has a distinctive experiential character; it too colors what it is like to be you during this episode.

---

[1] The "sense of agency" is sometimes used as a superordinate term for agentive experiences in general (e.g., Marcel 2003) and as a label for a particular component of agentive experience—roughly, the experience of authoring an action (see, e.g., Pacherie 2008). As should be clear from the foregoing, I use the term for a faculty (sensory system) that produces agentive experiences rather than as a term for (any species of) the experiences produced by this system.

This vignette contains reference to multiple forms of agentive self-awareness—states that I refer to as "agentive experiences."[2] There is no agreed taxonomy of such states. Among the various terms in use are the following: "the experience of control," the "experience of free will," "the experience of acting," "the experience of volition," "the experience of conscious will," "the experience of efficacy," "the experience of mental causation," "the experience of effort," and "the feeling of doing." Some of these terms are best understood as synonyms of each other; others are best read as picking out distinct elements or aspects of agentive experience. Each of these labels refers to forms of experience that are individuated by reference to features of agency.

I take agentive experience to have as its core the experience of a particular movement or mental event as realizing one's own agency. Surrounding this core are a number of other experiential components, the precise nature and number of which is very much an open question. Actions are sometimes experienced as effortful and at other times as effortless. Actions are sometimes experienced as deliberate and at other times as spontaneous. More controversially, we often experience our actions as autonomous—as "up to us" in some way. There is debate about the content of such experiences—are they compatibilitist or incompatibilist in nature?—but a strong case can be made for thinking that some form of free will is experientially encoded. One might add to this list the phenomenology of deliberating and also that of deciding or choosing (Holton 2006).[3]

The existence of agentive self-awareness can be highlighted by drawing attention to pathologies of agency in which it is lost or disturbed. In the anarchic hand syndrome, patients complain that they have lost control of a hand; they report that one of their hands has acquired a "will of its own" (Banks et al. 1989; Della Sala, Marchetti, and Spinnler 1991; Gasquoine 1993; Goldberg and Bloom 1990; Pacherie 2007). The hand in question might also appear to act in an anarchic fashion, by (say) grabbing food from a stranger's plate at a restaurant. Patients deny that such actions are theirs and may take steps to prevent the hand from moving by sitting on it or tying it down. Detailed reports of what it is like to have an anarchic hand are rare, but it is plausible to suppose that the syndrome involves an experience of alienated agency—an experience of one's hand as acting on its own accord.

Disturbances of agentive experience are also evident in the schizophrenic delusions of thought insertion and alien control (Mellors 1970;

---

[2] "The phenomenology of first-person agency" is also used as a synonym for "agentive experience." I prefer the former label over the latter, for "phenomenology" has often been used to refer to a method for studying consciousness rather than as a term for the phenomenal character of experience.

[3] See Bayne (2006, 2008), Bayne and Levy (2006), Hohwy (2004), Holton (2006), Horgan, Tienson, and Graham (2003), Marcel (2003), Nahmias et al. (2004), Pacherie (2008), and Siegel (2005) for further discussion of the contents of agentive experience.

Frith et al. 2000b). Patients suffering from these delusions complain that some of their thoughts and actions are no longer their own or are at least no longer under their control. "My fingers pick up the pen, but I don't control them. What they do is nothing to do with me"; "The force moved my lips. I began to speak. The words were made for me" (Mellors 1970, 18). "My grandfather hypnotized me and now he moves my foot up and down." "They inserted a computer in my brain. It makes me turn to the left or right" (Frith et al. 2000b, 358). These delusions appear to be grounded in abnormal experiences of agency (Pacherie, Green, and Bayne 2006), and if these syndromes involve experiences of alienated agency, then there is some reason to suppose that unimpaired agency might be accompanied by experiences of intact or unimpaired agency. Of course, the fact that there are experiences of alienated agency does not entail that there are—or even could be—experiences of impaired agency, but it surely provides some support for that thesis.

Where in the cognitive architecture should we locate such experience? They are not located within the central cognition, nor are they located within the systems responsible for programming and executing actions, nor are they located within the high-level reaches of any of the standard perceptual modalities. Instead, such states are the products of a dedicated perceptual system (or systems). These systems involve forward models of action control and operate along the following lines (Frith et al. 2000a, 2000b; Blakemore and Frith 2003). The forward models are fed a copy of the agent's motor commands and are then put to the following uses. First, they are used to predict the sensory consequences of the agent's movement. These predictions are used to filter sensory information and to attenuate the component that is due to self-movement. Second, the copy of the motor commands is also sent to a comparator (or comparators), so-called because they compare the predicted sensory consequences of the movement with sensory feedback. When there is a match between predicted and actual state, the comparator sends a signal to the effect that the sensory changes are self-generated; when there is no match (or an insufficiently robust match), sensory changes are coded as externally caused. Crucial to the comparator approach is the notion that agentive awareness can be generated by mechanisms that need not—and typically will not—have access to full-fledged intentions. It is very much an open question whether the comparator-based story can account for each and every one of the many components of agentive experience, but there is good reason to think that it lies at the heart of the phenomenon.[4]

Where in the cognitive architecture do these comparators fall? I take them to fall within perception, where that notion is very broadly construed. The representational states generated by these comparators play

---

[4] For further details see Bayne and Pacherie (2007), David, Newen, and Vogeley (2008), Haggard (2005), Hallett (2007), and Pacherie (2008).

the role of perceptions. Like other perceptual systems, the function of the sense of agency is to generate representations of some domain—in this case, one's own agency—and make those representations available to the agent's cognitive systems in an experiential format.

It is important to note that the perceptual model of agentive experience is *not* committed to a perceptual account of introspection. The model is a model of agentive experiences themselves; it is not a model of our access to agentive experiences. Giving an account of agentive experience is one thing; giving an account of introspection is quite another. Perceptual approaches to introspection are decidedly unpopular, but that unpopularity should in no way be taken to discredit the perceptual model of agentive experience. Note also that the perceptual model is not intended to cover everything that might be subsumed by the term "agentive self-awareness." There is a broad sense of agentive self-awareness that includes the conceptually articulated awareness of what one is trying to do (tie one's shoelaces, look for a book, reach for the salt). A full account of agentive self-awareness needs to address these high-level, conceptually articulated forms of agentive awareness, but I do not take on that task here. The perceptual model is intended to apply only to fairly low-level forms of agentive awareness of the kind introduced earlier.[5]

That, in a nutshell, is the perceptual model. I flesh the model out in more detail later (section five), but I turn now to its rivals.

THE DOXASTIC MODEL OF AGENTIVE EXPERIENCE

There will be those who think that the perceptual model gets off on the wrong foot by construing agentive self-awareness in experiential terms. According to what we might think of as the *doxastic model* of agentive self-awareness, such states are not really forms of experience at all; instead, they are states of thought. What it is to be aware of oneself as an agent is simply to have a conscious thought to that effect.

The doxastic model strikes me as intuitively implausible. Horgan, Tienson, and Graham's (2003, 324) description of agentive experience as "an aspect of sensory-perceptual experience, broadly construed" seems exactly right to me. The experience of acting is not exhausted by the conscious judgments one might have about what or how one is acting, if indeed one has any conscious judgments of that nature at all. Acting may frequently involve conscious judgment about what one is doing, but agentive self-awareness is not primarily a matter of judgment. Rather, it has the transparency, immediacy, and directness that characterizes our sensory engagement with the world. There might be good reasons to

---

[5] See Bayne and Pacherie (2007) for some discussion of how low-level and high-level agentive self-awareness might be related.

reject this view, but any such rejection would come at a significant cost to intuition.

Proponents of the doxastic model who are unmoved by the foregoing might find the following more convincing. If the doxastic view were right, then pathologies of agentive self-awareness would be pathologies of judgment rather than of experience. We should hold that the anarchic hand syndrome involves only a departure in the agentive judgments that the patient is prepared to make. Whereas a person whose hand has just taken food from a stranger's plate would normally be prepared to judge that they had performed the action (and perhaps confabulate a rationalization for it), anarchic hand patients are not prepared to make this judgment; instead, they insist that they did not move their hand—it moved of its own accord.

However, this does not seem to capture the situation. Although it is certainly true that anarchic hand patients are not (typically) prepared to admit that the action was theirs, it seems plausible to appeal to agentive experience—or the lack thereof—in order to *explain* why they deny having performed the anarchic actions. Surely it is the fact that the normal and expected experience of *doing* has been replaced by an experience of *happening* that leads these patients to judge that the action is not theirs. Whether or not one's denial of agentive ownership of the action is erroneous—and there is room for debate about this—the patient's pathology appears to be primarily one of *experience* rather than *thought*.

This objection can be reinforced by noting that experiences of alienated agency are unlikely to be cognitively penetrable. Suppose that an anarchic hand patient *does* take herself to be the agent of "her" anarchic actions. After all, she might reason as follows: "The movements of my anarchic hand are not guided by anyone else. They are actions, and where they are actions, there must be an agent. So, these actions must be mine." Such a patient might form the belief that the movements of her anarchic hand realize her own actions, but it seems unlikely that the acquisition of this judgment will suffice to correct their agentive experience. The patient can no more restore the missing experience of agency by forming the belief that their anarchic actions are truly her own than you or I can correct our visual experiences of the Müller-Lyer illusion by forming the belief that the lines in question are equal in length. Cognitive impenetrability, one of the key markers of the perception-cognitive boundary, speaks firmly against the doxastic analysis of agentive self-awareness.

The point generalizes. Patients suffering from depersonalization seem also to have lost the normal experience of themselves as agents. They "complain that they no longer have an ego, but are mechanisms, automatons, puppets; that what they do seems not done by them but happens mechanically" (Schilder 1953; Sierra and Berrios 1998). Nonetheless, they suffer from no delusions concerning agency: They know that their actions are their own. Phantom limb patients display what is in some sense the converse dissociation. They know that their "limb" is but a phantom, but they continue to experience themselves as acting with it. The history of philosophy provides us with additional examples of the cognitive impenetrability of agentive experience. Malebranche believed that God was the direct cause of his movements, but his commitment to occasionalism surely did not rob him of the experience of being the author of his deeds. Hard incompatibilists reject the reality of free will, but this has little impact on their experiences of freedom (see, e.g., Strawson 1986). Perhaps judgment can penetrate agentive experience under some conditions, but it seems clear that on the whole agentive experience exhibits the kind of doxastic impenetrability that is characteristic of perception. Agentive experiences are as distinct from the judgments to which they give rise as are visual experiences from the judgments to which they give rise. We might think of agentive experiences as "invitations to belief," but one should not confuse an invitation itself with that to which it is an invitation.

In response, the proponent of the doxastic model might hold that even if agentive experience is not a species of judgment strictly speaking, it does fall on the cognitive side of the perception-cognition divide. But what kind of cognitive state might agentive experience be if not a judgment? The only answer I know of is that it might be an entertaining of some kind. Suppose, when asked what the capital of Ethiopia is, the name "Addis Ababa" suddenly occurs to you. Do you judge that Addis Ababa is the capital of Ethiopia? Perhaps not. You might have no commitment whatsoever to the truth of that thought; it is merely that you "found yourself" with it when the question was put to you. Might agentive self-awareness involve states of this kind—thoughts that simply occur to one?

I think not. The difference between the case just discussed and agentive experience is as sharp as the difference between daydreaming about what it would be like to fly through the air unaided and actually experiencing oneself as being in this state. When it comes to daydreams and flights of fancy one has no tendency to take oneself as being in touch with how things really are; perception, by contrast, does involve such a sense, and that is surely what agentive experience is like. It is, we might say, *committal*. The experience of raising one's arm does not leave open the question of whether one might really be raising one's arm, but has instead the force of an assertion: "I *am* raising my arm."

THE TELIC MODEL OF AGENTIVE EXPERIENCE

Following Anscombe (1957) and Searle (1983), let us distinguish two ways in which mental states can be satisfied: in a thetic manner and in a telic manner. *Thetic* states are satisfied when they fit the world; they have a mind-to-world direction of fit. Judgments are paradigms of thetic states, for they are true (or veridical) when they fit the world and otherwise false (or nonveridical). Thetic states are in the business of responding to changes in the world. *Telic* states are satisfied when the world fits them; they have a world-to-mind direction of fit. Desires are the paradigms of telic states. They are in the business of bringing about a certain state of affairs. They are satisfied when they succeed; otherwise, they remain frustrated.

The perceptual model takes agentive experiences to have a thetic structure: They are representations (or "presentations") that matters are thus and so. By contrast, the telic model takes such states to have a telic structure. Searle himself endorses the telic model:

> As far as Intentionality is concerned, the differences between the visual experience and the experience of acting are in the direction of fit and in the direction of causation: the visual experience stands to the table in the mind-to-world direction of fit. If the table isn't there, we say that I was mistaken, or was having a hallucination, or some such. And the direction of causation is from the object to the visual experience. If the Intentional component is satisfied it must be caused by the presence and features of the object. But in the case of the experience of acting, the Intention component has the world-to-mind direction of fit. If I have this experience but the event doesn't occur we say such things as that I *failed* to raise my arm, and that I *tried* to raise my arm but did not succeed. And the direction of causation is from the experience of acting to the event. Where the Intentional content is satisfied, that is, where I actually succeed in raising my arm, the experience of acting causes the arm to go up. If it didn't cause the arm to go up, but something else did, I didn't raise my arm: it just went up for some other reason. (1983, 88; emphasis in original; see also 1983, 123f.)

Although Searle is perhaps the most explicit advocate of the telic line, a number of other authors appear to have some sympathy for at least a limited version of the view (O'Shaughnessy 2003; Peacocke 2003).[6] Proponents of the telic model might agree with Horgan, Tienson, and Graham's (2003) description of agentive experience as "an aspect of sensory-perceptual experience, broadly construed," but they will insist that this description must be construed very broadly indeed if it is to be accurate, for on this account the structure of agentive experience is diametrically opposed to that of perceptual states.

There are multiple ways in which we might get a fix on the dispute between the thetic and telic analyses of agentive experience. It can be read as a dispute about how to read the "of" in the phrase "the

---

[6] I find Peacocke's (2003, 2008) position difficult to pin down. On the one hand, Peacocke denies that agentive experience (what he calls "action-awareness") can be understood in perceptual terms. At the same time he grants that agentive experience is representational: "[I]n the sense that in enjoying action-awareness, it seems to the subject that the world is a certain way" (2008, 247). I am unsure how to reconcile these two elements of Peacocke's account, and it may be that his view is not really a form of the telic model despite appearances to that effect.

phenomenology *of* agency." The thetic theorist reads this "of" intentionally: The phenomenology of agency involves experiences that are intentionally directed toward agency. By contrast, the telic theorist reads
this "of" possessively: The phenomenology of agency is a matter of one's
actions (or tryings) themselves having experiential character. The dispute can also be captured by appeal to the contrast between transitive
and intransitive conceptions of experience. The thetic theorist takes a
transitive view of agentive experience (the phenomenology of agency is a
matter of experiencing that certain things are the case), whereas the telic
theorist takes an intransitive view of it (the phenomenology of agency
is a matter of one's actions, intentions, and the like having phenomenal
properties).[7]

How might we determine whether agentive experience is thetic or
telic? It is unclear whether introspection is competent to pronounce on
this question. According to one widely endorsed view, introspection provides us with access only to the contents of experience. Since the debate
between the thetic and telic accounts concerns the structure rather than
the contents of experience, introspection may be impotent here. Of
course, this view of introspection is highly contested, and many would
argue that there are introspectively accessible differences between experiences that outrun their contents. (What it is like to see something as
square is different from what it is like to feel it as square, but arguably the
two states share the same content.) Whether or not the current debate
falls within the domain in which introspection *could* deliver a verdict, it
is clear that introspection has not proven particularly useful in resolving
it. At best introspection is silent on the question of whether agentive
experience has thetic or telic structure, at worst it inclines theorists in a
telic direction and others in a thetic one.

We might hope to get more traction on this debate by asking how
agentive experiences could fail. States with a mind-to-world direction of
fit fail by being frustrated, whereas states with a world-to-mind direction
of fit fail by misrepresenting how things are. In what way—or ways—do
agentive experiences fail?

At least some forms of agentive experience fail (when they do) by
misrepresenting. This is surely what we ought to say about experiences
of free will. Whatever the exact content of experiences of free will, it
is surely an open question whether we are free in the way(s) in which
we experience ourselves as being free. Doubts about the veridicality
of experiences of free will are most pressing for those attracted to an
incompatibilist analysis of their content, but they can also be raised

---

[7] We might note in passing that the telic model of agentive experience is at odds with
standard representationalist conceptions of phenomenal character, for on such accounts
the phenomenal character of a mental state is fixed by how it represents the world as
being (see, e.g., Dretske 1995; Tye 1995). However, the telic model is consistent with the
spirit of such analyses, for it allows that facts about intentional content might fix facts
about phenomenal character.

within the context of compatibilist analyses. Indeed, Searle himself takes it to be very much an open question whether we actually possess the libertarian freedom that he thinks we experience ourselves as having (Searle 2001).

Experiences of effort can also be nonveridical: In principle, it seems possible that one might experience effortful tasks as effortless and vice versa. In fact, this possibility might not be merely theoretical. Naccache et al. (2005) describe a patient who performed normally on measures of cognitive load but experienced tasks involving high cognitive load as no more effortful than tasks involving low cognitive load. It is natural to suppose that in experiencing these tasks as effortless this patient was misrepresenting her own cognitive processing—they were effortful despite being experienced as effortless.

But what about the core components of agentive experience? Consider William James's case of a patient who is asked to raise his anesthetized arm. The patient's eyes are closed, and unbeknown to him his arm is prevented from moving. Upon opening his eyes he is surprised to discover that his arm has not moved. Although he tried to raise his arm, this attempt was a failure. What did James's patient *experience*? Searle describes his experience as one of *"trying* but *failing* to raise one's hand" (Searle 1983, 89; emphasis in original). I am not persuaded. Arguably, the patient was surprised to discover that his hand had not gone up because he experienced himself as raising it—the patient had an experience *as* of raising his arm. If this is right, then the experience of acting cannot be identified with acting "accompanied by certain phenomenal properties" (ibid., 92), for in this case there was no action for phenomenal properties to accompany. The case appears to demand a thetic analysis. On discovering that his arm has not moved, James's patient ought to treat his experience of acting in just the way he treats his perceptual experience of illusions—that is, as misrepresenting some aspect of reality.

The proponent of the telic model might reply that the patient's experience misleads him only insofar as it represents the *movement* of his arm—and there is nothing agentive, as such, about that content. We can see the futility of this response by considering the following variant of James's case. Suppose that the patient is paralyzed; he can try to raise his arm, but his trying will not be causally efficacious. However, a mischievous scientist with brain-reading technology can detect the patient's tryings and intervenes in his motor cortex so as to ensure that his tryings are successful. (This, of course, is the model that the occasionalists offered of all agency.) The patient will experience himself as raising his arm—after all, his arm goes up as and when he tries to raise it—but there is surely something nonveridical in his experience. This nonveridical element cannot be identified with the representation of the trajectory or location of his arm, for in this case these elements are veridical. Rather, it must concern his experience of *agency*—it must have something to do with the agent's role in producing the movement.[8]

Counterexamples aside, there is something rather odd about the thought that experiences (as) of acting successfully (unsuccessfully) could be identified with successful (failed) efforts. Why should agents have any first-person access to the success of their efforts merely in virtue of having successful attempts? Consider, as a parallel, the proposal that we should identify the experience of one's perceptions as veridical (nonveridical) with the veridicality (nonveridicality) of one's perceptions. Such a proposal is clearly a nonstarter: The veridicality of a perception is one thing, while the experience of it as (non)veridical is another. Identifying the experience of one's intentions as satisfied or frustrated with the event of them being satisfied or frustrated is similarly implausible.[9]

In my view, the proponent of the telic model ought to restrict the scope of the model to experiences of trying. Perhaps the experience of trying to do something is not a state that represents oneself as trying to do something but simply a trying "that possesses phenomenal character." In fact, there is some reason for taking Searle's phrase "the experience of acting" to refer to the experience of trying to act as opposed to the experience of acting, for it is this view that provides the most plausible reading of his position. At any rate, that it how I will understand his use of "the experience of acting."

Searle provides two arguments for the telic account of the experience of acting. First, he claims that it is part of the content of such experiences that they represent themselves as bringing about those actions with which they are associated: "If it [the experience of acting] didn't cause the arm to go up, but something else did, I didn't raise my arm: it just went up for some other reason" (1983, 88; see also 124). If this claim were true, it would provide an attractive argument for the telic account, for as we saw in the case of the mischievous scientist, the satisfaction conditions of trying to raise one's arm appear to include a self-referential component. Arguably, it is part of the content of the trying that it itself plays a direct role in causing one's arm to go up. It is not implausible to identify experiences of trying with tryings *if* indeed they share the same self-referential content.

---

[8] One can also arrive at this conclusion via a highly restrictive conception of actions, according to which actions are identified with attempts (Hornsby 1980). On this view, James's patient does in fact raise his arm, but it's just that the world fails to cooperate with his action. I assume here that this account of actions is incorrect, at least insofar as it is taken as an analysis of the content of the experience of acting.

[9] Telic theorists could go disjunctive at this point. They could reject the "common factor" assumption, according to which agentive experiences belong to a single kind whether or not they occur in the context of successful intentions ("the good case") or unsuccessful intentions ("the bad case"). Wading into the murky waters of disjunctivism is beyond the scope of this chapter, but suffice it to say that, if the telic theorist needs to go disjunctivist, then I do not want to go telic.

But do they share the same self-referential content? I doubt it. I can discern nothing in the phenomenology of the experience of trying to ϕ that represents that very experience as enabling me to ϕ. I am not convinced that experiences of trying contain any self-referential content, but, if they do, I am inclined to think that they represent themselves as being caused by tryings rather than representing themselves as causing actions. At any rate, I do not share Searle's intuition that in raising my arm I experience that experience as itself causing my arm to rise. In fact, I'm not sure that I experience *anything* as causing my arm to rise.

Searle's second argument for identifying experiences of tryings with tryings involves an appeal to failures of agency. He writes as follows: "[W]hen we have an experience [of acting] but the event doesn't occur we say such things as that I failed to raise my arm, and that I tried to raise my arm but did not succeed" (Searle 1983, 88). As I read it, the argument is that the telic account must be right because it correctly predicts that there is only a single "joint of intentionality" between experiences (as) of trying and actions. By contrast, the thetic account posits two such joints: one between experiences of trying and tryings themselves and another between tryings and their realization. If the thetic account were correct, it would follow that agents could experience themselves as trying to ϕ even when they did not ϕ for one of two reasons: Either their attempt at ϕ-ing was unsuccessful, or their experience as of attempting to ϕ was nonveridical. Searle's argument seems to be that experiences of tryings must be telic because we never countenance this second possibility.

I think that Searle is right to suggest that we do not generally recognize a gap between experiences of tryings and trying themselves; in this sense he may also be right to suggest that our folk conception of experiences of trying is, in some sense, telic. But perhaps the folk model of experiences of trying is incorrect. Perhaps we should be open to the idea that experiences of trying—no less than experiences of actually acting—can lead us astray.[10]

We can create space for this possibility by considering anosognosia for hemiplegia, a condition in which one is unaware that one is paralyzed on one side of one's body. When requested to perform an action that involves the paralyzed limb (such as clapping one's hands together), patients typically insist that they have performed the requested action despite the fact that they have moved only one hand. Among the various accounts of anosognosia for hemiplegia is the feedforward account, according to which this condition involves a deficit in the motor effector system (Heilman 1991, Gold et al. 1994; Adair et al. 1997).

---

[10] Perhaps the representational nature of experiences of trying has been overlooked for the same reason that the representational nature of experiences of pain has been overlooked: In each case, having the experience of being in the target state provides by far the best evidence that we are in the target state.

Proponents of this account argue that damage to the motor effector system has resulted in the loss of the ability to form intentions to move. It is tempting to gloss this account by suggesting that patients no longer try to move. Nonetheless, there is every reason to think that patients retain the *experience* of trying to move their limb, for they insist that they are moving (or have just moved) the limb. In short, there is some reason to think that anosognosia for hemiplegia may involve a situation in which a person's experiences of trying to do something are nonveridical: There is no trying here, not even a frustrated one, only an experience thereof. This account of anosognosia for hemiplegia might not be correct, but it does seem to be *coherent*, and its coherence suffices to undermine the claim that experiences of trying are, of conceptual necessity, telic.

The doxastic and telic models of agentive experience are the two leading competitors to the thetic model. If, as I have argued, these two models can be set to one side, then the intuitive case for the perceptual model that I sketched in §2 becomes all the more appealing. The next section reinforces the case for the perceptual model by responding to three lines of objection that might be leveled against it.[11]

OBJECTIONS AND REPLIES

The first objection concerns the relationship between agentive experiences and their intentional objects (that is, actions). The intentional object of a perceptual experience is typically independent of the experience itself. My visual experience of a dog is one thing while the dog itself is quite another; my auditory experience of a tree falling in the forest is one thing while the falling of the tree is quite another. One might take this independence—a fact that is arguably represented in the very contents of perception—to be a necessary feature of perceptual experience.

Are agentive experiences independent of their intentional objects? Some say "no." Mossel has recently rejected the perceptual model of what he calls "sensations of acting" on the grounds that such states are parts of actions and hence are not independent of actions in the way in which they would need to be were they to qualify as perceptions of agency (Mossel 2005, 134). Mossel is not alone in suggesting that agentive experiences are in some way internal to actions themselves. Searle states that "if my arm goes up, but goes up [without the experience of acting], I didn't raise my arm, it just went up" (Searle 1983, 88, see also 95). Striking a similar note, Ginet claims that a simple mental event is

---

[11] Another alternative to the thetic account conceives of agentive experiences as pushmi-pullyu representations. See Bayne (forthcoming) for discussion of this approach.

an action "if and only if it has an intrinsic phenomenal quality," which he dubs "the actish quality" (1997, 89).[12]

There is *something* to this line of argument. Many people are reluctant to regard physical or mental happenings that are unaccompanied by a basic "experience of doing" as actions. This reluctance is manifest in our intuitive response to the anarchic hand syndrome—as we saw, there is some temptation to deny that anarchic actions really are actions of the patient in question. Arguably this intuitive resistance is best explained by supposing that agentive experience of some kind is essential to agency.

But there is another side to the story. If anarchic hand actions do not qualify as the patient's actions, whose actions are they? One might deny that they are actions at all, but that seems implausible. Anarchic hand movements certainly *look* like actions, for they can be evaluated for success. (The attempt to take food from a stranger's plate might be frustrated by the waitperson's intervention!) Peacocke (2003) has suggested that anarchic hand actions are "orphans"— actions without an agent. This position has something to recommend it but it comes at some intuitive cost, for we tend to think that actions must come attached to agents. So perhaps we should admit that anarchic hand actions belong to the patient despite the fact that the patient experiences no sense of agency toward them. Some support for the view that actions need not be accompanied by agentive experiences derives from what Bach (1978) calls "minimal actions," such as tapping absentmindedly while listening to a lecture or walking to the shops while one's mind is on other matters. It is an open question whether minimal actions are always accompanied by an experience of agency. Would minimal actions that are not so-accompanied fail to qualify as bona fide actions? I do not see why they must.[13]

Although I reject the independence objection, I do not deny that agentive experiences of various stripes are often causally implicated in agency. Clearly, the experience of losing control of one's actions can lead one to attend more closely to what one is doing, which may in turn affect how (or indeed whether) one continues to act. Similarly, the experience of an action as effortful might lead one to either exert more effort or, alternatively, to abandon doing what one is trying to do. Indeed, perhaps

---

[12] Searle does not seem to have a settled position on this issue, for certain passages in *Intentionality* appear to allow that actions need not be accompanied by the experience of acting (see, e.g., 1983, 92).

[13] Although I have argued that the states of affairs represented by agentive experiences are independent of them, it may not be possible to give an analysis of what an action is that does not appeal in some way to agentive experience. However, even if this should turn out to be the case, it would still be possible for agentive experiences to be nonveridical. As a parallel, consider colors. Response-dependence conceptions of color hold that the analysis of colors must ultimately appeal to color experience, but such accounts allow that it is possible for an object to appear to be (say) green without being green. Similarly, a response-dependence conception of actions might allow that it is possible for something to appear to be an action without being an agent (and vice versa).

the experience of acting autonomously is in some way implicated in what it is to act autonomously. Just how agentive experience might be implicated in agency itself is a quite obscure issue, but it is not implausible to suppose that agency of the kind that we ordinarily enjoy would be unrecognizable in the absence of agentive experience; perhaps we would not even have the tools to conceive of ourselves as agents in the absence of agentive experience. Granting all this, there remains enough independence between agentive experiences and their conditions of satisfaction for it to be possible, in principle if not in practice, that such states are nonveridical.[14]

A second objection to the perceptual model focuses on the question of whether agentive experience involves the operation of a perceptual organ of the requisite kind. On the face of things, there does not seem to be anything that stands to agentive experience as the eyes stand to seeing, the ears to hearing, or the skin to touch. Might this fact scuttle the perceptual model?

To address the question we need to consider how the notion of a perceptual organ is to be understood. O'Dea (this volume, chapter 15) suggests that a perceptual organ is a mechanism over whose operation one has some degree of intentional control and whose mode of operation is implicitly represented in the very experiences it produces. On this proposal, perceptual experience involves some form of self-intimation of its own mode of acquisition: It is part of the content of visual experience that it is acquired via the deployment of the eyes, it is part of the content of tactile experience that it is acquired via the skin, and so on. O'Dea's account builds on a Gibsonian conception of perception, according to which perceptual organs are not mechanisms that passively register their input but tools by means of which we explore our environment.

O'Dea's analysis captures an important feature of the traditional senses—one that sets "the famous five" apart from other forms of sensory experience—but it is not the only viable notion of a perceptual organ. Consider proprioceptive, vestibular, and nociceptive experience. The mechanisms that lie behind these forms of experience are not open to view, and as a result of this they are not amenable to intentional control. There is nothing that one can do in order to get a better perspective on one's vestibular environment; there is no straightforward sense in which one can track the state of one's viscera. Nonetheless, there is a respectable sense in which these forms of experience do qualify as perceptual, for they are ways of gaining information about the state of the world (in this case, the state of the world that happens to coincide with one's own

---

[14] Perhaps the folk notion of action is not determinate enough for the question just examined to have an unequivocal answer. Our common-sense notion of action might simply have nothing to say about whether intentional goal-directed movement that fails to be accompanied by agentive experience qualifies as an action.

body). Furthermore, it is not clear that O'Dea's analysis even applies
to each of the famous five without qualification. Perhaps animals and
neonates can enjoy perceptual experience—they can see things, touch
things, and so on—without any awareness of how they come by this
information. O'Dea's analysis does capture something important, but
we should resist the suggestion that it gives us the only legitimate analysis of what it is to be a perceptual organ or, by extension, what it is to be
a perceptual sense.

A more liberal view of what it is to be a perceptual organ thinks of
organs as dedicated mechanisms that take as input energy of a distinctive
kind and generate as outputs representations in an appropriate format,
at least some of which are experiential. Does the mechanism responsible for agentive experience qualify as a perceptual organ even on this
more relaxed conception of a sensory organ? Even here one might have
qualms. On the comparator-based account introduced earlier, the sense
of agency takes as input not raw energy but motor representations and
representations drawn from the other perceptual modalities. So, there is
a real difference between the mechanisms responsible for agentive experiences and those that generate (say) proprioceptive, vestibular, and nociceptive experiences: The latter involve sensory transducers, whereas the
former do not. Nonetheless, I am not inclined to regard this difference as
particularly significant in the present context. The appropriate response
to it is to draw a distinction between basic and nonbasic perceptual systems, where the former take as input forms of energy, and the latter take
as input representations. The five traditional senses (and various forms
of proprioception and interoception) would qualify as basic perceptual
systems, whereas the sense of agency would qualify as a nonbasic perceptual system. Nonetheless, a nonbasic perceptual system is still genuinely
perceptual.

A third objection to the perceptual model is difficult to pin down
with any precision. Put most generally, the worry is that the approach
drains such experiences of their agentive nature. As Korsgaard puts it,
"to experience something is (in part) to be passively receptive to it, and
therefore we cannot have experiences of activity as such" (1996, 204).
More enigmatically, O'Shaughnessy writes as follows:

> If one is to relate as observer to anything then one has to be "without it,"
> whereas if one is intentionally to do anything then one has to be "within"
> the action we are attempting to observe, in which case we have an entirely
> empty and self-delusive experience of observation . . . or else we remain
> "without" in some less serious sense and genuinely seem to observe the
> action. But remaining "without," we lose the action as ours in gaining the
> observation: we lose any "withinness." (O'Shaughnessy 1980, 31)

I must admit that I fail to feel the force of the objection. There is no
doubt some sense in which perception is passive, but it is surely a gross
non sequitur to suppose that a passive state cannot represent agency.

After all, judgment is also passive, but there is no doubt that we can form judgments about our own agency. If it is possible for one's own agency to be represented in thought why should it not also be possible for it to be represented in experience? Why exactly would the perceptual representation of agency undermine its "withinness"?

I suspect that one of the worries behind this objection is the thought that on the perceptual model it must always be an open question whether the action being perceived as one's own really is one's own. Perceptual experience is not immune to error relative to the first person. For example, one can raise the question of whether the legs that appear to one in visual experience are one's own or those of another (Shoemaker 1968). But agentive experience *does* seem to be immune to error relative to the first person, for the question of whether the actions of which one is aware are one's own or someone else's seems to be puzzling at best and downright incoherent at worst. So, the objection runs, agentive experience is not perceptual. Engaging with this worry would lead us into deep waters that I cannot even begin to chart in this chapter; suffice it to say that the distinction between logical and de facto immunity to error might be of some help to us here. The objection requires that agentive experience is logically immune to error, whereas it may in fact be only de facto immune to error. We might compare agentive experiences to (say) proprioceptive experiences: we might be able to imagine scenarios in which these experiences track the states of another's body, but as things stand these experiences are restricted to states of oneself.

CONCLUSION

I have argued that there is much to be said on behalf of a perceptual model of agentive experience. The model does justice to its phenomenology; it receives some support from cognitive science; and it is able to meet the most pressing objections to it. Assuming that the perceptual model is on the right track, what lessons might we draw from it?

There are lessons to be drawn in two domains. First, the perceptual model opens up questions that are obscured by other analyses of agentive experience. How reliable is the sense of agency? Does agentive experience represent agency as it really is, or does the sense of agency lead us into error? To what degree is the manifest image of agency as encoded in agentive experience vindicated by the scientific image of agency? Versions of some of these questions can perhaps be posed from within the doxastic and telic models, but it is only the thetic model that brings them out into the clear light of day.

Second, the perceptual model encourages us to take a new look at perception's reach. If the sense of agency can be understood in perceptual terms how many *other* facets of human experience might also succumb to a perceptual treatment? Might it turn out that humans enjoy vomeronasal perception, as Keeley (2002/this volume, chapter 11) has suggested? Might it turn out that we possess a sense of echolocation, as Schwitzgebel and Gordon (2000) have suggested? Might various forms of cognitive feelings—the experience of having a word on the tip of one's tongue, of taking oneself to know what the answer to a question is, of taking someone to be familiar—also qualify as perceptual?

If, as some theorists do, one begins one's analysis of perception with the assumption that there are only five senses, then each of the forgoing questions must be answered in the negative.[15] It seems to me that this would be a rather unwelcome result. In my view, the question of how many senses we have should is one that should be left open for now. Vision, audition, olfaction, taste, and touch may be the paradigms of the perception, but there is good reason to doubt whether they exhaust the category. We need a nuanced account of perception, one that does justice not only to the famous five but also to their less celebrated siblings.[16]

References

Adair, J. C., R. L. Schwartz, D. L. Na, E. Fennell, R. L. Gilmore, and K. M. Heilman. 1997. Anosognosia: Examining the Disconnection Hypothesis. *Journal of Neurology, Neurosurgery, and Psychiatry* 63: 798–800.

Anscombe, E. 1957. *Intention*. Oxford: Blackwell.

Bach, K. 1978. A Representational Theory of Action. *Philosophical Studies* 34: 361–79.

Banks, G., P. Short, J. Martinez, R. Latchaw, G. Ratcliff, and F. Boller. 1989. The Alien Hand Syndrome. *Archives of Neurology* 46: 456–59.

Bayne, T. 2006. Phenomenology and the Feeling of Doing: Wegner on the Conscious Will. In *Does Consciousness Cause Behavior?* ed. S. Pockett, W. P. Banks, and S. Gallagher, 169–86. Cambridge, Mass.: MIT Press.

———. 2008. The Phenomenology of Agency. *Philosophy Compass* 3: 1–21.

———. Forthcoming. Agentive Experiences as Pushmi-Pullyu Representations. In *New Waves in the Philosophy of Action*, ed. J. Aguilar, A. Buckareff and K. Frankish. Palgrave Macmillan.

———, and N. Levy. 2006. The Feeling of Doing: Deconstructing the Phenomenology of Agency. In *Disorders of Volition*, ed. N. Sebanz and W. Prinz, 49–68. Cambridge, Mass.: MIT Press.

Bayne, T., and E. Pacherie. 2007. Narrators and Comparators: The Architecture of Agentive Self-Awareness. *Synthèse* 159: 475–91.

Blakemore, S.-J. and C. D. Frith. 2003. Self-Awareness and Action. *Current Opinion in Neurobiology* 13: 219–24.

---

[15] See, for example, O'Dea (this volume, chapter 15) and Nudds (2003 and this volume, chapter 16).

[16] I am very grateful to Frédérique de Vignemont, Elisabeth Pacherie, Michael Schmitz, Laura Schroeter, and especially Fiona Macpherson for comments on previous drafts of this chapter.

David, N., A. Newen, and K. Vogeley. 2008. The "Sense of Agency" and Its Underlying Cognitive and Neural Mechanisms. *Consciousness and Cognition* 17: 523–34.

Della Sala, S., C. Marchetti, and H. Spinnler. 1991. Right-Sided Anarchic (Alien) Hand: A Longitudinal Study. *Neuropsychologia* 29(11): 1113–27.

Dretske, F. 1995. *Naturalizing the Mind*. Cambridge, Mass.: MIT Press.

Frith, C. D. 1992. *The Cognitive Neuropsychology of Schizophrenia*. Hillsdale, N.J.: Erlbaum.

———, S. J. Blakemore, and D. M. Wolpert. 2000a. Abnormalities in the Awareness and Control of Action. *Philosophical Transactions of the Royal Society of London. Series B: Biological Sciences* 355 (1404): 1771–88.

———. 2000b. Explaining the Symptoms of Schizophrenia: Abnormalities in the Awareness of Action. *Brain Research Reviews* 31: 357–63.

Gasquoine, P. G. 1993. Alien Hand Sign. *Journal of Clinical and Experimental Neuropsychology* 15(5): 653–67.

Ginet, C. 1997. Freedom, Responsibility, and Agency. *Journal of Ethics* 1: 85–98.

Gold, M., J. C. Adair, D. H. Jacobs, and K. M. Heilman. 1994. Anosognosia for Hemiplegia: An Electrophysiologic Investigation of the Feed-Forward Hypothesis. *Neurology* 44(10): 1804–1808.

Goldberg, G., and K. K. Bloom. 1990. The Alien Hand Sign: Localization, Lateralization, and Recovery. *American Journal of Physical Medicine and Rehabilitation* 69: 228–38.

Haggard, P. 2005. Conscious Intention and Motor Cognition. *Trends in Cognitive Science* 9(6): 290–95.

Hallett, M. 2007. Volitional Control of Movement: The Physiology of Free Will. *Clinical Neurophysiology* 118: 1179–92.

Heilman, K. M. 1991. Anosognosia: Possible Neuropsychological Mechanisms. In *Awareness of Deficit after Brain Injury: Clinical and Theoretical Issues*, ed. G. P. Prigatano and D. L. Schacter, 53—62. New York: Oxford University Press.

Hohwy, J. 2004. The Experience of Mental Causation. *Behavior and Philosophy* 32: 377–400.

Holton, R. 2006. The Act of Choice. *Philosophers' Imprint* 6(3): 1–15.

Horgan, T., J. Tienson, and G. Graham. 2003. The Phenomenology of First-Person Agency. In *Physicalism and Mental Causation: The Metaphysics of Mind and Action*, ed. S. Walter and H.-D. Heckmann, 323–40. Exeter, UK: Imprint Academic.

Hornsby, J. 1980. *Actions*. London: Routledge and Kegan Paul.

Keeley, B. L. 2002. Making Sense of the Senses. *Journal of Philosophy* 99: 5–28.

Korsgaard, C. 1996. Creating the Kingdom of Ends: Reciprocity and Responsibility in Personal Relations. In *Creating the Kingdom of Ends*. New York: Cambridge University Press.

Marcel, A. 2003. The Sense of Agency: Awareness and Ownership of Action. In *Agency and Self-Awareness*, ed. J. Roessler and N. Eilan, 48–93. New York: Oxford University Press.

Mellors, C. S. 1970. First-Rank Symptoms of Schizophrenia. *British Journal of Psychiatry* 117: 15–23.

Mossel, B. 2005. Actions, Control, and Sensations of Acting. *Philosophical Studies* 124(2): 129–80.

Naccache, L., S. Dehaene, L. Cohen, M.-O. Habert, E. Guichart-Gomez., D. Galanaud, and J.-C. Willer. 2003. Effortless Control: Executive Attention and Conscious Feeling of Mental Effort Are Dissociable. *Neuropsychologia* 43: 1318–28.

Nahmias, E., S. Morris, T. Nadelhoffer, and J. Turner. 2004. The Phenomenology of Free Will. *Journal of Consciousness Studies* 11(7–8): 162–79.

Nudds, M. 2003. The Significance of the Senses. *Proceedings of the Aristotelian Society* 104(1): 31–51.

O'Shaughnessy, B. 1980. *The Will*, vol. 2. New York: Cambridge University Press.

———. 2003. The Epistemology of Physical Action. In *Agency and Self-Awareness*, ed. J. Roessler and N. Eilan, 345–57. New York: Oxford University Press.

Pacherie, E. 2007. The Anarchic Hand Syndrome and Utilization Behaviour: A Window onto Agentive Self-Awareness. *Functional Neurology* 22(4): 211–17.

———. 2008. The Phenomenology of Action: A Conceptual Framework. *Cognition* 107: 179–217.

———, M. Green, and T. Bayne. 2006. Phenomenology and Delusions. Who Put the "Alien" in Alien Control? *Consciousness and Cognition* 15: 566–77.

Peacocke, C. 2003. Awareness, Ownership, and Knowledge. In *Agency and Self-Awareness*, ed. J. Roessler and N. Eilan, 94–110. New York: Oxford University Press.

———. 2008. *Truly Understood*. New York: Oxford University Press.

Roessler, J., and N. Eilan, eds. 2003. *Agency and Self-Awareness*. New York: Oxford University Press.

Schilder, P. 1953. *Medical Psychology*. New York: Wiley and Sons.

Schwitzgebel, E., and M. S. Gordon. 2000. How Well Do We Know Our Own Conscious Experience? The Case of Human Echolocation. *Philosophical Topics* 28(2): 235–46.

Searle, J. 1983. *Intentionality*. New York: Cambridge University Press.

———. 2001. *Rationality in Action*. Cambridge, Mass.: MIT Press.

Shoemaker, S. 1968. Self-Reference and Self-Awareness. *Journal of Philosophy* 65(19): 555–67.

Siegel, S. 2005. The Phenomenology of Efficacy. *Philosophical Topics* 33(1): 265–84.

Sierra, M., and G. E. Berrios. 1998. Depersonalization: Neurobiological Perspectives. *Biological Psychiatry* 44: 898–908.

Strawson, G. 1986. *Freedom and Belief*. New York: Oxford University Press.

Tye, M. 1995. *Ten Problems of Consciousness: A Representational Theory of the Phenomenal Mind*. Cambridge, Mass.: MIT Press.

19

Cross-Modal Cuing and Selective Attention

Austen Clark

Experiments on cuing have long provided insights into the mechanisms of selective attention. A visual cue presented in a particular location can enhance subsequent visual discriminations at that location, making them faster, more accurate, or both. The standard interpretation of such experiments is that the cue attracts attention. Subsequent stimuli at that location are then more likely to be noticed as well, and thus they are more likely to receive quicker or more thorough processing.

Only recently has this paradigm been applied across modalities. In a cross-modal experiment, the cue is in one modality, and the target in another. The results are profoundly interesting: Across many pairs of modalities, a cue in one member of the pair can help direct attention in the other. Some of these results are described in this essay. They are interesting because they have profound implications about preattentive perceptual processing, the mechanisms that direct selective attention, and the character of the representations needed in order to do that directing successfully. The bulk of the essay draws these implications from the results.

1. SOME RESULTS

The argument focuses largely on the fascinating work done by Charles Spence, Jon Driver, and associates, starting in the 1990s. The experimental designs build on the "spatial cuing" paradigm of Michael Posner. A subject stares at a fixation point on a screen, and both cues and targets are presented on one side or another of that fixation point. Eye movements are controlled (perhaps tracked with an eye tracker), so that all of the orienting involved is "covert" orienting. Cuing can be of two sorts, which have come to be known as "endogenous" and "exogenous." In the "endogenous" form the occurrence of a cue is highly correlated with the subsequent presentation of a target on the same side. The subject is given time to learn this correlation and then, after each cue is presented, is given enough time to shift attention deliberately to the cued side. The deliberate shift of attention is "endogenous."

In contrast, "exogenous" cuing corresponds more closely to some salient or surprising stimulus that grabs one's attention reflexively and involuntarily. These experiments try to prevent the subject from forming or acting on an expectation based on the cue. They do this in two ways. First, the experiment is set up so that the cue is nonpredictive: All of the conditional probabilities of target location, given the cue, are the same. Second, the target also appears more quickly, within 100–300 milliseconds after the cue terminates.

Dependent variables are reaction times and accuracy. Posner found that, with a sufficiently salient cue, a target subsequently presented on the same ("congruent") side could be detected significantly faster than a target presented on the side opposite the cue ("incongruent"). Similarly, in the more leisurely and predictable endogenous cuing, a target presented on the same side as the cue could be detected more quickly and discriminated more accurately than targets presented on the opposite side. The interpretation of both effects is the same: The cue attracts selective attention to its location. Once one heeds that region, subsequent targets presented in the same region are more likely to be selected by selective attention for further, central processing. If targets receive more processing, they are discriminated more quickly, more accurately, or more thoroughly. So, the interpretation concludes, those targets are likely to be discriminated more quickly, accurately, or thoroughly than targets presented on the incongruent side.

Key features of this explanation have an even older lineage. Selective attention is thought to be a process that selects some representations but not others for further, "central" processing. To use various of the metaphors that have been suggested, it opens certain filters or gates or channels, or it allocates bandwidth or focuses the spotlight or adjusts the zoom lens, so that some stimuli are selected (and processed further), and others are not. Receipt of that further processing explains why some stimuli are processed more quickly, more accurately, or more thoroughly than others. In endogenous cuing the selection is deliberate, top down, and voluntary; in exogenous cuing the cue reflexively attracts or grabs attention and holds it to that region for a moment or two.

This same theoretical terminology is used throughout the reports of cross-modal cuing. The cross-modal experiments are similar to Posner's except that the cue is presented in one modality, and the target in another. For example, Spence and Driver (1996, 1997) have a subject staring at a fixation point in the center of a screen. At each of the four corners of the screen there is a light, and behind that light, a loudspeaker. The experimental task is to discriminate whether the light or the sound came from an upper or a lower corner. If one presents a nonpredictive visual cue on one side of the fixation point, a subsequent visual target on the same side is processed more quickly and accurately, just as Posner found. What is new is the finding that if one presents a nonpredictive visual cue on one side, a subsequent auditory target on the same side is likewise processed more quickly and accurately. Targets at incongruous locations are discriminated with less speed and lower accuracy.

Cross-modal cuing can work in the reverse direction as well (that is, from an auditory cue to a visual target). The mystery is: Which modality tells you how to do this? Audition cannot locate the light. Vision cannot place the sounds. The same problem recurs in all of the cross-modal effects. We seem to navigate effortlessly from one modality to another even though no one modality has the wherewithal to represent the entire route. So how do we do it?

The problem recurs across other pairs of modalities. Spence and Driver have demonstrated exogenous cross-modal cuing between vision and touch in both directions. In one design, for example, subjects hold a sponge in each hand between the index finger and the thumb. There is a small vibrator (a vibrotactile device) in the sponge near each digit and also small LEDs that can light up near each digit. A nonpredictive cue is given to one hand in one modality; then an up or down discrimination must be made in the other modality. Spence and Driver found that, just as with the audiovisual links, discriminations are faster if the cue is on the same side as the target. They have likewise found cross-modal cuing between touch and audition.

It should be emphasized that some experiments have failed to demonstrate exogenous cross-modal cuing; details of the task given to the subject and of the exact experimental paradigm used can make a big difference. Some cue-target pairs seem more delicate than others; visual cuing of auditory targets in particular has failed in a number of studies. Such cuing may arise only in specific experimental paradigms. Spence, MacDonald, and Driver (2004) summarize the situation as follows:

> The repeated positive findings of crossmodal exogenous spatial-cuing effects within paradigms that avoid many of the more obvious pitfalls inherent in the early research still provide existence-proof that such cross-modal influences can (sometimes) arise, as also confirmed with the various other methods that we review below. The existing failures to observe exogenous spatial-cuing effects for some particular pairings of modalities might reflect specific details of the paradigms used. (Spence, MacDonald, and Driver 2004, 291).

For the purposes of this essay, the important point is not whether cuing always occurs but that it can sometimes occur. In all of the pairwise combinations among vision, audition, and touch and in both directions, exogenous cross-modal cuing effects *sometimes* arise. To raise the conceptual issues, *once* would be enough.

1.1. Some Initial Unpacking

The first step in explaining these phenomena is to propose that the cue draws attention to its location: "[O]ur cuing effects must reflect a genuine improvement of localization in the cued region . . . owing to the cue attracting covert attention there" (Driver and Spence 1998b, 1320). The second premise of the explanation is that once drawn to a locale, attention "spreads." Within one modality it can spread from the "cued region" to regions in the vicinity. Even more powerfully, it can spread across modalities. At least that is the way Driver and Spence put it: "Our findings suggest that a strongly biased spatial distribution of endogenous attention in one modality tends to spread into other modalities as well, but at a reduced level" (ibid., 1325).

The locution is intriguing. What does it mean to say that attention in one modality tends to "spread" into other modalities? If one is spreading jam, for example, where can one find the toast that would connect sights to sounds?

To unpack this a bit, we need to know how to interpret talk about the "spatial distribution of attention" and about attention being "drawn" to a cue. It would be helpful to spell out how attention is disposed at a given moment, so that we can then describe how that disposition changes over time and in response to what. Attention at a given moment could be characterized by describing which representations it has selected and which it has not. Per hypothesis there is some selectivity operative at that moment: Some representations are selected for further, central processing, and some are not. What is this principle of selection, and how can one describe it? In the perceptual domain, at least, one could catalog it exhaustively by listing all of the stimuli that are possible at time t and, for each one, giving the probability that, at time t, it is selected for further, central processing. This would be a long list, and it would be impossible to complete, but the important point is that the list has to include some merely possible stimuli—stimuli that might have happened but did not.

The current state of selectivity of the system is a dispositional property; it includes propensities to respond to various possible stimuli. One might be paying very close attention to whatever sounds come out of a room but do nothing since no sound ever emerges. Nevertheless, sounds from that room would be processed with alacrity, were any to occur. What selectivity means is that one is disposed to process a certain subset of stimuli more thoroughly or quickly than others. To characterize that disposition adequately, the list must include some stimuli that in fact did not occur but might have.

I call such a list (of possible stimuli each associated with a probability of being selected) a "selection principle." It characterizes the current state of selectivity or the principle operative in the system at a moment: how the system is disposed to select some stimuli, and not others, for further, central processing.

The idea gives a simple way to describe the difference between "location-based" and "object-based" selection principles. Scan all of the stimuli possible at time t, and collect all of those whose probability of being selected for further processing is greater than some arbitrary cut-off value. If the selection is location based, then all those stimuli will be clustered in some region of space whose boundaries do not necessarily correspond to any identifiable object but are perhaps delimited in terms of spatial relations to the sense organs. Anything that might happen in that location is more prone to be selected subsequently. If the selection is object based, then all of those stimuli will cluster on some object (or objects) or proper parts thereof. Anything that might happen to some part of some selected object is more prone to be selected subsequently.

When the focus of attention changes, these odds change, but nothing else need change overtly. If a subject is told to pay attention to the lights, the odds that the subject will perform quick visual discriminations go up, and the odds of quick auditory discriminations go down. When the subject is faced with exactly the same stimulus array but told to pay attention to the sounds, the odds of quick auditory discrimination go up, but those of visual ones go down. This change in selectivity can happen in the absence of any overt behavior; our subject sits motionless in both cases but in one is paying attention to the sights and in the other to the sounds.

Now the fundamentally interesting finding of the vast literature on cuing and priming is that perception of a cue can *change* the selectivity operative in the system. Even more exciting are the cross-modal findings that it can change the selectivity operative in other modalities. How does it do this? More important for our purposes, what information must the system have available in order to implement those changing odds? It is vital to understand both *what* the system needs to represent in order to manifest such selectivity and *how* the system represents what it needs to represent to effect such changes in its own operating parameters.

1.2. How to Be Selective

An organism graced with selective attention can alter the flow of information within itself. With a shift in attention, some pathways are relatively enhanced or amplified, and others depressed or inhibited. Some bits of information are now more likely to receive central elaboration, others less so; some channels have faster effects, and others are demoted. Something within the system must bring about these changes in the way information flows within itself—changes in its selectivity—and let us call that functionally specified entity the "selectivity effector." It is that which effects the changes in selectivity that are manifest when the focus of attention shifts. There are various models of what a selectivity effector might be, and many use metaphors of gates and switches, amplifiers and filters, pathways and channels (see LaBerge 1995, 39). So a selectivity effector might be something like a "switch" in a computer network: a device that establishes different links between different parts of the network at different times, depending on the projected transmissions and the existing traffic. By opening and shutting gates and switches in different ways, such an effector could alter the flow of information within the system and thereby change the odds that some bits and not others receive further, central processing.

The job might get done in various ways, but however it is done, it is clear that the effector needs certain critical bits of information to do its job. If our experimental subject is to pay attention to the sights and not the sounds, for example, the selectivity effector must accurately register which gates and switches control visual processing and which ones control audition. It would be embarrassing and perhaps disastrous to confuse them. If a loud sound is to draw attention to its source, the selectivity effector must open just those gates and switches needed to allow the processing of stimuli from locations *near* that source. Here, too, mistakes might be disastrous. Rewiring oneself on the fly is a risky business.

The selectivity effector must then be guided—and guided well—when it does its job. If you are going to rewire yourself, you need accurate information about where the wires are and where they go. Let us drop the electrical metaphors, and try instead to characterize that which provides the information needed to direct the selectivity effector when it does its job. Such a "director" must extract and pass along the information needed in order for selective attention to make the appropriate selections. It does not make those selections itself. It passes that information along to whatever parts of the system change the selectivity operative at a given moment. The focus here is not how the selections are implemented but rather what sort of information is necessary for those selections to be appropriately sensitive to the environment.

Start with the very simplest case: exogenous location-based cuing within one modality. Cue x might be a flash of light, and target y a later flash nearby. The proffered explanation is that x attracts attention to its location, and, given the appropriate stimulus onset asynchrony (or SOA), a subsequent stimulus at that same location or nearby is thereby more likely also to be selected. The information needed to specify how subsequent targets are selected is, simply, their location. The selectivity director needs tell the selectivity effector where the cue occurred but nothing more.

Notice, though, that this description oversimplifies this simplest case. The mere fact that target y is in a region that cue x previously occupied will not suffice. We need to show that the system picks up and registers these facts. The cue must be perceived as occurring in region R, and the target must be perceived as occurring in or near the same region. If there is a cue in region R, but it is not perceived, then there is no cuing effect to explain. Conversely, it is not the actual location of the target stimulus that matters but rather the location it is perceived to have. It must be perceived to be in the same general location as the cue, and as long as it is so perceived, we can get a cuing effect.

These "regions" are, therefore, perceptual; they are locations *as* perceived, to be specified by whatever terms the given modality musters when it manages spatial discriminations. The boundaries of such regions are more or less vague, depending on the accuracy of spatial discriminations possible in that vicinity (or in that direction). Some of these regions might not have limits in all three orthogonal axes; they may be delimited in only two, or even one, such direction. "On the horizontal plane" identifies a region in this sense: We know the elevation of any point in that region, but that is the only axis that is specified. Its azimuth and depth are left unspecified.

Audiovisual cuing provides examples of regions that have vague boundaries along some spatial axes and totally lack such boundaries along others. Auditory discrimination of differences in the elevation of sounds is relatively poor, while discrimination of their azimuths is relatively good. So if a sound draws attention to a certain region, its horizontal extent is delimited more precisely than its vertical. Depth is very poorly discriminated and might not be needed at all to manage cuing. The region of the sound can be thought of as the *direction* it comes from: a perhaps irregularly shaped cone aimed roughly at azimuth theta, elevation epsilon, extending outward in space. Like "on the horizontal plane," this region does not specify a depth at all. Many points within that cone would qualify. Such a region might be the R_m picked out by auditory spatial discrimination.

However, with this amendment we get a possible location-based account. The cue attracts attention to a visually represented region R_m. Once attention is attracted to that region, it stays awhile and perhaps spreads a bit. Then, given an appropriate SOA, a subsequent target that is perceived as occurring in or near region R_m is more likely to be selected by selective attention. That is, given an appropriate SOA, the only information needed to specify whether a subsequent target is likely to be selectively enhanced is whether or not it is perceived as occurring in or near that same region. This is a simple, location-based selection principle.

In contrast, if selective attention works in an object-based way, then to write down its selection principles we must at least sometimes use terms identifying objects. Selection is not solely dependent on perceived location; instead, it sometimes ranges over elements that are perceived to be parts of the same object as things already selected. Of course, the theorist here has the burden of specifying what is meant by "same object." It will in any case be an object as perceived: something represented by the system as the same object. However, with that proviso, there is no dearth of accounts of what might constitute these "perceptual objects." The central idea is that target y is more likely to be selectively enhanced if it is perceived as being part of the same object as was x.

2. EXOGENOUS CUING WITHOUT REMAPPING

Now at last all the pieces are on the board, and we can consider the conceptual implications of cross-modal cuing. In this section and the next I list a number of these implications, which follow from the models and results reported in Spence and Driver (2004).

In the cross-modal case the cue is in one modality, and the target in another. I use subscripts to flag this fact. Cue x occurs in modality M, and it is perceived to be in region R_m. The cue might be a sound, for example, and it draws attention to an acoustically discriminated region. The subsequent target y occurs in some distinct modality N. The region in which it is perceived to occur is delimited by a modality that is different from the one that delimits region R_m. The target might be a light, for example, and its location is discriminated visually. So the region the target is perceived to occupy will be dubbed R_n—a region as discriminated by modality N.

For many pairs M, N, cuing in modality M can improve the speed and reliability of discriminations in modality N. It has been demonstrated in both directions and in every possible pairing among vision, audition, and touch. The first inference drawn from this is that cuing in modality M can help to direct attention in modality N. In particular:

> 2.1. Cuing in modality M can help one select some subsequent subset of representations in modality N for further, central processing.

Given the theoretical assumptions sketched earlier, this inference is straightforward. One finds that some discriminations in the target modality N are completed more quickly or more accurately given the cue in modality M. So the changes in selectivity given a cue are not confined to the modality of the cue. Furthermore, we can infer:

> 2.2. A cue in modality M can provide information sufficient to yield some principle in terms of which some representations in modality N are selected.

For shifts in selective attention to be adaptive, the mechanism that does the shifting (the selectivity effector) must be at least somewhat sensitive to features and events in the immediate surroundings. The task of picking out the next thing to be noticed itself requires perceptual information. If, for example, one is selecting targets found in some region, then information about the extent of that region must be accessible to guide selective attention. However it is done, there must be some route whereby some perceptual information can make it to the mechanisms that guide attention. Otherwise, the selections made would have no reliable correlation with any features of the perceptible environment.

Cross-modal cuing shows decisively that information gleaned from one modality can serve to guide the selections applied within other modalities. The selection principle seems to be overlap of location: The cue draws attention to a region, and one can then discriminate stimuli in other modalities in that same region more quickly, more accurately, or both. In common-sense terms, a sound can draw your attention to a region or vicinity, and, for a while thereafter, visible events in that vicinity are likely also to be perceived more quickly, more accurately, or both. Notice that any such common-sense description treats the region as something that contains both auditory and visual stimuli. Events in that region can be perceived by any of various modalities. Such a region is similar to a common-sense physical object, which is something that can be both seen and touched, for example. For this reason these regions or objects are sometimes called "distal," "allocentric," or "external," but the critical point is that these modifiers do not indicate that we have thereby identified some new kind of space. Instead, there is and always has been just one space in which anything that can be found is to be found. What these modifiers indicate are variations in the ways of identifying regions in that one space. A "visual location" is not a new kind of location but simply a visual way of indicating a location in the one and only space.

Cross-modal cuing requires that locations be indicated in ways not limited to any one modality; for example, a visual specifier of location and an auditory specifier of location can specify the very same place (or places that largely overlap), albeit in different manners.[1] It is by no means a trivial matter to establish that two distinct specifiers both point to the same region, yet it must be done and done correctly if selective attention is to be guided in an adaptive way.

The task then is to formulate, starting with modality M, a selection principle that can be applied to a distinct modality N. How might one pick out a visible region in acoustical terms? Or a visual region in tactile terms? In modality M one makes the spatial discriminations needed to delimit region R_m, but the target occurs in a different modality, and the extent of the region R_n in which that target occurs is delimited by entirely distinct features. So forging this link is the critical step for correctly guiding the formulation of a new selection principle. One needs to rely on the fact that the acoustic specifiers of location R_m pick out a region that largely overlaps the one indicated by the visual specifiers of location R_n. Such guidance must be something the system can represent and compute, with results that are mostly reliable. Only then could that which effects the selectivity of the system do so in an adaptive way.

---

[1] Identity would require the boundaries of the indicated regions to be exactly congruent, which would be rare in the cross-modal case, given the differences in spatial discrimination in the different modalities. Overlap does not require congruent boundaries but nevertheless implies a "partial" identification. That is, some of the places indicated by one modality are identical to some places indicated by the other.

One condition on possible solutions is relatively straightforward:

2.3. If the cross-modal selection principle is location based, then information about locations as represented in modality M must be commensurable with information about locations as represented in modality N.

By "commensurable with" I mean that one can be derived as a function of the other.[2] Unless they are commensurable, we cannot use these "specifiers of location" to formulate a cross-modal selection principle. If there were not even a statistical association between them, cues in one modality would not enable one to make any predictions at all about events in another.

Consider the cuing from auditory to visual events as an example. As mentioned, the auditory region might be specified purely in terms of a direction: a cone, roughly centered on some azimuth and elevation, giving the direction (relative to the two ears) from which the sound appears to emanate. Any point within that cone can qualify; depth is not even specified. Similarly, as long as we have a fixed eye position, many of the cuing tasks could be managed with nothing more than an analogous, visual "direction." In vision the azimuth and elevation might both be defined by angles from the visual fixation point, and both of them would be much more precisely delimited than is possible in audition. However, if an acoustic cue could be massaged to yield such a visual direction, then the cuing results could be explained. Visual depth is not relevant to the task; as long as we could direct selective attention to select any visual events occurring in or near that cone, we would selectively enhance the appropriate targets.

Proposition 2.3 implies that if we observe auditory cuing of visual discriminations, then these visual directions must be commensurable with auditory directions. Region R_m is the auditory direction (or cone); R_n the visual. Commensurability is easy: Given a fixed eye position, auditory azimuths and elevations can readily be converted into visual ones.

Notice that even if the locations R_m and R_n overlap, it is only if the system somehow trades on that overlap or relies on it that we can justifiably claim that the system represents them to *be* overlapping. The auditory system does not "know" that R_m overlaps a region that can be discriminated visually. So even though in fact these locations are (as always) locations within a "common space," to this point they are not yet represented *as* locations within a common space. To this point there is nothing to show that the system represents auditorally specified regions as being, even partially or potentially, the same as visually specified ones.

---

[2] The function might be probabilistic and error prone. At the very least we need some statistical association: One can be predicted from the other with odds that are at least somewhat better than chance.

However, if cross-modal selection principles are ever used, then the situation changes:

2.4. If the overlap of regions R_m and R_n is used by the system to generate a selection principle applied to targets in modality N, then the system represents those regions *as* overlapping.

That is, if the system is using its specification of R_m to create instructions so as to guide the system to select R_n, then the system itself is trading on the identification. We find downstream consumers of the information who rely on the world being as represented. Here the downstream consumer is selective attention itself.[3] It relies on the correct specification, in visual terms, of the region where the acoustic cue occurred. Specifically, the selectivity effector can do its job successfully only if the world is such that the region indicated by R_m overlaps that of R_n. So not only is it a region common to the two modalities; it is now also represented *as* a common region. Such talk is not justified until this stage, but here at last it is.

3. REMAPPING

The exogenous cross-modal cuing experiments discussed so far give rather weak grounds for thinking that the system is trading or relying on identification of locales. Those grounds are bolstered enormously when we consider the phenomena that Spence and Driver call "remapping." Remapping arises when we remove one of the constraints on the task assigned to the subject. So far all the experiments discussed require the subject to maintain a fixed posture. All the orienting is covert: The gaze does not shift, the head is fixed, and the arms are immobile, held in a neutral posture. What happens if we allow our subjects to move?

For example, all of the visuotactile experiments thus far proceeded with the subject's hands and arms in a neutral position, with the right hand on the right side of the body and the left hand on the left. But what happens if you cross your arms? The question seems a simple one, but only in retrospect: This experiment was first tried in 1996. If the selection functions were hard wired, then a vibration on the right hand might draw attention to regions on the right side of the body, no matter where that hand has wandered. If the system were a little better designed, a vibration on the right hand could draw attention to stimuli on the left side of the body, if that is where the hand happened to be. The latter is what was found.

Even more compelling is the converse result, using visual cues for tactile targets. In the neutral position the light on the right side will speed tactile discriminations on the right hand. If the arms are crossed,

---

[3] The methodology and terminology here both derive from "consumer" semantics, also known as *bio-* or *teleosemantics*. See Millikan (1984, 2004).

the light on the right side speeds tactile discriminations on the left hand, which is now located closer to that light than is the right hand. Notice that this "closer to" is a cross-modal relative distance: When a subject's arms are crossed, tactile stimuli on the left hand are now closer to the light source than are tactile stimuli on the right hand. This "closer to" cannot be assessed by touch alone or by vision alone; it requires representation of the place of the light and the place of the hands in a common space. We must locate the light in a system of places and relative distances in which we can also locate the tactile stimuli on the two hands. Otherwise, no sense could be given to the proposition that the light on the right side is now closer to the left hand. If the latter explains why attention "spreads" from the region of the light to the tactile stimuli on the left hand, then the system itself must have access to such "cross-modal" or "common" distances. Its representation of and facility with these cross-modal distances is revealed when it formulates a new selection principle, using the location of the light on the right side to direct attention to the left hand.

Similar results are found for audiovisual cross-modal cuing. Label the loudspeakers A, B, C, and D. Loudspeaker B is the second one from the left. In the first set of trials, the gaze is focused straight ahead between speakers B and C. Sounds from loudspeaker B will speed the processing of visual stimuli that occur to the left of the fixation point. The gaze is then shifted leftward to a point between speakers A and B. After that shift in gaze, if the system were well designed, sounds from loudspeaker B should speed the processing of visual stimuli in a region immediately to the *right* of the fixation point. The latter is what was found.

We already knew the selection principles include multiple modalities. Now we learn that creating a new cross-modal selection principle is not a hard-wired affair but is sensitive to and permuted by the current bodily position. Selectivity is modified on the fly as posture changes.

This adds a new wrinkle to the explanation of how a cue can improve the processing of a target in a different modality. If the subject's head position is constant, then sounds from loudspeaker B will, both before and after the shift in gaze, still draw attention to the auditorally defined direction R_m—a sound near the sagittal plane but a bit to the left. However, if visual stimuli in that same (unchanging) region are to continue to receive attentional amplification, something has to change when one shifts one's gaze. The visual relation between the (auditorally identified) target region and the visual fixation point changes with that shift in gaze. Where previously the auditory stimulus provided information that guided attention to visual stimuli to the left of the visual fixation point, now it must guide attention to visual stimuli to the right of the visual fixation point.

If we label the old visual specifiers of the target region S_n, then with the shift in gaze we need new visual specifiers S_n' if we are to continue to pick out visual stimuli in the same region R_m. What is the relation between the old S_n and the new S_n'? Or, to put it another way, after the eyeballs move, how does the system determine the visual locations of the regions to which auditory cues will now draw attention? Common sense has a short answer: The loudspeakers have not moved, and so attention will continue to be drawn to the same place. As Driver and Spence put it:

> Sounds drew visual attention in the "correct" direction with respect to external space, even when the eyes were deviated in the head. This entails that the mapping between auditory locations and retinal locations, which directed exogenous cross-modal attention, must have changed, to keep vision and audition in register as regards external space. (Driver and Spence 1998b, 1324)

It would again be a mistake for philosophers to read this as implying that "external space" is a kind of space to be contrasted with all the other kinds of space. Instead, the issue is how the one and only space is represented. If it is represented *as* external, then the routes to identifying locations within it are not confined to any one modality. One can locate within it at least some of the things one hears, some of the things one sees, and some of the things one feels. What remapping will add, critically, is that one can also identify some of the places within it proprioceptively, for some of those places overlap places where one's body is located. For now we can state remapping as follows:

3.1. When postures change, cross-modal selection principles can change so as to continue to direct attention to the same place.

The same place in "external space," if you like, though I hope in this context the modifier is redundant.[4] Principle 3.1 summarizes some of the experimental results just reviewed and gives us a simple method for determining the new visual specifier S_n', which is activated after a shift in gaze. To find it, find which visual specifier now specifies the same place that the old one did:

> [T]he spatial mapping between modalities gets updated when different postures are adopted. . . . The senses thus remain in useful register, with respect to each other and the outside world, despite changes in posture. (Driver and Spence 1998b, 1323)

Since we can do this, it follows that the system has information sufficient to do it:

3.2. After successful remapping, the system has information sufficient, given representations of stimuli in modality M, to select representations in modality N that are representations of the same place.

---

[4] The modifier is useful only if one wants to contrast "external space" (i.e., space represented *as* external) with "visual space" (i.e., space *as* represented visually). To avoid confusion, think of these modifiers as adverbs. They flag different ways of identifying places.

Some theorists describe the earliest visual maps as "retinotopic," which (strictly speaking) would imply that they are *about* the events on the retina. I urge that we think of them as retinocentric but *not* retinotopic. That is, they might use a retina-relative manner of identifying their subject matters, but that subject matter is resolutely distal. The maps are *about* events in front of the eyes, out there in external space. Remapping shows this. How? It shows that the system uses the visual specifiers of location (and auditory specifiers of location and so on) to track regions of external space. Downstream consumers of the feature maps can ignore the differences among the retinocentric specifiers and instead use them to track the one distal location that they specify. The visual system in effect "sees through" the retinocentric differences (it remaps them) so as to keep a clear eye on their subject matter: the same unchanging region specified.

With each shift in gaze the system that directs attention unceremoniously throws out the old visual specifiers of location and grabs new ones, and the new ones are precisely those that now specify the same external region that the old ones did. It manifests the utmost indifference to the differences among the specifiers; what matters is the region specified. Its loyalties are not retinotopic. This is precisely what shows us that those visual specifiers of location are used as specifiers; they are swapped in and out as need be to continue to track the region specified.

4. MEANS SUFFICIENT FOR REMAPPING

Since we can remap, it follows that we possess means sufficient for remapping. What then are those means? What sort of information does a subject use in order to remap?

When bodily posture changes, the selection principle that relates the cue in modality M to the target in modality N must be modified, so that the senses remain in register with regard to external space, and attention can be directed to the correct place. Evidently the subject perceives the changes in bodily position, and those perceptions can be used to effect the remapping. So (sometimes) proprioceptive input is used to change the cross-modal selection principle and to change it in such a way that it continues to select representations that are *of* the same place. Put another way, the selection principles operative between two modalities can be changed, given information arising from a third one.

4.1. Proprioceptive information can be used successfully to modify the operative selection principle, even in cases in which neither modality is proprioceptive.

Remapping is particularly straightforward in the audiovisual experiments. It is easy to see how an auditory direction is commensurable with visual ones. With a shift in gaze, an auditory direction must be associated with a new visual direction—a new visual specification of the region to which attention continues to be drawn. However, a shift in gaze is a shift in the *direction* of gaze, and this direction is just another direction commensurable with the other two. So a change in the direction of gaze could be used to remap auditory directions onto new visual ones. Here then is a particular example of 4.1:

> 4.1. Audiovisual. The auditory and the visual specifiers of location are both commensurable with a third set: the proprioceptive indicators of the direction of gaze. The latter can be used to adjust the link between the first two.

Oddly enough, even though the link that needs to be reforged connects audition to vision, the information needed to reforge that link is found in neither modality but instead in proprioception. Proprioceptive information about the direction of gaze can do that job, and sometimes it seems to be the only information available.

The same holds for all the visual-tactile experiments in which subjects are prevented from seeing their hands or arms. To determine which buzzing feeling is closer to the seen light, those subjects must employ proprioception:

> [T]he spatial mapping from particular retinal activations in vision, to somatic activations in touch, gets updated when the hands adopt different postures. This is presumably owing to an influence from proprioceptive signals specifying the current hand position. . . . Thus a third modality (here proprioception) can apparently influence the attentional interactions between two other modalities (here vision and touch). (Driver and Spence 1998b, 1322)

Why proprioception? Spence and Driver suggest a simple answer. Sensory receptors are spread across the body. Changes in posture are important in sensory terms when they change the spatial relations between one set of receptors and another. For remapping purposes, the important information is not about bodily posture per se but rather what it indicates about the altered spatial distribution of receptors. We need remapping when (and only when) a change in bodily posture changes the spatial distribution of one set of receptors relative to another.

> 4.2. The proprioceptive information needed to effect a remapping specifies the location of parts of one's own body; in particular the spatial disposition of one's receptors.

An overly fancy way to put it is as follows: Those receptors are represented as located within the same space as the auditory and visual stimuli that one senses.[5] A less fancy but more accurate statement is

---

[5] This is too fancy partly because of the suggestion that the receptors might be located in some space other than the one in which stimuli are found and also because the representations involved do not employ the concepts of "receptor" or of "space."

this: Information specifying the spatial disposition of receptor surfaces is commensurable with information specifying the location of stimuli in the various modalities. In these early, stimulus-driven, preattentive processes we seem already to find means of identifying locations that can comprise all of the various classes of auditory, visual, and tactile stimuli, as well as the various receptors they stimulate.

Remapping thus adds another sense in which the "common" space is common. Now within it one must also be able to locate one's own body or, in particular, one's own receptors. It includes not only the things one senses but also the receptors used to sense them. We must include the latter to keep straight all of the relations among the former. The point provides a simple, sensory analog for a feature of our conceptual framework that was noted by Kant and reemphasized by Strawson. Here is how Strawson described it:

> It is a single picture that we build, a unified structure, in which we our-selves have a place, and in which every element is thought of as directly or indirectly related to every other, and the framework of the structure, the common, unifying system of relations is spatio-temporal. By means of identifying references, we fit other people's reports and stories, along with our own, into the single story about empirical reality; and this fit-ting together, this connexion, rests ultimately on relating the particulars which figure in the stories in the single spatio-temporal system which we ourselves occupy. (Strawson 1963, 17)

I suggest that something analogous is found even in humbler surround-ings, where we do not yet have thoughts, identifying reference, reports, stories, or even words. It is found among the sensory systems of represen-tation employed in cross-modal cuing. They, too, must fit both the things sensed and the receptors used to sense them into one common framework of spatial relations. However, we do not need a conceptual framework of "material bodies" for this: It is built into our sensory mechanisms.

Even in that simpler, sensory setting, there are good reasons to think that the system uses its specifiers of location in something like the way that referring terms are used. I have argued elsewhere (Clark 2000) that the way they are used in solving the problem of feature integration (or "property binding") gives us grounds for thinking that the specifiers of location have at least a quasi-referential role. They serve to indicate the subject matter of the representations in ways that are independent of what the representations say about that subject matter.

However, cross-modal cuing, and in particular remapping, provide independent and stronger substantiation for this idea. The challenge is to guide selective attention in such a way that its selections will be adaptive. Cross-modal cuing shows that when a cue changes the state of selectivity operative in the system, the system maps the region of the cue to regions of potential targets even if the latter are specified in other modalities. It has to do so if a cue in one modality can selectively enhance the process-ing of targets in another.

Furthermore, remapping shows that the use of different specifiers of location is not idle but that the system is sensitive to and relying on identifications of what those specifiers specify. Relations between sets of specifiers in two different modalities depend upon bodily position. Remapping shows that the system is exquisitely sensitive to the proprioceptive registration of that position. It uses proprioceptive information to alter the mapping from a cue in one modality to a target in another. When posture changes, the system immediately swaps an old indicator for a new one, and the swap is made so that the new indicator specifies the same region the old one did. Such use demonstrates that all three sets of specifiers must be commensurable with one another and that they are being used to track locations in space. Otherwise, it is very hard to understand why the shifts in selective attention proceed as they do or how sensory mechanisms could possibly guide those shifts so that they remain adaptive.

5. LOCATIONS AND OBJECTS

A final nugget can be extracted from these results: They bear on the contrast between location-based and object-based models of selective attention. The difference between these is easy to describe in terms of selection principles. If selective attention were purely location based, then all of the principles of selection employed by selective attention could be written down with terms whose reference is confined to the locations of stimuli, whereas if selective attention is object based, then to formulate the selection principles one must employ terms that refer to objects of some sort. They might be "visual objects" or "proto-objects," but in any case these entities must be distinct from mere locations. One simple distinction is that objects can move, whereas locations cannot.

It is clear that there are object-based effects on selective attention. Consider, though, the more radical thesis that *all* of the selection principles are object based: that selection principles *always* employ terms that refer to some kind of object. The system never uses location-based selection. This thesis is suggested in places by Zenon Pylyshyn (2003):

> [F]ocal attention is typically directed at *objects* rather than at *places*, and therefore . . . the earliest stages of vision are concerned with individuating objects and . . . when visual properties are encoded, they are encoded as *properties of individual objects.* (Pylyshyn 2003, 181)

The cross-modal effects pose a difficulty for this claim. A system that always selects only objects runs into problems representing what it needs to represent to make cross-modal links. If, for example, the representations of "visual objects" represent just their visible features, then it becomes very difficult to explain how a visual object can serve as a cue that directs attention toward some sounds (and not others) or toward some tactile stimuli (and not others).

Part of the issue depends on what one means by a "pure object-based" system and what the representations thereof may or may not include. For Pylyshyn, for example, a "visual object" is just anything to which a visual index can be attached. The index may be purely demonstrative, and it might not include any representation of the location of its referent. However, if we do represent locations, this system treats them exclusively as properties of the indexed items. We have a small number of indexed visual objects, and each such object might have a location that is stored in its "object file."

A further question is whether the representation of visual objects allows for their location to be represented in anything other than visual terms. As far as I can tell, this is an open question for Pylyshyn; nothing commits him to an answer either way. Visual objects themselves typically have lots of nonvisual properties since (as Pylyshyn notes) visual objects typically turn out to be ordinary physical objects, and ordinary physical objects are more than merely visual. However, these are properties of the objects themselves; the question is still open whether visual *representations* of such objects do or do not represent anything other than visual features of them.

Both choices face difficulties. One might naturally assume that visual representations of visual objects represent only their visible features. The locations stored in a visual object file would be purely visual. In audition we would likewise have "acoustic objects," whose locations are represented purely auditorally, and "proprioceptive objects," whose locations are purely proprioceptive. The problem, however, is this: In no one of these systems could we represent or express a cross-modal identification. We could not represent that this visually identified object is in the same place as that tactile one. To represent such facts we need both systems, and we need to secure identifications between them.

The problem has been a familiar one since Berkeley's *New Theory of Vision*: "The extension, figures, and motions perceived by sight are specifically distinct from the ideas of touch, called by the same names; nor is there any such thing as one idea, or kind of idea, common to both senses" (Berkeley 1709, paragraph 127). I take the first claim to be inarguable: that visual ideas are not the same ideas as ideas of touch.

This problem is not insuperable; one can simply suppose that there is some extra- or supramodal mechanism that *can* correlate the two kinds of objects. The layered maps in the superior colliculus and multimodal neurons in the parietal cortex provide possible candidates. Nonetheless, there remains a deeper problem if we insist that all of the representations involved are object based—that information about locations or directions is always stored as locations or directions of *objects*. To explain cross-modal cuing, we need to represent cross-modal relative distances in a much more fulsome manner than seems possible in a small set of object files.

Consider the visual-tactile experiments, for example. A light goes on near the subject's left hand. Subsequent tactile stimuli on the left index finger or thumb are discriminated more quickly than those on the right hand. The location-based explanation is that visual attention is drawn to a region that is visually identified, and then tactile stimuli in or near that region are more likely to be selected for central processing. So tactile discriminations and reaction times for stimuli in that vicinity improve.

An object-based account would propose that attention is drawn to a visual object (the light), and then it spreads to tactile objects that are nearby. However, notice this last step requires that "nearby" must be assessed cross-modally. The left hand is relatively closer to the light than is the right hand. The system must have access to such cross-modal relative distances in order for attention to "spread" appropriately from visual objects to the appropriate tactile ones. Put another way, given the visual object, the system must have preattentive access to the relative distances between it and any of the discernible tactile objects, the discernible acoustic objects, the discernible proprioceptive objects, and so on. Otherwise, attention could not spread to the "closer" ones of the discernible candidates.

Unfortunately, once this problem has been recognized, it spreads everywhere. We cannot simply store one location per object since objects have disparate parts that are spread out in space. Stimuli that attract attention might be associated with any such part. It will not do, for example, to store exactly one location for the entirety of the felt left hand; the up/down discriminations require one to discriminate the vibrations on the tip of the index finger from the ones on the side of the thumb. One can imagine innumerable variations of this experiment employing tactile stimuli on many different places on the hand. For these we would need to represent relative distances among the perceptibly distinct places of all the different parts of the hand. If these are distinct "tactile objects," then tactile objects essentially become equivalent to discriminably distinct places. Any place of any part of the hand that one can feel to be distinct from any other such place would qualify. That recipe yields a plethora of places.

It would be impracticable to store all of these relative distances as properties within each object file.[6] Each such file would have to include distances from each part of the object to all of the current visual, proprioceptive, or auditory stimuli that might attract attention. Finally, the specifiers of location must be cast in terms that all three modalities can employ, so that the cross-modal relative distances can be expressed.

---

[6] One might object that they do not need to be stored since the distances are out there in the world, and to update them one need merely probe the world perceptually. The problem with this response is that such relative distances have preattentive effects. Directing a perceptual probe at the world requires attention already to be directed correctly.

I submit that the upshot is essentially equivalent to a location-based system. That a vibration on the hand can cue auditory attention to a particular region requires a preattentive capacity to compare locations and distances across the two modalities. It can be described rather awkwardly as relative distances between tactile objects and auditory objects, but the system of relative distances required is one that cannot be confined to any one modality, so the talk of "tactile objects" and "auditory objects" becomes otiose. Much simpler, then, is to acknowledge that the specifiers can specify locations, and do so independently of what particular objects or what kinds of object occupy those locations.

The audiovisual cuing experiments provide vivid examples of what I mean by saying that visual objects and auditory objects would become otiose. Such cuing could be accomplished with nothing more than specifiers of visual and auditory *directions*. Suppose, as in the later experiments, we use designs in which differences in elevation drop out as irrelevant. Then we need the direction of the gaze relative to the head, the angle between the focal point of the gaze and the visible stimulus, and the direction of the sound relative to the head. The task reduces to converting an auditory azimuth to a visual one or vice versa. So the audiovisual cross-modal cuing effects require that one compare directions of sounds to those of visual stimuli, but nothing more than that.

The parsimonious hypothesis is that we have what we need, but no more. We need visual and auditory directions to solve this problem, but we do not need visual or auditory objects. Even if visual and auditory objects exist for other reasons and could be put to work, they would not gain employment when this problem needs to be solved. It can be solved on a skimpy basis—a skimpy *ontological* basis.

In short, starting with a pure object-based model, we seem forced to embrace a system of specifiers of location with the following properties. They must be available for any discriminable place of any part of any object. They must be comparable across all the relevant pairs of modalities.; The comparisons must be computable without regard to which "objects" occupy those locations. Finally, the comparisons can be completed preattentively. If we have all that we basically have variables that range over locations, and do so independently of what objects are found at those locations.

6. CONCLUSIONS

My conclusions fall into three broad categories. First, the evidence for cross-modal cuing supports the view that a number of different modalities transact significant business in a location-based way. Information about locations in one can be transformed into a principle that selects stimuli in another.

Second, the remapping studies in particular support the view that the locations represented by the various modalities that can participate in cross-modal cuing are locations in external space and that they are represented as such. They are not locations within mind-dependent "sensory" spaces, nor are they places on the retina. They are at best retinocentric, but not retinotopic. With a change in posture, specifiers of location within an affected modality are swapped so that new specifiers continue to specify the same region. This is the critical finding needed to show that the system is using those specifiers *as* specifiers and that what they specify are locations in external space.

Finally, a pure object-based system does not seem to have the wherewithal to express the content of the identifications needed in order to secure cross-modal mapping. We have to represent information about locations in a fuller way than is therein allowed.

References

Berkeley, G. 1709. An Essay towards a New Theory of Vision. In *George Berkeley: Philosophical Works*, ed. M. R. Ayers, 1–59. London: Dent, 1975.

Clark, A. 2000. *A Theory of Sentience*. Oxford: Oxford University Press.

Driver, J., and P. G. Grossenbacher. 1996. Multimodal Spatial Constraints on Tactile Selection Attention. In *Attention and Performance XVI: Information Integration in Perception and Communication*, ed. T. Innui and J. L. McClelland, 209–35. Cambridge, Mass.: MIT Press.

Driver, J., and C. Spence. 1998a. Attention and the Cross-modal Construction of Space. *Trends in Cognitive Sciences* 2: 254–62.

———. 1998b. Cross-modal Links in Spatial Attention. *Philosophical Transactions of the Royal Society of London B* 353: 1319–31.

———. 2000. Multisensory Perception: Beyond Modularity and Convergence. *Current Biology* 10: R731–R735.

———. 2004. Crossmodal Spatial Attention: Evidence from Human Performance. In Spence and Driver 2004, 179–220.

Kennett, S., C. Spence, and J. Driver. 2002. Visuo-tactile Links in Covert Exogenous Spatial Attention Remap across Changes in Unseen Hand Posture. *Perception and Psychophysics* 64: 1083–94.

LaBerge, D. 1995. *Attentional Processing*. Cambridge, Mass.: Harvard University Press.

Ladavas, E. 1987. Is the Hemispatial Deficit Produced by Right Parietal Lobe Damage Associated with Retinal or Gravitational Coordinates? *Brain* 110: 167–80.Millikan, R. 1984. *Language, Thought, and Other Biological Categories*. Cambridge, Mass.: MIT Press.

———. 2004. *Varieties of Meaning*. Cambridge, Mass.: MIT Press.

Pylyshyn, Z. 2003. *Seeing and Visualizing: It's Not What You Think*. Cambridge, Mass.: MIT Press.

Spence, C., and J. Driver. 1994. Covert Spatial Orienting in Audition: Exogenous and Endogenous Mechanisms Facilitate Sound Localization. *Journal of Experimental Psychology: Human Perception and Performance* 20: 555–74.

———. 1996. Audiovisual Links in Endogenous Covert Spatial Attention. *Journal of Experimental Psychology: Human Perception and Performance* 22: 1005–30.

———. 1997. Audiovisual Links in Exogenous Covert Spatial Orienting. *Perception and Psychophysics* 59: 1–22.

————, eds. 2004. *Crossmodal Space and Crossmodal Attention.* Oxford: Oxford University Press.

Spence, C., J. MacDonald, and J. Driver. 2004. Exogenous Spatial-cuing Studies of Human Crossmodal Attention and Multisensory Integration. In Spence and Driver 2004, 277–320.

Strawson, P. F. 1963. *Individuals.* New York: Anchor.

————. 1974. *Subject and Predicate in Logic and Grammar.* London: Methuen.

Index